A Handbook for
TEACHING & LEARNING
IN
HIGHER EDUCATION

Enhancing Academic Practice

A Handbook for
TEACHING & LEARNING
IN
HIGHER EDUCATION

Enhancing Academic Practice

HEATHER FRY
STEVE KETTERIDGE
STEPHANIE MARSHALL

Crest Publishing House

(A JAICO ENTERPRISE)
G-2, 16 Ansari Road, Darya Ganj
New Delhi-110 002

Published by :
KOGAN PAGE INDIA PVT. LTD.
(For Crest Publishing House)
2/13 Ansari Road,
Darya Ganj, New Delhi-110002.

A HANDBOOK FOR TEACHING & LEARNING
IN HIGHER EDUCATION
—Enhancing Academic Practice
ISBN 81-242-0432-2

First Indian Edition : 2004

Printed by :
Efficient Offset Printers
215, Shahzada Bagh Industrial Complex
Phase-II, Delhi-110035.

Contents

Contributors

THE EDITORS

Heather Fry is Head of the Centre for Educational Development at Imperial College London. After teaching and lecturing in Nigeria she worked at the Institute of Education, London, and at St Bartholomew's and Royal London School of Medicine and Dentistry, Queen Mary's. She teaches, publishes and researches on a range of aspects of pedagogy and educational development in university and professional settings, especially in relation to medicine and dentistry. Recent research and publications focus on learning through clinical simulation, using technology with campus-based students, and progress files. She is joint editor with Steve Ketteridge and Stephanie Marshall of *The Effective Academic: A Handbook for Enhanced Practice*, Kogan Page (2002).

Steve Ketteridge is Director of Educational and Staff Development at Queen Mary, University of London where he was formerly a lecturer in microbiology. He has extensive experience of teaching at undergraduate and Masters levels, working with students from across the life sciences and civil engineering. His main interest is in the development of academic practice and he has worked with research staff and students in many research-led universities and research institutes. More recently his interests have extended into academic management and leadership. He is joint editor with Stephanie Marshall and Heather Fry of *The Effective Academic: A Handbook for Enhanced Practice*, Kogan Page (2002).

Stephanie Marshall is Director of Staff Development and Provost of Goodricke College at the University of York. Her latter role has led to an active interest in supporting students who are 'let loose' on project and dissertation research, requiring an outside facilitator to assist them in project management skills. Prior to her current post, she was a lecturer in Educational Studies. Since then, she has retained an active interest in both educational, leadership and management development, teaching, publishing and researching on various aspects of the pedagogy of both higher education and management development. She is joint editor with Steve Ketteridge and Heather Fry of *The Effective Academic: A Handbook for Enhanced Practice*, Kogan Page (2002).

THE AUTHORS

Professor Liz Beaty is Director of Learning and Teaching at the Higher Education Funding Council for England. She was formerly Head of Learning Development at Coventry University, responsible for courses for teaching staff and for projects developing new approaches to teaching and higher education research.

Margot Brown is National Co-ordinator at the Centre for Global Education, York St John. She has worked with teachers and student teachers in developing global perspectives and active learning strategies for use in classroom and college courses.

Sylvia Alexander is a lecturer in Informatics at the University of Ulster. Her research interests are in the area of computer science education, particularly pedagogic and technological innovation. In 2002 she completed her PGCUT (Certificate in University Teaching) by APEL.

Professor Vaneeta D'Andrea is Co-Director of the HEFCE Teaching Quality Enhancement Fund, National Co-ordination Team and Director of Educational Development Centre at City University, London. She has published and consulted globally on professional development programmes on teaching/learning in higher education.

Stephen Fallows is Research Co-ordinator for the Centre for Exercise and Nutrition Science at Chester College of Higher Education. He returned to his initial academic discipline (nutrition science) in 2001 after almost 10 years' work in educational development at the University of Luton. He is co-editor (with Christine Steven) of *Integrating Key Skills in Higher Education*, also published by Kogan Page.

Adam Feather is a Consultant Physician in Medicine for the Elderly at Newham General Hospital. He is also a lecturer in medical education at St George's Hospital Medical School and has written several medical undergraduate assessment text books.

Della Freeth is Reader in Education for Health Care Practice in the St Bartholomew School of Nursing and Midwifery, City University, London. Her main interests are in interprofessional learning, learning through simulated professional practice and means of supporting evidence-informed practice.

Hazel Fullerton was formerly Head of Educational Development Services at the University of Plymouth and co-chair of the Staff and Educational Development Association. She has wide experience of supporting teaching and learning, including the observation of teaching across many disciplines. Hazel is currently revisiting her former career as an artist in South West England.

David Gosling is Co-Director of the National Co-ordination Team for Teaching Quality Enhancement at the Centre for Higher Education Practice at the Open University. His research interests include philosophical approaches to educational development and the management of change in higher education.

Carol Gray is Lecturer in Modern Languages in Education, University of Birmingham. She is involved in the development of initial and in-service training for modern languages and publishes on a range of related topics.

Sandra Griffiths is Director of the Educational Development Unit at the University of Ulster. With a background in teaching in several sectors of education, she has been much involved in developing and teaching on a postgraduate certificate for university teachers.

Jennifer Horgan is Student Services Manager with the Open University in Wales where she has responsibility for the provision of generic Associate Lecturer Support and Development. She was previously Director of Staff Development at the University of Wales, Aberystwyth and has taught across many sectors of education, including providing initial teacher training for science teachers.

Dr Sherria Hoskins is a Senior Lecturer in Psychology at the University of Portsmouth. Her research interests include qualitative and quantitative differences in student motivation, with a specific interest in the impact of the learning environment.

Professor Dai Hounsell is Professor of Higher Education at the University of Edinburgh and previously Director of the Centre of Teaching, Learning and Assessment at that University. He publishes and advises widely on teaching and learning matters and is an editor of the international journal *Higher Education*.

Professor John Klapper is Director of the Centre for Modern Languages, University of Birmingham. He has published materials for the teaching of German and Russian and has written on various aspects of foreign language pedagogy and teacher development.

Joseph Kyle is Senior Lecturer and Director of Learning and Teaching in the School of Mathematics and Statistics at Birmingham University; Mathematics co-ordinator for the LTSN Mathematics, Statistics & Operational Research Network, and an editor for *Teaching Mathematics and its Applications*.

Ursula Lucas is Principal Lecturer at the Bristol Business School, University of the West of England. Her research interests are in higher education and learning in the professional workplace. In 2001 she was awarded an ILT National Teaching Fellowship.

Professor Philip Martin is Director of the Learning and Teaching Support Network (LTSN) English Subject Centre, at Royal Holloway. He has a particular interest in the development of interdisciplinary work, and is an editor of the inter-disciplinary journal *Literature & History*.

Robin Mason is Professor of Educational Technology in The Open University's Institute for Educational Technology and chairs a module in the MA in Open and Distance Education, called *Learning in the Connected Economy* (in joint development with Cambridge University). She also contributes to the development of the UK e-University and writes extensively about educational technology.

Gerry McAllister is Director of the National LTSN Centre for Information and Computer Sciences at the University of Ulster. His research interests include new methods of detection and correction for Hearing Acuity and the use of Technology in Teaching and Assessment.

Judy McKimm is Head of Curriculum Development at Imperial College School of Medicine. She manages a number of overseas and UK-based projects concerning health management, staff development and quality management. She is an accreditor for the ILT and was a medicine subject reviewer for the QAA and Welsh Funding Council.

Peter Milford is Head of the School of Accounting and Finance at Bristol Business School, University of the West of England. His teaching specialism is financial management and his research interests include accountability and control in the public sector. He has consultancy experience in the pharmaceutical industry and the health sector.

Professor Stephen Newstead is Dean of the Faculty of Human Sciences at the University of Plymouth and was President of the British Psychological Society during 1995 and 1996. His research interests include the psychology of assessment and learning in higher education.

Tina Overton is a Senior Lecturer in Chemistry at the University of Hull and the Director of the LTSN Subject Centre for Physical Sciences. She is interested in all aspects of chemical education, particularly critical thinking, problem solving and problem-based learning.

Pam Parker is Senior Lecturer: Educational Developments in the St Bartholomew School of Nursing and Midwifery, City University, London. Her main interests are in the assessment of clinical practice and interprofessional education.

John Pettit is a lecturer in The Open University's Institute of Educational Technology. He is chair of an online module in IET's MA in Open and Distance Education, and is also chairing a team providing staff development in online teaching/learning.

Richard Wakeford is the University Staff Development Officer at the University of Cambridge. He is an experienced researcher, teacher and presenter, having worked in the fields of education and medicine, and he now runs staff development activities on student assessment, selection, and teaching and learning. He is best known for his work and publications in the fields of the assessment of medical competence and in medical education generally.

Case study authors

Dr Claire Adjiman, Chemical Engineering, Imperial College London
Dr Pat Bailey, Chemistry, University of Manchester Institute of Science and Technology
Dr Mike Beeby, Bristol Business School, University of the West of England
Dr Simon Belt, Environmental Sciences, University of Plymouth
Dr Charles Booth, Bristol Business School, University of the West of England
Sam Brenton, Educational and Staff Development, Queen Mary, University of London
Irene Brightmer, University of Derby
Dr Liz Burd, Computer Science, University of Durham
Nick Byrne, Director, Language Centre, London School of Economics
Dr Hugh Cartwright, Chemistry, University of Oxford
Dr Elizabeth Davenport, St Bartholomew's and the London School of Medicine and Dentistry, Queen Mary's
Dr Louise Grisoni, Bristol Business School, University of the West of England
Dr Jane Harrington, Bristol Business School, University of the West of England
Professor Lee Harvey, University of Central England, Birmingham
Dr Beverley Hopping, School of Engineering, University of Manchester

Dr Siobhan Holland, English Subject Centre LTSN, Royal Holloway, University of London

Dr Desmond Hunter, Music, University of Ulster

Professor Reg Jordan, Director of LTSN-01, University of Newcastle

Dr Mike Joy, Computer Science, University of Warwick

George MacDonald Ross, Philosophy, University of Leeds

Dr Jean McPherson, School of Medicine, University of Newcastle, Australia

Caroline Mills, Geography, University of Gloucestershire

Dr Peter Morgan, Management Centre, University of Bradford

Dr Ailsa Nicholson, LTSN for Business, Management and Accountancy, University of East Anglia

Professor Gus Pennington, Education and Management Development consultant

Derek Raine, Physics, University of Leicester

Dr Mark Ratcliffe, Computer Science, University of Wales, Aberystwyth

Dr Frank Rennie, Development Director of the University of the Highlands and Islands

Dr Patricia Reynolds, GKT Dental Institute, King's College London

Peter Washer, Educational and Staff Development, Queen Mary, University of London

Penny White, South Bank University

Acknowledgements

The editors wish to acknowledge all those who have assisted in the production of this book. We are especially grateful to our team of expert contributing authors and those who have supplied the case studies that enrich the text.

The encouragement and support of Professor Gus Pennington is also warmly acknowledged by the editors.

Finally, we thank Jonathan Simpson from Kogan Page for his help in the management of this project.

Heather Fry
Steve Ketteridge
Stephanie Marshall

1

A user's guide

Heather Fry, Steve Ketteridge and Stephanie Marshall

PURPOSE OF THIS BOOK

This book is intended primarily for relatively inexperienced teachers in higher education. Established lecturers interested in exploring recent developments in teaching, learning and assessment will also find the book valuable. It has much to offer others in higher education and beyond (for example clinicians in the National Health Service) who have supporting roles in teaching and learning. It will be of interest also to computing and information technology staff, librarians, technical staff, researchers, graduate teaching assistants, and foreign language assistants. Those coming into the sector from overseas, business, industry or the professions will find the book a useful introduction to the practice of teaching in universities in the UK. Senior managers in the sector may also find it a useful way of updating themselves about current imperatives and practices. The handbook also has much to offer others working with adult learners.

The book is informed by best practice in teaching, learning, assessment and course design from across the higher education sector, underpinned by appropriate reference to research findings. The focus is primarily on teaching at the undergraduate level in the UK, but with much of many chapters having considerably wider applicability. A particular strength of this book is that it reviews generic issues in teaching and learning that will be common to most practitioners, and also explores practices in a range of major disciplines.

It is likely that those taking induction programmes, or certificates or diplomas in teaching in higher education will find the handbook useful and thought provoking. It introduces not only general methods for teaching, but also considers the distinctive elements of pedagogy in a number of disciplines and discusses aspects relating to professional practice and its assessment, including observation of teaching and portfolio building. The handbook is likely to support all those seeking to enhance their teaching practice, including those wishing to obtain or maintain membership of appropriate professional bodies, such as the Institute for Learning and Teaching in Higher Education. Staff who are in, or may move into, positions of greater seniority, with responsibility for course teams, research groups and similar, and wish to take a broader view of teaching and the wider role of the academic, may wish to dip into *The Effective Academic* by the same editors (Ketteridge, Marshall and Fry, 2002).

This second edition of the handbook has been considerably revised and updated to reflect the changing higher education sector, to mention recent research and publications, to incorporate some new case studies and to include consideration of teaching in a wider range of disciplines. Since the first edition the use of learning technologies in teaching and learning, especially of virtual learning environments, has moved forward very rapidly and this is reflected in new case studies and chapters and the updating of text and examples of practice. The new edition is also able to take greater cognizance of the Learning and Teaching Support Network (LTSN), as it has evolved since the first edition. The expertise of the LTSN and its generic and discipline-specific subject centres is reflected in the inclusion of new authors and reference to the relevant Web sites. The first edition, however, remains a very valuable resource.

The book draws together the accumulated knowledge and wisdom of many experienced and influential practitioners, researchers and educational developers in the sector. Authors come from a range of disciplinary backgrounds, from a range of higher educational institutions, and from across the UK. They have taken care in writing to avoid over-use of jargon, but to introduce key terminology, and to make the text readily accessible to staff from all disciplines. The handbook aims to take a scholarly and rigorous approach, while maintaining a user-friendly format.

This handbook has been written on the premise that readers strive to extend and develop their practice. It endeavours to offer a starting point for teaching: provoking thought, giving rationales and examples, encouraging reflective practice and prompting considered actions to improve and enhance one's teaching. It does this through inclusion of a mix of research evidence, successful examples of practice, an introduction to some key educational concepts and consideration of the major issues confronted by lecturers in their teaching role, with similarities and differences of disciplinary context also being given prominence.

For the purposes of the handbook the terms 'academic', 'lecturer', 'teacher' and 'tutor' are used interchangeably and should be taken to include anyone engaged in the support of student learning in higher education.

THE CONCEPT OF ACADEMIC PRACTICE

This book is premised on the recognition of the multifaceted and complex role of all those working in higher education. It acknowledges and recognizes that academics have contractual obligations to pursue excellence in several directions at the same time, most notably in teaching, research and scholarship, academic management and, for many, maintenance of standing and provision of service in a profession (such as teaching or nursing). Academic practice is a term used throughout that encompasses all of these facets. Hence teaching is recognized as being only one of the roles that readers of this book will be undertaking.

The authors recognize the fast pace of change in higher education in the UK. The last decade has seen a significant increase in student numbers, greater diversity in the undergraduate student population and in the prior educational experience of students, further pressure on resources, requirements for income generation, improved flexibility in modes of study and delivery, and new imperatives related to quality and standards. A further challenge facing the sector is the expectation to prepare students for the world of work and to make a contribution to the local community. A key recent change has been an increase in student debt, with increasing numbers of students being employed for longer hours during term time than previously. At the same time the pressures of research have become even more acute for many academics in the sector. All of these features have implications for the nature of teaching in higher education, and all have brought increased stress and demands on staff time.

NAVIGATION OF THE HANDBOOK

The handbook has four sections. Each chapter is written so that it can be read independently of others, and in any order. Readers can readily select and prioritize, according to interest, although reading Chapter 2 early on will be helpful.

Part 1: Development of practice

This introductory chapter describes features of the book and how to use it, and the section contains 13 further chapters, each of which explores a major facet of teaching and/or learning. Each aspect is considered from a broad perspective, rather than adopting the view or emphasis of a particular discipline. These chapters address most of the repertoire essential to the teaching, learning and assessment of students in higher education.

Part 2: Development of the academic for teaching and learning

This section addresses the development of the academic as a teacher. It is concerned with how teachers can learn, explore, develop and enhance their practice. It provides guidance to help lecturers scrutinize their understanding of underpinning theory and its implications for practice. There are suggestions for giving and receiving feedback, for self-auditing one's practice, for evaluating teaching, developing reflective practice and building a portfolio. This section considers many of the building blocks essential to continuing professional development.

Part 3: Working in discipline-specific areas

The third section considers teaching and learning from the perspective of different fields of study. It seeks to draw out, for several major disciplinary groupings, the characteristic features of teaching, learning and assessment. These chapters are most useful when read in conjunction with chapters in other parts. They also provide the opportunity for individuals working in one discipline to explore and benchmark across other disciplines.

Glossary

The final section is a glossary of acronyms and technical terms. This may be used in conjunction with reading the chapters, or separately.

DISTINCTIVE FEATURES

The book has a number of features.

Interrogating practice

Chapters feature one or more instances where readers are invited to consider aspects of their own institution, department, courses, students or practice. This is done by posing questions to the reader under the heading 'Interrogating Practice'. This feature has several purposes. First, to encourage readers to audit practice with a view to enhancement. Second, to challenge readers to examine critically their conceptions of teaching and workplace practice. Third, to ensure readers are familiar with their institutional and departmental policies and practices. Fourth, to give practitioners the opportunity to develop the habit of reflecting on practice. Readers are free to choose how, or if, they engage with these interrogations.

Case studies

In each part of the book the chapters include case studies. The case studies exemplify issues, practice, and research findings mentioned in the body of the chapters. The majority are real cases and examples drawn from a wealth of institutions, involving the everyday practice of authors and colleagues, to demonstrate how particular approaches have been used successfully. Some of those contributing case studies are at the leading edge of teaching in their discipline, others report on research into learning and teaching.

Further reading

Each chapter has its own reference section and suggested further reading. Readers are referred also to Web sites, resource materials, videos, etc.

The glossary – more details

A further distinctive feature is the glossary. It contains the main terms encountered in teaching and learning in higher education and some commonly used acronyms. In the text the first usage in each chapter of these 'technical terms' is indicated by **bold type**. All terms are succinctly explained in the glossary at the end of the book. This may be used as a dictionary independent of any chapter.

IN CONCLUSION

This second edition of the handbook builds upon and updates the first, while retaining its key features. In this spirit, the chapter on learning (Understanding Student Learning, Chapter 2), itself updated, remains, in the view of the editors, a central feature, underpinning much that follows, and as such is a useful starting point.

FURTHER READING

Ketteridge, S, Marshall, S and Fry, H (2002) *The Effective Academic: A handbook for enhanced practice*, Kogan Page, London

Part 1
Development
of practice

<table>
<tr><td>

2

</td><td>

Understanding student learning

</td></tr>
</table>

Heather Fry, Steve Ketteridge and Stephanie Marshall

INTRODUCTION

It is unfortunate, but true, that some academics teach students without having much formal knowledge of how students learn. Many lecturers know how *they* learn best, but do not necessarily consider how *their students* learn and if the way they teach is predicated on enabling learning to happen.

Learning is about how we perceive and understand the world, about making meaning (Marton and Booth, 1997). Learning may involve mastering abstract principles, understanding proofs, remembering factual information, acquiring methods, techniques and approaches, recognition, reasoning, debating ideas, or developing behaviour appropriate to specific situations.

Despite many years of research into learning, it is not easy to translate this knowledge into practical implications for teaching. This is because education deals with students as people, who are diverse in all respects, and ever changing. Not everyone learns in the same way, or equally readily about all types of material. The discipline and level of material to be learnt also have an influence on learning. Students bring different backgrounds and expectations to learning. There are no simple answers to the questions 'how do we learn?' and 'how as teachers can we bring about learning?' Our knowledge about the relationship between teaching and learning is still incomplete, but we do know enough about learning to be able to make some firm statements about types of action that will usually be helpful in enabling learning to happen.

Most lecturers will recognize that motivation and assessment both play a large part in student learning in higher education and these topics are considered in more detail in, respectively, Chapters 5 and 4.

We draw on research specific to students in higher education and also mention some aspects of **adult learning**. However, higher education teachers need to be aware that less mature students (in age or behaviour) may not be 'adult learners' and that some of the evidence about adult learning is less than robust.

This chapter is not written for (or by) academic psychologists but is intended to give a simplified overview of what we know about student learning and the implications this has for teaching. It sets out to (a) present and review some of the common models and ideas related to learning in higher education and (b) indicate the broad implications of these ideas for selecting teaching and assessment methods and strategies.

Interrogating Practice

As you read this chapter, note down, from what it says about learning, what the implications for teaching might be in your discipline. When you reach the last section of the chapter, compare your list with the general suggestions you will find there.

VIEWS OF LEARNING

In the literature there are several schools of thought about how learning takes place. Of these the most prominent is **constructivism**.

Constructivism

Most contemporary psychologists use constructivist theories of one type or another to explain how human beings learn. The idea rests on the notion of continuous building and amending of previous structures, or schemata, as new experience, actions and knowledge are assimilated and accommodated. Constructivism stems in part from the work done by Kant over 200 years ago, who thought that experience leads to the formation of general conceptions or constructs that are models of reality. Unless schemata are amended, learning will not occur. Learning (whether in **cognitive, affective, interpersonal** or **psychomotor domains**) is said to involve a process of individual transformation. Thus people actively construct their knowledge (Biggs and Moore, 1993). Piaget (1950) and Bruner (1960, 1966) are two of the 20th century's most prominent constructivists. For example, Bruner's ideas relating to inducting students into the modes of thinking in individual disciplines and his notion of revisiting knowledge at ever-higher levels of understanding, leading to the idea of a spiral curriculum, have been very influential. In the discipline of history, for instance, Bruner is often cited as the inspiration for changing the focus of history teaching in schools. This shifted the balance from regurgitation of factual information to understanding. Some of the ways in which this was done were to encourage learners to understand how the past is reconstructed and understood, for example by learning how to empathize and to work from primary sources. Most of the current ideas about student learning, including **experiential learning,** the use of **reflection**, etc, are based in constructivism.

Constructivism tells us that we learn by fitting new understanding and knowledge into, with, extending and supplanting, old understanding and knowledge. As lecturers we need to be aware that we are rarely if ever 'writing on a blank slate', however rudimentary, or wrong, pre-existing related knowledge and understanding are. Without changes or additions to pre-existing knowledge and understanding, no learning will have occurred.

Very frequently learning is thought of in terms only of adding more knowledge, whereas lecturers should be considering also how to bring about change or transformation to the pre-existing knowledge of their learners (Mezirow, 1991). Additions to knowledge, in the sense of accumulated 'fact', may sometimes be possible without substantial transformation, but any learning of a higher order, involving understanding or creativity, for example, can usually only happen when the underlying schemata are themselves changed to incorporate new understanding. Such change will itself be likely to facilitate retention of facts for the longer term (see approaches to study, below). Chalmers and Fuller (1996) provide a succinct and useful account of some of these ideas.

Interrogating Practice

Think of one or two occasions when you feel you have gained real mastery or insight into a particular aspect of your discipline. Would you say that this was only by addition, or involved a change of pre-existing understanding?

Other schools and views

Rationalism (or idealism) is an alternative school, or pole, of learning theory still with some vogue. It is based on the idea of a biological plan being in existence that unfolds in very determined directions. Chomsky was a foremost member of this pole. Associationism, a third pole, centres on the idea of forming associations between stimuli and responses. Pavlov and Skinner belong to this pole. Further details of such theories may be found in Richardson (1985).

Lave and Wenger (eg 1991) are associated with a social theory of learning called **situated learning**. Situated learning focuses on understanding knowledge and learning in context, and emphasizes that the learner engages with others to develop/create collective understanding as part of a community of practice. Their view of learning is thus relational, and rejects, or at least downplays, the importance of the continuous reformation and transformation of the schemata of individuals. Supporters of situated learning view learning as a social practice and consider new knowledge can be generated from practice. The latter perspective is a view also shared by others.

Case Study 1: Lecturers' views of learning

Queen Mary, University of London

Below are some statements about student learning. We have used these to challenge attitudes of new staff and help them unpack their perceptions of learning. Staff (during a workshop in the induction phase) are asked for their reaction to each statement.

Student learning is:

- quantitative increase in factual knowledge;
- memorization and reproduction;
- applying and using knowledge.
- acquisition of skills and methods;
- making sense and understanding;
- abstracting meaning;
- understanding or comprehending the world in a different way;
- performing well in assessment;
- solving problems;
- developing creativity;
- extending imagination;
- developing an analytical approach;
- changing within oneself as a consequence of understanding the world differently.

We asked staff to think about their own views, to discuss them with their neighbours and then to participate in a whole group discussion. Initially, discussion usually highlighted differences between disciplines in the importance attached to individual statements. However, as discussion progressed, a consensus view usually emerged in which most staff, irrespective of discipline, strongly supported the view that student learning involves most of these things.

(Heather Fry and Steve Ketteridge)

ADULT LEARNING THEORY

It is questionable how far there really are theories of adult learning. On one hand it is debatable how far the learning of adults is sufficiently distinct from the learning of others, and on the other hand, some of the axioms of adult learning are indeed axioms rather than theory (see Bright, 1989, especially Brookfield). Despite this, there are propositions concerning the learning of adults which have had much influence on higher education, if only to cause teachers in that sector to re-examine their premises and adjust some of their views. Adult learning theories are thought by some to be increasingly relevant, as non-traditional participants (whether considered by age, mode of study or ethnic, economic or educational background) increase as a proportion of traditional students.

Malcolm Knowles is associated with the use of the term **andragogy** (despite its much earlier aetiology) to refer to this area. His most quoted definition of andragogy is as the 'art and science of helping adults learn' (Knowles, 1984). One of the complications of the area is that he has changed his definition over time. From his work spanning more than 30 years, andragogy is considered to have five principles:

- As a person matures they become more self-directed.
- Adults have accumulated experiences that can be a rich resource for learning.
- Adults become ready to learn when they experience a need to know something.
- Adults tend to be less subject-centred than children; they are increasingly problem-centred.
- For adults the most potent motivators are internal.

There is a lack of empirical evidence to support these views. Despite many critiques of andragogy and the problems of its definition (eg, see Davenport, 1993) it has had considerable influence. Many 'types' of learning that are much used and discussed in higher education, including experiential learning, student **autonomy** in learning and **self-directed learning**, belong in the tradition of adult education. (Furthermore, considerable areas of work in higher education around the student experience, supporting students, and widening participation are also closely linked to work that has its origins in adult education, eg, barriers to entry and progression.)

EXPERIENTIAL LEARNING

It is self-evident that experience gained through life, education and work plays a central role in the process of learning and this perspective on learning is called 'experiential learning' or 'learning by doing' (see also Chapters 10 and 23). Probably the most popular theory of learning from experience can be attributed to Kolb (1984), who developed ideas from other models of experiential learning.

An appreciation of experiential learning is necessary to underpin many of the different types of teaching activity discussed elsewhere in this book, including **work-based learning** and **placement learning**, teaching **laboratory** and practical work, **action learning, role play** and many types of **small group teaching**. The Kolb model frequently appears in the literature, often modified to accommodate particular types of learning (or training) experiences and using alternative or simplified terminology (eg see Chapter 23).

Experiential learning is based on the notion that understanding is not a fixed or unchangeable element of thought but is formed and re-formed through 'experience'. It is also a continuous process, often represented as cyclical, and, being based on experience, implies that we all bring to learning situations our own ideas and beliefs at different levels of elaboration.

The cyclical model of learning that has become known as the 'Kolb Learning Cycle' (see Figure 2.1) requires four kinds of abilities/undertaking if learning is to be successful. Learning requires:

- concrete experience (CE);
- reflective observation (RO);
- abstract conceptualization (AC);
- active experimentation (AE).

But what do these terms mean? First, learners are involved fully and freely in new experiences (CE). Second, they must make/have the time and space to be able to reflect (RO) on their experience from different perspectives. It is this element in the cycle that will be strongly influenced by **feedback** from others. Third, learners must be able to form and re-form, process their ideas, take ownership of them and integrate their new ideas into sound, logical theories (AC). This moves towards the fourth point (AE), using understanding to make decisions and problem solve, test implications in new situations, all of which generate material for the starting point for the next round, the concrete experience again. Thus the experiential

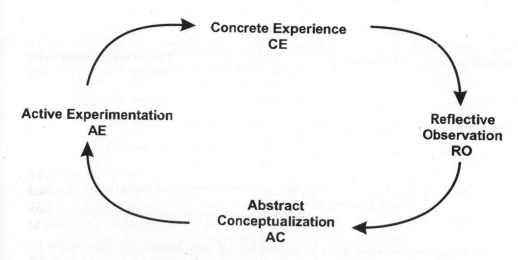

Figure 2.1 The Kolb Learning Cycle

cycle does not simply involve doing, but also reflecting, processing, thinking and furthering understanding. By extension, this cyclical process has a part to play in even the most abstract and theoretical disciplines where the academic is concerned to help the learner acquire the 'tools of the trade' or the modes of thinking central to the discipline, such as in philosophy or literary criticism.

All four stages of the process are necessary for effective learning to be achieved. This leads to the question: is it possible to be at two points in the cycle at one time? For example, can one act and reflect at the same time? Is it possible to be at the concrete experience stage in the cycle and be undertaking abstract conceptualization together? These are pairs of very different types of ability, described by some as polar opposites in the learning process, and the learner may have to choose which one to allow to dominate in the particular learning situation (see Chapter 15). The way in which the learner resolves these tensions will have an effect on the learning outcome and the development of different types of strength in the learner and, as will be seen, may pertain to personality traits and/or disciplinary differences.

Wolf and Kolb (1984) have suggested that learners develop different learning styles that emphasize preference for some modes of learning over others, leading to particular characteristics (see Table 2.1).

Clearly those responsible for organizing learning need to be able to create opportunities for learning that are sensitive to these different styles of learning. However, it should not be forgotten that even though learners may have different preferences, for effective learning they will need to be encouraged to move through all the constituent elements in the learning cycle.

Table 2.1 Learning styles (based on Wolf and Kolb, 1984)

Learning Style	Strengths	Dominant Learning Ability
Convergent	Practical application of ideas	AC and AE
Divergent	Imaginative ability and generation of ideas	CE and RO
Assimilation	Creating theoretical models and making sense of disparate observations	AC and RO
Accommodative	Carrying out plans and tasks that involve them in new experiences	CE and AE

The preferred learning style of an individual may have a relationship to the particular disciplinary framework in which the learning is taking place. Becher (1989) brings together the work of two principal authors as the 'Kolb–Biglan Classification of Academic Knowledge'. This classification would seem to suggest that the preferred learning style might be attributable to a relationship with a particular disciplinary framework. Accepting this classification implies that encouragement in different elements of the learning cycle needs to be taken into account when planning experiential learning opportunities in different disciplines.

The distribution in the four quadrants shown in Table 2.2 is interesting, in that those studying the disciplines in quadrants 1 and 2 are described as showing some preference for reflective practice. However, we must ask ourselves, noting that some of the disciplines mentioned in quadrants 3 and 4 are now strongly associated with reflective practice, just how useful this classification really is. Perhaps the lesson to learn is that there are likely to be disciplinary differences in these

Table 2.2 Classification of academic knowledge

1. Abstract Reflective
  AC–RO
  Hard Pure
  Natural Sciences
  Mathematics
	2. Concrete Reflective
	  CE–RO
	  Soft Pure
	  Humanities
	  Social Sciences

3. Abstract Active
  AC–AE
  Hard Applied
  Science-based professions, Engineering,
  Medicine and other healthcare
  professions
	4. Concrete Active
	  CE–AE
	  Soft Applied
	  Social professions
	  Education, Social Work
	  Law

Based on the Kolb–Biglan Model described by Becher (1989)

characteristics that may be difficult to classify. How far students acquire, are attracted to, or bring with them to a subject any of the associated ways of thinking, or 'frames of mind', is a difficult matter (see Gardner's classic work, 1985). There is another issue concerning transitions in students' learning styles and Nulty and Barrett (1996) present some research findings in this area.

Reflection and **reflective practice** are not easy concepts for lecturers in higher education, either in respect of their own professional development or the learning of their students. Support in their development is often necessary (see Chapters 10 and 15). Schon (1987), in examining the relationship between professional knowledge and professional **competence**, suggests that rather than looking to another body of research knowledge, practitioners should become more adept at observing and learning through reflection on the artistry of their own particular profession (see Chapter 15). Reflection on practice (on experience) is central to the development of professions for two reasons: first, recognized 'experts' in the field exhibit distinct artistry and, second, this artistry cannot be learned through conventional teaching models – it requires observation of competent practitioners, experience in carrying out all the tasks of one's job and reflection upon that practice. Such reflective practice is likely to follow Kolb's pattern of cyclical conceptualization and reconceptualization as part of a continuous process. Several researchers have considered the difficulties inherent in developing reflective practice (eg Boud and Walker, 1998). The development of reflection as part of learning is a key aspect of **lifelong learning**.

Interrogating Practice

Call to mind three occasions when conscious reflection on something you have experienced (in the street, the laboratory, on the television, from reading, etc) has enhanced your understanding or ability to carry out a particular task.

STUDY, APPROACHES TO LEVELS OF UNDERSTANDING AND LEARNING STYLES

Approaches to study

In the 1970s, Marton (1975) conducted empirical work that has subsequently gained much credibility and currency in higher education. Considerable subsequent work has taken place, eg, by Marton and Saljo (1984). This research, investigating the interaction between student and a set learning task, led to the conclusion that students' approaches to the task (their intention) determined the extent to which they engaged with their subject and this affected the quality of outcomes. These approaches to study/learning were classified as deep or surface.

The former, the **deep approach** to learning, is typified as an intention to understand and seek meaning, leading students to attempt to relate concepts to existing experience, distinguishing between new ideas and existing knowledge, and critically evaluating and determining key themes and concepts. In short, such an approach results from the students' intention to gain maximum meaning from their studying, which they achieve through high levels of cognitive processing throughout learning. Facts are learnt in the context of meaning.

The latter, the **surface approach** to learning, is typified as an intention to complete the task, memorize information, make no distinction between new ideas and existing knowledge; and to treat the task as externally imposed (as extrinsic). Rote learning is the typical surface approach. In summary, such an approach results from the students' intention to offer the impression that maximum learning has taken place, which they achieve through superficial levels of cognitive processing. Facts are learnt without a meaningful framework.

The following illustrates these concepts. The learning outcomes for, say, social science students, who adopt a deep approach to the task of reading a set text, would include full engagement with the central theme of the text and an understanding of contributing arguments. In contrast, those who adopt a surface approach would fail to identify the central themes – primarily because they would be engrossed in progressing through the text sequentially, attempting to remember the flat landscape of facts.

The conceptions of deep and surface learning have increased in sophistication with further research, most notably the work of Biggs (1987) and Ramsden (1988). Ramsden (1992: 47–48) provides useful examples of statements from students in different disciplines exhibiting deep and surface approaches; these are helpful in showing the differences between the approaches.

Biggs and Ramsden turned learning theory on its head in that rather than drawing on the work of philosophers or cognitive psychologists, they looked to students themselves for a distinctive perspective. Ramsden (1988) suggested that approach to learning was not implicit in the make-up of the student, but something between the student and the task and thus was both personal and situational. An approach to learning should not, therefore, be seen as a pure individual characteristic but rather a response to the teaching environment in which the student is expected to learn. Biggs (1987) identified a third approach to study – the **strategic**, or **achieving approach**. Here the emphasis is on organizing learning specifically to obtain a high examination grade. With this intention, a learner who often uses a deep approach may adopt some of the techniques of a surface approach to meet the requirements of a specific activity such as a test. Thus taking a deep approach is not a fixed and unchanging characteristic. The achieving approach is intimately associated with assessment.

One of the greatest misconceptions on the part of many students entering higher education is their belief that a subject consists only of large amounts of factual knowledge and, to become the expert, all one need do is add new knowledge to one's existing store. It is the responsibility of the lecturer to challenge and change such conceptions and to ensure that their teaching, the curricula they design, and the assessments they set, do not echo this perspective. Biggs (1999) is one of the foremost proponents of the view that approaches to learning can be modified by the teaching and learning context, and are themselves learnt. He has also developed a taxonomy (SOLO) for classifying levels of understanding that can be applied across all disciplines.

The SOLO taxonomy of levels of understanding

SOLO stands for structure of the observed learning outcome. The taxonomy is based on the study of learning outcomes from a variety of academic content areas and the principle that as students learn, the outcomes of their learning pass through similar stages of increased complexity (Biggs and Collis, 1982; Biggs, 1999). The changes are in the amount of detail and the quality of learning. Quantitative changes occur first, and then the learning changes qualitatively. The taxonomy may be used to describe the increasingly complexity of learning tasks as academic complexity increases. As such it can be used as a framework for classifying **learning objectives** and student achievement. Like Bloom's taxonomy, with which it can be aligned, it is concerned primarily with the cognitive domain (see Chapter 3 for further discussion of learning objectives and Bloom).

The SOLO taxonomy is an hierarchical classification in which each level is the foundation for the next. It defines five levels of understanding, each of increasing complexity:

- *Prestructural* – understanding at the individual word level. Students at this level may miss the point or use tautology to cover lack of understanding. Here, students show little evidence of relevant learning. Such understanding should be rare in the context of higher education.
- *Unistructural* – responses deal with terminology. Such responses meet only part of the task and miss out important attributes.
- *Multistructural* – many facts are present, but they are not structured and do not address the key issue/s.
- *Relational* – consists of more than a list of details, addresses the point and makes sense in relation to the topic as a whole. This is the first level at which understanding is displayed in an academically relevant sense. It involves conceptual restructuring of components.

- *Extended abstract* – a coherent whole is conceptualized at a high level of abstraction and is applied to new and broader contexts. It is a level of understanding in which a breakthrough has been made and it changes the way of thinking about issues. It represents a high level of understanding.

Application of the SOLO taxonomy to learning in higher education would result in describing quantitative increases in knowledge as unistructural or multistructural and qualitative changes as relational or extended abstract. The SOLO taxonomy may be used to describe levels of understanding and thus to inform curriculum development and the articulation of learning outcomes and assessment criteria. (It is important not to confuse Biggs' levels with the **levels** for qualifications set out in the **Framework of Higher Education Qualifications** – see Chapter 13). One implication of Biggs' work is that higher levels of the SOLO taxonomy are unlikely to be achieved by those adopting a surface approach to learning.

Learning styles

There have been several different categorizations of learning style. That of Wolf and Kolb is described above, another categorization is described in Chapter 15, and many readers will have heard of a third which opposes serialist and holist learning styles (Pask, 1976). A serialist is said to prefer a step-by-step approach and a narrow focus while holists prefer to obtain the 'big picture' and work with illustrations and analogies.

However, perhaps the best known categorization of learning style is that of Honey and Mumford (1982). They offer a four-fold classification of activist, pragmatist, reflector, and theorist:

- Activists respond most positively to learning situations offering challenge, to include new experiences and problems, excitement and freedom in their learning.
- Reflectors respond most positively to structured learning activities where they are provided with time to observe, reflect and think, and allowed to work in a detailed manner.
- Theorists respond well to logical, rational structure and clear aims, where they are given time for methodical exploration and opportunities to question and stretch their intellect.
- Pragmatists respond most positively to practically based, immediately relevant learning activities, which allow scope for practice and using theory.

It is anticipated that the preferred learning style of any individual will include elements from two or more of these four categories.

An awareness of learning styles is important for the lecturer planning a course module, as a variety of strategies to promote learning should be considered. Teachers also need to be aware that changing firmly established patterns of behaviour and views of the world can prove destabilizing for the learner who is then engaged in something rather more than cognitive restructuring (Perry, 1979).

Approaches and styles

Many of those who have worked with learning styles and approaches to learning have developed questionnaire-type taxonomies, or inventories, for identifying the approach or style being used by the learner. These have limited use if one regards the underlying concepts and understanding of whether the characteristics are learnt or inherent, as in a state of flux. This has not prevented lecturers using them to 'diagnose' student learning. Their use does have the advantage of helping students to think about how they best learn and whether they would benefit from trying to modify their behaviour. Those who are interested might wish to see the 'Approaches to Study Inventory' (Entwistle and Ramsden, 1983) or Honey and Mumford (1982).

Whenever encountering the term 'learning style', it is important to be clear about which categorization is being referred to, and not to confuse learning style with approaches to study/learning. It is also essential to bear in mind that there is a major contrast between approaches and styles, at least in the view of their main proponents, in the degree of immutability of these qualities. The contrast is between approaches to learning (which are modifiable) with learning styles (which are fixed and part of personality characteristics and traits). There has been much debate and publication in this area in recent years. For further discussion and consideration of the implications see Prosser and Trigwell (1999). The current state of play dictates that neither approaches nor styles should be regarded as fixed, ie both may be modifiable, but that both may be habituated and hard to change.

Interrogating Practice

Think of occasions when you have chosen to use a deep approach to learning. Think of other occasions when you have used a surface approach and consider how many of these involved an achieving intention.

Teaching for learning

'It is important to remember that what the student does is actually more important in determining what is learned than what the teacher does' (Sheull, cited in Biggs, 1993). This statement is congruent with a constructivist view and also reminds us that students in higher education must engage with and take some responsibility for their learning. The teacher cannot do all the work if learning is to be the outcome; congruently, the teacher must ensure that course design, selection of teaching and learning opportunities and assessment help the learner to actively construct knowledge. As designers of courses and as teachers, if we want to 'produce' graduates of higher education able to think, act, create and innovate at a relatively high level, then we need to consider how we lead learners beyond being regurgitator, copyist or operative. Learning requires space for thinking or reflecting 'in your head' and for interaction with others, and learning from and with peers and experts. Barnett (eg 1994, 1997) has highlighted these and many other related issues. These imperatives, coupled with those of our discipline, should affect our view of what constitutes good teaching in higher education.

All too often, discussions of teaching in higher education centre on the premise that learning is only, or primarily, about the acquisition of more and more factual information. But what is, arguably, more important is the way learners structure information and how well that enables them to use it (Biggs, 1999). For example, how well can a learner recall their learning, combine parts of it together, make judgements based on it, synthesize, extrapolate, apply, and use it to be innovative and creative. The onus is on us as teachers to be discriminating in selecting methods of teaching, assessment and course design to bring about the types of learning we desire. General advice about teaching should not be plucked out of thin air, but grounded in and aligned with theories about learning. Notable among the precepts that emerge from what we understand about how students learn are the following:

- Learners experience the same teaching in different ways.
- Learners will approach learning in a variety of ways and the ways we teach may modify their approaches.
- Teachers may need to extend/modify the approach of many learners.
- Learners have to be brought to 'engage' with what they are learning so that transformation and internalization can occur.
- Learners bring valuable experience to learning.
- Learners may be more motivated when offered an element of choice.
- Learners need to be able to explain their answers and answer 'why?' questions.
- Learners taking a discipline that is new to them may struggle to think in the appropriate manner (an important point in modular programmes).

- Teachers need to understand where learners are starting from so that they can get the correct level and seek to correct underlying misconceptions or gaps.
- Teachers and learners are both responsible for learning happening and students must take/have some responsibility for learning.
- Teachers need to be aware of the impact of cultural background and beliefs on learner behaviour, interpretation and understanding.
- Feedback and discussion are important in enabling the teacher and learner to check that accommodations of new understanding are 'correct' (peer feedback is important too).
- Prior knowledge needs to be activated.
- Discussion of what is being learnt in a peer (small) group can be a powerful learning tool.
- Learning best takes place in or related to a relevant context (to facilitate the 'making of meaning').
- When planning, specifying outcomes, teaching or assessing, lecturers need to consider all appropriate domains and be aware of the level of operations being asked for.
- The learning climate/environment in which learners learn affects the outcomes (eg, motivation, interaction, support, etc).
- Teachers must reduce the amount of didactic teaching.
- Teachers should avoid content overload; too much material will encourage a surface approach.
- Basic principles and concepts provide the basis for further learning.
- Assessment has a powerful impact on student behaviour.

OVERVIEW

What is important about teaching is what it helps the learner to do, know or understand. There are different models of learning that teachers need to be aware of. What we do as teachers must take into account what we know about how students learn.

REFERENCES

Barnett, R (1994) *The Limits of Competence*, Society for Research into Higher Education/Open University Press, Buckingham

Barnett, R (1997) *Higher Education: A Critical Business*, Society for Research into Higher Education/Open University Press, Buckingham

Becher, T (1989) *Academic Tribes and Territories*, Society for Research in Higher Education/Open University Press, Buckingham

Biggs, J (1987) *Student Approaches to Learning and Studying*, Australian Council for Educational Research, Hawthorn, Victoria

Biggs, J (1993) From theory to practice: a cognitive systems approach, *Higher Education Research and Development* (Australia), **12** (1), pp 73–85

Biggs, J (1999) *Teaching for Quality Learning at University*, Society for Research into Higher Education/Open University Press, Buckingham

Biggs, J and Collis, K F (1982) *Evaluating the Quality of Learning: The SOLO taxonomy*, Academic Press, London

Biggs, J and Moore, P (1993) *The Process of Learning*, Prentice-Hall, New York

Boud, D and Walker, D (1998) Promoting reflection in professional courses: the challenge of context, *Studies in Higher Education*, **23** (2)

Bright, B (ed) (1989) *Theory and Practice in the Study of Adult Education: The epistemological debate*, Routledge, London

Brookfield, S (1989) The epistemology of adult education in the United States and Great Britain: a cross-cultural analysis, in *Theory and Practice in the Study of Adult Education: The epistemological debate*, ed B Bright, pp 141–73, Routledge, London

Bruner, J S (1960) *The Process of Education*, Harvard University Press, Cambridge, Mass.

Bruner, J S (1966) *Towards a Theory of Instruction*, Harvard University Press, Cambridge, Massachusetts

Chalmers, D and Fuller, R (1996) *Teaching for Learning at University*, Kogan Page, London

Davenport, J (1993) Is there any way out of the andragogy morass?, in *Culture and Processes of Adult Learning*, eds M Thorpe, R Edwards and A Hanson, pp 109–17, Routledge, London

Entwistle, N and Ramsden, P (1983) *Understanding Student Learning*, Croom Helm, London

Gardner, H (1985) *Frames of Mind*, Paladin, London

Honey, P and Mumford, A (1982) *The Manual of Learning Styles*, Peter Honey, Maidenhead

Knowles, M and Associates (1984) *Andragogy in Action*, Gulf Publishing Co, Houston

Kolb, D A (1984) *Experiential Learning*, Prentice-Hall, Englewood Cliffs, New Jersey

Lave, J and Wenger, E (1991) *Situated Learning: Legitimate peripheral participation*, Cambridge University Press, Cambridge

Marton, F (1975) On non-verbatim learning – 1: Level of processing and level of outcome, *Scandinavian Journal of Psychology*, **16**, pp 273–79

Marton, F and Booth, S (1997) *Learning and Awareness*, Lawrence Erlbaum Associates, Mahwah, New Jersey

Marton, F and Saljo, R (1984) Approaches to learning, in *The Experiences of Learning*, eds F Marton, D Hounsell and N Entwistle, Scottish Academic Press, Edinburgh

Mezirow, J (1991) *Transformative Dimensions of Adult Learning*, Jossey-Bass Publishers, San Francisco

Nulty, D D and Barrett, M A (1996) Transitions in students' learning styles, *Studies in Higher Education*, **21**, pp 333–44

Pask, G (1976) Learning styles and strategies, *British Journal of Educational Psychology*, **46**, pp 4–11

Perry, W (1979) *Forms of Intellectual and Ethical Development in the College Years*, Holt, Rinehart and Winston, New York

Piaget, J (1950) *The Psychology of Intelligence*, Routledge and Kegan Paul, London

Prosser, M and Trigwell, K (1999) *Understanding Learning and Teaching: The experience in higher education*, Society for Research into Higher Education/Open University Press, Buckingham

Ramsden, P (1988) *Improving Learning: New perspectives*, Kogan Page, London

Ramsden, P (1992) *Learning to Teach in Higher Education*, Routledge, London

Richardson, K (1985) *Personality, Development and Learning: Unit 8/9 learning theories*, Open University Press, Milton Keynes

Schon, D (1987) *Educating the Reflective Practitioner: Toward a new design for teaching and learning in the professions*, Jossey-Bass Publishers, San Francisco

Wolf, D M and Kolb, D A (1984) Career development, personal growth and experiential learning, in *Organisational Psychology: Readings on human behaviour*, 4th edn, eds D Kolb, I Rubin, and J McIntyre, Prentice-Hall, Englewood Cliffs, New Jersey

FURTHER READING

Biggs, J (1999) As above. A lucid exposition of student learning and how to constructively align this with teaching.

Chalmers, D and Fuller, R (1996) As above. Part One is a useful introduction to student learning and its impact on teaching and assessment. The rest of the book considers the teaching of learning skills.

Gibbs, G (ed) (1994) *Improving Student Learning*, Oxford Centre for Staff Development, Oxford. Many contributions from leading authorities on student learning.

Ramsden, P (1992) As above. Still much valuable discussion of student learning, despite the publication date.

Rowland, S (2000) *The Enquiring University Teacher*, Society for Research into Higher Education/Open University Press, Buckingham. Explores learning how to be a university teacher from a collaborative and reflective perspective.

3 Organizing teaching and learning: outcomes-based planning

Vaneeta-marie D'Andrea

ORGANIZING TEACHING AND LEARNING

Organizing teaching is really about designing learning. Designing learning is one of the most fundamental activities of a university teacher. Often, due to pressures of time, preparing to teach is given less time and consideration than implementing and evaluating the teaching/learning process. Furthermore, the language of pedagogic design has historically been off-putting to most academics, seeming little more than educational jargon at best, and 'mumbo-jumbo' at worst. Despite the jargon, the aim of pedagogic design to assist in the development of conscious and purposeful teaching and learning is a laudable one, especially if the learning outcomes achieved are improved by so doing.

Teaching involves helping students to know something not known before, it constitutes a process of change. These intentions are most often implicit or inferred. The conscious planning of teaching and learning make these intentions explicit. As will be discussed, making teaching/learning intentions more explicit improves the learning experience of students. The current terminology for approaching the design of teaching and learning in this fashion is 'outcomes-based planning'. The discussion that follows will focus on the use of this approach for the organization of teaching and learning in higher education.

AIMS, OBJECTIVES/OUTCOMES OF THIS CHAPTER

The primary aim of this chapter is to review the principles and practices of **course/module** design in order to provide higher education staff, with teaching responsibilities, with a foundation for developing an outcomes-based planning approach to the organization of teaching and learning.

The **objectives**/outcomes of this chapter can be specified as follows. It is expected that as a result of working through this chapter, the reader will be able to:

- State the rationale for using an outcomes-based approach to organizing teaching and learning in higher education.
- Write learning objectives/outcomes for a course/module that clearly communicate to those with responsibilities for teaching and to students and other interested parties, the explicit intention of a teaching and learning experience.
- Identify the links between objectives/outcomes, student characteristics, course/module content, teaching and learning strategies, course/module assessment methods.
- Evaluate the usefulness of an outcomes-based approach to teaching and learning, for students, themselves, their subject, and other interested benefactors of higher education provision.

OUTCOMES-BASED PLANNING: THE BACKGROUND

The findings of the Higher Education Quality Council (HEQC) Graduate Standards Programme (Gaymer, 1997) and the Dearing Report (NCIHE, 1997) echo decades of debate, both in the UK and abroad, on the importance of making the teaching and learning process more explicit and transparent to both teacher and students alike and, most recently, other benefactors of higher education provision. The earliest discussions of making teaching and learning more explicit centred on the development of learning objectives. These originated in the field of behavioural psychology. The debates surrounding the use of behavioural objectives in higher education have been ongoing for several decades and at times have been quite vociferous (Mager, 1962). Arguments for and against their use are listed in Table 3.1.

Defining learning objectives requires teachers to make conscious choices about a wide range of teaching and learning considerations. The process of identifying teaching/learning objectives essentially defines what it is *the teacher* wants the student to learn. The focus of this planning is on the inputs to the learning experience and can be described as teacher-centred. For educators who subscribe to a learner-centred pedagogy, learning objectives are less acceptable than the notion

Table 3.1 Teaching and learning objectives: pros and cons

Pros	Cons
Behavioural objectives:	Behavioural objectives:
Make learning focused and achievable	Focus too narrowly on minutiae, which can trivialize learning
Give direction to student learning	Focus on measurable objectives to the neglect of attitudes, values, motivation and interests
Provide a positive contract between the teacher and student, avoiding digressions	Are difficult and time-consuming to write
Allow for specific intervention if objectives not met	Are teacher-centred
Allow for flexibility in learning activities	Limit opportunities from spontaneous unintended outcomes occurring during learning experiences
Help to focus on essential concepts and skills in the subject	Result in educational achievements being confounded by issues of accountability
Possibly increase learning (suggested by the literature)	

of learning outcomes. In this case the outcomes equal outputs and focus on what *the students* will be able to do at the end of their programme of study (Otter, 1992; Walker, 1994).

References to learning outcomes, *per se*, are becoming more and more prevalent in higher education literature, especially with regard to developments related to the recommendations of the Dearing Report (NCIHE, 1997), eg, the articulation of **programme specifications**. Outcomes may viewed as a middle ground between statements of learning which are considered over-generalized (learning aims) and those which are over-specified (learning objectives) (Walker, 1994).

It is not uncommon when reading the literature on organizing learning in higher education to find the terms 'objectives' and 'outcomes' used interchangeably or together, as objectives/outcomes. The distinctions are frequently overlooked because, despite the variations in how they have been defined, when used, both require greater explicitness and transparency with regard to planning the teaching/learning process. The pedagogic value of objectives/outcomes for planning is discussed in the section to follow.

Table 3.2 Five approaches to course/module design

Type of Approach	Description
Systematic	Proceeds from identifiable needs to predictable outcomes. It follows a planning sequence with a feedback loop for changing and improving the design each time the course is taught.
Intellectual	Examines the subject matter in terms of assumptions held in the discipline with regard to a particular body of information, attitudes and skills. It asks questions such as: should the course be taught at the macro- or micro-level of conceptual analysis?
Problem-based	Identifies one or more specific problems to be addressed. It is not objective-defined but objective-based through inference. It eventually gets to a systematic approach but not sequentially. It places an emphasis on the process of understanding the problem.
Creative/experiential	Involves teaching/learning by experience and generally through the dynamics of a group process. Outcomes are defined in the existential moment of learning.
Training/workshop-based	Outcomes are defined by the skills acquired through the training workshop.

MODELS OF COURSE/MODULE DESIGN

When asked how they go about planning, academics often identify a process described as the 'intellectual approach'. That is, they start by listing topics they wish to cover in a course/module, placing primary emphasis on disciplinary content (see Table 3.2). Subject specialists in the arts and humanities often report using the 'experiential approach' to planning and those in the physical sciences and medicine tend to report using a 'problem-based approach'. Others may use a combination of approaches when planning courses. Knowledge of the various approaches to learning design is useful when reviewing and assessing teaching practice.

Interrogating Practice

If you have had some teaching experience, a good place to start when thinking about reviewing your present approach to course/module planning, is to answer the questions below. (If you are just starting to think about this area, then put the questions in the future tense.)
How do you typically go about planning a course/module?
Why do you do it the way you do?
How satisfied are you with your approach?
How successful is it for your students' learning?

(Based on Young, 1978)

SYSTEMATIC APPROACH AND OUTCOMES-BASED PLANNING

Among the various planning approaches commonly used in higher education, the systematic approach to course/module planning is most closely linked to the outcomes approach to teaching and learning. In fact, the specification of outcomes is the first step in the systematic approach. Figure 3.1 illustrates each of the component parts of a systematic approach to course/module design. It demonstrates that integral to this approach is the interrelationship of the various steps, ie, each part links to and informs the others in an iterative fashion. Because the first step in this planning process starts by stating the objectives/outcomes, followed by the second step of identifying and sequencing the topics to be considered, the emphasis of this model is clearly on the outcomes to be achieved by the student, not the content to be imparted. It also shifts the focus used by the intellectual model of course/module planning from the knowledge base of the teacher to the knowledge needs of the student, thus creating a more learner-centred educational experience.

In addition to shifting the focus of the course/module planning to the needs of students, another advantage of the systematic model shown in Figure 3.1 is that by following the sequence of tasks outlined, planning occurs in incremental steps. It addresses the complex task of course/module planning by helping to organize a body of knowledge into manageable components, thus making a challenging activity one which is eminently more achievable. As one staff member in higher education stated: 'When starting to plan a course I tend to look at everything at once, which can be overwhelming. By using the systematic approach I can pinpoint my focus and make some progress. Otherwise I do little or nothing constructive about planning my course/module.'

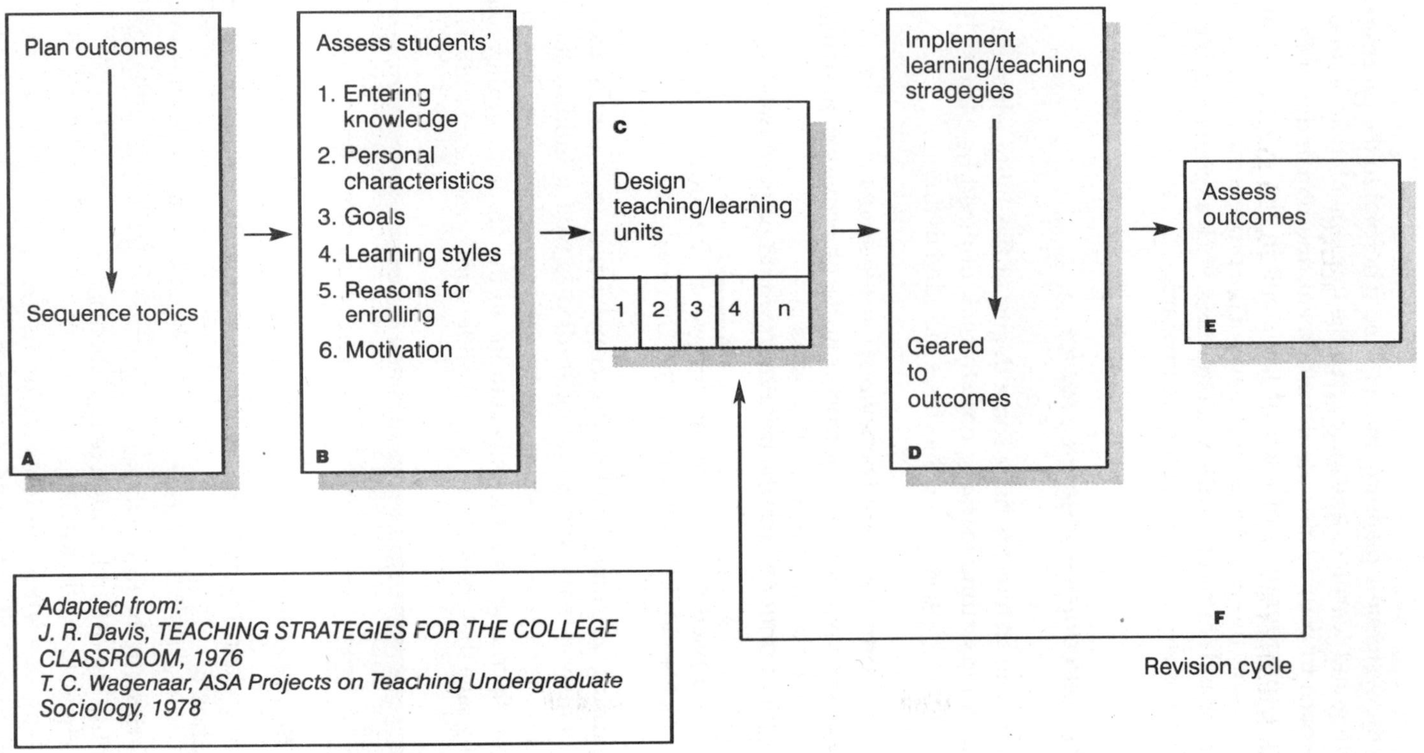
Plan outcomes
Sequence topics
A
Assess students'
1. Entering knowledge
2. Personal characteristics
3. Goals
4. Learning styles
5. Reasons for enrolling
6. Motivation
B
C
Design teaching/learning units
1
2
3
4
n
Implement learning/teaching stragegies
Geared to outcomes
D
Assess outcomes
E
F
Revision cycle
Adapted from:
J. R. Davis, TEACHING STRATEGIES FOR THE COLLEGE CLASSROOM, 1976
T. C. Wagenaar, ASA Projects on Teaching Undergraduate Sociology, 1978

Figure 3.1 Systematic approach to course / module planning

Because the systematic planning model is both helpful to the process of organizing teaching and learning, and promotes the implementation of an outcomes-based approach to course/module development, the remainder of this chapter focuses on a consideration of each of the steps in the systematic approach. However, for some models of teaching, parts of the process may occur in a slightly different order and/or receive different emphasis, such as courses using problem-based learning or work in some of the creative arts.

Step A: plan outcomes – sequence topics

Learning outcome statements have some degree of flexibility when compared to the rigid rules for writing learning objectives as outlined by Mager (1962). The expectations for writing learning objectives included defining:

- who is to perform the desired behaviour (eg, the student);
- what actual behaviour would demonstrate the objective (eg, to write);
- the result of the behaviour (eg, the product);
- the conditions under which the behaviour would be performed (eg, in a two-hour exam);
- the standard used to evaluate the success of the product (eg, 70 per cent correct) (Goldsmid, 1976; Robert Gordon University, 1996).

Effective **learning outcomes** are less prescriptive and are meant to facilitate the student's orientation to the subject being studied as well as guiding the choice of teaching/learning/assessment strategies for the course/module. They are meant to communicate course/module expectations to the student, so they should be stated in language that the student would understand (see Case Study 1).

Case Study 1: Writing learning outcomes

Oxford Brookes University

Well-written learning outcomes will need to satisfy a number of key criteria and should:

- be written in the future tense;
- identify important learning requirements;
- be achievable and assessable;
- use language which students can understand;
- relate to explicit statements of achievement.

Some examples of learning outcomes:

History

- Provide causal analysis of particular events or issues that presuppose a familiarity with the major historical processes which have shaped modern British and European societies.
- Use a wide range of potential historical resources, and avoid the pitfalls which these may present.

Occupational therapy

- Explain your own responsibilities under Health and Safety at Work legislation and act accordingly.
- Recognize and apply the implications of professional ethics (for example, in relation to confidentiality, plagiarism, syndication and copyright).

(Walker, 1994, pp 5–7)

Levels of outcomes

Concern for levels of achievement as an element of stated learning outcomes was considered by Bloom as early as 1956 and preceded the current debate in the UK on levels descriptors by decades. Bloom's taxonomy of learning objectives (outcomes) is considered a major work in this field of inquiry. Bloom's levels were arranged hierarchically with more complex learning listed at the higher levels (see below). Levels are 'an indicator of relative demand; complexity; depth of study and learner autonomy' (Gosling and Moon, 2001) and add to the transparency and clarification of the learning process. 'Level descriptors provide a structure to higher education by giving a more practical meaning to progression in learning.' (Moon, 2002).

Bloom's original taxonomy of learning levels was focused on what he called the cognitive domain of learning. Bloom suggested that in the cognitive domain understanding ranged over six levels of learning, from the lowest level which he termed factual knowledge to increasingly more difficult cognitive tasks, through comprehension, application, to analysis and synthesis, up to the highest level, evaluation of information.

This taxonomy, although useful for planning and writing learning outcomes, was criticized because it excluded other domains of learning. Bloom and his colleagues (Krathwohl, Bloom and Masica, 1964) and Kibler (1970) set out to extend the taxonomy to include what they called the affective and psychomotor domains as well. Others have extended them further and there are now taxonomies of the perceptual, experiential and interpersonal domains (Moore, 1969; Steinaker and Bell, 1979; Menges and McGaghie, 1974).

Four 'domains' of intended learning outcomes for programmes of study in higher education in the UK, proposed in the Dearing Report (NICHE, 1997, recommendation 21), have been used for a variety of purposes, including organizing teaching and learning. They include:

- knowledge and understanding;
- key skills: communication, numeracy, IT, learning to learn;
- cognitive skills (eg, ability in critical analysis);
- subject-specific skills (eg, laboratory skills).

For some disciplines and in some universities, specification based on these four 'domains' would present no problem because current practice is very similar. For others this specification would mean radical change and would raise issues of acceptability in relation to the teaching of the discipline. Understanding the domains of learning, whatever the classification, is the first step in establishing levels of learning outcomes, but more important are the levels themselves.

Research on **deep** and **surface approaches** (eg, Biggs, 1987) to learning (Chapter 2) has also influenced thinking on levels of outcomes and views all learning as having five levels delineated as:

- an increase in knowledge;
- memorizing;
- the acquisition of procedures;
- the abstraction of meaning;
- understanding reality.

When the teaching and learning outcomes focus on the first three levels, this is called a 'surface' approach to learning. When they focus on the last two levels, this is called a 'deep' approach to learning. The major difference between the two types of learning is the level of meaning placed by the student on knowledge acquisition. Bloom's taxonomies of learning are useful in helping to write outcomes that also take into account deep and surface approaches to learning.

Practical advice for writing learning outcomes

In order to assist the student produce the result which is appropriate for the level of achievement intended, it is important to word outcomes carefully. Table 3.3, which uses Bloom's cognitive domain categories as an example, lists some of the

Table 3.3 Suggested words for outcome level statements (cognitive domain)

Level	Suggested Words
Evaluation	Judge, appraise, evaluate, compare, assess
Synthesis	Design, organize, formulate, propose
Analysis	Distinguish, analyse, calculate, test, inspect
Application	Apply, use, demonstrate, illustrate, practice
Comprehension	Describe, explain, discuss, recognize
Knowledge	Define, list, name, recall, record

(Adapted from Bloom, 1956)

possible words that have been identified as useful for this purpose. It is easy to see that a common characteristic of all of these words, no matter what the level, is that they are unambiguous action verbs.

A useful, and more detailed, 'How to…' booklet by Gosling and Moon (2001) on writing learning outcomes and assessment criteria, which includes level descriptors, is noted in the Further Reading section at the end of this chapter.

Some systematic course/module planning models include defining the broader aims of teaching and learning in advance of defining the outcomes. When this is done, words such as understand, appreciate, and grasp are used. A comparison of words commonly used in writing aims and those that may be used in writing outcomes is given in Table 3.4. The two lists help to identify the differences between aims and outcomes and their use in planning and designing learning.

Table 3.4 Comparison of words used in writing aims and outcomes statements

Aims	Outcomes
Know	Distinguish between
Understand	Choose
Determine	Assemble
Appreciate	Adjust
Grasp	Identify
Become familiar	Solve, apply, list

Interrogating Practice

Writing learning outcomes:

1. You are teaching a foundation course and you want your students to remember some important terms. Write a leaning outcome statement that you hope will achieve this and involve a deep approach to learning.

2. You are teaching about a specific concept in your subject area. You want your students to reach an *analytical* level in their thinking. Choose one outcome that you want students to accomplish and write a learning outcome for this session.

3. You are teaching at the foundation level about a theoretical area important to understanding your subject. What you want your students to be able to do is to reach the level of *evaluation*. Write a learning outcome for this session.

(Based on D'Andrea, 1996; Schnable, 1993)

Sequencing topics

Once the outcomes are written, the remainder of the systematic approach is fairly straightforward and involves more of a matching exercise than anything else. The match must be made between the stated outcomes and all subsequent stages. First, the topics chosen need to match the outcomes before they are organized into the sequence which will be followed during the period of study.

Interrogating Practice

Using the format illustrated in Figure 3.2 start by completing the first two sections for a unit of your teaching. Then, following the description of Steps C, D and E which follow, complete the rest of the sections. Once completed, check to see that the various sections match against each other, both in terms of inherent logic and their relationship to each other, particularly in contributing to the achievement of the outcomes stated.

Course/module aims:
Associated objective/outcome:
Teaching/learning strategy:
Assessment strategy:

Figure 3.2   Framework for linking aims, outcomes and strategy

Step B: assessing student characteristics

The next step in the systematic approach to organizing teaching and learning is to identify the major categories of student characteristics that affect the learning experience of students. Some of the characteristics that have been found useful to the planning process include: knowledge on entry, personal characteristics, demographics, variables and **learning style** (see Table 3.5). Once identified, a match can be made between student needs and learning outcomes. For example, knowledge on entry will clearly help determine the topics to be examined and the depth of their consideration in a course/module. If getting information on the students for your specific course is difficult, aggregate information on students at the institution can prove quite useful. Some institutions are well equipped to provide a wide range of information on students enrolled on specific programmes; others are not.

If all available information is taken into account when designing the teaching/learning units and choosing the strategies to implement them, it is much more likely that effective strategies will be employed to enhance the students' learning experience.

Interrogating Practice

Table 3.5 lists a few examples of student characteristics that can be used to assist with the planning of a course/module. It also suggests sources of information and how they can be used in the planning process. Using this as a guide:

1. Identify the sources of information on students available at your institution.

2. Specify how the information available could be used in your course/module planning.

Table 3.5 Categories of student characteristics

1. Knowledge on Entry
   (i) Knowledge and skills relevant to the outcomes of the course/module (eg, IT skills for a statistics course).
   (ii) Possible source of information: student self-report, pre-test (**diagnostic test**), result of previous course(s)/module(s).
   (iii) Use of information: to alter outcomes, provide learning development activities, decide on concrete versus abstract presentation of information; pace of presentation.

2. Personal Characteristics
   (i) Characteristics which result in orientation to subject matter and work habits which influence learning. Examples: academic self-concept, 'beliefs' about the subject, course, unit/lesson's relevance and worth to a student (eg, two-year experience as a juvenile case worker prior to a course in juvenile justice system).
   (ii) Possible source of information: student self-report, interview, observation, standardized and self-developed instruments, beginning of course questionnaire, informal conversations.
   (iii) Use of information: assessment and development of affective objectives. Special attention to some students. Relate course material to experiences, interests, and aspirations as a way to make it meaningful, ensure concrete experience before presenting abstractions, use skills and experiences in the course.

3. Demographic Information
   (i) Examples: age, academic status, work status, residence, degree programme, class/work schedule.

Table 3.5 continued

(ii) Possible source of information: self-report questionnaire, oral introduction at first class session.

(iii) Use of information: assess teaching/learning methods and activities.

4. Learning Style
   (i) Characteristic way a student processes information and/or participates in learning activities. Example: as a learner, a student might be independent, collaborative, dependent, avoidant, competitive or participative.
   (ii) Possible source of information: student self-report, observation, learning style inventory (Chapters 2 and 15).
   (iii) Use of information: understanding of student behaviour, design methods of teaching and learning to use, or to alter student's preferred style.

Steps C, D and E: designing teaching/learning units, implementing teaching/learning strategies and assessing outcomes

In a systematic approach to course/module planning, designing the teaching and learning units, choosing and implementing teaching and learning strategies, and assessing the teaching and learning are the critical steps which need to be directly linked to the outcomes planned. Each unit should be related to at least one outcome and the teaching, learning and assessment methods should be chosen so that the outcomes can be achieved. For example, a course with practical outcomes should adopt practical methods of teaching and learning and assess students' learning in practical situations. On the other hand, courses with the aims to develop students' ability to undertake independent studies within a discipline should include significant elements of independent study assessed by project work, rather than a lecture-based course assessed by unseen exams (D'Andrea, 1996). There is no correct teaching and learning strategy and there may be many possible routes to this end. Whatever is chosen, it should be the one that can help students achieve the stated outcomes for the course/module.

Step F: revision cycle

The systematic approach also includes a revision cycle. This is meant to allow for the improvement of the course/module delivery and achievements of students' learning. In this case, results of students' assessments are used to inform the changes to be made. Again, these would of necessity be directly linked back to the outcomes stated in Step A. It is also important to reappraise the learning outcomes themselves at regular intervals in order to establish whether they continue to reflect the needs of the subject and / or the students. If not, then it is time to revisit them in order to renew and update them and to begin the systematic planning cycle again (Robert Gordon University, 1996).

OVERVIEW

Using an outcomes-based approach to organizing teaching serves a multitude of purposes. It allows teachers to clarify for themselves the implicit outcomes that are always part of any teaching and learning activity. It allows for a reflective interrogation of all aspects of the pedagogical practice and assists in the selection of appropriate teaching / learning and assessment strategies. It allows students to have a clearer understanding of what they can expect from their educational pursuits and avoids any unnecessary guessing games about what is important to learn. Both these last points will assist students through potentially greater motivation to learn, which in turn can lead to improved performance in the process of learning. Collectively such approaches should foster and facilitate improved communication between teachers and students.

REFERENCES

Biggs, J B (1987) *Student Approaches to Learning and Studying*, Australian Council for Educational Research, Melbourne

Bloom, B (1956) *Taxonomy of Educational Objectives Handbook I: Cognitive domain*, McGraw-Hill, New York

D'Andrea, V (1996) *Course design workshop materials*, Roehampton Institute, London

Gaymer, S (1997) *Levels, Credits and Learning Outcomes Article*, Higher Education Quality Council, Quality Enhancement Group Memorandum, London

Goldsmid, C A (1976) *Components/Characteristics of Instructional Objectives*, American Sociological Association Projects on Teaching Undergraduate Sociology, Oberlin, Ohio

Gosling, D and Moon, J (2001) *How to Use Learning Outcomes and Assessment Criteria*, Southern England Consortium for Credit Accumulation and Transfer, SEEC Office, London (http://www.seec-office.org.uk/)

Higher Education Quality Council (1997) *Graduate Standards Programme Final Report*, Volumes 1 and 2, Higher Education Quality Council, London

Kibler, R J (1970) *Behaviorial Objectives and Instruction*, Allyn and Bacon, Boston

Krathwohl, D R, Bloom, B S and Masica, B B (1964) *Taxonomy of Educational Objectives: Handbook II: Affective domain*, David McKay, New York

Mager, R F (1962) *Preparing Instructional Objectives*, Fearon, Palo Alto, California

Menges, R J and McGaghie, W C (1974) Learning in group settings: towards a classification of outcomes, *Educational Technology*, **14**, pp 56–60

Moon, J (2002) *How to Use Level Descriptors*, Southern England Consortium for Credit Accumulation and Transfer, SEEC Office, London (http://www.seec-office.org.uk/)

Moore, J W (1969) Instructional design: after behavioural objectives what? *Educational Technology*, **9**, pp 45–48

NCIHE (1997) (Dearing Report) *Higher Education in the Learning Society*, National Committee of Inquiry into Higher Education, HMSO, London (also to be found at: http://www.leeds.ac.uk/educol/ncihe)

Otter, S (1992) *Learning Outcomes in Higher Education*, Unit for the Development of Adult and Continuing Education, London

Robert Gordon University (1996) *Specifying the Outcomes of Student Learning: A course booklet for the postgraduate certificate in Tertiary Level Teaching*, Educational Development Unit, The Robert Gordon University, Aberdeen

Schnable, J (1993) Exercise on Writing Learning Objectives, American Sociological Association, *Teaching Techniques and Strategies: How to Revive the Classroom*, Cincinnati, Ohio

Steinaker, N N and Bell, M B (1979) *The Experiential Taxonomy: A new approach to teaching and learning*, Academic Press, New York

Walker, L (1994) *Guidance for Writing Learning Outcomes*, Oxford Brookes University, Oxford

Young, R E (1978) *Course Planning: A workable approach to course design*, Virginia Commonwealth University, Richmond, Virginia

FURTHER READING

Allan, J (1996) Learning outcomes in higher education, *Studies in Higher Education*, **21** (1), pp 93–108. A very useful summary on the history of learning objectives/outcomes.

Davis, J R (1974) *Learning Systems Design*, McGraw-Hill, New York

Gosling, D and Moon, J (2001) *How to Use Learning Outcomes and Assessment Criteria*. See above. A useful and up-to-date 'how to' guide for development of learning outcomes and related assessment criteria with specific reference to practice in the UK.

Entwistle, N (1992) *The Impact of Teaching on Learning Outcomes in Higher Education, A Literature Review*, UCoSDA, CVCP, Sheffield. A useful reference list on the subject of learning outcomes.

Mager, R F (1962) See above. Essential reading for anyone wishing to start at the beginning of the objectives/outcomes debate.

Walker, L (1994) See above. For practical advice on writing learning objectives/outcomes, including examples from a range of subjects.

4 Principles of student assessment

Richard Wakeford

INTRODUCTION

The **assessment** of students' learning is a not well understood and, in most disciplines, an under-researched aspect of higher education. This is understandable – teachers may feel that their educational energy is being sapped by curricular and pedagogical demands, and what's wrong with the present assessment system, anyway? – but it is not tolerable. Why not? Why is it important to include a discussion of student assessment in a handbook for teachers in higher education?

It is important for two quite different reasons. First, assessment is an integral component of the teaching and learning system. Assessment may be used explicitly to guide students in their study. But also, student perceptions of what is rewarded and what is ignored by more formal examination procedures will have a substantial impact upon their learning behaviour and thus upon the outcomes of a course.

Second, for a variety of reasons, assessment needs to be accurate – and if it is not itself examined, then we cannot know how accurate it is. We need assessment to be accurate because it is pointless and unfair to students if it is otherwise. We need it to be accurate for internal and external quality assurance purposes; and we need it to be accurate to defend the increasingly likely legal challenges from disaffected students who feel they have been unfairly judged, classified or even excluded.

Thus assessment may be seen as informal and **formative** (see also Chapter 12), within the teaching process, or **summative**, making formal decisions about progress and level of achievement. While the distinction may not always be a true one – less formal assessments may be summated and included in summative assessment, and failing a summative assessment may be most formative – this chapter concentrates on the formal, summative assessment and the principles underpinning it.

As part of its recent (1998–2001) and final round of **Subject Reviews**, the Quality Assurance Agency for Higher Education (**QAA**) asked the following questions within its inspections (QAA, 1997), making it clear that it regards assessment as a central component of the teaching and learning process.

How effective are assessment design and practice in terms of:

- clarity, and students' understanding of assessment criteria and assignments;
- promoting learning (including the quality of feedback to students);
- measuring attainment of the intended learning outcomes;
- appropriateness to the student profile, level and mode of study;
- consistency and rigour of marking;
- evidence of internal moderation and scrutiny by external examiners?

A few years ago, a senior examiner in an old university wrote to his examiners as follows about changes to degree classification conventions: 'May I emphasize that this year beta/alpha, alpha/beta and alpha/alpha/beta are functioning, respectively, almost exactly as beta/beta/alpha, beta/alpha and alpha/beta did last year. Markers familiar with last year's conventions should adapt to the new nomenclature (designed to make Firsts look more like Firsts to outsiders) and not stint their leading alphas.' Unfortunately for him, the memorandum fell into the hands of *Private Eye*, resulting in freedom for this small but telling piece of information. The assumption is that all those being communicated with would automatically understand the arcane secret language of examination procedures.

The post-Dearing reforms in UK universities will lead to increased expertise among (at least) recently appointed staff in all matters relating to teaching, learning and assessment. Coupled with the interest of external accrediting bodies, such as the QAA, generally, and also subject-specific ones (for example, the General Medical Council, resulting in almost wholesale reform of curricula and examinations in UK medical schools), these developments will certainly cause higher education institutions and their staff to take a greater interest in the topic. This will inevitably reduce the 'if it ain't broke, don't fix it' attitude of many, which can extend to a presumption that if a system has been in existence for decades (or even centuries), then it must be all right.

The requirements upon educational providers under the Disability Discrimination Act, the Special Educational Needs and Disabilities Act, and the Race Relations (Amendment) Act, to provide fair and equitable services to all university students (and applicants), will make the need to understand the issues surrounding the assessment of students that much greater.

So what makes student assessment bad, good or better?

ASSESSMENT CONCEPTS AND ISSUES

Depending upon the aims of assessment policies of an individual institution or department, effective assessment will reflect truthfully some combination of an individual's abilities, achievement, skills and potential. Ideally it will permit predictions about future behaviour. To be effective, assessment will need to reflect programme content, and be **valid**, **reliable** and **fair**.

In the past, tests have often been constructed by the fairly haphazard compilation of a set of questions, using whatever assessment method(s) existed. It is now recognized that assessment needs to reflect course or programme content accurately by being blueprinted onto it, at both a general and detailed level. At a general level, the nature of assessment will reflect the general **objectives** (or intended outcomes) of a teaching course or programme. For example, a course designed to teach problem-solving skills would use approaches to assessment which permit assessment of problem-solving abilities, not knowledge recall; a course emphasizing cooperative activities and personal presentation skills would probably need to use testing techniques other than written ones. At a more detailed level, the questions or items used within an assessment component need to be created according to some form of blueprint. The nature of the blueprint will depend upon the subject, but might look something like the example in Table 4.1, where a test item is to be generated for each cell in the table.

Effective assessment procedures need to be at once valid (or appropriate) and reliable (or accurate and consistent). Validity can be seen as having three aspects: face validity, construct validity and impact validity. Face validity is to do with the appropriateness of the content of a test for the audience and level used. Construct validity concerns the nature of the broader constructs tested – for example, recall of knowledge, demonstration of teamwork skills, oratorical persuasive powers. A carefully blueprinted test should have good face and construct validity. Impact validity is about the impact which an assessment procedure has upon the behaviour of the learners, and is probably closely related to students' perceptions of what is rewarded by the test methods used. For example, in a postgraduate examination, an essay test was modified so as to assess explicitly candidates' ability to evaluate published research papers: very significant changes in learner behaviour took place, emphasizing group discussions of primary source material (Wakeford and Southgate, 1992).

Thus validity is judged largely qualitatively; but the reliability of an assessment procedure is calculated mathematically. Depending upon the nature of the assessment method, there are many sources of unreliability in assessment: these include inadequate test length, inconsistency of individual examiners (poor intra-examiner reliability), inconsistencies across examiners (poor inter-examiner reliability), and inadequacies of individual test items used. Inter- and intra-examiner reliabilities can be evaluated straightforwardly, given the raw data. Correlation

Table 4.1 Blueprinting assessment

Teaching Content as Specified in Course Handbook

	Topic A.1	Sub-topic A.11	Sub-topic A.12	Topic A.2	Topic A.3	Topic B.1
Knowledge recall (multi-choice test)						
Application to professional practice (short answer questions)						
Technical problem-solving (computer-based test)						
Critical evaluation of theories (essay)						

matrices will enable test item performance to be evaluated when using open-ended written tests; commercial software exists to enable examiners to evaluate the performance of items in computer-marked tests such as multiple choice tests. The more open-ended assessment is, in general, the harder it is to determine reliability in these ways.

Such techniques will permit judgements about aspects or components of a test (eg, 'Dr X marks differently to all his colleagues'; 'The question on the rise of Irish nationalism needs re-thinking'), but examination boards will increasingly need some overall evaluation of the reliability of a test. What is needed is an answer to the question: to what extent would the same results have been achieved with a similar, parallel form of the same test? A statistical technique that estimates this will give an indication of the robustness of the rank order of candidates produced by a test (Coefficient alpha, or 'Cronbach's alpha', is a good one – it needs to be above 0.8) and other statistics can be used to assess the robustness of pass/fail decisions or degree classifications.

An assessment can be well blueprinted, valid and reliable, but care must be taken to ensure that it is fair both to all individuals and to groups of individuals. For example, examiners may have different marking tendencies so that candidates are likely to be unfairly treated in open-ended written tests if the marking arrangements assume that such differences are insignificant.

There is also evidence that different groups may perform differentially according to assessment methods used. Overall, women appear to perform less well than men in multiple choice type tests, for example, with the reverse difference for free response items, such as essays. Consider the following unpublished data

(Table 4.2) from a national postgraduate examination in medicine, involving a free-response essay-type paper and a multiple true/false multiple choice question (MCQ) paper.

The men/women differences are statistically highly significant ($p<.001$ in each case), but differences will not inevitably follow this pattern. In Cambridge University, an ongoing research project seeks to understand the apparent under-performance of women in the end-of-year examinations which is manifest in many though by no means in all subjects. The implication is that all examination boards would be well advised to set in place appropriate quality assurance monitoring procedures and never rely upon a single examination modality.

ASSESSMENT METHODS

A large number of assessment methods are available for use in higher education. They are listed and described in detail in the principal texts on assessment (see Further Reading section). Those most likely to confront new university teachers are long essay questions, short answer questions, so-called multiple choice questions (MCQs) of many varieties, the assessment of practical or laboratory exercises and quite possibly oral examinations.

As the use of information technology is becoming ubiquitous in the classroom, so it is increasingly being used to support assessment. All of these question formats are amenable to the use of software applications which may enhance examination presentation, analysis and quality monitoring, as well as in the provision of course and student feedback (eg, see www.questionmark.com, www.speedwell.co.uk).

Essay questions

Description

Questions inviting extended written responses (each taking from half-an-hour to an hour or more to answer).

Table 4.2 Differences in test scores by gender and type of test

	Mean MCQ Mark	Mean Essay mark	Number of Candidates
Men	50.11	48.20	1609
Women	48.78	51.69	1482

Variations

The opportunities to vary the testing approach according to the subject are legion, subject only to the examiners' imagination. For example: write a newspaper article with an audience in mind (eg, explaining a current controversy or scientific development for the *Telegraph*, the *Sun*); book review; grant application. The method may be varied by setting topics in advance (the '168-hour examination', Gibbs, Habeshaw and Habeshaw, 1988) or using the open book approach, whereby a limited number of texts are permitted to be brought into the examination room.

Marking systems

Essays are traditionally marked by academic instinct. More recently it has been found that the use of model answers may make for more consistent and fair marks, but this may also over-emphasize what is omitted, not rewarding clever ideas not thought of by the question-setter, and encourage 'grapeshot' answering approaches (ie, flinging everything faintly relevant onto the page in the hope of occasionally hitting the examiner's model). A compromise, where examiners agree a list of five to six themes or constructs for an essay question, on each of which each candidate's essay is rated on a standard scale, may be better.

Advantages

They are readily set and should be able to test high-level cognitive skills (eg, the ability to bring different ideas or theories together and create a synthesis).

Drawbacks

It may be difficult to permit enough essays to reflect realistically the examination blueprint. To achieve adequate reliability, testing time needs to be long (eg, three hours) and multiple marking may be required. Poor exam questions may be unclear ('Write a letter to Wundt's grandson' – Wundt, in case you didn't know, was a turn-of-the-century phrenologist) or, even if clear, simply invite/reward regurgitation of lectures. Candidates may interpret the question in different ways, making fair marking difficult. Fair marking is difficult, anyway. Choice of question makes fair marking almost impossible and this may enhance the impact of differential examiner marking tendencies.

Short answer questions

Description

Questions inviting limited written responses, not normally more than a page in length and often less; which can be short notes or diagrammatic in nature. Response time is 5 to 10 minutes per item.

Variations

Possibilities are relatively limited. An open book approach is possible, with reference materials permitted to be brought in to the examination room.

Marking systems

Model answer systems are typically used (answer supplied by question-setter), but there is no guarantee of accurate or consistent marking. The 'theme/construct' system, see above, is again recommended.

Advantages

Such questions are readily set and are reasonably quick to mark. They can cover a broad test blueprint. The number of questions can give adequate reliability in (often) a couple of hours of testing time.

Drawbacks

It is not easy to produce items which test at cognitive levels higher than simple recall.

Multiple choice questions

Description

Classically, an item stem with four or five completions, with the candidate being invited to identify the most correct one (the 'single correct response' type). Generally, responses are entered on a computer-readable card.

Variations

There are many. Multiple true/false items are common in some disciplines in the UK (each item must be identified true or false), though many testing experts frown on these, arguing that matters are rarely completely true or completely false. Extended matching items (EMIs) are the current vogue in medicine (see Chapter 23), with a more or less extended stem being followed by a number of linked and sophisticated MCQ completion items (Case and Swanson, 1998).

Marking systems

Different approaches imply different systems. Controversy over whether there should be penalties for incorrect responses ('students shouldn't be encouraged to guess') or whether there should not ('otherwise we test confidence/personality as well as what we're trying to test'). Such issues are discussed in detail elsewhere (Case and Swanson, 1998).

Advantages

MCQs allow quick coverage of broad test blueprint. Results are available quickly. This method removes marking error and encourages examiner pre-agreement over correct/incorrect responses. Items can be banked for future use.

Drawbacks

MCQ testing often provokes fierce hostility from traditionalists, for 'dumbing down assessment'. It is hard to write good items and to develop approaches which test at higher cognitive levels. True/false items are impossible in some disciplines. MCQs must be monitored statistically (when it is frequently found that technical errors have been made) and there is an arguable need for security with respect to the item bank.

Assessment of laboratory/practical work

Description

The use of a laboratory situation to assess aspects of a student's work that may not appropriately be assessed by regular paper-based tests. A wide variety of testing objectives are possible and Brown, Bull and Pendlebury (1997) offer a long list of potential objectives which may need to be included in assessment. As a result of deciding what exactly it is that needs to be assessed, the teacher must decide whether any simple paper-and-pencil test method is adequate, or whether the laboratory needs to be the venue for assessment. Typically, students are required to perform some experimental procedure, note the results and evaluate their findings (see Chapter 18).

Variations

Many, including 'dry practicals', where the results of a laboratory experiment are presented and students are required simply to analyse them and to evaluate and comment on them. Group work is increasingly a feature of many undergraduate programmes, reflecting the importance of collaboration skills as a course aim. But the assessment of group work brings a variety of problems (Wood, 1991).

Marking systems

These vary, depending upon the approach. Main problems surround how to balance assessment of process versus outcome/analysis/evaluation and standardizing this. The classic science paradigm (methods, results, conclusion) may assist in producing assessment criteria. Work in the assessment of medical students using objective, standardized approaches may also be helpful (Harden and Gleeson, 1979).

Advantages

This method allows assessment of a uniquely important aspect of many subjects, the 'real world' of scientific enquiry.

Drawbacks

There are practical difficulties towards making assessment equitable for all students: what happens if a student's experiment 'goes wrong'. The cost of this method of testing may be high. It is also difficult to determine assessment priorities (eg, process versus outcome) and rewards.

Orals

Oral or **viva voce** examinations, though commonly used in professional and post–graduate assessment, are the subject of great concern to test developers and psychometricians – especially when loosely described criteria such as 'sparkle' are mentioned. Orals have their attractions, but are subject to all the well-known biases and problems of selection interviews, and should only be used in the full knowledge of these problems and how these effects may be minimized. The new practitioner in higher education is counselled to beware of and avoid orals, certainly until he or she has read some of the literature (eg, Wakeford, Southgate and Wass, 1995).

QUALITY MONITORING: CURRENT ISSUES iN ASSESSMENT

Making assessment decisions more defensible

UK universities have yet to experience substantial challenges by students to their assessment decisions, but there are signs that this may change. With payment of fees, students are increasingly starting to look like customers, and may well start to behave like them. Academics themselves, moreover, are starting to challenge university decisions made about them on matters such as promotion (Evans, 1999; Evans and Gill, 2001).

With little 'case law' available in the UK, we can do little but look to the United States to see what the bases of such challenge may be. McManus (1998) has summarized the bases of candidates' successful legal challenges there as:

- Candidates being denied the possibility of re-sitting an assessment because of an arbitrary limit on the number of attempts allowed.
- Candidates arguing that they were not, as learners, in a position to learn the things which the assessment procedures assessed.
- Candidates asserting that the test was not valid for the purpose for which it was being used (and possibly had been devised in an inadequate way).
- Candidates asserting that the test had inadequate reliability.
- Candidates arguing that the test was discriminating unfairly against some group (to which the plaintiffs belonged).
- Candidates stating that due process had not taken place (ie, rules and regulations had not been properly observed).
- Candidates arguing that the pass mark had been set inadequately.

The US evidence (Mehrens and Popham, 1992; Downing and Haladynia, 1997) comes from countries with different legal traditions to the UK and should thus be treated cautiously, as it itself suggests, especially for 'high stakes' examinations such as vocational qualifications and assessments contributing to degree classifications. For example, the US literature goes so far as to recommend the use of procedures such as routine 'bias-sensitivity review' for which UK academics may not yet be ready. Translated into the local culture, the implications are that, for assessment in higher education:

- Contemporary good practice in assessment should be adopted (or at least pursued) generally.
- Examiners should receive training on assessment generally, detailed information about the procedures in which they are to be involved, and receive feedback on their performance.

- The function of different components of an assessment system (eg, essay tests, oral examinations, MCQs) should be explicit (and plausible).
- Course designers should be able to defend how the content of an assessment procedure – the questions or items – has been arrived at: how has it been blue-printed?
- Examination procedures – due process – should be specified in detail.
- There should be explicit assessment criteria for test procedures which involve examiner judgement.
- Assessment procedures should be routinely quality assessed, including measures of reliability.
- Multiple assessment methods should be used to counter possible bias associated with individual methods.
- There should be explicit justification for any use of choice-of-question in tests, the methods of equating of standards described.
- The issue of differential examiner marking tendencies must be addressed.

Some current issues in assessment

A number of issues in assessment are currently viewed as important ones which need addressing by universities. They include:

- Controlling for the variability among examiners in the marks which they award to candidates.
- Setting standards for pass/fail and degree class examinations.
- Difficulties caused by the use of student-selected options (eg, 'answer one out of five questions').
- Difficulties caused by the increasingly varied cultural background of students.
- The need to comply with the spirit of the Race Relations (Amendment) Act, etc.
- Increasing argument about the appropriateness of single degree classifications.

There is a persuasive literature attesting to the tendency of examiners to mark in different ways (eg, Wakeford and Roberts, 1984). Almost all examiners can be classified on two dimensions – hawks versus doves (mean or generous markers), and theatrical versus restrained (giving extreme marks or showing little mark variation); and most are consistent in these behaviours. Occasionally, examiners can be found whose marks simply disagree in direction with those of their colleagues.

Case Study 1

The author was working some years ago with examiners from a medical Royal College. They asserted that, with their well-understood general guidelines for grading, together with the explicit marking guidelines for individual questions, they did not believe that there would be substantial differences in the marks given by different examiners.

We undertook a marking experiment to explore these matters. Each examiner re-marked, blind, the same 10 scripts from a recent examination, selected so as to represent a range of abilities. These experienced examiners used the usual general marking guidelines (out of 25; pass mark = 10; distinction mark = 20 and above) and the specific guidance for the question. Four examples of examiners' overall marks were:

Examiner	Average Mark	Standard Deviation	Minimum	Maximum
01	11.5	3.5	7	16
02	19.7	2.9	15	23
06	13.8	1.1	12	16
11	12.2	7.0	4	24

Individual examiners, even armed with explicit guidelines, were readily identifiable as hawks (01) or doves (02), and as theatrical (11) or restrained (06).

The clear implications for university examination committees are: (a) that, in the interests of fairness, individual examiners should each be responsible for awarding only a portion of the marks received by each student (ie, examiners should *not* mark the entire scripts of just a few students; rather, they should mark the answers to a single question, say, for all students); and (b) marks should routinely be analysed by the examiner (this can provide especially helpful feedback when scripts are double-marked). It is thus important neither to give in to the pleas of examiners to make their marking more interesting by giving them different questions to mark nor to accede to the assertions of examination administrators that splitting up student scripts into answers to individual questions is unreasonable.

The way in which **standard**-setting has traditionally taken place in UK university examinations has typically been left up to individual examiners, armed either with guidelines from a question setter or by means of their own internal standards of judgement, possibly supported by general university-wide guidelines.

Unfortunately, such arrangements can often be shown not to work: consider the following case study data relating to the final year examinations in a physical science at an old university.

Case Study 2

One hundred and fifty-five students all took four compulsory unseen essay papers (numbered 1–4), but had, as part of a variety of options, all to take either optional unseen essay paper A or optional unseen essay paper B. The mean marks (and standard deviation) for A were 70.12 per cent (10.31) and for B were 59.53 per cent (15.76).

The university had assumed that the students who had opted for A were cleverer than those opting for B. However, a subsequent analysis of the marks on papers 1–4 showed that the difference was, significantly, in the opposite direction – the average mark on these papers for students taking A was 60.0 per cent and for those taking B was 70.5 per cent. The students taking B were actually the cleverer group. Students were not being treated fairly because effective 'test equating' had not been instituted.

Now it is actually very difficult to set equitable standards when students sit different tests, other than by straightforward statistical manipulation. It is important, though, to recognize the problem and, where possible preclude it (by not including marks from options in summated examination marks), or alternatively to arrange a defensible system for catering for it. Allowing options in assessment, though often desirable educationally, makes for psychometric difficulties.

In general, standards should be set by an examination committee (or examiner group) discussing criteria for degree classes by sharing their expertise and judgements at the level of individual questions.

Providing equitable arrangements for students from different cultural backgrounds may be even more difficult. Certainly, minority groups may feel discriminated against by assessment procedures (see Wakeford *et al*, 1992 for a case study). We are now beginning to realize some of the difficulties when working on the development of oral examinations in postgraduate medicine (see Roberts *et al*, 2000): people raised in different cultures may, for example, not engage in eye contact similarly, with differential inferences being made by examiners; and they may not pick up examiners' cues similarly – for example, to start and to stop role-play. But the differential, even discriminatory trends are almost certainly present in all other forms of assessment.

The need to comply with the spirit of the Race Relations (Amendment) Act and other recent acts designed to ensure fair treatment by ethnicity and gender will have major but as yet unclear impacts on university testing procedures. But certainly, examiners should be provided with training on gender, ethnicity and disability issues in assessment. And examination results should be routinely analysed towards assessing whether fair treatment is being provided. Further analyses should investigate possible causative influences (eg, by bias sensitivity review of items), towards discussion by relevant examination committees.

Challenging the orthodox notion that a single degree classification is helpful to most employers of graduates is an uncomfortable but real discussion which is addressing the attention of many of those concerned with assessment in higher education. Helpful to universities, selecting graduate students, it may be. But the debate will probably outlive the longevity of this edition of our handbook.

Case Study 3: Reviewing a course's end-of-year examinations

A second-year bioscience course taken by 185 students was assessed using two three-hour unseen examinations – a 60-question multiple true/false objective test (in each question, five items were to be marked 'true' or 'false') and a 15-question short essay question test.

A spreadsheet was constructed to facilitate manipulation of the examination data. The departmental secretary created this and inserted the students' examination reference numbers into the first column. Into column 2 she put each candidate's gender, and into column 3 a classification of their ethnicity.

The objective test involved students in marking a response sheet using pencils: this sheet was then read by an optical scanner, the results were input into a commercial computer marking package, and the mark for each item added into the spreadsheet. Each of the 15 short essays was marked by a different member of staff. The secretary added these marks to the spreadsheet so that for each student there were 300 columns relating to the objective test (each with a mark of 1 or 0) and 15 columns relating to the short essay question test, each showing a mark out of 25 (the customary arrangement).

The new departmental statistical expert then used her statistical package to process and analyse the data. She produced a percentage mark for each student on both tests, after transforming the marks on the objective test so that a student who guessed randomly on the whole test would have obtained zero marks.

The statistician's initial action was to prepare a scatter plot representing each candidate's scores on the two tests (see Figure 4.1). Immediately, two things became obvious: first, there was a general high correlation between the two scores; and second, something was apparently wrong with four students' computer-marked test scores. The optically marked cards were inspected and it was found that the four students had used inappropriately hard pencils whose light marks the scanner had failed to read: the marks were made darker, the cards re-scanned, the database updated (at considerable inconvenience), and the percentage scores re-computed.

Before computing an overall mark for each student (the average of the two test scores), the statistician examined the distributions of marks for the two tests. These were:

	Mean Mark	Standard Deviation
Objective Test	45.7	11.7
Short Essay Test	58.9	11.2

She advised that, as the spread of marks on each test was similar – as evidenced by the standard deviation – that they would have an equal impact on the summated score, and that they should simply be averaged to obtain a final mark. This was done, and a class list produced which showed traditional proportions of students obtaining each degree class. Using her statistical package, it took her a few moments to estimate the reliability or consistency of each of the exam components – Cronbach's alpha for the objective test was 0.85 and for the essay test was 0.87.

To examine fairness of the assessment procedures with regard to gender and ethnicity, the statistician examined the distribution of marks by ethnic group and gender for each examination component. An analysis of variance, she said, showed no significant differences on scores by either of these variables.

Upon publication of the class lists, a student noticed that the percentage of students achieving each degree class was identical to those of the three previous years. He threatened to request a judicial review of the department's assessment procedures, claiming that this was *de facto* evidence of normative rather than criterion-referenced testing. In the event, he was awarded a university graduate studentship and lost interest in these matters.

The Examination Committee met early in the summer vacation. It resolved:

- that test reliability was good for both components;
- that the analyses were most helpful and that they be developed and used by the department as the basis of standard examination quality assurance arrangements;
- that it was content with the tests' fairness to students, currently;
- that examiners should continue each to mark the answers to a single essay question for all students;
- that standard-setting procedures need to be reviewed towards the setting of explicit criteria for the classification of answers to individual questions;
- that the functions of the two assessment components needed to be differentiated;
- that the performance of the objective test items needed to be examined;
- that the marks output from the optical scanner always be examined immediately to see whether any scripts may have been incorrectly read.

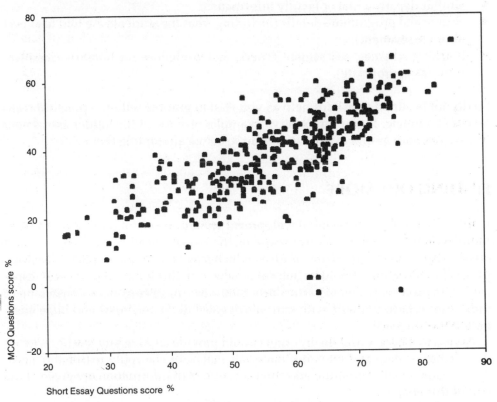

Figure 4.1 Scatter plot showing candidates' scores in two tests

As in other areas of endeavour in higher education, it seems that the future will involve more bureaucracy (and work) to achieve the worthy goal of assured high quality.

BECOMING AN EXAMINER YOURSELF

Most university teachers rapidly find themselves required to take part in their university's formal assessment procedures, often more rapidly than they feel comfortable with. What guidance might they be offered?

The most important and general point is to refuse to be intimidated and to join a conspiracy of misunderstanding and silence. When told that you are to be an examiner, request direction towards:

- any university information for examiners, including relevant rules and regulations, appeals procedures, policies on unfair practices by candidates, codes of practice, and any general guidance;
- similar departmental or faculty information;
- course and programme details (including what the students are told to expect about assessment);
- marking schemes, assessment criteria and guidelines for honours classifications (as appropriate).

So do not be afraid to ask for help as you start to grapple with the practical realities of examining. If you can observe examples of some of the harder assessment techniques such as oral examinations, do so before attempting them.

FINDING OUT MORE

Universities will provide staff development sessions on examinations and assessment which will help flesh out some of the issues raised by this chapter and enable discussion of problems or ideas which may be relevant to particular disciplines. Such sessions should be helpful to new staff. But some subject areas – especially the professions, most particularly medicine – have considerable assessment industries related to them, with journals devoted to the business, and huge international conferences.

Access to a library and the Internet should provide a university teacher with all the further reading and reference materials that he or she could reasonably need. Some leads into the literature and Internet sources of information are given at the end of this chapter.

OVERVIEW

What, then, are the most important principles of assessment?

First, the function or purpose of any assessment procedure needs to be clear, eg, formative or summative, and clearly related to the course teaching and learning. Second, the approach needs to be valid and appropriate to that purpose – this is a largely qualitative judgement. Third, it needs to be reliable or consistent in its application. Fourth, to achieve these ends, assessment procedures need to be discussed and themselves examined.

Using these four principles as questions to evaluate any part of the assessment system with which they are involved could enable university teachers to start involving themselves in what, with likely increasing consumerism in higher education and associated legal challenges, seems likely to be a hot academic topic for the years to come.

Interrogating Practice

What are the three most important questions that you now need to ask about your departmental assessment procedures?

REFERENCES

Brown, G, Bull, J and Pendlebury, M (1997) *Assessing Student Learning in Higher Education*, Routledge, London

Case, S M and Swanson, D B (1998) *Constructing Written Test Questions for the Basic and Clinical Sciences*, National Board of Medical Examiners, Philadelphia (available only electronically, but gratis, from: www.nbme.org)

Downing, S M and Haladynia, T M (1997) Test item development: validity evidence from quality assurance procedures, *Applied Measurement in Education*, **10** (1), 61–82

Evans, G R (1999) *Calling Academia to Account*, Society for Research into Higher Education and the Open University Press, Buckingham

Evans, G R and Gill, J (eds) (2001) *Universities and Students: A guide to rights, responsibilities and practical remedies*, Kogan Page, London

Gibbs, G, Habeshaw, S and Habeshaw, T (1988) *53 Interesting Ways of Assessing your Students*, Technical and Educational Services, Bristol

Harden, R M and Gleeson, F (1979) Assessment of clinical competence using an objective structured clinical examination, *Medical Education*, **13**, 51–54

McManus, I C (1998) Personal communication

Mehrens, W A and Popham, W J (1992) How to evaluate the defensibility of high stakes tests, *Applied Measurement in Education*, **5** (3), 265–83

Quality Assurance Agency for Higher Education (QAA) (1997) *Subject Review Handbook* (QAA 1/97), QAA, Bristol

Roberts, C *et al* (2000) Oral examinations, equal opportunities and ethnicity: fairness issues in the MRCGP, *British Medical Journal*, **320**, 370–74

Wakeford, R *et al* (1992) Does the MRCGP examination discriminate against Asian doctors? *British Medical Journal*, **305**, 92–94

Wakeford, R E and Roberts, S (1984) Short answer questions in an undergraduate qualifying examination: a study of examiner variability, *Medical Education*, **18**, 168–73

Wakeford, R and Southgate, L (1992) Postgraduate medical education: modifying trainees' study approaches by changing the examination, *Teaching and Learning in Medicine*, **4**, 210–13

Wakeford, R, Southgate, L and Wass, V (1995) Improving oral examinations: selecting, training and monitoring examiners for the MRCGP, *British Medical Journal*, **311**, pp 9331–35

Wood, R (1991) *Assessment and Testing: A survey of research*, Cambridge University Press, Cambridge

FURTHER READING

Books are a prime source of theory and evidence in assessment. My selection is as follows:

Brown, G, Bull, J and Pendlebury, M (1997) *Assessing Student Learning in Higher Education*, Routledge, London (particularly recommended)

Brown, S and Glasner, S (eds) (1999) *Assessment Matters in Higher Education*, Society for Research into Higher Education/Open University Press, Buckingham

Case, S M and Swanson, D B (1998) See above (the best guide in the world on writing objective test items)

Heywood, J (2000) *Assessment in Higher Education*, London, Jessica Kingsley Publishers (an updated and wide-ranging text by the author of an earlier classic)

Streiner, D L and Norman, G R (1995) *Health Measurement Scales: A practical guide to their development and use*, 2nd edn, Oxford University Press, Oxford (the science behind objective testing: sampling, reliability, etc)

Wood, R (1991) *Assessment and Testing: A Survey of Research*, Cambridge University Press, Cambridge (a good reference source on assessment based upon a more general review of assessment – ie, beyond higher education)

THE INTERNET

The Internet is increasingly the prime source of information on experiments and developments in education, generally, and assessment, specifically. But as many sites, links and references have only a short lifetime, it is inappropriate in a book to list many. The most currently useful UK higher education sites are undoubtedly those of the generic and subject-specific Learning and Teaching Support Network (LTSN) centres, accessed via www.ltsn.ac.uk – the Generic Centre has just published a series of useful guides on student assessment. 'DeLiberations' at London Guildhall University – www.lgu.ac.uk/deliberations/home.html – is a Web site specifically for academics and educational developers and where assessment is a permanent discussion issue. People with a specific subject-based student assessment interest should try entering their subject and 'student assessment' (or 'examinations') into a search engine such as Google (www.google.com for an international search, www.google.co.uk for UK sites only): with any luck, they will find someone with a parallel interest and/or expertise.

5 Encouraging student motivation

Stephen E Newstead and Sherria Hoskins

INTRODUCTION

A few years ago one of us was involved in a programme of research on student cheating in higher education. The research team had a strong suspicion that incidents of cheating were related to student motivation and wanted to test out this hypothesis. We were thus faced with the problem of how to measure student motivation. We were struck by how little research had been done in this area, by how few measures of student motivation there were, and in particular by how difficult it was to obtain a quick and readily usable indication of what students' motives were in studying at university. This led us to consider how we could identify, first, what motivates students, and second, differences between **intrinsic** and **extrinsic motivation**.

To this end, we devised a very quick and simple (but totally unvalidated) measure: we simply asked students to indicate what was the single main reason why they were studying at university. The responses were, of course, many and varied, but we were able to categorize the great majority of them into three main categories, which we called 'stop gap', 'means to an end' and 'personal development' (Newstead, Franklyn-Stokes and Armstead, 1996). These categories are summarized in Table 5.1. The percentage figures give the proportion of students who were placed into each category out of a university sample of 844 students whose responses could be categorized.

Those classified as stop-gap students (10 per cent) were studying because they could think of nothing else to do, wanted to defer taking a decision, or simply wanted to enjoy themselves for three years. Those classed as means-to-an-end students wanted to achieve something through their degree, whether this was a better paid or more interesting job, or simply qualifications to put after their names. This was much the most common category, with two-thirds of our sample

Table 5.1 Reasons for studying

	Percentage of Students
Stop gap	10%
Avoiding work	
Laziness	
Allowing time out to decide on career	
Social life	
Fun and enjoyment	
Means to an end	66%
Improving standard of living	
Improving chance of getting a job	
Developing career	
Getting a good qualification	
Getting a worthwhile job	
Personal development	24%
Improving life skills	
Reaching personal potential	
Gaining knowledge for its own sake	
Furthering academic interest	
Gaining control of own life	

being classified in this way. Personal development students (nearly a quarter of our sample) were ones who were interested in the subject itself or wanted to use their degree to realize their own potential or to develop their personal skills.

While the classification was largely *post hoc*, and was carried out with incomplete knowledge of existing educational theories of motivation, it is striking how similar our classification is to those arrived at by other researchers. For example, a key distinction is often made between intrinsic and extrinsic motivation. Intrinsically motivated students enjoy a challenge, want to master the subject, are curious and want to learn; while extrinsically motivated students are concerned with the grades they get, external rewards and whether they will gain approval from others (Harter, 1981). While the fit is not perfect, the parallels with our own classification system are clear, with intrinsic motivation corresponding closely to personal development and extrinsic motivation corresponding to means to an end.

Other major distinctions that have been made in the literature also map closely onto our categorization. Dweck and Elliott (1983) have drawn the highly influential distinction between performance goals and learning goals. Students with performance goals are motivated primarily by obtaining good marks, while learning oriented students wish to actually learn something from their studies.

Performance goals are linked to means to an end (and extrinsic motivation), while learning goals are linked with personal development (and intrinsic motivation). Other distinctions in the literature related to Dweck's are those between ability and mastery goals (Nicholls, 1984) and between ego involvement and task involvement (Ames, 1984). There are, of course, important differences in emphasis in all these approaches, but there is enough similarity between them, and enough overlap with the distinctions made in our own characterization, to conclude that the concepts underlying them are reasonably consistent and widespread.

Interrogating Practice

What do you know about the motivation of the students you teach? If they are training for a specific career, does this affect their motivation in a particular way?

AMOTIVATION AND ACHIEVEMENT MOTIVATION

Stop-gap motivation was not especially common in our student sample, but it did occur. While this has not been extensively discussed in the literature, the related concept of **amotivation** has received some attention. Deci and Ryan (1985) describe amotivated students as ones who do not really know why they are at university, think themselves incompetent and feel that they have little control over what happens to them. In a real sense, then, these students show an absence of motivation.

This highlights another aspect of motivation: that it has strength as well as direction. Thus far we have looked at motivational goals, in other words what students' aims are. But even students with identical goals may have very differing strengths of that motivation. A simple example would be two students, both of whom were studying to get a better job, for one of whom it was their lifelong and heartfelt ambition, and for the other of whom it was little more than a passing interest. Although their motives would be the same, the different strengths of these motives might be expected to lead to very different behavioural outcomes, for example in their ability to persevere in adversity.

Many educational writers discuss **achievement motivation** as one of the principal factors influencing outcomes in higher education (Entwistle and Ramsden, 1983). A student who is high in achievement motivation can be seen as lying at the opposite end of the scale from an amotivated student. The former student is concerned primarily with achieving a successful outcome at the end of his or her studies. This cuts across many of the dimensions discussed earlier, in that both extrinsically and intrinsically motivated students can be high or low in achievement motivation. In other words, achievement motivation is largely a measure of the strength of motivation, rather than of its direction.

It is a gross over-simplification, but nevertheless it seems reasonable to suggest that our own research and the existing literature have identified three main types of motivation: intrinsic, extrinsic and achievement motivation (with amotivation simply being the opposite end of the continuum to achievement motivation). Clearly, however, it is of little use knowing what students' motives are unless the impact of these on how students behave is known.

MOTIVES AND BEHAVIOUR

There is surprisingly little evidence as to the behaviour associated with different motives. Some fairly simplistic predictions can be made. For example, one might expect that students high in achievement motivation will actually achieve higher grades. Furthermore, given that intrinsic motivation seems so central to higher education, one would surely expect that students with this motivation should perform better academically than those with extrinsic motivation. One might also predict that the study strategies would be different in different groups of students; for example, intrinsically motivated students might be expected to develop a deeper understanding of the material than extrinsically motivated ones, and perhaps also to be more resistant to discouragement in the light of a poor mark. There is, surprisingly, little clear-cut evidence on any of these predictions.

One line of evidence concerning the relationship between motives and behaviour derives from the work on students' approaches to studying (eg, Entwistle and Ramsden, 1983). Research into these approaches, using the **approaches to studying inventory**, is arguably the most extensively researched area in higher education in recent years. The main focus of this research has been on the distinction between **deep** and **surface** approaches to studying. A deep approach is concerned with conceptual understanding of the material, and incorporating this into one's existing knowledge; whereas a surface approach is characterized by rote learning of material, with the intention of reproducing this in another context (eg, an examination). Each of these approaches is linked to a certain type of motivation, with deep approaches being associated with intrinsic motivation and surface approaches with extrinsic motivation.

Crucially from the present perspective, these associations were derived empirically, through the use of factor analysis. What this means is that specific types of motivation and specific approaches to studying tended to be associated with each other in the responses given by students to questionnaire items. Subsequent research has shown the main factors to be remarkably robust. However, the link between motives and strategies may not be as neat as it seems at first sight. Pintrich and Garcia (1991) found that intrinsically motivated students did indeed use strategies designed to develop a conceptual understanding of material, but that extrinsically motivated students did not, as would have been predicted, use more rehearsal strategies.

In addition to deep and surface approaches, another approach consistently emerges in the analysis of responses to the Approaches to Studying Inventory. This is usually termed the **strategic approach**, and it is closely related to achievement motivation. Strategic students vary their approach depending on the circumstances; if they judge that a surface approach is necessary in one situation, they will use it, but in others they might use a deep approach. Their main aim is to secure high marks and they will adapt their strategy in whatever way they see fit to try to achieve this aim.

Australian research by Biggs has also identified achieving orientation as a major factor in students' approaches to learning. Biggs (1987) characterizes the achieving motivation as a desire to obtain high grades even when the task to be completed does not inspire interest. Biggs states that this motive is facilitated by competition which provides students with the opportunity to increase their self-esteem.

In the same way as Entwistle and Ramsden (1983), Biggs associates this type of motivation with a specific learning strategy, which he terms the achieving strategy but which is very similar to the strategic approach.

The relationship between motivation and academic success has been investigated by Pintrich and Garcia (1991), and the picture that emerges is not a simple one. Overall, there was no direct relationship between intrinsic motivation and academic success, but instead an interaction between motivation and the strategy adopted. In essence, students who lack intrinsic motivation can still perform well, providing they adopt appropriate study strategies to compensate for this. Research into students' approaches to studying has produced mixed results. While some authors have reported a correlation between deep approaches and academic success (eg, Entwistle and Ramsden, 1983) this is not always found to be the case (eg, Clarke, 1986). Hence there is little evidence to support the claim that intrinsic motivation leads to academic success. As we shall see, one possible reason for this is that intrinsic motivation, while valued by lecturers, is not necessarily rewarded in the assessments they give students.

Interrogating Practice

Reflect on the correlation between motivation and academic achievement as demonstrated by students you teach. How well do your intrinsically motivated students perform?

MEASURING STUDENT MOTIVATION

In addition to the measures of achievement motivation contained within the instruments developed by Entwistle and Ramsden (1983) and Biggs (1987), a small number of other motivation measures has been developed specifically for use with students in higher education. The two most important of these are the Academic Motivation Scale developed by Vallerand *et al* (1992) and the Motivated Strategies for Learning Questionnaire developed by Pintrich *et al* (1993).

The Academic Motivation Scale consists of 28 items which are designed to assess three types of intrinsic motivation, three types of extrinsic motivation, and amotivation. It would appear to have reasonable reliability and validity (Vallerand *et al*, 1992), and its short length means that it can realistically be used in educational research.

The Motivated Strategies for Learning is a much longer scale, containing 81 items, with rather more sub-scales. It is also US-oriented, and thus far seems to have not been used in this country. Although the scale has good reliability and validity, it is rather too long to be of great use in educational research, at least outside the United States.

THE DEVELOPMENT OF MOTIVATION

We have seen the kinds of things that motivate students, leading us to consider their motivation through the years of a degree course.

Interrogating Practice

In your experience, do students come to university with high motivation? What happens to their motivation during their stay at university? Does your department inspire them to ever higher levels of motivation? If so, how?

One measure of students' motivations on arriving at university is Entwistle's (1998) Approaches to Study Skills Inventory for Students (ASSIST). Part of this involves questions about reasons for entering higher education. In a study carried out at the University of Plymouth, this inventory was administered to some 600 first-year students, with the results as given in Table 5.2.

Table 5.2 Percentage of students agreeing strongly or fairly strongly with questions on the ASSIST scale

Reason for Entering Higher Education	Students Agreeing
The qualification at the end of this course would enable me to get a good job when I finish	92%
The course will help me develop knowledge and skills which will be useful later on	89%
I wanted a chance to develop as a person, broaden my horizons and face new challenges	63%
The opportunities for an active social life and/or sport attracted me	63%
I would be able to study subjects in depth, and take interesting and stimulating courses	61%
I basically wanted to try and prove to myself that I could really do it	46%
Having done well at school, it seemed to be the natural thing to go on to higher education	39%
It would give me another three or four years to decide what I really wanted to do later on	37%
I suppose it was a mixture of other people's expectations and no obvious alternative	9%
I rather drifted into higher education without deciding it was what I really wanted to do	7%

Taken from Sharpe *et al*, in submission

These results are broadly consistent with the findings obtained using a very different method (and on students already in higher education) by Newstead, Franklyn-Stokes and Armstead (1996). The main reasons for entering higher education were to get a good job and to develop useful skills (ie, means to an end). Next most frequent were reasons relating to personal development, such as to study subjects in depth and develop as a person. Less frequent were the stop-gap reasons, such as to delay taking a decision or simply drifting into higher education. The only slight mismatch is in the high ranking given in the Sharpe study to an active social and sporting life. This is probably because the reason is indeed an important one for many people, but is seldom the single most important reason (the Newstead study asked simply for the single main reason for studying).

The similarity of the findings in these two studies might suggest that students' motives do not change a great deal over the course of their degrees. There is direct support for this contention in the research of Fazey and Fazey (1998). They used Vallerand's Academic Motivation Scale to carry out a longitudinal investigation of students' motivation over the first two years of their degree courses at the University of Bangor. Their results indicated that students were high on both intrinsic and extrinsic motivation on entry to university but much lower on amotivation. From the present perspective, the interesting finding was that the levels of these three types of motivation showed virtually no change over the first two years at university. In a sense this is a disappointing finding since one might have hoped that higher education would have led to students becoming more intrinsically motivated by their subject. It is of course possible that this does happen to some students but is offset by an equal number who become less intrinsically motivated. A similar finding emerged in a study by Jacobs and Newstead (2000) who found that students' interest in their discipline seemed, if anything, to decline over the course of their studies.

ENCOURAGING STUDENT MOTIVATION

Lecturers frequently bemoan the lack of student motivation and ask what they can do to improve this. We hope that the foregoing overview will have at least hinted that there is no quick fix. Indeed, before even addressing this issue it is necessary to ascertain what aspect of student motivation needs to be addressed. Most lecturers would agree that a complete lack of motivation of any kind – amotivation – is highly undesirable. Further, most lecturers would claim that intrinsic motivation is more desirable than extrinsic. Hence these are the two principal questions that will be addressed in this section.

First, then, how can we avoid students becoming amotivated? For some students, this will be next to impossible, since they may have entered higher education with the sole aim of enjoying the social life. But there is also evidence that what we do to students at university can lead to their becoming amotivated. Hoskins (1999) has recently completed a research programme investigating students' approaches to essay writing, and has discovered through a combination of focus groups and questionnaires that certain factors of this process lead to students losing motivation. Of particular importance is the feedback given, both in terms of the mark awarded and the written feedback provided.

One group of students approached essay writing with an understanding motivation, in that they enjoyed writing, had an intrinsic interest in the essay and tended to read extensively. Because of the amount of reading they did, they often had problems focusing their essay and adhering to the word limit. As a result they tended to receive poor marks but had difficulty in understanding where they had gone wrong or what skills they needed to overcome the problems. These students felt that marking was often inconsistent and contained insufficient detail to be helpful. In consequence, they avoided using an understanding motivation on the grounds that they felt it unlikely to lead to a good mark.

One of the most prominent themes in the focus group data collected by Hoskins was the almost unanimous perception of essay marks as unsatisfactory. Students often felt that there was no relationship between the amount of effort they put into an essay and the mark they were awarded, and that it took a disproportionate amount of effort to achieve small percentage increases. They were highly critical of what they regarded as a 'glass ceiling' – an unwritten rule which seems to prevent them getting marks higher than an upper second. Since they found it relatively easy to produce an essay which got a high lower second or low upper second mark, there was little incentive to do any extra work given the existence of this glass ceiling. The belief that the range of marks awarded for essays is too limited given the potential range available was also a constantly recurring theme.

It is only part of the answer to this problem, but it would appear that one way of avoiding amotivation is to make sure that students are given full and appropriate feedback; and, if it is clear that they have put in extra work and not received a particularly high mark, then feedback on why this has occurred needs to be given. When terms such as 'developing an argument' are used, there needs to be some explanation of what this means. One way of achieving this might be by setting up a database of examples which could act as an essay feedback bank that staff could draw on. This would enable them to demonstrate what aspects of an essay are likely to attract good marks. The use of marking schemes also has the potential to improve the quality of the feedback, though there is the danger here of 'downsliding' (Collins and Gentner, 1980), where students (and perhaps staff also) focus on low level activities such as correcting spelling mistakes at the expense of more complicated revisions such as trying to develop an argument.

Of course, lecturers will argue that they have insufficient time to do all this, and there is undoubtedly truth in this. What may be required is an overhaul of assessment systems so that lecturers are able to give appropriate feedback. If the assessment process is so overwhelming that proper feedback cannot be given, then there is surely something wrong with the system.

Interrogating Practice

What does your feedback do to your student's perceptions of their own ability? Does it encourage motivation or amotivation?

The second issue is that of how to encourage intrinsic rather than extrinsic motivation. There is much evidence to suggest that the majority of students tend to adopt surface approaches (of which extrinsic motivation is a part) at university (Ramsden, 1992). The evidence presented in Table 6.1 (in Chapter 6) also indicated the extent to which means-to-an-end motivation was prevalent in one group of students.

Again there is no easy or guaranteed solution to this, and some authors are rather pessimistic as to what can be achieved by individual lecturers or even groups of lecturers. Biggs (1993) points out that university education is part of a system, and that most systems are resistant to change, instead tending to return to the state of balance that has developed within them. What this means is that students' approaches to study and their motives are determined by a number of aspects of the higher education system, including their perception of the department and university they are in, and even of the university system in general. Trying to change students' motives by changing the way one module or group of modules is taught is unlikely to be effective, since all the other aspects will be working against this change. Similar rather disappointing conclusions come from attempts to train students to approach their studies in different ways. Norton and Crowley (1995) found that the training programme they devised had little effect on how students studied. Purdie and Hattie (1995) found that their training programme led to a temporary improvement in approaches to studying but that these rapidly reverted after the training came to an end.

However, there is one aspect of higher education which does seem to be crucially important in students' motivation, and that is the assessment system (see Chapter 4). Entwistle and Entwistle (1991) describe how final year students start with good intentions, are intrinsically motivated and attempt to adopt deep approaches to their studies; however, as examination time approaches they become increasingly extrinsically motivated and adopt surface, rote learning approaches. Similar findings have emerged in research by Newstead and Findlay (1997). One way of changing this might be if the assessment system were to be one which encouraged conceptual understanding as opposed to rote learning. It would appear that the standard three-hour essay-based examination does tend to produce surface approaches, despite the best intentions of lecturers. This might be altered through the increased use of problem solving, case studies and the like, where knowledge has to be used rather than just learnt. What is more, such assessments could take place under formal examination conditions, thus avoiding some of the problems associated with continuous assessment (such as student cheating, which is where this chapter began).

Finally, it may be possible to guide students to help themselves by encouraging them to adopt strategies which will keep up their motivation. A recent study by Wolters (1998) investigated the kinds of strategies that students used to regulate their own motivation, and found that these varied between students and as a function of the task in question. Among the most common strategies were reminding themselves of the extrinsic rewards (usually the need to do well in an exam), cognitional strategies such as reading through notes and preparing new notes, and changing the environment in which studying was taking place (eg, taking breaks or moving to a quieter room). It is not known which of these strategies were the most effective and it is probably the case that they will not be equally effective for all students, but informing students of the self-regulatory strategies available might conceivably be of some help.

OVERVIEW

This chapter has provided a brief insight into some of the research findings regarding student motivation. In simple terms, students can be motivated or amotivated, reflecting the extent to which they want to succeed. In addition, they can be intrinsically motivated and/or extrinsically motivated. Intrinsically motivated students want to learn for learning's sake, while extrinsically motivated students study for external rewards.

However, these factors are not easy to measure, and as a result there are few measures of motivation in higher education and relatively little research in this field. One might expect that motivation would correlate with both student behaviour and with academic achievement but research has produced inconsistent results. In addition, one might expect students to become more highly motivated and more intrinsically motivated during their time in higher education; once again, however, results are inconclusive.

In this chapter we hope to have highlighted the importance of ascertaining how motivated students are by the specific tasks set, and also of determining the kind of motivation that these tasks elicit. We have no ready panacea for solving the problems of student motivation, but it seems reasonable to suggest that the provision of high quality feedback and the adoption of appropriate assessment systems are at least part of the answer.

REFERENCES

Ames, C (1984) Competitive, co-operative, and individualistic goal structures: a cognitive-motivational analysis, in *Research on Motivation in Education:* Volume 1, *Student motivation*, eds R Ames and C Ames, pp 177–207, Academic Press, San Diego

Biggs, J (1987) *Student Approaches to Learning and Studying*, Australian Council for Educational Research, Victoria

Biggs, J (1993) What do inventories of students' learning processes really measure? A theoretical review and clarification, *British Journal of Educational Psychology*, **63**, pp 3–19

Clarke, R M (1986) Students' approaches to learning in an innovative medical school: a cross-sectional study, *British Journal of Educational Psychology*, **56**, pp 309–21

Collins, A and Gentner, D (1980) A framework for a cognitive theory of writing, in *Cognitive Processes in Writing*, eds W Gregg and E R Steinberg, Lawrence Erlbaum Associates, Mahwah, New Jersey

Deci, E and Ryan, R M (1985) *Intrinsic Motivation and Self-determination in Human Behavior*, Plenum, New York

Dweck, C S and Elliott, E S (1983) Achievement motivation, in *Handbook of Child Psychology: Socialization, personality and social development*, ed E M Hetherington, **4**, pp 643–91, Wiley, New York

Entwistle, N J (1998) Motivation and approaches to learning: motivating and conceptions of teaching, in *Motivating students*, eds S Brown, S Armstrong and G Thompson, pp 15–23, Kogan Page, London

Entwistle, N J and Entwistle, A (1991) Contrasting forms of understanding for degree examination: the student experience and its implications, *Higher Education*, **22**, pp 205–27

Entwistle, N J and Ramsden, P (1983) *Understanding Student Learning*, Croom Helm, London

Fazey, D and Fazey, J (1998) Perspectives on motivation: the implications for effective learning in higher education, in *Motivating Students*, eds S Brown, S Armstrong and G Thompson, pp 59–72, Kogan Page, London

Harter, S (1981) A new self-report scale of intrinsic versus extrinsic motivation in the classroom: motivational and informational components, *Developmental Psychology*, **17**, pp 302–12

Hoskins, S (1999) The development of undergraduates' approaches to studying and essay writing in higher education, PhD thesis, University of Plymouth

Jacobs, P and Newstead, S E (2000) The nature and development of student motivation, *British Journal of Education Psychology*, **70**, pp 243–54

Newstead, S E and Findlay, K (1997) Some problems in using examination performance as a measure of student ability, *Psychology Teaching Review*, **6**, pp 14–21

Newstead, S E, Franklyn-Stokes, A and Armstead, P (1996) Individual differences in student cheating, *Journal of Educational Psychology*, **88**, pp 229–41

Nicholls, J G (1984) Achievement motivation: conceptions of ability, experience, task choice and performance, *Psychological Review*, **91**, pp 328–46

Norton, L S and Crowley, C M (1995) Can students be helped to learn how to learn? An evaluation of an approaches to learning programme for first year degree students, *Higher Education*, **29**, pp 307–28

Pintrich, P R and Garcia, T (1991) Student goal orientation and self-regulation in the classroom, in *Advances in Motivation and Achievement*, eds M Maehr and P R Pintrich, **7**, pp 371–402, JAI Press, Greenwich, Connecticut

Pintrich, P R et al (1993) Reliability and predictive validity of the motivated strategies for learning questionnaire (MSLQ), *Educational and Psychological Measurement*, **53**, pp 801–13

Purdie, N M and Hattie, J A (1995) The effect of motivation training on approaches to learning and self concept, *British Journal of Educational Psychology*, **65**, pp 227–35

Ramsden, P (1992) *Learning to Teach in Higher Education*, Routledge, London

Sharpe, R et al (in submission), Attitudes and approaches to studying in entry level undergraduate students (article submitted for publication)

Vallerand, R J *et al* (1992) The academic motivation scale: a measure of intrinsic, extrinsic and amotivation in education, *Educational and Psychological Measurement*, **52**, pp 1003–17

Wolters, C (1998) Self-regulated learning and college students' regulation of motivation, *Journal of Educational Psychology*, **90**, pp 224–35

FURTHER READING

Brown, S, Armstrong, S and Thompson, G (eds) (1998), *Motivating Students*, Kogan Page, London. This is an edited book stemming from a Staff and Educational Development Association (SEDA) conference on Encouraging Student Motivation, offering some interesting and useful contributions.

Hartley, J (ed) (1998) *Learning and Studying: A research perspective*, Routledge, London. A well-written book covering a range of wider issues relevant to student motivation. It draws on up-to-date research, providing useful examples. It provides good insight into how psychologists investigate learning to include their findings.

6 Lecturing for learning

Jennifer Horgan

INTRODUCTION

The growth in participation in higher education during the last decade and measures to widen access are bringing into the university system students from a broad spectrum of ability and from diverse backgrounds. These factors present an enormous challenge to university lecturers who are expected to 'combine the talents of scholar, writer, producer, comedian, showman and teacher in ways that contribute to student learning' (McKeachie, 1994).

This chapter looks at the lecture method as a means of promoting student learning and considers ways of making lectures more effective. The case studies illustrate how a number of university teachers have adapted their approach to lecturing by making students take a more active part in class. The reasons for adopting this approach are discussed, and students' views of good teaching are explored and compared with those expressed by practitioners. This chapter also includes a brief discussion on handling disruptive behaviour by students, which is a problem emerging in some universities.

This chapter does not consider the lecture from a performance perspective. In lecturing, the importance of aspects, such as using your voice effectively, reinforcing your message and building a rapport with your audience, should not be under-estimated. One way in which lecturers can gain feedback on all the different elements of their craft is by exposing their teaching to observation by a peer or other professional observer. This is now recognized as an important means of improving practice and it is discussed fully in Chapter 16.

Many lecturers now choose to use PowerPoint presentations as part of their lectures and for the production of handouts. The use of PowerPoint does add an air of professionalism to presentations and lectures, though lecturers should use it only to a level with which they are comfortable, lest an attempt to employ the software's 'bells and whistles' distract from the content or hinder the delivery of the lecture. Its more sophisticated functions, such as the ability to animate images and build up a composite, layered diagram on screen, are useful for those types of delivery which need to use complex graphical representations, but more generally it is best used to present a simple textual backdrop to the lecture, and as such is cosmetically far more appealing than the traditional overhead projector and transparencies.

REASONS FOR LECTURING

The demise of the lecture method has long been predicted, yet it still remains the most widely used teaching method in higher education. It is not hard to see why lectures are popular with those charged with organizing university education as they provide a cost-effective means of teaching large groups of students. However, university teachers in many disciplines also argue that a lecture approach is an absolutely essential component of any **course** and they cite compelling pedagogic reasons for choosing this method of teaching. Primarily, lectures are seen as necessary for providing background information and ideas, basic concepts, and methods required by students before they can learn much on their own and become effective participants in classroom discussion.

Interrogating Practice

Why are lectures important in your discipline? How do your reasons for using the lecture method match up with those given below? Have you any other reasons to add to the list?

Cashin (1985) lists the following reasons for using the lecture method:

- Lectures can provide new information, based on original research and generally not found in textbooks or other printed sources.
- Lectures can be used to highlight similarities and differences between key concepts.
- Lectures can help communicate the enthusiasm of teachers for their subjects.
- Lectures can model how a particular discipline deals with questions of evidence, critical analysis, problem solving and the like.
- Lectures can organize subject matter in a way that is best suited to a particular class and course objectives.
- Lectures can dramatize important concepts and share personal insights.

LECTURE METHOD COMPARED WITH OTHER TEACHING METHODS

Many research studies have compared the effectiveness of the lecture method with other methods of teaching. McKeachie *et al* (1990) concluded that the lecture method is only as efficient as other methods of teaching as a means of transmitting knowledge. Teaching methods where active discussion is used are found to be more effective when the following are measured:

- retention of knowledge after the end of a course;
- transfer of knowledge to new situations;
- problem solving and thinking;
- attitude change.

Bligh (2002), in a very comprehensive review of the literature, also concluded that the lecture is as effective as other methods as a means of transmitting information, but not more so. It is less effective than other methods for promoting thought and changing students' attitudes.

In spite of these findings, it seems likely that the lecture will retain its place as the most widely used teaching method for some time to come. If limitations of the lecture method are recognized, what strategies can be used to improve the quality of student learning?

MAKING LECTURES MORE EFFECTIVE

The traditional lecture

Common sense and our own experience tell us that people learn better if they think about what they are learning and have an opportunity to engage with the material, rather than simply get the chance to see it and hear about it. Research into learning supports this common sense view and is discussed in more detail in Chapter 2. As Ramsden (1994) points out, 'Active engagement, imaginative inquiry and the finding of a suitable level are all much more likely to occur if teaching methods that necessitate student activity, student problem-solving and question-asking, and co-operative learning are employed.' However, in the traditional lecture the student often takes a largely **passive** role and there is little opportunity for **active learning** such that the learner can engage with the subject matter being presented. Many lecturers feel that the traditional lecture is the most effective way of 'covering the material' but this approach is rarely satisfactory from the learner's point of view. It has been said that most of us are so busy ' covering the material' in a lecture that we miss the chance to 'uncover it'. In fact, Ramsden (1992) argues that the use of the traditional lecture may actually be detrimental to the quality of student learning, in that it leads students to expect learning to be a passive experience and does not provide them with opportunities to engage in **deep** processing of the subject matter. Initially students may object to lecturers who choose a more active approach, but as they get used to the approach they respond well, a point borne out by evaluation comments outlined in Case Study 1.

Ramsden (1994) suggests that many new lecturers see teaching as the efficient transmission of knowledge from the teacher to the learner and rarely think of the impact of this approach on students' learning. The initial focus for the new lecturer is, quite naturally, on the quality of the presentation and the skills involved in classroom management. It is only later when confidence has built up that many new lecturers feel able to turn their attention to the needs of the student as learner.

Attention levels during lectures

Various studies on attention levels during a 50-minute lecture reveal that during the first 10 minutes attention levels are high, but as the lecture proceeds attention levels drop and continue to do so if students are not actively involved in some way. Research studies on memory and retention of material show that students frequently forget, or never learn, much of the material presented to them during a typical 50-minute traditional lecture. Learning of material can be consolidated if students are given an opportunity to use it within a short time of its initial presentation.

Bligh (2002) refers to research carried out on factors that cause students to forget and concludes that facts presented during the middle of a lecture are not remembered as well as those at the beginning or the end. He suggests that lecturers need to take this into account by introducing novel points and/or contrasting approaches during the middle of a lecture. The material is recalled more effectively if key points are flagged up in advance, using what Brown (Brown and Atkins, 1988) refers to as 'advance organizers'.

Note taking is used by students as a means of maintaining attention during a lecture, as an aid to memory and as the basis for revision of the material covered. Bligh (2002) uses the terms 'encoding' to describe the use of notes to aid memory and finds that there is overwhelming evidence to support the view that note-taking during a lecture aids memory of the lecture. He also cites studies that support the view 'that students who have notes to revise from, will do better in examinations than students who do not'.

The need for a structured approach

Students will learn and remember much more if their learning is organized and many would argue that the main role of the lecture is to enable students to find a framework in which to fit new facts and ideas. McKeachie (1994) suggests that in order to be effective 'the lecturer needs to build a bridge between what is in the students' minds and the structures in the subject matter'. This is one of the main themes in Bruner's theoretical framework, discussed under constructivism in Chapter 2. He describes learning as an active process in which we construct new ideas or concepts based on our current/past knowledge. If this is the case, the role of the teacher is to translate the information to be learnt into a format that fits into the learner's current state of understanding.

However, it is important to give students opportunities to develop their own way of structuring new material rather than imposing a rigid framework on them, and McKeachie (1994) argues that some students do not learn well if the lecturer is too highly organized. We need to encourage students to take more responsibility for their own learning, 'our teaching should consist of guiding rather than governing student learning'. This point needs to be kept in mind. .

Interrogating Practice

What approaches have you experienced or used in lectures that you believe encourage student learning? How can bridges be built between structures in the subject matter and students' understanding? How can we help students make new meaning of the material presented to them?

Putting ideas into practice

How can this information on attention levels, active learning and structure help us to improve our lecturing technique? In other words, how can we make the lecturing less like a lecture (passive, rigid, routine knowledge transmission) and more like active communication between teacher and students?

Case Study 1: Active learning in first-year lectures in computer science

University of Wales, Aberystwyth

In this case study the lecturer uses an interactive approach in all his lectures as a means of promoting active learning. With first year undergraduates taking the module Introduction to Programming, there are lectures on Java programming punctuated with questions to the whole class. At the beginning of the academic year when students do not know each other the lecturer divides the lecture theatre into areas and takes answers from each couple of rows in turn. Care is taken to prevent students feeling overwhelmed by answering in such an arena. After week 5 of the course when students have been away on a team-skills weekend, questions are targeted at named students. The lecturer then finds enthusiastic students wave their arms in the air before he has even posed the question. Students are encouraged to ask questions during the lecture. Lectures are punctuated with questions at roughly 10-minute intervals and the whole class is expected to work on the answer to ensure they are all actively thinking about the material. This approach keeps interest high throughout the class and ensures that everyone is involved in the topic being presented. Students learn well in this demanding classroom environment.

Those who have not used this approach before may wish to be cautioned that it is important to have a clear structure so that student questions feed into the lecture and take it on step by step as it is easy to be side-tracked. Student evaluation reports show a high level of satisfaction with this approach.

(Dr Mark Ratcliffe)

General points

The literature abounds with ideas for making lectures more effective, especially when dealing with large numbers of students (eg, Gibbs, 1992; Brown and Race, 2002)). The main points to consider are listed below, although some of these will not necessarily be relevant or applicable to all disciplines:

- Structure the lecture carefully; so that you provide a solid framework into which students can fit new knowledge. Show students an outline of this framework.
- Ensure that you provide students with clear signals to help them appreciate direction, links and points of separation between parts of the content. These are called **signposts**. Make sure that they can 'see the wood as well as the trees'. Make links between the present lecture and past or future lectures.
- Make some statement of educational intent at the outset. Ideally state your **aims, objectives/learning outcomes** (see Chapter 3) so that students will know what you wish them to achieve.
- Make sure that your lecture is not overloaded with content. For example, Russell, Hendricson and Herbert (1984) have shown that students learn more when information density is not too high. You may not cover as much as you wish, but if the material is understood and can be applied, your time has been well spent.
- Organize your lecture so that you change the demands made on students every 10 to 15 minutes. This should ensure that attention levels are kept high.
- Make your lectures more participatory, and adopt this approach right from the start of the course when norms and expectations are being established. A good example is shown in Case Study 1.
- As the lecture proceeds, continue to show students the lecture outline on an overhead transparency so that they can chart their way through and note the significant elements.
- Provide a summary of the main points as you complete each section and an overall summary at the end of the session (this can be used profitably at the beginning of the next lecture to remind students of what has already been covered).
- Give students an opportunity to interact as soon as possible with the new material being presented so that they are able to make links between the new material and what they have learnt in the past. You may wish students to work individually or in a **buzz group** for short periods during the lecture, or you may give them follow-up work to be completed outside class.
- Help students to take good lecture notes – concept maps, spray diagrams and mind maps are alternative ways of taking notes that students may wish to explore with your help. Many lecturers now publish full lecture notes on their Web sites. You may wish to pause occasionally and allow students to check their notes against those of the person sitting next to them.
- Make good use of handouts – these may be gapped handouts where you leave space for students to add their own notes. You may wish to provide students with diagrams, references or articles for further reading.

Structuring a lecture

Brown and Atkins (1988) suggest the following checklist of questions for use after a lecture has been prepared:

- What are the central questions of the lecture?
- What do you expect students to learn or understand from your lecture?
- What lecture methods will you use?
- Will the opening be clear and interesting?
- Are the sections of the lecture clearly organized and clearly linked?
- Are the main key points clear, accurate and linked?
- Are your examples and illustrations apt?
- Will any reservations and qualifications you plan to make be clear and apt?
- Will your section summaries and final summary be clear and coherent?
- What activities will students have to carry out during the lecture?
- What possible weaknesses are there likely to be in the presentation?
- How do you plan to combat these possible weaknesses?
- Are any audio-visual resources you might need going to be available?
- How will you evaluate (see Chapter 14) the effectiveness of your lecture?

Case Study 2 illustrates an approach one lecturer has used to get feedback on problem areas, as an alternative to asking students to pose questions in class.

Case Study 2: Getting feedback from large introductory classes

Battles (2000) describes an approach she has used to gain input on problematic areas of the course from a large introductory class in Geological Sciences. Students are asked to submit, on an optional, weekly basis, a notecard on which they have identified a topic/concept from the lecture, reading or laboratory work that they did not understand. The notecards are reviewed and the most problematic topic/concept is dealt with in the next lecture. This use of notecards provides a simple means of finding out the most pressing difficulties and as Battles points out it reinforces good study habits as it encourages students to review their notes and/or text. There is a high level of student participation in this feedback.

Ways of varying student activity in lectures

The following suggestions are offered as means of engaging students with the subject matter being presented. Several of these devices are illustrated in the Case Studies:

- Give students a question or problem to be tackled individually and then ask them to share their ideas in small groups, commonly called buzz groups.
- Change the way in which you use your time in the lecture theatre. Case Study 3 gives an example where lectures have been radically redesigned to enable students in Chemical Engineering to develop problem-solving and teamwork skills.
- Show a video/DVD clip with instructions on what to look for (see Case Study 4).
- Present material live from the Internet with instructions on what to look for, what data to collect, etc.
- Demonstrate a task or device and include instructions on what to look for.
- Set a brief multiple choice question (**MCQ**) test. If possible ask a colleague to help with administering this – it can be a very effective way of providing almost instant feedback on students' understanding of the topic being discussed.
- Solve a problem collectively.
- Ask students to discuss briefly, in groups of two or three, a research design or interpretation of a set of findings.
- Ask students to frame questions in relation to data or to make estimates (eg, percentages of various crimes, range of accuracy of instruments). Students can compare their ideas in small groups. You can then show them the correct figures.
- Ask students to invent examples and compare them with those of another student.
- Ask students to consider briefly likely advantages and disadvantages, or strengths and weaknesses of a procedure or theory. Then outline the advantages and disadvantages so that they can compare these with their views.
- Turn a part of your lecture into a question and answer session – this needs courage and you may lack confidence to do this with a large group in the early stages of your career. It is possible to get around this by providing students with a 'question box' so that you have prior notice of questions and an opportunity to think about the answers. It may be advisable to pump-prime the box with some good questions!

(The points in this list are adapted from Brown and Atkins, 1988)

Case Study 3: Problem-solving in small groups in Chemical Engineering lectures

Imperial College London

The Process Analysis module (Level 1) in the MEng in Chemical Engineering is the first experience students have of chemical engineering when they arrive at Imperial College London, and the course aims to give them a better understanding of the way an engineer approaches problems. The learning outcomes include not only the acquisition of new technical knowledge, but also the development of problem-solving and teamwork skills. It is therefore essential for students to be given first-hand experience of solving problems in groups, through tutorials and project work, *and* in lectures. Given the large class size (100 to 120 students) and the limited time available in lectures, it is important for the students to receive clear instructions on how to conduct small group work and for individual students not to monopolize the lecturer's attention while group work is going on. We have therefore implemented a group work structure which can be repeated at each lecture and which the students adapt to quickly.

In all academic tutorials, students are split in groups of five to six people. At the beginning of each Process Analysis lecture, a transparency is shown to indicate where each tutorial group should sit in the lecture theatre. Each group is split over two rows so that students can turn around and form a small discussion group. This takes some time in the first lecture, but students soon know where they should be sitting. The handouts for almost every lecture contain one or more problems the students are expected to solve in small groups. Students are told how much time is available. They are asked to attempt the problem within their groups. They are told to call the lecturer when they have a problem that they cannot resolve as a group or when they have finished the problem. *Individual* students who call upon the lecturer are asked to reconsider the question with the rest of their group. This allows the class size to be reduced from 100 to 120 units (students) to 20 units (groups) and makes it possible for a single lecturer to move between groups as the students work.

The duration of the exercise should be set so that the average group has had some time to identify the difficulties in solving the problem. However, it is important to end the exercise before most groups have had the chance to fully solve the problem. Once they have identified a solution strategy, students tend to lose their focus and it becomes more difficult to bring the class back to attention. Once the class is attentive, the problem is solved (fully or in outline) on the board. At this point, input is requested from students. Rather than asking for individual student participation, groups can be asked to contribute an answer. This is much less threatening for students and ensures greater response.

Some lectures are entirely dedicated to solving a large problem. However, to make sure that all students benefit from this, it is important to identify natural breaks in the problem-solving process and to bring the students back to attention to solve sub-problems. This allows the strong groups to check their approach and the weaker groups to consider all aspects of the problem during the lecture time.

What is distinctive about this strategy is that the students work in the same groups in tutorials and take problems and experiences from the lectures to their small groups to consolidate and extend their learning there.

(Dr Claire Adjiman)

Case Study 4: Improving learning in Geography lectures

University of Derby

This case study describes a module on the Geography of Health and Disease to a class of over 60 second-year students at the University of Derby. The timetable slot involves three hours of teaching time so the lecturer uses a variety of strategies to keep students actively involved.

The lecturer often uses video footage to illustrate points and emphasizes the need to help students use video as a learning resource, rather than as a source of entertainment. Students are given suggestions about how they should take notes from the video and provided with a list of points that they should look out for. The subject matter presented on overhead transparencies during the lecture often requires students to look at tables of data collected from a number of different countries. The strategy here is to break students into pairs and ask each pair to look for trends and contrasts between years, etc. This approach enables students to learn from each other and prevents them taking a passive role. Whenever possible the lecturer starts a topic off by asking students to volunteer information based on their own experience, eg, 'Think of the number of people you know who have died from degenerative diseases/infectious diseases, etc'.

It should be noted that this approach is risky as you are not always entirely in control of the situation, but the lecturer here is convinced that students learn more by being actively involved. In this module students comment adversely on the fact that they have to work too hard in lectures.

(Irene Brightmer)

DISRUPTIVE BEHAVIOUR

One of the issues that has come to the fore in recent years in many institutions is that of disruptive behaviour in large classes, especially in large lectures. Such disruptive behaviour in a higher education class is likely to be more subtle than that experienced at secondary school level, but when it occurs it can cause significant problems to the lecturer and other students. The use of the mobile phone for text-messaging stands out as a new form of disruption to enter the classroom in recent years in the UK and beyond (eg, Edwards, Smith and Webb, 2001: 37). Case Study 5 explores the problem of disruptive behaviour in more detail and offers some strategies for use by lecturers.

> ### Case Study 5: Dealing with disruptive students in lectures

In my experience, both as a lecturer and as someone who now advises other lecturers on learning and teaching, the problem of disruptive students is not uncommon. During lectures, students will sometimes chat to each other, send each other written notes, even text-message each other. More extreme forms of disruptive behaviour (for example, students throwing paper darts or engaging in heated shouting matches with lecturers) are rare but not unknown. These behaviours can be disconcerting for the lecturer and distracting for those students who do want to learn. And while students chatting in lectures may not be uncommon, lecturers may be reluctant to ask for advice in how to deal with it as there is a perception that 'good' lecturers should be sufficiently inspiring, authoritative or entertaining to avoid the problem. The situation is often particularly acute for those new to lecturing, not only because of their inexperience, but because new lecturers may be given the Level 1 classes, which in practice may have large numbers of students crammed into lecture theatres (which can sometimes be hot, badly lit and poorly ventilated). New lecturers always need to be well prepared and this means familiarizing themselves on their departmental policies on such things as use of mobile phones.

Research from the compulsory education sector indicates that the causes of disruptive behaviour in schools may be both teacher and student induced. In the university context, the disruptive student may have genuine complaints about the performance of the lecturer. Some university lecturers prioritize their research and may not give the same attention to their teaching. This lack of enthusiasm for teaching is often clearly evident to the students. Or the students may be dissatisfied with the content of the curriculum. For example, on vocational courses, students may ask: 'Why do we need to learn this in order to become...' If that type of concern is at the root of the disruption, then it may be worth the time in the lecture to explain the links between what the lecturer is covering now and subsequent parts of the course. If the disruptive student's concerns are any wider than that, these are probably best dealt with outside of the lecture.

Some of the more routine problems such as students chatting can be headed off by the type of routine good teaching practice outlined in this book, particularly any method to make the lectures as interactive as possible, as well as paying attention to lesson plans with appropriate timings, breaks and a variety of teaching methods. Many of the strategies for successfully dealing with small groups (see Chapter 7) are good practice for larger lecture contexts. Ground rules negotiated between students and lecturer at the start of a module can be useful. Establishing discipline through a 'tough' start may avoid students 'testing the limits' of a new lecturer. Examples of appropriate ground rules would be: that students will be admitted to the lecture up to 10 minutes late but no later; or that there will always be a question and answer period at the end of lectures.

No matter how exemplary the lecturer's practice, disruptive students and difficult situations will always arise and present challenges. When they do, the best strategy is always to tackle a problem early. While the lecture is going on, scan the crowd, and make eye contact with the students. If a couple of students start to talk to each other, a direct gaze in that direction may be enough to stop it. If it continues, then pause at an appropriate point and ask if anyone has any questions about what has been covered so far in the lecture – again looking in the direction of the students who are talking. The purpose here is not to embarrass the disruptive students, but to flag up that they are distracting and to offer them a face-saving way of stopping. If they still continue to talk, then again pause at an appropriate point and ask the student directly if they have any problems with what's been covered. Remember never to show annoyance (keeping a neutral tone of voice) and always be tactful and diplomatic. If they still don't stop, then have a quiet word with them after the lecture. It is important to scale up sanctions gradually. Cases have been known of a lecturer walking out of a lecture due to disruptive students, but this should really be a final resort. It may also be counterproductive, as the lecturer will probably have to return and face the students, and ultimately deal with the underlying problem.

(Peter Washer, Queen Mary, University of London)

STUDENT VIEWS OF 'GOOD' LECTURING

Having looked at the research evidence on how to improve the quality of learning in lectures, and in the case studies seen how some experienced university lecturers have developed their teaching to incorporate good practice, let us now turn to students' views of 'good lecturing'.

A study carried out at the University of Lancaster looked at student perceptions of good teaching (Ramsden, 1992). The most frequent descriptions of good lecturing commented on the lecturer's ability to pitch material at the right level, to provide a clear structure and to maintain an appropriate pace. The most striking aspect of comments from students related to the effect of a lecturer's on a student's approach to learning, enthusiasm and his or her ability to provide good explanations.

Parallels can be drawn with a more recent survey carried out at the University of Virginia, where a cross-section of undergraduate students was asked to give opinions about lecture methods and about the qualities that the students found most appealing in a lecturer (Lacoss and Chylack, 1998). The students were also asked to comment on which aspects of lecture style, format and environment they found most conducive to learning and retention of material.

Students consistently praised those professors who introduced variety, interaction, structure and intensity into their lectures. No one style of lecture was singled out as being more effective than any other and, in fact, students appreciated variety in lecturing style. The ability of the lecturer to make use of examples, demonstrations and changes of tone ('to break the trance') was thought to be more important than the style used.

Particularly appreciated were lecturers who incorporated responses from students by soliciting questions during lectures, made themselves available afterwards, or who collected feedback from a bulletin board on the Web. The comments made by students about lecturers attempts to 'connect with them', were particularly interesting. They welcomed attempts to jolt them out of the passive role in lectures and agreed that such interactive advances were 'well worth the initial awkwardness they felt'. This approach was said by the group to promote better student preparation and result in greater respect and enthusiasm. Lecture techniques identified by students as particularly helpful were:

- use of outlines and lists;
- delivery paced to allow note-taking;
- pauses to allow clarification;
- short intermissions for review of material / personal reactions / questions;
- repetition of the main points;
- final recap of the key points.

Finally, students saw the lecturer as providing 'an active example of learning and processing information that, in turn, helped them to digest the material on their own'.

OVERVIEW

Effective lectures need to be structured, well-planned learning experiences that shake students out of the passive, stenographic role and provide a challenging learning environment. The experienced practitioners whose approaches have been examined in the case study material in this chapter have reached the same conclusions about what constitutes good lecturing in higher education. No one pretends that this approach is easy and many experienced lecturers will feel cautious about such change and feel uneasy about teaching in a less controlled environment than previously. The best advice that can be given to anyone contemplating a change, from a traditional lecture to a more interactive approach, is to suggest that step-by-step change works best for both students and the lecturer. If your first attempt does not work as you had planned, do not abandon the idea, but rather reflect on why this was so and try again.

REFERENCES

Battles, D A (2000) Use of notecards as a technique for enhancing the quality of large introductory classes, *Journal of Geoscience Education*, **48**, p 30

Bligh, D (2002) *What's the Use of Lectures?* Intellect, Exeter

Brown, G and Atkins, M (1988) *Effective Teaching in Higher Education*, Methuen, London

Brown, S and Race, P (2002) *Lecturing: A practical guide*, Kogan Page, London

Cashin, W E (1985) *Improving Lectures*, idea paper 14, Manhattan, Center for Faculty Evaluation and Development, Kansas State University

Edwards, H, Smith, B and Webb, G (2001) *Lecturing, Case Studies, Experience and Practice*, Kogan Page, London

Gibbs, G (1992) *Lecturing to More Students: Teaching more students, part 2*, Polytechnic and Colleges Funding Council, Oxonian Rewley Press, Oxford

Lacoss, J and Chylack, J (1998) *In Their Words: Students' ideas about teaching*, http://www.virginia.edu/trc/lacoss.htm

McKeachie, W J (1994) *Teaching Tips: Strategies, research and theory for college and university teachers*, Heath and Co, Lexington, Massachusetts

McKeachie, W J *et al* (1990) *Teaching and Learning in the College Classroom: A review of the research literature*, 2nd edn, MI: NCRIPTAL, University of Michigan, Ann Arbor

Ramsden, P (1992) *Learning to Teach in Higher Education*, Routledge, London

Ramsden, P (1994) Current challenges to quality in higher education, *Innovative Higher Education*, **18** (3), pp 177–87

Russell, I J, Hendricson, W D and Herbert, R J (1984) Effects of lecture information density on medical student achievement, *Journal of Medical Education*, **59** (1), pp 881–89

FURTHER READING

Bligh, D (2002). See above. The latest edition of this classic in the field which comprehensively reviews the literature on lecturing.

Brown, S and Race, P (2002). See above. A user-friendly book that covers all aspects of the art of lecturing.

Gibbs, G (1992). See above. A quick and easy practical guide to lecturing, concentrating on approaches with large classes, by an influential figure in higher education.

7 Teaching and learning in small groups

Sandra Griffiths

BACKGROUND AND DEFINITION

In the UK there have been numerous attempts to define precisely what is meant by **small group teaching** in higher education (Abercrombie, 1970; Bligh, 1986). From a historical perspective, some of these attempts were linked to the fact that small group teaching often took place in association with the lecture method. Many of the aims and practices of small group teaching reflected this link. This led to the view that the method existed only insofar as it supported the proper business of teaching: the formal lecture (see Chapter 6).

Attempts to define the concept using the words '**seminar**' and '**tutorial**' are problematic. These names are often used interchangeably. This led some writers to abandon their use in favour of the term 'group discussion'. The use of group discussion is congruent with a major objective of the activity, that is to teach students to think and to engage with their own and others' learning through the articulation of views (Stenhouse, 1972; Bligh, 1986).

In this chapter, consideration is given to the enormous and unique potential of the small group to promote learning. It is viewed as an exciting, challenging and dynamic method open to use in a variety of forms and to serve a range of purposes appropriate to different disciplines. Therefore terms will be explored in their most diverse and flexible forms. The process is identified not as a didactic one but rather as a participative experience, in which students are encouraged to take responsibility, along with tutors, for their own learning. Electronic discussion groups may also promote learning (see Chapter 11).

A HIGHLY SKILLED ACTIVITY

Many writers (Bligh, 1986; Griffiths and Partington, 1992) argue that small group teaching is among the most difficult and highly skilled of teaching techniques. In addition to the primary objective of teaching students to think, the tutor must have a number of subsidiary objectives if the small group is to function. Writers generally agree that the method requires a wide knowledge of subject matter and ability to attend to detail while keeping an eye on the overall picture. Appreciation of how groups function, openness of spirit, accommodation of different views, receptivity to new ideas and maturity to manage a group of students without dominating them, are all necessary for effective small group teaching. These attributes are best thought of as skills to be developed over a period of time.

Not only do tutors have to learn how to teach using small group methods but also students have to learn how to work in small groups. Here, it is assumed that it is the tutor's job to assist students to learn, to equip them with self-confidence and facilitate group cohesion. Therefore, a tutor using these methods is much more than a subject matter expert.

In recognizing that small group teaching is a difficult and highly skilled teaching technique, it is important to know that it is also one of the most potentially rewarding teaching and learning methods for tutors and students alike.

GROUP SIZE

Small group teaching, broadly speaking, is any teaching and learning occasion which brings together between 2 and 20 participants. The participants may be students and their tutors, or students working on their own. Because of the relatively small numbers of students involved, the financial cost of the method can be high.

CONTEXT

In recent years the experience of small group teaching and learning has come under threat. With the expansion of student numbers in higher education, class sizes have increased dramatically; tutored small group teaching is expensive when compared with the lecture. A resulting re-examination has had a profound impact on small group teaching and learning. It has led many tutors to re-evaluate critically the nature of the method and to maximize its potential to the full with some quite interesting and innovative results. **Peer tutoring, peer assessment,** peer learning and **peer support** have become more common, (for example Griffiths, Houston and Lazenbatt, 1996). In defence of the method, it has been necessary for assurances to be made that time devoted to teaching in this format is well organized and well spent.

This re-examination has also coincided with other changes in the external environment. The implementation of accreditation of university teachers has grown rapidly since the establishment of the Institute for Learning and Teaching in 1999, and is resulting in a considerable culture shift. Part of this shift involves a growing recognition by lecturers that they are responsible not only for what is taught but also, in part, for how students learn.

LEARNING IN SMALL GROUPS

The interpersonal and interactive nature of small groups makes them a challenging and appropriate vehicle for engaging students in their own learning. Students are engaged in small groups, both as learners and as collaborators in their own intellectual, personal and professional development. Furthermore, there is strong evidence from students themselves that they benefit from, and enjoy, the experience in a whole range of different ways (Rudduck, 1978; Luker, 1989; Griffiths, Houston and Lazenbatt, 1996). These might best be summed up as both cognitive and affective in nature. Alongside understanding and knowledge benefits, students suggest that participation, belonging and being involved are all important dimensions of the experience. The implications of these findings are that the process of building and managing groups, and assisting with the development of relationships, is of paramount importance.

The small group is viewed as a critical mechanism for exploring the development of a range of **key skills** (see Chapter 9). It is within the small group that self-confidence can be improved, and teamwork and interpersonal communication developed. Development of these group work and other skills are reported by students (Griffiths, Houston and Lazenbatt, 1996) to foster conditions whereby they can observe their own **learning styles**, change these styles to suit different tasks and engage more deeply with the content of their subject. These latter attributes are often cited as prerequisites for a **deep approach** to learning. This revitalized interest in key skills has succeeded in according group work a new status.

Despite moves towards mass participation and larger classes in higher education, the quality of the learning experience, the need to deliver key skills and the potential for innovation, have contributed to the retention and enhancement of the small group method. Small groups are used extensively, and in many different ways, eg, in **problem-based learning** approaches (see Chapter 23).

PLANNING

Successful small group teaching and learning does not happen by chance. Planning for effective small group teaching is as important as planning any other teaching activity. This point sometimes goes unrecognized because the actual activity of learning in small groups can at first glance appear unstructured. Some lecturers are put off by the seemingly informal, loose or open-ended nature of small group learning. Others fear this informality will be a recipe for chaos or that the group will develop into a therapy session. All types of teaching must be planned as part of a coherent package, with appropriate use of different methods within each component.

This appearance of informality is deceptive. Behind the facade of the informal group lies a backdrop in which all the learners are playing within a known set of rules which are spoken or unspoken. The approach might better be described as a kind of structured spontaneity. In other words, the creative flow of ideas is possible precisely because the lecturer or leader has a clear framework, deliberately planned to meet the **objectives** of the session. Within this framework, students feel safe to develop their ideas. Equally important, staff feel safe to try out and practise the skills of small group teaching.

Planning for small group teaching may take many forms. It will have much in common with features of planning for any learning occasion. Typically the teacher might consider the intended **learning outcomes**, selection of suitable type of small group teaching method and learner activity.

Beyond these general features the session plan will be dependent upon the requirements of specific disciplines, the culture of the institution, the overall context of the programme or module and the particular learning needs and prior knowledge of the students.

Whatever form the plan takes, it is critical that precise intentions for small group work are outlined. It is salutary to ask often whether what is being aimed at, and undertaken in small groups, is qualitatively different from that which is being carried out in other delivery modes. The gains for the students should justify the extra costs incurred. In short, the aims and content of the teaching session should dictate and justify the means.

Interrogating Practice

Using your own experience as a learner in small groups, identify strengths and weaknesses of different approaches used in your discipline.

PREPARING LEARNERS

In a study into peer tutoring in higher education (Griffiths, Houston and Lazenbatt, 1996) staff indicated that they had recognized the need for student preparation on the 'knowledge of subject' side but had not recognized, prior to their action research, the extent to which students would need training, and ongoing facilitation, to work in the new ways. These new ways refer to working within learner groups. This finding concurs with evidence from other quarters (Griffiths and Partington, 1992), where students offering advice to lecturers say that lecturers too often assume that they, the students, know how to work in groups. It is just as important for teaching staff to prepare students to work in groups as it is to prepare themselves.

Interrogating Practice

How do you assist learners to organize small group sessions where you are not present? How could you improve on your current practice?

Preparing students to work in small groups can mean providing specific training for students on how groups work. Such training will develop an understanding that all groups go through a number of stages. Hence, when conflict arises in the group, for example, it can be understood and dealt with as a natural feature to be resolved, rather than perceived as a descent into chaos. Preparation can also mean affording structured opportunities at strategic points within the teaching programme to examine how the group is functioning, what problems exist and how resolution can be achieved. Some lecturers achieve this by providing guidelines (ground rules) at the beginning of a small group session or at the beginning of a series of seminars or workshops. Some lecturers go further, believing that students (either individually or as a group) can themselves effectively be involved in establishing and negotiating ground rules and intended outcomes. Such activities may constitute a **learning contract**.

Such a learning contract is an important way of effecting a safe and supportive learning environment. Establishing the contract may involve tutors and students in jointly:

- Setting, agreeing and understanding objectives.
- Agreeing assessment procedures and criteria (if appropriate).

- Allocating tasks to all participants, tutors and students.
- Developing ground rules for behaviour within the group.

The staff/student contract provides a mechanism for continuing review. It is recommended that time be set aside every third or fourth meeting to evaluate the progress and process of the group's working against the original contract.

PHASES OF GROUP DEVELOPMENT

Social group theorists describe the initial phases in the life of a group using a variety of terms such as inclusion, forming and approach–avoid ambivalence (eg, Adair, 1996; Tuckmann, 1965). These works discuss the behaviour of individuals working in groups. What is also recognized is the conflicting tendency to avoid the situation of joining groups because of the demands, the frustration and even the pain it may bring about. This 'moving towards, pulling away' behaviour can easily create tension in the early stages of a group if it is not handled sensitively. Certain behaviours may be a natural part of the initial joining stages rather than a conscious act of defiance or withdrawal by a student. Understanding how students are likely to behave can assist the tutor to provide a framework that fosters confidence and allows trust to develop.

The ending of the group often brings to the surface many issues to do with termination. How intervention is handled at this stage will have a bearing on helping the members to move on. The tutor needs to be aware of appropriate ways of ending different types of group activity. For discussion and guidance on managing behaviour in groups see Jaques (2000).

Interrogating Practice

Consider small group teaching sessions you have facilitated. Think about the different types of individual and group behaviour you have witnesses. What were the possible causes?

SIGNIFICANCE OF THE SETTING

Few tutors in higher education work in an ideal setting with tailor-designed group workrooms. A great deal can be done, however, in setting up the room to encourage participation and interaction. The research into the influence of environmental factors on interaction has been fairly extensive and shows that physical arrangements have a powerful effect. For example, Korda (1976) documents the effect on encounters when one person is seated and the other is not.

It is well known that communication increases if the differences in social level or status are small. Therefore, part of the tutor's task is to play down the differences in roles and, in particular, play down his or her own authority. This will facilitate the free flow of discussion. It is not a straightforward matter since the tutor must relinquish authority while all the time remaining in control. This knowledge about the need to minimize social status differences has an impact on where the tutor actually sits within the group.

In fact, it is possible to arrange a room so that certain desired effects are achieved. Three situations (Griffiths and Partington, 1992) serve as examples of this point:

- Nervous students can be encouraged to participate more readily if their place in the group is opposite (ie, in direct eye-contact) to either a sympathetic tutor or an encouraging, more voluble student peer.
- A dominating, vociferous student can be quietened by being seated immediately next to the tutor.
- The level of student participation and of student–student interaction can be affected by the choice of room itself. Is the tutor's own room with all his or her paraphernalia of authority likely to be more or less conducive to student participation? What is an unadorned, stark seminar room with a rectangular table and a special high-backed lecturer's chair at one end likely to dictate for the processes of the group?

Interrogating Practice

Visualize yourself in a room where you teach small groups. Where should you sit to maximize your interaction with the group? Where might a student sit to avoid interaction with the tutor or with other students? Where might a student sit if he or she wishes to persuade others of a point of view?

TYPES OF SMALL GROUP TEACHING

A specific method selected for small group teaching will derive from the objectives set. There are many different methods of small group teaching; some methods are more suited to certain disciplines than others. However, few methods are peculiar to one subject alone. A large number of methods can be adapted for use in any subject. It is important to remain flexible and open to try out a variety of methods drawn from a wide repertoire. It may be necessary to overcome a tendency to find one method that works well and use this method frequently. The effect on learners of over-exposure to one method of teaching is worth considering.

Below is a brief description of various ways of working with small groups. It is not intended to be comprehensive, nor are all types mutually exclusive. Some methods are described in terms of a special setting that encourages the application of principles or techniques; for example, brainstorming is a structured setting for the use of lateral thinking. Other methods are described in terms of their size or purpose:

- *Brainstorm session* – generation of ideas from the group to foster lateral thinking. There is no criticism of ideas until they are logged.
- *Buzz group* – two or three people are asked to discuss an issue for a few minutes. Comments are usually then shared with a larger group.
- *Cross-over groups* – used for brief discussions then transfers between groups.
- *Fishbowl* – small groups are formed within a large, observation group, followed by discussion and reversal.
- *Free discussion* – topic and direction comes from the group; the tutor or leader observes.
- *Open-ended enquiries* – students determine the structure as well as reporting back on outcomes.
- *Peer tutoring* – students learn from one another and teach one another.
- *Problem-based tutorial group* – involves small groups using problem-based learning.
- *Role-play* – use of allocated or self-created roles. It is important to facilitate students to enter and come out of role.
- *Self-help group* – run by and for students; the tutor may be a resource.
- *Seminar* – group discussion of a paper presented by a student (note that this term is often used in different ways).
- *Simulation/game* – structured experience in real/imaginary roles. Guidelines on the process are important and feedback is critical.
- *Snowballing* – pairs become small groups then become larger groups.
- *Step-by-step discussion* – a planned sequence of issues/questions led by student or tutor.
- *Structured enquiries* – the tutor provides lightly structured experiments and guidance.
- *Syndicate* – involving mini-project work, followed by reporting to the full class.

- *Tutorial* – a meeting with a very small group, often based on feedback to an essay or assignment (note that this term is often used in different ways).
- *Tutorless group* – the group appoints a leader and may report back; may focus on discussion or completion of some other type of set task.

(This list has been adapted from several sources, but owes much to Habeshaw, Habeshaw and Gibbs, 1988.)

There are several approaches not mentioned above that can be used in small or large groups. The main determining factor is the amount of interaction that is desirable. Apart from that it is necessary to ensure that in a larger group all members can see, hear, and so on. Case studies, **problem classes** and demonstrations fall into this category.

Interrogating Practice

Study the list, noting methods you are familiar with and methods you have employed. Select one or two methods you have not used before and work out how you can try them out in the near future.

Case Study 1: The use of small groups in teaching and learning on an undergraduate music degree at the University of Ulster

Course: BMus (Hons)
Year of study: 2
Module: Renaissance Studies
Delivery: lectures/classes, seminars and workshops
Class size: 20–25 students

Seminar programme

For this part of the **module** the class is divided into five groups. The tutor, ensuring a mix of personalities, determines the formation of the groups. Each group delivers two presentations to the whole class. The higher of the two marks awarded contributes towards the module assessment. The assessment criteria are negotiated with the class. Each group is asked to maintain a diary, recording meetings and discussion and their management of particular tasks.

Structure of each one-hour seminar:

Group presentation (15–20 minutes).
Listening groups consider presentation and agree questions (10 minutes).
Questions and discussion (15 minutes).
Reports completed (10 minutes).

As the presentation is a group endeavour, groups are encouraged to involve each member, not only in the presentation and delivery of the presentation but also in the response to questions during the seminar. Students are reminded to think of interesting ways in which the presentation might be delivered to engage the attention of their audience. The 'presentation' might take the form of a panel discussion or a debate, it might be modelled on a game show programme. Each presenting group is required to submit a one-page summary one week prior to the seminar. This is copied to the other groups to familiarize them with the treatment of the topic.

At the end of the seminar each of the listening groups completed a report which invites comments on the effectiveness of the presenting group's management of the situation and their knowledge of the topic, including their response to questions. The tutor monitors the proceedings and completes a separate report. The marks awarded by the students and the tutor are equally weighted in the final assessment.

(Dr Desmond Hunter, Module Tutor)

SKILLS FOR EFFECTIVE SMALL GROUP TEACHING

Among important skills for teachers, those of listening, asking and answering questions and responding are paramount in small group settings.

Questioning

The skills of asking and answering questions are not as simple as they might appear at face value. Many general teaching and social skills communication texts deal with the skill of questioning, for example Brown and Atkins (1988). Good questioning techniques require continuing preparation, practice and reflection by students and teachers alike. Preparation of a repertoire of questions in advance will allow the teacher to work effectively and flexibly in the small group.

Similarly, student-to-student interactions in groups is enhanced if students prepare questions at the outset or end of a class. The confidence of students is often boosted through preparation of content in the form of key and incisive questions on a topic.

The type of question asked is also linked to promoting or inhibiting learning. Questions may be categorized in different ways such as:

Open	Closed
Broad	Narrow
Clear	Confused
Simple	Complex
Reflective	Recall
Probing	Superficial
Divergent	Convergent

Interrogating Practice

Broadly speaking, which categories do your questions fit into? Make a list of probing questions relevant to an important concept in your subject.

How you ask questions is also important in fostering student responses. Body language displaying an indifferent, aggressive, closed or anxious manner will be less effective. An open, warm challenging or sensitive manner may gain more responses of a thoughtful nature.

Interrogating Practice

When asked a question by a student what are some of the things you can do other than directly answering the question?

The above activity concentrates on your reactions to student questions. Some of these reactions may result in students being able to answer their own questions. However, there will be times when you will directly answer the question. Directly answering questions during a group meeting takes less time than attempting to encourage the student or group to come up with the answers. If you choose to answer directly, make your answer brief and to the point. After responding you may wish to check that you have really answered the question by saying something like: 'Does that answer your question?'

The timing of asking questions, the use of pause and silence are also important in developing the skills of answering and asking questions. Taking these matters into consideration may in part address the common problem teachers in higher education report – that students do not contribute during small group sessions.

Listening

The mental process of listening is an active one that calls into play a number of thinking functions including analysis, comprehension, synthesis and evaluation. Genuine listening also has an emotional dimension since it requires an ability to share, and quite possibly understand, another person's feelings, and understand his or her situation.

Intellectual and emotional meanings are communicated by the listener and speaker in both verbal and non-verbal forms. So how you listen will be observable through gestures and body language. Your listening skills may be developed by thinking about all the levels of a student's comment, in this way:

- what is said: the content;
- how it is said: tone and feelings;
- when it is said: time and priority;
- where it is said: place and environment.

Listening attentively to individual students in the group and to the group's mood will heighten your ability to respond. This may require a new approach, one that demands practising silence, but if you persevere you will find this an attainable skill, through which remarkable insights can be gained.

Interrogating Practice

Consider how much time you spend listening to students and encouraging students to listen to one another. Check out your perceptions of your real talk time / listening time by asking students for feedback.

Responding

Listening in silence by paying undivided attention to the speaker is an active process, engaging and heightening awareness and observation. The other aspect of positive listening is of course to intervene in a variety of ways for a variety of purposes. The more intense our listening is, the more likely it is that we will know how to respond, when to respond and in what ways.

There are many ways of responding and many reasons for responding in a certain way. Appropriate responses are usually made when the tutor has considered not only the cognitive aims of the session but also the interpersonal needs of the group and the individual learner's level of confidence and knowledge. Different responses will have different consequences for the individual student and for the behaviour of the group as a whole. Therefore, an appropriate response can only be deemed appropriate in the context of the particular small group teaching session.

Interrogating Practice

Along with a small group of colleagues, determine what skills you might usefully develop to increase effectiveness as a facilitator of groups.

OVERVIEW

This chapter has considered a selection of appropriate group methods; mentioned a range of group formats; referred to individual and group behaviour; and offered an opportunity for teachers to consider how they might develop and enhance their practice, including by offering suggestions for further reading.

REFERENCES

Abercrombie, M (1970) *Aims and Techniques of Group Teaching*, SRHE, London

Adair, J (1996) *Effective Motivation*, Pan, London

Bligh, D (ed) (1986) *Teaching Thinking by Discussion*, SRHE and NFER Nelson, Guildford

Brown, G and Atkins, M (1988) *Effective Teaching in Higher Education*, Routledge, London

Griffiths, S, Houston, K and Lazenbatt, A (1996) *Enhancing Student Learning through Peer Tutoring in Higher Education,* University of Ulster, Coleraine

Griffiths, S and Partington, P (1992) *Enabling Active Learning in Small Groups: Module 5 in effective learning and teaching in higher education,* UCoSDA/CVCP, Sheffield

Habeshaw, S, Habeshaw, T and Gibbs, G (1988) *53 Interesting Things to do in your Seminars and Tutorials,* 3rd edn, Technical and Educational Services Ltd, Bristol

Jaques, D (2000) *Learning in Groups: A handbook for improving group work,* Kogan Page, London

Korda, M (1976) *Power in the Office,* Weidenfeld and Nicolson, London

Luker, P (1989) Academic staff development in universities with special reference to small group teaching (unpublished PhD thesis), University of Nottingham

Rudduck, J (1978) *Learning Through Small Group Discussion,* SRHE, University of Surrey

Stenhouse, L (1972) Teaching through small group discussion: formality, rules and authority, *Cambridge Journal of Education,* 2 (1), pp 18–24

Tuckmann, B (1965) Developmental sequences in small groups, *Psychological Bulletin,* 63 (6), pp 384–99

FURTHER READING

Griffiths, S and Partington, P (1992). See above. An in-depth look at the topic. Useful interactive exercises and video to highlight skills.

Habeshaw, S, Habeshaw, T, and Gibbs, G (1988). See above. Very useful for practical advice and activities.

Race, P and Brown, S (2002) *The ILTA Guide, Inspiring Learning about Teaching and Assessment,* ILT in association with *Education Guardian,* York. Contains a lively and practical section on small group learning and teaching.

8 Supervising projects and dissertations

Stephanie Marshall

'The waiter analogy is useful [when considering what constitutes good project and dissertation supervision]: a good waiter in a good restaurant is around enough to help you when you need things but leaves you alone enough to enjoy yourself' (Murray, 1998).

Readers undoubtedly will agree with the sentiments expressed above, as would students reflecting on their desired role for their supervisors in the supervision of projects and dissertations. But how is such a fine balance achieved, and is it really possible for a supervisor to attain the ideal of knowing when to be 'hands on' and when to be 'hands off'? This chapter seeks to explore this question, first, by providing a background to the use of projects and dissertations in undergraduate teaching (for an exploration of postgraduate dissertation supervision see Taylor, 2001), moving on to consider a working definition; and second, by mapping out the terrain – that is, the key issues supervisors need to think through and be clear about prior to introducing such a strategy for promoting learning; then, finally, summarizing the key management and interpersonal skills required of the supervisor in order to promote efficient and effective supervision of projects and dissertations.

WHY PROJECTS AND DISSERTATIONS?

Over the past decade, the use of projects and dissertations in university curricula has been seen as increasingly important for a number of reasons. Projects and dissertations have always been viewed as an effective means of research training and of encouraging a discovery approach to learning, through the generation and analysis of primary data. Such an approach is aimed at the development of higher level cognitive skills such as analysis, synthesis and evaluation. Alongside this obvious rationale, projects and dissertations are also seen as an effective means of:

- diversifying assessment;
- addressing concern to promote transferable skills and skills for employability (see Chapter 10);
- empowering the learner;
- motivating students.

Projects and dissertations have come to be seen as an important component of degree programmes across the disciplines, due to such a rationale as above, and the clear emphasis they place on the learner taking responsibility for his or her own learning.

DEFINITIONS

Projects and dissertations are often discussed as one in the educational development literature (Day, Grant and Hounsell, 1998; Wilkins, 1995). It is worth considering both distinctions and similarities prior to offering a working definition.

A project as distinct from a dissertation is generally defined as aimed at generating primary data (Williams and Horobin, 1992). Dissertations, on the other hand, are categorized as generating secondary data, often in the form of a long essay or report (Parsons and Knight, 1998).

Henry (1994) researched extensively the use of projects in teaching on behalf of the Open University. She offers a six-point definition of a 'project' which I would suggest is not dissimilar to a dissertation, stating that: 'The student (usually) selects the project topic; locates his or her own source material; presents an end product (usually a report and often for assessment); conducts an independent piece of work (though there are also group projects). The project lasts over an extended period and the teacher assumes the role of adviser' (1994: 12).

The similarities between projects and dissertations are obvious, in that both require project management skills: scheduling, action planning, time management, and monitoring and evaluation. Over recent years the term 'dissertation' in the context of undergraduate work has come to be employed less, and use of the term 'project', incorporating the notion of project management, employed more. Case Study 1, drawing on the University of York 2002 prospectus, exemplifies this trend.

Case Study 1: Definitions of projects as offered in the University of York undergraduate prospectus

Electronics

'The individual final year project is usually chosen from a range of suggestions from staff, although many others are suggested by students... The essence of the project is to provide open-ended and flexible opportunities for students to explore those subject areas where they most want to specialize at an advanced level, and for them to be able to show initiative, originality and project management skills over a prolonged period of time.'

History

'In a few courses on collaborative project work, students work together; they have a tutor for consultation and guidance, but are themselves primarily responsible for shaping and producing the project they have been set... students quickly find that there is very little "spoon feeding". Self-reliance is strongly encouraged. Our task is to help students learn how to find things out for themselves, to organize their work independently and to develop their own interest in historical scholarship.'

Music

'At the heart of the course is a series of projects which offer opportunities for you to work at your own pace and to contribute to the group-study of a topic... You will have considerable freedom in your choice and timing of projects... The organization varies from one to another, but all have the same general pattern...'

All three explanations of project work offered in Case Study 1 emphasize project management skills on the part of the student. Such a definition suggests that both projects and dissertations are a piece of project management with an emphasis on the students determining the parameters within which they will operate to deliver a time-bound externally described output – a project or dissertation of a certain length and format. Within this specified time framework, students determine the parameters of their own work and are offered the potential to pursue their own interests within a given discipline area. The role of the supervisor thus moves away from that of teacher providing the format within which students will be expected to perform to that of facilitator. Further to the Research Councils and QAA's concern for professional supervisor practice *Effective Academic* (BBSRC;

QAA Code of Conduct for Research), there has been a wealth of applied research into best practice in postgraduate dissertation supervision (Beattie, Hutchinson and Marshall, 2001), but research into undergraduate project and dissertation supervision remains under-developed. Nevertheless, many of the interpersonal skills issues on the part of the supervisor are transferable, and inform the discussion which follows.

Despite the growth of concern to build more opportunities for students to combine their learning of discipline-specific knowledge to the 'real world', which will be of subsequent use in the workplace (Holmes, 1995; NCIHE, 1997), there is little evidence of concern to explore the distinction between the supervisor as teacher and supervisor as facilitator.

Such a distinction is between the supervision of projects and dissertations and that of the routine supervision of students by teaching staff. The former requires a time-bound, managed activity that requires project management skills on the part of both supervisor and supervisee. The latter requires self-awareness (eg, of one's personality style, gender, class and race) combined with an ability to engage in reflective practice and acute sensitivity to the needs of the student. It is this distinction that warrants further consideration.

Projects and dissertations clearly offer a teaching and learning strategy which passes the onus for learning onto the students, thus requiring supervisors to reposition themselves away from the role of teacher, moving vertically up the axis to that of facilitator, as illustrated in Figure 8.1. The implications of this shift in role offer the greatest potential for student learning at the same time as offering the greatest potential for role conflict on the part of the supervisor. As Day, Grant and

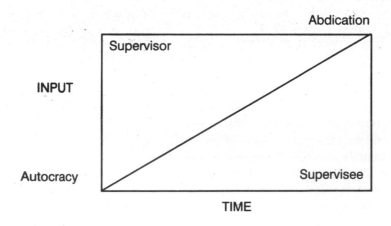

Figure 8.1 The supervisor–supervisee relationship

Hounsell (1998: 51) suggest, 'avoiding the twin traps of over- or under-supervising is never easy'.

Establishing and agreeing the appropriate working relationship between supervisor and supervisee – a highly complex and under-explored area at the undergraduate level – offers the key to maximizing the learning capacity of projects and dissertations. How to achieve such a working relationship is explored in detail in the next section.

MAPPING THE TERRAIN

Prior to embarking on the introduction of projects or dissertations, supervisors should review their own project management skills. There would appear to be four key questions that supervisors need to address:

* their own motivation in choosing a project or dissertation as a learning strategy;
* whether to opt for a structured or unstructured project or dissertation;
* their role as supervisor;
* ways of broadening support for supervisees.

THE AIMS AND OBJECTIVES OF THE LEARNING STRATEGY

In planning any project or dissertation, supervisors must be clear as to why they are choosing such a method of teaching and learning to promote the aims of the learning programme. The labour intensity and potential for undue pressure on the supervisor further to pursuit of the project method have been discussed elsewhere (Henry, 1994). All Quality Assessment Overview Reports (NISS, 1997) suggest that projects and dissertations form an important part of any departmental repertoire of teaching and learning strategies. Furthermore, projects and dissertations do appear to feature as distinct evidence of a significant piece of student-centred learning in course programmes which might otherwise appear rather traditional. There is general agreement that projects and dissertations are best left until the latter part of the degree programme (Jaques, 1989; Thorley and Gregory, 1994; Hammick and Acker, 1998), and, indeed, 'for most students, the single most significant piece of work carried out is the final-year research project or dissertation. Not only can it assist with the integration of subject material, but it provides an introduction to research techniques and methods' (QO 10/95). It is this unique feature of projects and dissertations – ie, the shift in control from supervisor to supervisee – which can offer the greatest challenge to both student and supervisor. This shift is explored further in Part 3.

Interrogating Practice

Reflect on projects or dissertations you have supervised or, indeed, have recently completed. How was this learning strategy used to promote the aims of the curriculum?

STRUCTURED VERSUS UNSTRUCTURED

There has been much written both in favour of structured and in favour of unstructured projects and dissertations. At one end of the spectrum, it is agreed that providing students with a structure reduces the risk of failure at the same time as making the supervisory role easier in the sense that the supervisor will be able to monitor student progress through clearly prescribed stages (Race and Brown, 1998). The main critique of such a method is that projects and dissertations can appear insufficiently open-ended, thus being too prescriptive, offering a rationalist approach to learning rather than a constructivist and presenting a number of students with little real challenge (QO 2/95). At the other end of the spectrum, it is agreed that providing students with extended project and dissertation work allows them to collect a range of evidence, proceeding on to test a range of theories and explanations, to promote a deep approach to learning and allowing the potential for students to progress along a hierarchy of understanding such as that offered by the SOLO taxonomy outlined in Chapter 2. The result should thus be a demonstration and familiarity with key theories (which at best will be conceptualized at a high level of abstraction), and an awareness of the importance of using sufficient evidence (QO 8/96). However, the main critique of adopting the unstructured approach is that students, in being given too much choice and scope, may flounder. Alongside student autonomy, academic staff will be forced to supervise too great a range of projects, thus testing the facilitatory supervision skills of some staff. Both these factors can result in a compromise of quality (QO 10/95).

Interrogating Practice

Reflect on the parameters offered for projects and dissertations within your department. Would you classify these as structured or unstructured? What are the strengths and weaknesses of the approach adopted by your department?

THE ROLE OF PROJECT AND DISSERTATION SUPERVISOR

Determining how to supervise projects and dissertations offers a great challenge. As with any project, 'front loading' (putting the most time in at the beginning) at the planning stage – both initially on one's own and then with the supervisee(s) – is essential. Stone (1994) refers to the 'walk-through' approach as offering an essential planning tool. By this he means that the supervisor should mentally walk through every step of the project, considering such issues as phasing and likely time allocation. It would seem most appropriate to pursue this method to promote dialogue with supervisees (particularly as one of the regular complaints from supervisors with respect to unstructured projects and dissertations is that students choose overly ambitious topics, wholly naïve as to the breadth of the topic but also as regards phasing and costing out the different activities – eg, literature review, research, writing up, etc – within a fixed timescale).

There are four key features of the supervisory framework which will require planning for and sharing with the supervisee(s). First, determine and agree educational objectives; second, determine and agree specific objectives to include formative deadlines; third, agree set targets; and, finally, review and ensure understanding of the assessment criteria (see Case Studies 3 and 4). Within this framework, time allocation for supervision needs to be made clear to avoid any possible future confusion. Most departments offer details of supervisors' office hours (NISS, 1997). Within these dedicated supervisory hours, the supervisor needs to ensure equity of quality time for supervisees, and thus should spend some time going through a few simple calculations.

Interrogating Practice

Reflect on how much time, to include planning, delivery, supervision, and review, you would normally spend on a taught course which equates in credit value to the project or dissertation you are or will be supervising. What does this mean in terms of hours a week you should make available for project or dissertation supervision? What does this mean in terms of time allocation for each of your supervisees?

Once a framework for supervision has been determined as above, legal (eg, health and safety regulations, special educational needs and disability requirements), ethical (eg, issues of confidentiality) and financial (eg, restricted budgets for science experiments) constraints should be addressed. Such issues undoubtedly will be addressed in departmental guidelines for project and dissertation completion, and can be reviewed elsewhere (Williams and Horobin, 1992). As more additional guidance data to inform the execution of projects and dissertations is gathered, it ultimately will save the supervisor much time in the long run by establishing and codifying his or her own clear guidelines and criteria, offering these to supervisees as either a handout or a Web page, or both.

Supervising unstructured or semi-structured projects and dissertations implies assisting students in formulating research questions; second, choosing methods; and finally, scoping the means of data collection. As the end product should be the supervisees' intellectual property, the supervisor must be sensitive to the supervisees' ability to determine these for themselves. There is a fine line between guiding and telling, and much will depend on the ability and vision of the student, combined with the sensitivity of the supervisor.

Interrogating Practice

Reflect on your role. At which stage(s) of the project or dissertation will you take on a 'teaching' role, and at which stage(s) a facilitatory role? Consider the skills required at both ends of the spectrum.

Focusing on the facilitatory role should prompt a response which includes: asking supervisees open-ended questions, reflecting questions back and encouraging supervisees to explore strategies to take their work forward. Facilitation skills have been written about extensively, as they do not necessarily require supervisors to demonstrate their own technical skills but rather interpersonal skills, which can prove far more difficult to learn (Williams and Horobin, 1992; Hammick and Acker, 1998). Furthermore, with the increase in student numbers, it is highly likely that supervisors will be required to supervise a group of students working outside what the supervisor might perceive to be his or her own area of expertise.

Interrogating Practice

Reflect on your own departmental practices. How do students choose their supervisor, or are students allocated to a supervisor? Will you be expected to supervise students outside your area of expertise?

Further to supervisory responsibility being determined, the supervisor and supervisee should establish an agreed, appropriate working relationship. At the first meeting, the supervisor and supervisee should discuss expectations in terms of apportioning responsibility. The most recognized formalized approach to agreeing a working relationship is that of a learning contract, or what Williams and Horobin (1992: 43) refer to as creating a 'we culture'. Ryan (1994) offers a template for a supervisor checklist and student contract which itemizes the range of responsibilities to which both parties agree: eg, timetabled regular meetings, writing up supervisory meeting notes, ethical issues, submission of progress reports, and involvement in peer group support.

WAYS OF BROADENING SUPPORT

With the massification of higher education, and the recognition of the value of teamwork, peer support has increasingly been viewed as a learning strategy that should be promoted within the curriculum (Thorley and Gregory, 1994) for a range of reasons. For example, working in project teams provides moral support at the same time as promoting teamwork skills. Such an approach is becoming more widespread, eg, in problem-based medical education (see Chapter 23). The group often has a greater range of total experience and skills than any one individual. It is particularly beneficial to be able to draw on a range of students' skills such as an exceptionally IT literate student, a student capable of sophisticated statistical analysis, or a student capable of maintaining morale when the going gets tough. It could be a requirement of the department that peer support teams meet at prescribed times to provide feedback. Jaques (1989: 30) advocates this method, suggesting that:

> Many of the issues to do with the progress of a project can be just as well dealt with by students themselves, provided they have a reasonably clear structure to work with. In the case of individual projects, students can report and be quizzed in turn by the rest of a peer group at regular meetings on matters like: ...What are you proposing to do?... How can you break that down into manageable steps?... What or who else could help you?... '

He advocates using a similar set of guidance questions towards the end of the project, moving on to suggest ways of engaging these peer groups in summative evaluation, prior to formal submission of the project. Clark (1992: 7), writing about the supervision of group work projects in the History Department at the University of York, advocates the supervisor being close on hand to offer interventions if requested by students, noting that when he dropped in on his first ever project group to offer advice on writing-up, he was told with much amusement, 'Go away, we don't need you.'

Other ways of broadening support include the setting up of a Virtual Learning Environments (VLEs – see Chapter 11), a Web site poster board with guidance notes (eg, format, word length) and frequently asked questions (FAQs), and encouraging students to post up queries (Web sites such as WebCT, COSE, MERLIN). However, the supervisor will need to monitor the poster board to make appropriate interventions, ensuring accurate resolution of problems takes place. Finally, there are an increasing number of books on the market targeted at the student population, providing additional guidance and 'how to' tips (eg, Parsons and Knight, 1998).

MANAGING SCHEDULING

The pressure of time will be felt by both supervisors and supervisees when working to deadlines. In order to keep projects and dissertations on track, a range of documentation can prove useful. The use of guideline criteria and learning contracts as initial documentation was referred to in the previous section. Schedules, action plans and checklists similarly are useful tools. Some useful examples are provided by Day, Grant and Hounsell (1998) and a simplistic version of a checklist offering a 'walk-through' approach to supervision is illustrated in Case Study 2. Checklists and documentation are most useful to avoid memory overload, but also to provide a written record of the meeting to include agreed action points. Such written records are invaluable in cases of student appeals.

> ### Cast Study 2: Checklist for preparation for project and dissertation supervisory meetings

University of York

The checklist that follows results from brainstorming sessions with academics enrolled on staff development workshops aimed at promoting professional supervision of dissertations and projects.

Planning for the supervision – how will you tackle the following?

- discussing current strengths and weaknesses;
- encouraging the student to plan for taking the work forward;
- setting a short-term objective (to include contingency planning) within an action plan;
- setting up a more detailed time and action framework.

What will your agenda be?

- agree action plan and/or
- review progress against action plan;
- give feedback on performance;
- troubleshoot, problem solve;
- revisit assessment criteria;
- revisit and re-define action plan and timescale.

What information will you need to refer to?

- supervisee's written progress reports;
- supervisee's draft material;
- departmental project regulations and assessment criteria.

Arrangements for the supervision meeting:

- ensure 'quality time' free from interruptions;
- ensure the venue is conducive to open discussion.

The supervision meeting must be structured and well organized:

- opening – use this to clarify purpose and agree the agenda;
- middle – you should facilitate discussion of ideas, discuss specific issues, monitor progress, give constructive feedback, question effectively, set and agree objectives leading to the next supervision meeting;
- end – you should record an action plan, to include short-term objectives; and end on a positive note.

(Stephanie Marshall)

By adopting such methods as offered in Case Study 2 and checklists presented elsewhere (Day, Grant and Hounsell, 1998; Wilkins, 1995), both supervisor and supervisee will share a sense of purpose and progress. Another means of assisting rigour in approach is to ensure that there are open and transparent assessment criteria, which will aid the supervisor to assist the supervisee in ensuring that adequate attention is paid to the weighting of various components. An example of such rigour is offered in Case Study 3, which offers a marker's assessment pro-forma, and Case Study 4, which offers a student's self-assessment pro-forma.

Case Study 3: Assessment pro-forma

UCL Department of Computer Science

MSc Computer Science Project Mark Sheet, 1999

Student's Name:

Title:

Marker 1:   Marker 2:

Mark the project report as 'excellent', 'satisfactory' or 'unsatisfactory' according to each of the twelve criteria below. Where a report is *totally* deficient in some respects, leave a row blank. Use the intermediate columns as needed.

The terms down the left are intended for projects of the traditional design and implementation sort; those on the right for design studies that did not include implementation. If the project does not fit either of these patterns, ignore the table and explain your mark in the comments section.

Implementation-based projects   Excellent   Satisfactory   Unsatisfactory   *Design-based projects*

Implementation-based projects	Excellent		Satisfactory		Unsatisfactory	Design-based projects
Background reading. General understanding of the subject area						(as left)
Report organization and structure						(as left)
Clarity of expression						(as left)
Reasonable and well justified conclusions Critical appraisal of the work						(as left)
Key problems identified and solved						(as left)
Documentation (user / system manuals, design documents etc as appropriate)						(as left)
Completeness. Objectives achieved fully						(as left)
Overall system design						Requirements and objectives well understood and presented
Appropriate use of data structures and algorithms						Appropriate use of design methodology

Appropriate use of tools, libraries, existing codes etc						Overall quality of the final design
Well structured and readable implementation						Evaluation and/or verification of the design (eg, by prototyping)
System testing and/or verification						Practicality of the design
Count the ticks in each column						
Multiply each count by these weights	×8	×5	×4	×3	×1	
Add weighted counts together						
Multiply total weighted count by $^{25}/_{24}$ to yield agreed mark					%	

(Developed by members of the UCL Computer Science Department)

Case Study 4: Assessment pro-forma

University College London

Faculty of Mathematical and Physical Sciences

Course Assessment

Q5 Project/Dissertation [1998/99]   Department of Computer Science

Supervisor(s)..

Course code D99
Year of study (1, 2, 3).....1....
Group or Individual work (G, I) ...I...

After all the material connected with your project/dissertation has been submitted please complete this assessment **and submit with your project**. Your replies will not be analysed until after the final examiners' meeting to ensure your full and frank cooperation.

In the next 3 sections please rate your assessment in the range –2 to +2 by placing a tick in the appropriate box.
In what follows the word 'project' should be interpreted as dissertation where appropriate.

(1) PREPARATION AND TRAINING		-2	-1	0	+1	+2	
The aims of the project were	unclear						clear
Preparation for practical aspects of the project was	poor						good
The theoretical background preparation was	poor						good
The training in presentational skills was	poor						good
The preparation for data interpretation was	poor						good
The training in time management was	poor						good
The quality of supervision was	poor						good
The amount of supervision was	too little						too much
(2) CONTENT AND FACILITIES		-2	-1	0	+1	+2	
The project workload was	too low						too high
Your interest in the project was	low						high
The required report length was	too short						too long
Library facilities were	poor						good
Computing facilities were	poor						good
Laboratory facilities were	poor						good
(3) OVERALL ASSESSMENT		-2	-1	0	+1	+2	
Overall, my view of the project was that it was	very poor						very good

(4) GENERAL COMMENTS

Please write down overleaf any comments that you feel will be helpful in improving the project/dissertation in future years. Please do not be inhibited; anonymity is assured.

Thank you for taking the time to complete this questionnaire.

(Developed by members of the UCL Computer Sciences Department)

By supervisors adopting a rigorous approach to project and dissertation completion that entails, first, transparency in formative and summative assessment criteria, combined with, second, professional supervisory skills, supervision will be viewed as a constructive means of monitoring the milestones on the route to successful project and dissertation completion.

OVERVIEW

This chapter examined the greater use made of projects and dissertations across disciplines and endeavoured to provide a working definition. Projects and dissertations were described as offering a unique learning opportunity in that, first, they are sufficiently time-bound to afford students the opportunity to demonstrate their project management skills and, second, they are clearly a student-centred learning experience which requires the supervisor to take on the role of facilitator. It was argued that for supervisors to offer effective and efficient supervision of projects and dissertations, they would have to examine and refine their own management and interpersonal skills. In the case of the former, a range of planning tools was offered. In the case of the latter, it was suggested that the supervisor should broaden support for the student, so that the supervisor could take on the role of facilitator, prompting and encouraging the student to seek out his or her own solutions and strategies for moving forward. It is this combination of unique features which makes the use of projects and dissertations such a powerful learning tool.

REFERENCES

Beattie, C, Hutchinson, S and Marshall, S (2001) What makes for effective PhD training and supervision in the Arts and Humanities? *English Subject Centre Newsletter*, (2), August

Biotechnology and Biological Sciences Research Council (BBSRC) (2002) BBSRC, www.bbsrc.ac.uk

Clark, C (1992) Group projects in the department of history, *Staff Development and Training Newsletter*, Staff Development Office, York

Day, K, Grant, R and Hounsell, D (1998) *Reviewing Your Teaching*, CTLA & UCoSDA, Edinburgh

Hammick and Acker (1998) Undergraduate Research Supervision: a gender analysis, *Studies in Higher Education*, **23** (3), pp 335–47

Henry, J (1994) *Teaching Through Projects*, Kogan Page, London

Holmes (1995) quoted in Livingston and Lynch (2000), 'Group Project Work and Student-centred Active Learning: two different experiences', in *Studies in Higher Education*, **25**, (3), pp 325–45

Jaques, D (1989) *Independent Learning and Project Work*, Open Learning, Oxford

Murray, R (1998) *Research Supervision*, Centre for Academic Practice, Strathclyde

NCIHE (1997) (Dearing Report) *Higher Education in the Learning Society*, National Committee of Inquiry into Higher Education, HMSO, London

NISS (1997) Quality Assessment Overview Reports, http://www.niss.ac.uk/education/hefce/qar/overview.html

Parsons, T and Knight, P (1998) *How to do your Dissertation in Geography and Related Disciplines*, Chapman & Hall, London

Quality Assessment Agency (QAA) *Codes of Practice*, www.qaa.ac.uk

QO 2/95 Subject Overview Report – Chemistry, in NISS (1997) Quality Assessment Overview Reports, http://www.niss.ac.uk/education/hefce/qar/overview.html

QO 8/96 Subject Overview Report – Sociology, in NISS (1997) Quality Assessment Overview Reports, http://www.niss.ac.uk/education/hefce/qar/overview.html

QO 10/95 Subject Overview Report – Environmental Studies, in NISS (1997) Quality Assessment Overview Reports, http://www.niss.ac.uk/education/hefce/qar/overview.html

Race, P and Brown, S (1998) *The Lecturer's Toolkit*, Kogan Page, London

Ryan, Y (1994) Contracts and checklists: practical propositions for postgraduate supervision, in *Quality in Postgraduate Education*, eds O Zuber-Skerritt and Y Ryan, Kogan Page, London

Stone, B (1994) The academic management of group projects, in *Using Group-Based Learning in Higher Education*, eds L Thorley and R Gregory, Kogan Page, London

Taylor, S (2001) Postgraduate supervision, in *The Effective Academic*, eds S Ketteridge, S Marshall and H Fry, Kogan Page, London

Thorley, L and Gregory, R (1994) *Using Group-Based Learning in Higher Education*, Kogan Page, London

Wilkins, M (1995) *Learning to Teach in Higher Education*, Coventry Printers, Warwick

Williams, M and Horobin, R (1992) *Active Learning in Fieldwork and Project Work*, CVCP USDTU, Sheffield

FURTHER READING

Day, K, Grant, R and Hounsell, D (1998) See above. Chapter 7 deals specifically with supervising projects and dissertations, and has some examples of useful pro-forma.

Habeshaw, S, Habeshaw, T and Gibbs (1989) *53 Interesting Ways of Helping Your Students to Study*, Technical and Educational Services Ltd, Bristol

Henry, J (1994) *Teaching Through Projects*, Kogan Page, London. A comprehensive and thorough examination of the use of project work to inform extension of this practice by the Open University.

Rudestam, K and Newton, R (1992) *Surviving Your Dissertation*, Sage, London

Zuber-Skerritt, O and Ryan, Y (1994) *Quality in Postgraduate Education*, Kogan Page, London

Williams, M and Horobin, R (1992) See above. As with all the contributions to this extensive volume of aspects of active learning, useful to dip into, particularly to examine the changed role of the supervisor in projects and dissertations.

C&IT learning environments to assist in promoting peer support and monitoring of projects and dissertations – Internet addresses:

WebCT (http://www.webct.com/)

COSE (http://www.staffs.ac.uk/COSE)

MERLIN (http://www.hull.ac.uk/merlin/welcome.html)

<table>
<tr><td>9</td><td>

Teaching and learning for student skills development

</td></tr>
</table>

Stephen Fallows

INTRODUCTION

Sometimes, as teachers in higher education we become so involved with our own subject discipline that we forget the basic fact that the major proportion of graduates never revisit the subject of their degree after graduation. A science graduate progresses into accountancy, a history graduate becomes a personnel manager, a philosophy graduate moves to a management consultancy business, a law graduate becomes a teacher and so on; the permutations are endless.

The statistics indicate that of all graduates, those who remain within the confines of their academic degree discipline are in the minority. For some disciplines, this is self-evident (for instance, there are few mainstream positions for philosophers). But even for those academic disciplines for which there is apparently a direct link to a career path (such as electronic engineering or dietetics) there are many graduates who seek alternative routes to employment either immediately on graduation or subsequently.

So, what is it that graduates are taking from higher education as they move into employment? They will all obviously have gained the specialist knowledge of their subject (with a greater or lesser degree of success) – after all, that is the material that has taken time and effort to teach them and which they have used in order to complete their assessments. Some will be able to use this knowledge directly in their new professional lives as doctors, surveyors, linguists, research scientists, physiotherapists and so on. Others will be able to give direct application to their subject-specific knowledge as teachers, advisers or specialist commentators. But for many it has to be accepted that their study of a discipline is merely a means to a different end; these students will have used their subject as a means to demonstrate their abilities as learners. They will have been endowed with something over and above a knowledge of literature, biochemistry or history.

If as teachers we have been really successful all our graduates will have developed a wide portfolio of high level skills that are not only useful in the higher education context but are also transferable beyond the confines of the academic world. These skills will have been developed through the variety of activities that the students undertake whilst in higher education.

This chapter will describe the generic skills needed for the world of work and presents a framework developed at the University of Luton to ensure that these skills are integrated into programmes of study. The chapter is based on a major review of the integration of such skills in higher education undertaken by the author (Fallows and Steven, 2000). For a discussion of the evolution of the skills agenda in higher education see Noble (1999), Drew (1998) and CVCP (1998).

THE EMPLOYERS' VIEW

The world of employment is changing rapidly. In the past, many new graduate employees looked forward to a career within a specific organization and where, in the right circumstances, progression up the internal corporate career ladder could be expected. This model may still exist for some, but for the majority of graduates the model will be quite different. The new career model is not one of permanence within an organization with planned progression, but one that involves life with several organizations and often within several sectors – public, commercial, industrial.

Furthermore, the general business environment is changing rapidly. New opportunities are emerging as fast as old businesses die away; a large proportion of the working population is employed by businesses that simply did not exist a couple of decades ago (eg, the mobile phone or Internet sectors). No one can predict with certainty what will be the new big growth areas of business 20 years hence; all that can be predicted with any certainty is that today's students will be playing a big role in these new organizations.

Employers have been outspoken for many years about their needs for new graduate employees to 'hit the ground running'. The concept of extended, structured training programmes for graduates is probably available to just a small elite minority; everyone else has to arrive as fully functional as possible. These thoughts are especially true for the smaller and medium-sized enterprises ('SMEs') that are representing an ever-larger proportion of job opportunities.

In order to be fully functional in employment, modern graduates need to be equipped with a range of skills and clearly understand the scope of their skills. There has been much discussion about what should be included in this category of skills and there are many publications in this area, but for an extended and critical review see Bennett, Dunne and Carré (2000).

SKILLS FOR THE WORLD OF WORK

There is broad agreement that skills are required though there is significant variation in the terminology used to describe these; the following are widely used in the UK – **key skills, transferable skills, common skills, core skills**. Around the world other terms are used to describe the additional skills outcomes; for example 'Abilities' – Alverno College, Milwaukee, 'Springboard competencies' – Bowling Green State University, Bowling Green, Ohio, and 'Tertiary literacies' – University of Wollongong, Australia.

Whichever term is used as the collective noun, there appears to be a universal acceptance that students should develop the following during their time in higher education:

- communication skills, using a range of approaches;
- information management skills (retrieval, evaluation, analysis and utilization);
- use of modern communication and information technologies (C&IT);
- people skills (such as team/group working, ethics and recognition of diversity);
- personal skills (time management, personal responsibility and the ability to continue to learn).

HIGHER EDUCATION RESPONSES

Higher education institutions have adopted a range of strategies with respect to skills development and are at differing stages of implementation. Some institutions have taken the view that skills develop naturally during the students' studies and thus no particular action need be taken. At the other extreme, certain institutions have taken a much stronger and proactive position and have put the development of skills as a high priority in their teaching and learning strategies.

For those institutions that have embraced the skills agenda there are several models which can be summarized as follows:

- The totally embedded model. Here skills development takes place within the general curriculum and across the range of modules or courses offered. There is often an institutional understanding that all teachers will work towards a common set of skills expectations, regardless of subject discipline. This model suits an institution with a centrally managed modular curriculum that allows its students a wide choice of options.

- The targeted skills model. Here the institutional position is that different subject discipline areas have 'naturally occurring' skills development opportunities and similarly have different requirements. This model most often applies in traditional universities in which considerable autonomy is devolved to individual departments.
- The skills module model. Here the institution has taken the decision to offer its students a specific module or course that focuses specifically on skills development (eg, see the case study by Partridge in Fry and Marshall, 2002). This model can be further sub-divided into the generic and template approaches. In the generic approach, a single module or course is directly applicable, independent of subject discipline and may be taken by mixed groups drawn from several subject disciplines. In the template approach, an outline skills module is provided which can be 'tuned' and made specific to the students' academic interests.
- The external model. Here the students are encouraged (or even required) to gain skills relevant to future employment through work experience or other extra-curricular activity. This may be formally included as a module or other element of the students' programme of study, or may be a quite separate activity that in turn may receive separate certification.

There are some other important issues to be considered along with models of skills development. Should skills be specifically assessed and certificated? Or should skills be acknowledged in the students' end of programme transcript? Should poor skills performance lead to more general failure of the degree? There can be no definitive responses to these and similar questions; however, it is far more straightforward to give a specific skills grade in those instances where the skills module approach is adopted. In practice, it is unavoidable that proficiency in certain skills (for instance information management) will yield the student higher grades in standard assignments or that failure to develop these skills will be detrimental to a student's progression.

Should skills expectations rise as the student progresses through higher education? The embedded model allows for skills descriptors to become more demanding as the student moves from induction to graduation. By contrast, the skills module approach almost by definition suggests a single level of expectation rather than one of continuing development.

Progress files

Since the publication of the Dearing Report (NCIHE, 1997) government has taken an increasing interest in the development of students employability skills. One way in which this has been exhibited is through **progress files** (see also Chapter 13). The part of the progress file which relates to development and demonstration of skills for employability is called the personal development plan (see also Chapter 12). These build on the idea of personal development logs and they help students to develop and document their skills. Many institutions have Web-based systems for students to use in developing and recording skills that relate to employability. Such generic tools are not without their difficulties, some of which are considered by Fry *et al* (2002).

TEACHERS' RESPONSE

The considerations outlined in the previous paragraphs are generally outside the remit of the typical teacher in higher education. They are generally points that are raised within working parties or advisory groups where they are considered within the context of the institutional mission. The working parties and advisory groups may publish reports and consultation papers, but in practice most teachers are too busy other than to give them more than a passing glance.

However, once the institutional strategy is in place, it generally falls to the individual teacher to implement the chosen approach. But how to do this? For the established teacher the question will be, 'How do I add a focus on skills without destroying years of curriculum development?', while for the newcomer it will be, 'It's difficult enough developing my teaching materials to cover the curriculum content without having to think of skills – how will I cope?'

Similarly, there are often worries about dilution of the curriculum with the skills agenda taking up time that could be used to add further curriculum content. This worry has often indicated doubt that implementation of institutional skills initiatives will compromise the academic quality of programmes through the additional workload (on teachers and students alike).

In practice, much of this skills debate is not new; it has just become more overt. Ever since formal education began many centuries ago, teachers have required students to communicate, to engage with information (using the relevant literature) and to work with their peers; other elements have emerged only in recent years (such as communications and information technology).

PRACTICAL IMPLEMENTATION

In order to consider the practicalities of implementation, it is useful to take a specific institutional example as an extended case study and to use this as a convenient framework for discussion. The example used here is based upon the model adopted by the University of Luton from the mid- to late-1990s. This choice is based essentially on familiarity of the author with the system; it is not a particular endorsement of the Luton model over that of other institutions.

At the University of Luton, the approach adopted was to set out in some detail a set of skills descriptors for each level of undergraduate study. Figure 9.1 gives details of the descriptors ('**level descriptors**') chosen by the institution and the expectations placed on its students at Level 3 – that is in the final stages of an undergraduate degree. The figure sets out the University of Luton skills expectations in some considerable detail and with step-wise reference to operational contexts, to cognitive matters and to a set of core skills descriptors. (Similar tables are available for Levels 1 and 2.)

The descriptors divide into four broad expectations that are subsequently subdivided into 13 key points of reference.

Planning and problem solving

It is expected that 'the learner will be able to take a well-defined problem, apply given tools and methods both accurately and creatively to a set of abstract data or concepts and produce conclusions appropriate to those data'.

It is the teacher's role to define the problem and supply the tools and methods but from then on it is the students' responsibility to derive the skills outcome. Planning and problem solving can be divided into four skill areas.

Decide on action plans and implement them effectively

This is concerned with developing self-organization in order to ensure that all necessary tasks are completed as required. Work needs to be planned, staged and undertaken in manageable doses. Similarly students need to become organized in the management of their various study materials.

This is a skill that will have been built up through the students' time with the institution. On arrival, students are likely to be disorganized, but by the time that they undertake a research dissertation as part of Level 3 studies it is reasonable to expect this skill to be well developed. After all, the preparation of a dissertation is as much an exercise in skills development as a research project. To achieve success the student will have had to define a logical programme of work, in step-wise manner, negotiate

	CHARACTERISTIC OF CONTEXT	RESPONSIBILITY	ETHICAL UNDERSTANDING
1. Operational Contexts	At Level 3 the Learner: Should be working within complex and unpredictable contexts demanding selection and application from a wide range of innovative or standard techniques.	Should be autonomous in planning and managing the learning process within broad guidelines.	Should be aware of personal responsibility and professional, codes of conduct and be able to incorporate a critical ethical dimension into a major piece of work.

	KNOWLEDGE & UNDERSTANDING	ANALYSIS	SYNTHESIS/CREATIVITY	EVALUATION
2. Cognitive Descriptors	By the end of Level 3 the Learner: Should be able to demonstrate confident familiarity with the core knowledge base of his/her discipline(s) and an awareness of the provisional nature of knowledge.	Should be able to analyse new and/or abstract data and situations without guidance, using a wide range of techniques appropriate to the discipline(s).	With minimum guidance, should be able to transform abstract data and concepts towards a given purpose and be able to design novel solutions.	Should be able to critically review evidence supporting conclusions/recommendations, including its reliability, validity and significance, and investigate contradictory information and/or identify reasons for the contradictions.

	INFO. RETRIEVAL & HANDLING		COMMUNICATION & PRESENTATION		PLANNING & PROBLEM SOLVING		SOCIAL DEV. & INTERACTION	
3. Core Skills Descriptors	By the end of Level 3 the Learner: Should be able to seek, describe and interpret information within the context of the discipline(s). In particular:		Should be able to communicate effectively in context both orally and on paper. In particular:		Should be able to apply given tools/methods accurately and carefully to a well defined problem and draw appropriate conclusions. In particular:		Should be able to work with and meet obligations to others (tutors and or other students). In particular:	
	– identify own information needs to support complex problem requirements	I1.3	– produce a complex piece of work which demonstrates a grasp of vocabulary of the subject and deploys a range of skills of written expression appropriate to the subject	C1.3	– decide on action plans and implement then effectively	P1.3	– formulate effective strategies for achieving goals when working with others	S1.3
	– complete an information search using a range of appropriate primary and secondary sources. Draw accurate conclusions independently using the subject methodology	I2.3	– assess the quality of his or her own oral communication and identify areas for improvement	C2.3	– manage time effectively in order to achieve intended goals	P2.3	– participate effectively in the operation of a team an collaborate with members of the team	S2.3
	– analyse data, using appropriate techniques	I3.3	– deliver a paper or presentation which succeeds in communicating a series of points effectively.	C3.3	– clearly identify criteria for success and evaluate his or her own performance against those criteria	P3.3		
	– use appropriate IT resources independently to support previously identified areas.	I4.3			– produce creative and realistic solutions to complex problems	P4.3		

Figure 9.1 University of Luton – Modular Credit Scheme – Level 3 generic descriptors and core skills

access to the necessary resources (particularly the case for laboratory studies), complete the work to a professional standard and present the required reports.

Manage time effectively in order to achieve intended goals

A key element of planning is time management. This is a skill that is demanded by most if not all employers; it is also a skill that can present problems for many students. It is not uncommon for assessed work to be completed at the last minute, with requests for time extensions to the deadline. The imposition of rigid deadlines on students' work directly mirrors the 'real world' requirements for delivery of outputs to a predetermined timescale.

Developing time management skills is not easy, particularly when the deadline is some time off. One technique that may be adopted is to give the students short time-constrained activities on a regular basis. For example, the preparation of brief summary notes on 'gapped handouts' can not only break up the formal lecture or tutorial but can also offer the chance to develop tight use of time. Poor time management is particularly a problem with research theses and dissertations (see Chapter 8). Early negotiation of interim reports, draft papers and use of formal scheduled supervision tutorials can help to ensure that materials are presented on time.

Clearly identify criteria for success and evaluate their own performance against those criteria

Criteria for success equate to what is required for the student to reach particular grades or achieve specified outcomes. The requirements (of necessity) become progressively more stringent as progress is made in the system. It is essential that at each step the criteria are defined clearly and presented in a manner that is understandable to the students. In some instances it will be appropriate for students to engage in the assessment process by provision of grades on their own and colleagues' performance. This is perhaps easiest achieved in oral presentations with students providing feedback to their peers on specific criteria.

An alternative approach is to provide the students with an item of academic writing and then ask them to act as reviewers in a manner equivalent to that used by a peer-reviewed journal – in this exercise, students can be given the specific review criteria used by a named journal from their subject discipline. This approach goes somewhat further than the simple production of a standard review of a published paper.

Produce creative and realistic solutions to complex problems

Problem solving is fundamental to many employment roles and is most appropriately addressed through the use of experiential activities.

While the expectation is that students will be able to deal with complex problems, there is often great merit in the development of this skill by offering, in the first instance, a series of simple and perhaps even trivial problems. The use of these simple problems in groups allows students not only to complete the task but also to discuss and debate the mechanisms through which the solution was achieved. It is desirable that 'real world' examples are used in problem-solving as complexity is increased but in the initial consideration of problem-solving this is not necessary.

Information retrieval and handling

It is expected that 'the learner should be able to find, describe and interpret information within the context of the discipline(s)'.

Again this expectation is sub-divided into four elements.

Identify their own information needs in order to solve complex problem requirements

The skill described previously focused on problem solving and acquisition of relevant information is critical to success in this activity. The key matter for students to address is the need for appropriate information; it is essential that the skill of efficient data collection is developed. This skill is directly transferable into employment where the pressures of time require that problem solving is rapid, with use of specifically identified information rather than the often 'blunderbuss' approach that is common in less experienced students.

The question for teachers is how to steer students to the identification of the information that is relevant to their academic needs, with a view to providing for their future professional needs. Tutorial or whole class exercises can be used to draw up lists of the information that might be useful in resolving problems or completing tasks. Once the lists of potential sources have been drawn up they can be prioritized in relation to the task. It is generally useful in such activities to use tasks that allow for many sources to be considered in the prioritization exercise.

Complete an information search using a wide range of appropriate primary and secondary sources

In the past an information search was essentially limited to the paper-based library sources. Nowadays access to electronic resources, either locally or via the Internet, has greatly increased access to information.

Students can be asked to identify a set number of documents on a given topic from each of a number of sources (say, from peer-reviewed journals, newspapers and the Internet) and to discuss the strengths and weakness of the materials collected. The challenge for students is to identify materials of quality and to be able to sort these out from the less authoritative ones. The Internet, in particular, can offer some excellent materials but can also present students with material of a less than academic nature.

Analyse data using appropriate techniques

Data analysis will inevitably vary from discipline to discipline. For some subjects traditional statistics courses will be provided with an emphasis on numerical analysis. For other disciplines the data used will be of a more qualitative nature. The key issue with data analysis exercises is to use data that is of interest to the students rather than merely hypothetical lists of numbers. Data that present challenges to commonly held views or which deal with controversial subjects can be particularly appealing. If it is possible for students to generate their own data (rather than merely being provided with data from others); this provides ownership and can aid subsequent discussions.

Nowadays it is usual to use computer software packages for statistical analysis; here it is important that the emphasis does not move to a focus on the software at the expense of the more substantive matters of selection of the most appropriate test and subsequent interpretation of the result.

Use appropriate IT resources independently to support previously identified areas

The use of IT has become a universal fact of life in employment. Almost all graduates will be required to use the standard software suites of word processor, spreadsheet, databases and presentation software. Such usage is also almost universal across higher education and increasingly so in the lower phases of education. However, it is not enough for students to be able to create (for example) spreadsheets or databases; they must also be enabled to use such resources for the data-handling exercises referred to previously.

IT resources also include a variety of learning materials from focused computer assisted learning (CAL) packages through to the more diverse use of online learning environments (see Chapter 11) which allow for materials and ideas to be shared between students and their teachers.

Specialist software is available for many disciplines from dietary analysis packages for those studying nutrition to computer-aided design packages for engineers. It is essential that the students' learning experience includes use of such relevant resources.

Communications and presentation

The general expectation is that 'learners... should be able to communicate effectively in context, both orally and on paper'.

Context here has relevance to both subject discipline and level of expression which should be appropriate to the task. There are three elements.

Produce a piece of work that demonstrates that they have… the vocabulary of the subject [and can] deploy a range of skills of written expression appropriate to the subject

Each academic discipline has its own specialist knowledge and the graduate must be competent in the use of this vocabulary. Traditionally this has been demonstrated in the production of written assignments that use this vocabulary in essays, reports and dissertations. Requiring students to prepare a range of documents on a topic can extend this. For example, in addition to the conventional academic paper, students can be asked to prepare a brief summary in lay terms.

It is especially important that students are able to comprehend written materials that use specialized vocabulary and translate these into everyday language. One activity that works well is to provide students with a recent article from an appropriate academic journal and ask them prepare a short newspaper article based upon it.

Assess the quality of … own oral communication and identify areas for improvement

Communication in this context will include both formal presentations and contributions to class or group discussion. For presentations it can be useful to get students to provide each other with informal feedback. Providing feedback on others can often be a valuable learning exercise (and has the added benefit of requiring additional concentration on the material presented by peers).

Develop [an oral] paper or presentation that succeeds in communicating a series of points effectively

Surprisingly, many teachers have difficulty with this requirement. It is not uncommon to attend academic conferences where experienced lecturers read the outputs of their personal research in the most boring and uninspiring manner. A good method to develop this skill is to ask students to read and analyse an academic paper. Key points can be identified and organized by the students into a series of slides suitable for presentation to a specified audience. Video recording of students' presentations allows them to analyse their personal performance at a later time.

Social development and interaction

The general expectation is that learners 'should be able to work with and meet obligations to others (tutors and/or other students'.

This expectation is discussed in two elements.

Formulate effective strategies for achieving goals when working with others

This is essentially the first step in the skill of working in a group. Group work, either as a learning activity or a formal element of assessment, has become a standard element of most higher education programmes. In many instances the groups work well but on occasion there can be difficulties. Where there are difficulties this is invariably due to failure to designate roles and responsibilities. 'Working with others' should be interpreted in a range of contexts. It can include reference to other members of the institution (librarians, technical staff, etc), participant subjects in research studies or clients in the professional setting.

Participate effectively in the operation of a team and collaborate with other members of the team

Team working is seen as central to current employment practice in many organizations; this is tempered by the individual's urge to succeed. The students need to learn how to work with their peers, recognizing each other's strengths and limitations. Interaction between members of the team requires the ongoing giving and acceptance of constructive criticism as tasks are undertaken to a deadline.

Where team activities are undertaken in role then it is generally a good strategy to provide each team member with an incomplete set of information (paralleling the real world); in order to complete the task effectively there has to be collaboration.

Students can be encouraged to participate in other teams in order to develop skills in this area; this can include teams from outside the institution such as would be experienced on work placements or external research projects.

Interrogating Practice

Having considered your institution's skills strategy, which areas need strengthening in the teaching of your own discipline?

OVERVIEW

Whichever institutional model of skills teaching is used, it is always best to remain with examples and tasks that fit within the context of the students' primary subject discipline and its core knowledge base. Similarly, where relevant, professional values and requirements should be taken into account; for instance, the development of oral communication skills is particularly important for anyone seeking employment in one of the caring professions but may be less so for others.

Looking at the Luton model used in this chapter, it will be apparent that in practice it is rare for any skill to be developed in isolation. For example, most assignment tasks will use skills such as planning and problem-solving, information retrieval and handing, and finally communication and presentation. In this chapter (and in skills-related documents produced by others) it has been appropriate to separate the skills to ease discussion and to highlight specific points.

The major challenge facing all teachers is to incorporate skills development in a way that engages with students' interests. Some students may fail to appreciate the value of oral (or even written) communication skills while others may underestimate the need for skills with numerical data. Clearly there will be variation in the extent to which individual skills will be used but what cannot be avoided is that fact that nowadays the skills referred to in this chapter are an essential feature of every graduate's portfolio.

REFERENCES

Bennett, N, Dunne, E and Carré, C (2000) *Skills Development in Higher Education*, Society for Research into Higher Education, Open University Press, Buckingham

Committee of Vice-Chancellors and Principals (CVCP) (1998) *Skills Development in Higher Education, Full Report*, CVCP, London

Drew, S (1998) *Key Skills in Higher Education: Background and rationale*, SEDA Special No 6, Birmingham.

Fallows, S and Steven, C (eds) (2000) *Integrating Key Skills in Higher Education: Employability, transferable skills and learning for life*, Kogan Page, London

Fry, H, Davenport, E, Woodman, T and Pee, B (2002) *Progress Files: A case study*, Teaching in Higher Education 7, 97–111

Fry, H and Marshall, S (2002) Revitalizing the curriculum, in *The Effective Academic: A handbook for enhanced practice*, eds S Ketteridge, S Marshall and H Fry, Kogan Page, London

National Committee of Inquiry into Higher Education (NCIHE) (1997) (Dearing Report) *Higher Education in the Learning Society*, NCIHE, HMSO, London (also to be found at: http://www.leeds.ac.uk/educol/ncihe)

Noble, M (1999) Teaching and learning for employability, Chapter 10, in *A Handbook for Teaching and Learning in Higher Education: Enhancing Academic Practice*, eds H Fry, S Ketteridge and S Marshall, Kogan Page, London

FURTHER READING

Fallows and Steven (2000). See above. A review of the material covered in this chapter, but in far greater depth.

10 Supporting learning from experience

Liz Beaty

INTRODUCTION

The value of practical experience within higher education programmes has a long history. Laboratory classes and experiments are used in science and engineering, simulations and games have been a feature of management and social science courses, while many art and design courses develop technical skills alongside knowledge and aesthetic appreciation. Projects are a feature of many final year degree programmes and are an essential ingredient of most Masters programmes. Beyond these methods are 'sandwich' courses, which use placements to give students experience in the workplace as part of their academic studies. Health professionals have integrated programmes where they undertake academic study alongside supervised practice in hospitals. Such approaches are based on the premise that **experiential learning** should be an important part of a degree programme, especially those which have a professional or applied orientation.

Many vocational courses plan for experiential learning to take place outside of the university as **work-based learning**. This chapter will focus on learning from experience in both the university environment and natural settings where the experience is the stimulus for learning.

Employability is a key issue for graduates from higher education (see Chapter 10). The importance of the experiential base of a degree is therefore increasingly acknowledged as important in building employment-related skills. In teacher training, for example, there has been a move to increase the importance of classroom practice with mentoring from practising teachers. In nursing, however, the growing importance of the knowledge base has resulted in a move in the opposite direction.

Degree programmes assess and award credit for learning based on experience gained inside the university. Increasingly, credit is also being awarded for learning gained from experience on **placements** outside of the university. This will become more important as degree programmes become more flexible and with more use of systems of credit accumulation and transfer including assessment of prior (experiential) learning (AP(E)L).

The challenge is to bring experiential learning into courses so that students leave the university able to transfer their learning into their future life and work. This development requires more than simply putting theory into practice. Acting professionally as a doctor, producing saleable art work or designing a robust bridge requires a complex interweaving of knowledge, technical skills and application of professional ethics. This requires something akin to wisdom, which is usually attributed to learning over a long period of time through worldly experience and thoughtful contemplation. Experiential learning is holistic; it acknowledges the student as a person. Championing experiential learning is fundamentally about nurturing people in order to enhance their life and the society within which they live.

This chapter describes different models for using experiential learning in higher education and offers suggestions for course design which can successfully integrate theory with practice. It goes on to describe the skills needed by teachers in supporting students in experiential learning through supervision, mentoring, tutoring and facilitation of action learning.

ACADEMIC LEARNING AND EXPERIENTIAL LEARNING

There is a difference between learning in the natural world and learning in the constructed world of higher education. Learning from everyday experience is serendipitous, what we learn and how we learn is situated and context dependent. In an academic environment, learning is intentional; what is to be learnt is prescribed and how it is to be learnt is carefully structured: 'Academics want more to be learned than that which is already available from experiencing the world. The whole point about articulated knowledge is that being articulated it is known through exposition, argument, interpretation; it is known through reflection on experience and represents therefore a second order experience of the world' (Laurillard, 1993: 25).

If learning in the academic context is to affect positively how individuals approach the world, ie their future actions, academic learning must be perceived as relevant, and be learnt in a way which promotes transfer. The learner must understand enough to know when and how to transfer this knowledge to his or her future activity. As well as understanding the ideas, the student must understand the significance of the ideas. Teachers, therefore, need to use examples, case studies and practical experiments, running alongside theoretical ideas, to set them in a context and to make them relevant. If the relevance is directly experienced by the students themselves, then the learning will be reinforced.

Experience does not always lead to learning and theories of experiential learning have focused on the importance of reflection. The most well-known model is based on Kolb's **learning cycle** (1984) (see Chapter 2) which suggests that in order to learn effectively from experience, there must be a movement through reflection on experience where observations on the features of and issues in the context are brought to conscious attention. There follows a focus on generalizing from these experiences and understanding them. This part of the cycle is where theories and ideas are brought to bear on the experience. In the third part of the cycle there is an attempt to evaluate the experience and to plan for change through experimentation. The following step takes us back into experience, but this time the experience is informed by the learning cycle so that the result is different due to learning that has taken place through the cycle.

If experience in the natural environment is to result in learning which promotes enquiry, critical thinking and understanding, the experience must be interrogated and reflected on in the light of theory. This means that experience is not, on its own, enough to support learning. Rather, deliberate and conscious reflection is a requirement for effective experiential learning to take place. Teachers, therefore, need to work alongside students in supporting this reflection and critical appraisal of experience in order that students learn from it.

The learning cycle takes place over a period of time and is a *post hoc*, deliberate approach to learning from experience. This large reflective cycle involves reflection on action. In giving students opportunities to learn from experience we are also helping them to become conscious of the relationship between ideas and action. In experiential learning, the process of learning takes precedence over the content.

BRINGING EXPERIENTIAL LEARNING INTO COURSES

There are two basic ways of making experiential learning an integral part of course design. The first is to provide opportunities for experience in the form of structured and pre-planned practical work which will develop skills and technique within the controlled environment of the university. The second way is to give students the opportunity to learn from experience within a naturalistic environment in a work placement. In both cases, the key to effective learning is the support given to the student to draw out learning from the experience and in linking **critical incidents** in the experience to ideas and theories which shed light on them.

Practical exercises and project work will lead to little learning if they do not actively help students to integrate their studies. Similarly, work-based learning will be sterile if not adequately supported through a cycle of action and reflection and underpinned by a critically addressed knowledge base.

USING EXPERIENCE INSIDE THE UNIVERSITY

Methods that promote experiential learning inside the university include:

- laboratory experiments (Chapter 18);
- simulations;
- case studies, including problem-based learning (**PBL**);
- micro teaching;
- projects (Chapter 8).

Each of these examples uses mainly teacher-designed experiences within the course to allow practice of technical or interpersonal skills and to promote understanding of the relevance of the course to the 'real world'.

Laboratory experiments

Laboratory experiments require the student to undertake a series of tasks in order to observe the results. These can be individual or team-based experiments. The methods are usually prescribed and the expected results known. The point of undertaking the experiment is not 'real science' but practice of technique, skill of observation and recording, while demonstrating the relevance of theory to outcomes. Such a method, particularly when students are working in teams, offers much scope for **deep learning** in that it derives from a critical reflection of the experience and deliberate focus on the significance of observations.

Simulations

Simulations are attempts to create a realistic experience in a controlled environment. They can be very simple and require only the participation of the students within a described scenario or they can be elaborate rule-governed games which demonstrate complex relationships. Simulations have been created using computer technology to show how altering variables affects complex machinery. Other types of simulations involve case scenarios of interpersonal relationships to demonstrate how certain behaviours produce different reactions. These latter types are used extensively in areas like management and social work education, and often involve role-play. The advantage of simulation is that the experiences are real but there is no lasting effect on the external world. So the simulation can involve making mistakes, say, in bridge building or controlling nuclear power plants, operating on a patient or managing a redundancy programme, without a real disaster. They create powerful learning opportunities but they also require a great deal of careful planning and construction. A good simulation can take many months of development but, once developed, it can be used again and again.

Two important considerations for teachers in using simulations are as follows. First, to make sure that the learning which comes from undertaking the simulation is linked back to the objectives of the course, otherwise the students may learn that effects take place without critically analysing why and how. Second, in role play simulations, although the context is simulated, the feelings of people within the simulation are real. It is important to debrief properly these events both in terms of how people reacted to the case and their role within it, as well as in terms of the learning objective.

Case studies

Case studies are complex examples which give an insight into the context of the example as well as illustrating the main point. These are used extensively in vocational degrees where an understanding of complex relationships is important. Case studies can be either real or imaginary. If they are based on reality, source material may come from newspapers, journals or non-published reports (where permission will be needed for use within the course). Imaginary cases may take a good deal of preparation from the teacher. The aim is to build up a picture of an issue or problem through a case study and then give the students exercises and tasks to complete in relation to the case. The exercises will require the student first to understand the nature of the case and then to analyse the appropriate features of it in order to complete the task. This can make a rich learning experience. Again, case studies lend themselves to teamwork where multiple perspectives on a case can support critical appraisal and broader understanding. Extensive use of case studies can support a complete course design. Problem-based learning uses teams working on a series of case studies as the primary focus of learning (see Chapter 23). Concepts and theories from discipline areas are studied as they arise through the case.

Micro teaching

Micro teaching involves intensive practice of a skill under observation. Usually the practice is videotaped and then reviewed with a mentor giving feedback. The practice can be in a real situation or more usually in an artificial practice room. This is used extensively in training: eg, presentation and interview skills. The recording allows feedback to be given in relation to specific behaviours and the student is able to see what the mentor sees, also making the teaching session more focused on individual characteristics. Feedback on micro teaching is usually given in a one- to-one tutorial.

Projects

Projects are used where teachers want to give students scope to study a topic in depth. Projects can give students experience of research, analysis and recording as well as valuable practice in writing reports. In the example which follows, experiential learning is brought to a course through intensive group projects which are carefully structured by the tutors to support integration.

> ### Case Study 1: Integrating team project, civil engineering, University of Brighton

Context

Integrative projects (IPs) are used at various times throughout the degree programme in civil engineering. Their purpose is to integrate aspects of academic studies such as separate subjects or writing skills with technical skills and also to create an experience which integrates human aspects by forcing students to work to a sharp deadline with other people. In this way the projects simulate work experience within a real environment but under the control and structure provided by the teacher.

Short intensive projects usually last for one week. Students work in groups of four or five, selected by the tutor. The specific aims of the project differ throughout the three years of the course. For example, one is based on integration of design skills, another on the skills involved in undertaking a feasibility study.

The projects begin with a briefing and students are given documentation which describes the project and gives a schedule for the week. The schedule includes site visits, client interviews, discussion sessions and formative assessment tasks. This documentation also details health and safety procedures and rules for the workplan. The week is scheduled with times for various events and visits, allowing sufficient freedom for teams to organize their time and to cooperate and undertake different tasks within the project. Tutors are available for consultation throughout the week.

The assessment of the project involves a final report, a group presentation and interview with a panel of tutors.

USING EXPERIENCE IN A NATURAL SETTING

Methods that promote experiential learning outside the university are:

- field trips;
- placements;
- work-based learning projects.

Field trips

Field trips combine work in university and work in a naturalistic setting. For example, geography students may be taken to a particular landscape to do tests and collect samples, taking their observations and collections back to the university for further analysis. Field trips may also allow questions to local people, collection or copying of documentation, etc. The advantage of field trips is that the visual and physical impact of the surroundings bring the theory to life. Field trips allow many secondary learning objectives to be met. As in the example of the integrative project above, the effect of going away as a group and being together in one place for an extended time can offer opportunities for teambuilding and cooperation. It is important for the success of the field trip that planning is thorough and briefing is carefully handled. The purpose and scheduling of the trip must be transparent to both tutor and student.

Placements

Placements give the student experience of a working environment over a period of time. Placements usually give students a role within the organization, which is supervised and chosen to allow them to participate in a meaningful way. The organization offering the work placement needs to be able to rely on getting a suitable and adequately prepared student able to undertake the assigned role. The university needs to be sure that the organization will fulfil its agreement in helping the student gain appropriate work experience along with necessary mentorship. Articulating and agreeing expectations are therefore crucial.

Placements can be affected greatly by the attitudes of the various parties to the agreement. Students need to get involved, be reasonably flexible and willing to learn from their experienced colleagues. Similarly, the balance of helpfulness and constructive criticism from colleagues in the workplace will support learning. A good relationship between the university tutors and managers in the workplace is essential to ensure that the placement offers the right degree of challenge and support to the student. Effective administration is also crucial to success in setting up and managing the placement experience.

Work-based learning projects

Work-based learning projects create a client relationship between the student and the organization. For undergraduate degrees, the students undertake projects for a client organization but without being employees. The role of the university is to ensure that learning is generated from the experience of project work regardless of the success of the project itself. The role of the university in the relationship with the client organization varies considerably. In some cases the student is totally in control of the relationship, while in other cases the teacher carefully controls and documents any agreements made. Clients are sometimes involved in the assessment of work-based learning through attending presentations or reporting on aspects of the project outcomes. As with placements, the control is shared three ways and the clarity of roles and responsibilities is a key to the successful outcome. In work-based projects there is a danger that work on the project dominates, with learning from experience of doing the project taking second place. The role of the teacher is to focus student attention on the learning potential throughout the life of the project and to inform the process with relevant academic content. Designing work-based learning can be particularly fruitful where there are potential or existing research and consultancy relationships between the university and employers. This form of partnership is increasingly a feature of the modern university and should be encouraged within the teaching and learning function. In particular, postgraduate study can be enhanced through more fluid connection between the world of study and the world of work.

ACTION LEARNING AS A SUPPORT FOR WORK-BASED PROJECTS

Using action learning as a group process to support students' learning from their experience can be highly supportive of the individual and the project because the emphasis is on learning and on action.

Action learning is based on the relationship between reflection and action. It involves regular meetings in groups (known as sets) where the focus is on the issues and problems that individuals bring, and planning future action with the structured attention and support of the group. Put simply, it is about solving problems and getting things done.

McGill and Beaty (1995) define action learning as 'a continuous process of learning and reflection, supported by colleagues, with an intention of getting things done. Through action learning individuals learn with and from each other by working on real problems and reflecting on their own experiences. The process helps us to take an active stance towards life and helps to overcome the tendency (merely) to think, feel and be passive towards the pressures of life'.

In the action learning set, students can learn through reflection on their progress and in many ways they learn about themselves as well as about the project they are undertaking. Because it is a group method, they also learn a great deal by listening to other group members discussing their projects.

The key components of action learning are as follows:

- Individuals meet together in a set. For ease of working, about five to seven people make up the set.
- Each individual brings a real issue or project to the set that they wish to work on.
- The whole set works on progressing each project one at a time, sharing the time evenly between them.
- The aim is for each student to be able to take action on his or her project and to learn from reflection on experience.
- Regular meetings three to four hours every four to six weeks for a cycle of meetings over an agreed period (for example 6, 9 or 12 months).
- The set will create explicit ground rules to ensure effective working.

Action learning is thus based on the idea that effective learning and development come from working through real-life problems with other people. As a support for experiential learning it stresses the dual importance of understanding and action.

> ## Case Study 2: Example of a work-based learning project based on an action learning MA in work-based learning, Coventry Business School

The Coventry Business School Masters course in work-based learning offers valuable lessons that are transferable to undergraduate programmes of study. This programme was designed to give managers the opportunity to study as they undertake a project at work. The course is run over one year and is based on project work supported by action learning and tutored workshops. A module on work-based learning is taken during the first term and followed by two terms' work on the project. Participants work in action learning sets which support their learning throughout the programme. Each participant chooses a project which they have authority to undertake and which could be expected to yield outcomes within one year. Examples include 'introduction of performance measures, managing absence in an organisation, introduction of an appraisal system, recruitment and retention of volunteer persons' (Johnson, 1998). Participants meet in their sets for half a day on a four-weekly cycle. In these sets they discuss progress and blockages with their projects and take away a number of action points to be dealt with by their next meeting. In the set meetings there are opportunities to identify any knowledge or skills that they need which could be provided by the university, the employers or other participants on the course. The sets are facilitated by an experienced member of the course team whose role is to link each set with the course, but the lead is taken by the students themselves. The focus of the course is on the learning rather than the project. The course is popular with industry and public sector employers as it gives value to the organization at the same time as providing professional development for individual managers.

ONLINE LEARNING SUPPORT FOR THE EXPERIMENTAL LEARNER

The rapid growth in use of virtual learning environments (VLEs – see Chapter 11) is good news for the support of experimental learning. At last there are ways in which learners working at a distance can be in touch with their peers and tutors without travelling to the campus. There are many experiments with use of the Web for learning and the most fruitful areas for the support of experimental learners seem to be in the communications through bulletin boards and Intranet mail. Within a fully functioning VLE there is scope for academic support to be constantly available to students while they are in employment and this will greatly enhance the ability of tutors to support work-based learning and student placements. It offers also the opportunity for students to contact each other while they are away from the university and thus maintain peer group support throughout their placement or project periods of study. The technology offers the opportunity to bring employers and other off-campus experts into courses in a way only dreamt about previously. Although the Web-based communications technology is now well established, however, the use of it is still in its infancy and both universities and employers will need to experiment with the designs that can be most appropriate and enabling of true networked learning. The vision is of a world where the academy integrates with work and leisure in a fully functioning and supportive networked learning environment. While we are not there yet, modern technology already offers the opportunity for experiential learning in natural settings to become part of the core course for most learners.

THE TEACHER'S ROLE

This section describes the roles of the teacher in supporting learning from experience. As experiential learning is essentially about student activity, the teacher's role will be in the form of structuring that experience and facilitating learning through appropriate interventions. Roles for the teacher in supporting experiential learning can be as tutor, coach, trainer, mentor, supervisor or facilitator. These roles are often combined, with one teacher taking on multiple roles.

Tutoring

In this role the teacher is concerned with the structure of the learning experience. The process of the learning has been pre-specified at least in terms of what is to be covered (in work placements the timing of when things are covered will not necessarily be under tutor or student control) and the tutor's job is to make sure the experience is as useful as possible. The tutor is seen by the student as being in charge of the learning environment and particularly as a guide to the assessment of learning.

Coach or trainer

The role of coach is often to promote practical skills, where the student is taken through the steps of learning how to perform some action, and skill is developed mainly through practice. It is the role of the coach to notice where the student is going wrong or being ineffective and where intervention would be helpful. The coach will call 'time out' on an activity to demonstrate good practice and to go carefully and slowly through steps where mistakes could easily be made. This type of teaching is very important in areas of professional practice where the development of technical skills goes hand in hand with understanding the context.

Mentor

The mentor is often a more experienced version of the student, an older or more knowledgeable peer. Mentorship therefore often involves observation both by the mentor and of the mentor. Feedback is supplemented by discussion and debate with a feeling of more comradeship and less hierarchy than is evident with the other roles. Mentorship is a growing function with many professional areas requiring mentors for induction and for people taking on new responsibilities. As with many of the roles that support experiential learning, it succeeds or fails on the basis of the relationship that is established between the mentor and mentee.

Supervision

Supervisors require many of the same skills as the mentor, but while mentors act as guides, working alongside the student, supervisors are more remote and act as monitors of progress. Supervision requires a clarity about the nature of the learning that is required and supervisors are usually experts carrying responsibility for the working area and for students' progress. The issue for supervisors is often about when to intervene and when to allow students to learn through discovery (see Chapter 8). Individuals attack problems in different ways and have different **learning styles**. Supervisors, therefore, must be sensitive to the way in which the student is tackling the problem and not impose their own approach inappropriately.

Facilitation

In experiential learning the word facilitator is often used in preference to the word teacher. Facilitation implies that the activity is one of support rather than initiating. The experience belongs to the student and the facilitator helps the student to get most out of the experience by providing appropriate resources and intervening in support of the learning. There are different models of facilitation where at one extreme the student is an autonomous learner, in total control of content and process, with the facilitator supporting.

In most courses in higher education the facilitator will have control of the process. This allows students to follow up their interests by choosing the topic of a project, but the timing, the rules for undertaking it and the assessment of the project are in the control of the teacher.

In general, experiential learning requires more facilitation and less direct teaching than academic learning. The process of learning comes to the foreground and the content emerges from the experience.

Tutoring online

Facilitation is crucial in using online learning to support experimental learning off campus. Here the facilitator must gauge how far to stimulate discussion and how far simply to monitor it. The tutor's presence online must also be allowed for in any workload negotiation of support for experiential learning.

OVERVIEW

Academic courses which do nothing to link theory into practice through situated cognition and harnessing learning from experience will be sterile.

Experiential learning can take place in departments in the form of projects, experiments, working with case studies, or it can be external to the department as work-based learning, field work and practice placements.

To be effective, experiential learning within a naturalistic environment involves an intentional cycle of action and reflection. Experiential learning which is based on deliberate teaching events such as laboratory experiments and simulations must be carefully linked to theoretical study within the course.

The challenge for modern higher education is not simply to train the next generation of academics, it is rather to tie learning from experience inextricably to academic study and vice versa in a strong lifelong process of learning which develops the person and society. That is why attention to supporting experiential learning within course design is crucial.

REFERENCES

Beaty, E, France, L and Gardiner, P (1996) Consultancy style action research: a constructive triangle, *International Journal for Academic Development*, **2** (2)

Johnson, D (1998) Workbased learning qualifications at Master's level: academically valid or the emperor's new clothes?, MA dissertation, Coventry University

Kolb, D A (1984) *Experiential Learning*, Prentice-Hall, Englewood Cliffs, New Jersey

Laurillard, D (1993) *Rethinking University Teaching*, Routledge, London

McGill, I and Beaty, L (2001) *Action Learning: A guide for professional, management and educational development*, revised 2nd edn, Kogan Page, London

FURTHER READING

Jarvis, P, Holland, J and Griffin, C (1998) *The Theory and Practice of Learning*, Kogan Page, London

Moon, Jennifer A (1999) *Reflection in learning and professional development: Theory and practice.* Kogan Page, London

Schon, D (1987) *Educating the Reflective Practitioner*, Jossey-Bass, San Francisco

Staff and Educational Development Association (1996) *Induction Pack for Teachers in Higher Education*, SEDA, Birmingham

Sutherland, P (1997) *Adult Learning*, Kogan Page, London

Weil, S W and McGill, I (1989) *Making Sense of Experiential Learning*, Society for Research into Higher Education/Open University Press, Milton Keynes

<table>
<tr><td>11</td></tr>
</table>

Virtual space, real learning: an introduction to VLEs

John Pettit and Robin Mason

INTRODUCTION: A QUICK TOUR OF A VIRTUAL LEARNING ENVIRONMENT (VLE)

A **VLE** is a world of learning populated by real people who think, read, type in their comments and questions in online discussions, laugh, feel pleased or disappointed, plan their study and occasionally fall out with each other (see Figure 11.1). It is also a world that more and more learners and teachers are experiencing – and not just in distance education of the kind illustrated in Figure 11.1. In the UK the Dearing Report (**NCIHE**, 1997) reflected and gave encouragement to the increasing use of communication and information technologies (**C&IT**) in what were once regarded as 'conventional' settings – campuses. As a result of this trend, many more teachers and learners face questions about how to orient themselves to VLEs. This chapter aims to provide just such an orientation for teachers new to VLEs – whether these are in-house environments as in Figure 11.1, or commercial products such as WebCT and Blackboard.

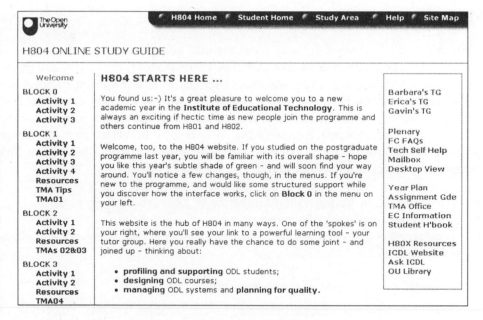

Figure 11.1   Plenty of choices for the student – menus to left, to right and top – in this virtual learning environment; reproduced by kind permission of The Open University

The VLE in Figure 11.1, developed by The Open University, has many features in common with environments used around the world. It allows students to choose, on one screen, from a large range of study-related options. In the left-hand menu, for example, they can click on descriptions of the activities they are being asked to do. When they want to carry them out, they click on the name of their tutor (Barbara, Erica or Gavin) at the top of the menu on the right. This brings them to their online tutorial group where they type in their activity messages and read other people's. If they want to 'meet' all the students on the course, however, they click on 'Plenary' in the second cluster on the right. In the Plenary they can also discuss with visiting experts online, and socialize with fellow students in the online café.

To help students organize their time, there is a Year Plan at the top of the third cluster in the right-hand menu: if they click on that, they can see when each block begins and when assignments are due. And what *are* the assignments? The Assignment Guide ('Assignment Gde'), just underneath, provides the questions and assessment criteria. Below that is 'TMA Office' where students deliver and collect their assignments. The final cluster in that right-hand menu takes students to an online collection of papers and book chapters, to a database, to an enquiry service and – at the very bottom – to the main Library.

VIRTUAL AND REAL

With any VLE, finding their way from tutorial group to assignment office to library may take students a while – as it does when students first arrive at a physical campus. But although VLEs are often described as virtual campuses, there are limits to the analogy between a Web site and a campus of trees, car parks and concrete. 'Virtual' implies that the Web-based environment is in some sense mimicking a 'real' campus. It is probably more helpful to recognize that *both* are learning environments, with differing characteristics and strengths. Taking this perspective, this chapter will provide:

- scenarios of how students might integrate VLEs into their daily lives;
- case studies of actual VLEs in use;
- some pointers as to how teachers and students can work enjoyably and effectively with VLEs.

First, though, a clarification of the terminology.

VLE OR MLE?

It is important to distinguish a virtual learning environment from a **managed learning environment (MLE)**, though confusingly VLE and MLE are sometimes used interchangeably. The JISC (2001) gives a lucid explanation of the difference, but essentially the VLE is a space where – as in Figure 11.1 – students work, sometimes alone, sometimes in a group, sometimes with their teacher.

An MLE is a bigger system: it *includes* the VLE (if there is one), but also covers areas where administrative and clerical staff input data – about courses, enrolment, fee income and so on – and from where management data can be extracted.

Obviously these can be big systems, and a college or university may well develop an MLE that is 'VLE-independent': if at some point it decides to switch from one VLE to another, or to incorporate more than one, it can do so without jettisoning the entire MLE. Now that this terminology has been clarified, the remainder of the chapter will focus on those who use VLEs – starting with students.

STUDYING ON CAMPUS AND FROM HOME

The following scenarios illustrate how VLEs might impact on two students' lives. They also give a context for deciding your own position in relation to the Interrogating Practice questions below.

Student A

She is on campus working at a computer, not her own but one of a bank provided by the university. She is reading through a VLE Web page in which her teacher invites the class to explore five online readings introducing a new topic. He has asked each student to find one reading that particularly interests them, and then to send a message to the online tutorial group explaining their interest – as preparation for a face-to-face discussion and debate. As she considers each reading in turn, Student A uses the on-screen Edit/Find button to search for phrases that she thinks are important. Finally, having picked one reading, she prints it out for closer study.

Interrogating Practice

Put yourself in the position of Student A. What – for you – are the pros and cons of using the VLE in this way on campus?

Student B

He is following the same course, but has transport difficulties and does not get to campus often. Tonight he is studying at home, using a laptop connected to the same VLE and looking at the same Web pages as Student A. Each Web page takes longer to arrive than it does for her, though, because his computer is connected via an ordinary phone line and basic modem. Now he clicks to the online tutorial group where he reads some recent messages – fellow students' reactions to the new readings. These set him thinking for tomorrow's face-to-face discussion: it is one he cannot afford to miss. He also reminds himself, from the VLE calendar, of when his next assignment is due. Hmm, sooner than he thought. Better check out the online café to see who else is sweating …

Interrogating Practice

What are the pros and cons of using the VLE off-campus, like Student B?

FOUR ISSUES

A number of issues arise from those two scenarios. Here are four issues; you may have picked out others:

- *Flexibility and access:* for various reasons, students may not be able to get to campus very often. Like Student B they may not live in easy reach of campus, they may be restricted by disability, or they may have to combine education with caring responsibilities or employment. For them VLEs bring an important flexibility. If they feel they are missing out on informal learning (the 'discussion in the bar'), a VLE can at least partly compensate with a virtual café – perhaps with graphic images of steaming coffee cups.
- *Learning styles:* if VLEs are integrated with face-to-face classes, that may suit a wider range of learners. For example, learners who are shyer in a face-to-face class may be able to contribute more confidently to an online conference. Non-native speakers may find that an online conference gives them the extra time they need to read and to respond to messages in English. And for all students (including the two in the scenarios) the slower pace of an online discussion may encourage more reflection. There are a lot of 'mays' because these issues are not clear-cut. Just because a technology such as online conferencing affords the possibility that the shy will blossom, and that learners with an 'activist' style will spend more time reflecting, it does not follow that this will happen (Mason, 2001). Much will depend on the students, the design of the course, and the contribution of the teacher.
- *Costs:* printing costs are borne by students, unless their department allocates them some free printing, and off-campus students also pay for the phone line; not all students can afford a home computer.
- *Integration:* the VLE, in the scenarios given, is integrated with more conventional face-to-face teaching; this integration is explored later in the chapter.

WHICH VLE?

Most discussions turn before long to the question, 'Which VLE do *you* use?' Is it Blackboard, or WebCT, an in-house development or...? Case Studies 1 and 2 feature two of the current 'big names', and Figure 11.1 illustrates an in-house development. Each VLE will have its champions, but in any choice there are trade-offs and compromises:

> The main problem with these big, commercial companies, as expressed by stakeholders during [our research], is that they are too prescriptive in terms of pedagogical approach. Some of the smaller systems, including UK-developed CoMentor and COSE, have been specifically developed to allow more flexibility for the develop-

ment of courses. As is often the case with technology, the choices seem to come down to big, easy to use and well supported versus small but more finely tuned to local user needs.

(Currier, Brown and Ekmekioglu, 2001: 29)

Often the choice does not lie with the individual teacher or department: it may be made by institutional managers on various grounds including licence cost and scalability. In such circumstances, it is important for teachers not to feel that the quality of their practice will be wholly determined by the particular VLE they are using. The course design, the teacher's skill and sensitivity, the institutional climate and the quality of technical support are also extremely important. When VLEs are implemented in particular contexts (see the case studies below), many factors come into play, not all of them to do with the attributes of competing software.

Case Study 1: The Highlands and Islands, an ideal candidate for a VLE

Levels: Access; FE; undergraduate; Masters; PhD
Number of students: c4,250 students in higher education; more in FE
VLE: Blackboard
Delivery: face-to-face; audio- and **video-conferencing**; e-mail; message-based conferencing

With the second-lowest population density in Europe, the Highlands and Islands appear well suited to a VLE. Interestingly, though, most courses of the University of the Highlands and Islands (UHI) combine online interaction with face-to-face technical support at local learning centres – rooms in outlying areas, containing computers and other hardware and software for use by the local community. Often, local academic mentoring is also available.

UHI uses Blackboard as its VLE and, in addition, major centres have video-conferencing links. Dr Frank Rennie, an experienced course designer and tutor with UHI, comments on this mix: 'We can offer students the type of support that best fits their circumstances. We have found that the form of support has changed over the years: in the early days we relied on only one type – for example, video-conferencing. Now we use a mix, including e-mail, audio- and video-conferencing, and message-based conferencing'.

(Dr Frank Rennie, UHI development director, and the authors)

> ## Case Study 2: More contact and better data, on the Bachelor of Dental Surgery degree course at King's College London

Programme: Applied Dental Science 3
Years: 4 and 5 of a five-year programme
Course: Therapeutics
VLE: WebCT
Delivery: lectures (**Webcasts**) and group study online; practical work; self-directed study
Class size: c150

Case Study 2 also demonstrates how a VLE can draw together a community – in this instance, staff and 150 students scattered across three London campuses. Paradoxically teachers and students now spend less time together in face-to-face lectures, many of which are recorded and viewable in the VLE.

Staff now have the opportunity to interact with students online. They can do this at times that suit them, rather than having to leave their clinics to travel from one campus to another to deliver an optional, and not always well-attended, lecture. But to keep the online load on teachers manageable, students are also encouraged to work in groups (see Figure 11.2). The course organizer Pat Reynolds, who introduced the VLE, reports: 'I encourage students to write about their clinical experiences and to invite discussion from others, with tutors adding the occasional bit of advice and giving direction rather than just giving the answers. For example, students discussed how to reduce panic attacks in dental-phobic patients and how to avoid a diabetic coma.'

This groupwork can generate surprising insights:
'The students' first injection practical in Year 2, supported by the College Ethical Committee, is on each other. Many have such good teeth that they have never had a dental injection. Students described on the **bulletin board** how it felt to receive the injection, but more importantly discovered that the person giving the injection often felt more faint than the recipient!'

Through the VLE, the course organizer can observe where students lack understanding or have insufficient training – for example, in the area of alternative therapies. She can also collect valuable data about student activity, for quality assurance.

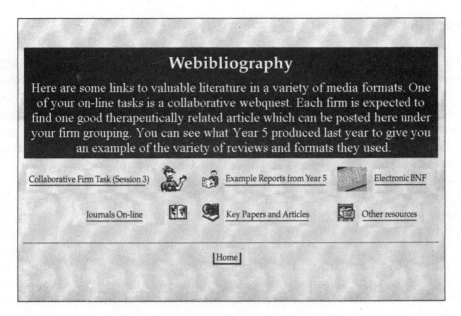

(Dr Patricia Reynolds, course organizer, and the authors)

FROM NEW TEACHERS TO SUCCESSFUL TEACHERS

Case Studies 1 and 2 illustrate the versatility of VLEs, and present insights from two experienced VLE users. Moving from there to offer advice to new users is not straightforward: general guidelines risk being banal, detailed suggestions too context-specific. The next part of the chapter aims to deal with that problem by asking you to develop connections between your own values and the way in which you might use a VLE.

The point about values is crucial. Teaching online can be a threat or an opportunity, a straitjacket or a useful set of tools and templates. It can offer creative extension of professional practice, or a sterile obligation to conform to an institutional blueprint. Collis and Moonen put it well when they identify the importance of teachers' 'personal engagement': 'Take care that the first experiences of working with the technology "fit" with the instructor's experience and beliefs about the learning process [and] build the instructor's self-confidence by starting with a successful experience' (2001: 56).

They are writing here from the point of view of institutional decision-makers and staff developers, but in this instance it is a point of view that teachers need to share if they are to gain professional satisfaction. What follows are a number of issues and questions. In answering them for yourself, you may develop your own way of finding a fit with your experience and beliefs.

WORKING WITH THE STUDENTS' CONTEXT

Where students live, how much money they have, whether they have to care for others and/or take paid employment, how they prefer to relate to their fellow students... all these are important influences on how successfully the VLE will mesh with their daily lives. The VLE, in other words, is not a tool that stands or falls according to its technical capabilities. It has to succeed in a range of contexts.

Another crucial contextual element – in addition to these broader financial, logistical and social dimensions – is the course of study itself, and particularly two key and related elements: assessment; and your communication with students.

A number of researchers (eg, Thorpe, 1998) have stressed that assessment influences, even distorts, the way in which many students perceive a course, the teaching material, what is worth spending time on, and so on (see also Chapter 2). In trying to negotiate this, students may look to you for signals as to what you expect. As Laurillard puts it: 'it means that in setting work for students we must think of them not necessarily as grappling with the intriguing ideas we have put before them, but as trying to second-guess what we want of them' (2002: 200).

Not all students will be equally skilled at this second-guessing, and even if teachers know what they want and think they have communicated it, students will not all have received the same message. Add that to the diversity of students' previous experience, and communication can look rather uncertain. This makes it more not less important that teachers should be clear in their own minds about why they want to teach online – just as they need to be clear about any other aspect of their teaching (see Chapter 3).

Interrogating Practice

Reflect on your own reason(s) for wanting to know more about – and use – VLEs. How far is your motivation self-generated, and how far the result of external pressure?

REASONS FOR WANTING TO KNOW MORE ABOUT VLES

Reason 1: Institutional push

The least satisfactory reason for using a VLE is that you are under external pressure. Institutional managers may be attracted to VLEs for a variety of reasons:

such environments appear to offer savings on costly face-to-face time, for example, and can be integrated with larger information systems to form a managed learning environment as was mentioned earlier. Institutions may feel that they need to introduce a VLE – or watch students defect to a rival institution that has one. Such a push is captured by Collis and Moonen as the 'You can't not do it' argument (2001: 29–43). Few of us can ignore such considerations, but Reasons 2 and 3 below are more solid.

Reason 2: Curiosity

Professional curiosity is a stronger personal motivation than institutional push, provided that in the longer run it is sustained by teaching success. If you are new to VLEs you may be curious to try them, to develop new skills by becoming comfortable with new technologies and new ways of teaching, to see how you can integrate your face-to-face sessions and VLEs, to help students get to grips with other ways of learning, and so on.

Reason 3: A desire to develop your teaching

If you can answer Yes to one (or preferably more) of the following, or can find equally strong teaching-related reasons of your own, that will provide a yet sounder basis for sustained innovation:

- Can you see that the VLE will facilitate learning that is different from what is possible in a face-to-face session? This is not to devalue either mode, but to identify the strengths of each. As Edwards and Usher put it, 'it is the growth of significance of the virtual that has brought to the fore the value of the face-to-face' (2001: 64).
- Can you identify how using the VLE will be convenient for students and / or you, or will bring you benefits in managing information about students' participation (as in Case Study 2, for example)?
- Can you specify how the contribution of the VLE will dovetail with other elements of the course, including the demands of assessment?

The next section looks at how some of these elements might be worked out in practice.

YOUR TEACHING

Suppose you want to introduce your students to a new topic and some background reading. This is similar to the task in the two scenarios depicted earlier, but this time approached from the point of view of the teacher. You could present your introduction in a number of ways (see Table 11.1).

Table 11.1 Five ways of introducing a new topic

Possible Approach	Some of the Pros and Cons
(a) You could give a face-to-face introduction with slides and questions, recommend five readings and ask students to find and study one that interests them	Pros: for some students, face-to-face teaching is the most comfortable form; you can quickly gauge students' apparent level of understanding Cons: you and the students have to meet at a particular time; some students may not attend, and some attendees may not track down the recommended readings
(b) As above, but you also provide a handout backing up your introduction, plus handouts of the five readings	Mainly as above, and: Pros: the handouts ensure that attendees receive the readings and can review your introduction; attendees can read the handouts at any time and anywhere (if they don't lose them) Cons: potentially large amount of photocopying
(c) You could create a Web page in the VLE containing your basic introduction with slides, plus hyperlinks to the five readings; ask students to find and study one reading that interests them	Pros: neither you nor your students have to attend a particular place at a particular time; students have great flexibility; participation can be monitored Cons: reading on screen is harder for many people than reading a printed handout; students need to find an on-campus computer that is available, or need a computer at home whose phone line is not being used by someone else
(d) As in (c) but you do not list the readings; instead you divide students into groups and ask each group to search for suitable readings online, rather like the 'collaborative Web quest' in Figure 11.2; ask students to discuss their findings online	Pros: for some students, the groupwork provides motivation; the task involves additional skills such as searching and evaluating online readings, and also group discussion online; Cons: the same issues arise, as in (c), over computer access – but more so since online discussion takes time
(e) You set up a face-to-face session, where students discuss and debate their chosen reading(s)	Similar pros and cons as for (a)

It is interesting to note that the familiar technology of handouts still has a number of strengths: printed material is usually easier to read than its on-screen equivalent, is portable, and requires no access to a computer or personal digital assistant. On the other hand, the VLE offers a way for you to deliver the material to students who cannot easily get to campus, so you may find it helpful to use two or more approaches: a combination of (a) and (c) could enable you to reach more of your students.

A second point to note is that the five approaches are not straight equivalents. The opportunities for learning change as you move down the table (as does your role), and a combination of (c) and (e), for example, could enable the teaching to mesh with the learning styles of more of your students.

Approach (d) most obviously exploits some of the potential of the VLE, and is an activity that the authors have often used on The Open University's MA in Open and Distance Education (see Figure 11.1). But in exploiting the potential of the VLE, you need to make sure that you are not exploiting yourself, which raises the question of time.

YOUR TIME

As you saw in Figures 11.1 and 11.2, a VLE offers great potential. You can set up collaborative activities for groups of students, provide an online café, deliver online papers, bring in visiting experts, provide a calendar and space for e-mailing, and so on. This is what creates such a rich environment, a feast, a treasure-house – and a potential black hole of time. For example, e-mailing can be very time-consuming, and if you use e-mail you would be advised to set out clearly, at the beginning of the course, what students can expect from you – perhaps a reply to e-mails within two days. You may also find it useful to gather some basic information into Frequently Asked Questions and direct students here first. Encourage students to send their questions to the VLE so that (1) there is a chance that one of their peers can supply the answer, and (2) your response is likely to be read by more than one person.

It is also important to decide how much time you and your students can afford overall. Collaborative online activities, for example, are wonderful when the computer conference is buzzing. But you need to be clear, and to state, why you are creating them and how they relate to learning outcomes. It may be better to start small, as in (c) in Table 11.1, and invest more time as you get feedback on what works for you and your students. This process of improvement can be both rewarding and surprising. As Oliver concludes, looking back on his early work in online teaching, 'Now I know that any innovation will return at least a dozen variations in form when implemented, and I actively look to see which forms support learning and which don't' (2001: 87).

CONCLUSION AND OVERVIEW

For the moment at least, VLEs are the standard medium for online teaching. But the hype surrounding them may lead to disappointment – for managers, teachers and students – if a guarantee of quick success is looked for. Online work demands new skills for teachers and students. Implementing a 'mixed economy' of face-to-face and online classes, as in the two scenarios earlier in the chapter, can also add to the load on teachers (Halfpenny and Wellings, 2001).

Faced with the prospect of being squeezed between unrealistic expectations and an ever-heavier workload, teachers need to be clear about why they are using the VLE and what it will add to their students' experience. But for every rule like that there is a particular context where things do not quite work out as expected. A mix of trial and error on the one hand, with some clear setting out of pros and cons on the other, probably offers the best way forward for most of us engaged in teaching in a VLE. Using a VLE can then enrich and transform experience of higher education – for students, as well as for teachers and tutors.

REFERENCES

Collis, B and Moonen, J (2001) *Flexible Learning in a Digital World: Experiences and expectations*, Kogan Page, London

Currier, S, Brown, S and Ekmekioglu, F C (2001) *INveStigating Portals for Information Resources And Learning* (INSPIRAL: final report to the JISC), Centre for Digital Library Research and Centre for Educational Systems, University of Strathclyde. Online: http://inspiral.cdlr.strath.ac.uk/ (15 March 2002)

Edwards, R and Usher, R (2001) *Globalisation and Pedagogy: Space, place and identity*, RoutledgeFalmer, London and New York

Halfpenny, P and Wellings, S (2001) Can virtual seminars be used cost-effectively to enhance student learning?, *ALT–J*, **9** (3), pp 43–52

JISC (2001) *MLEs and VLEs Explained*, Joint Information Systems Committee, Briefing Paper No. 1. Online: http://www.jisc.ac.uk/mle/reps/briefings/bp1.html (15 March 2002)

Laurillard, D (2002) *Rethinking University Teaching: A conversational framework for the effective use of learning technologies*, 2nd edn, Routledge Falmer, London and New York

Mason, R (2001) Effective facilitation of online learning: the Open University experience in, *Teaching and Learning Online: pedagogies for new technologies*, ed J Stephenson, Kogan Page, London

NCIHE (1997) (Dearing Report) *Higher Education in the Learning Society*, National Committee of Inquiry into Higher Education, HMSO, London (also to be found at: http://www.leeds.ac.uk/educol/ncihe)

Oliver, R (2001) It seemed like a good idea at the time, in *Online Learning and Teaching with Technology: case studies, experience and practice*, eds D Murphy, R Walker and G Webb, Kogan Page, London

Thorpe, M (1998) Assessment and 'third-generation' distance education, *Distance Education*, **19** (2), pp 265–86

FURTHER READING

Hammerich, I and Harrison, C (2002) *Developing Online Content: The principles of writing and editing for the Web*, John Wiley, Chichester

Lockwood, F and Gooley, A (eds) (2001) *Innovation in Open and Distance Learning: Successful development of online and Web-based learning*, Kogan Page, London; accounts of risk and innovation.

McVay Lynch, M (2002) *The Online Educator: A guide to creating the virtual classroom*, RoutledgeFalmer, London; step-by-step advice.

Murphy, D, Walker, R and Webb, G (eds) (2001) *Online Learning and Teaching with Technology: Case studies, experience and practice*, Kogan Page, London; reassuring tales of struggle (see Oliver, 2001, above).

12 | Supporting student learning

David Gosling

INTRODUCTION: LEARNING WITHIN A DIVERSE SECTOR

Higher education in the UK is moving rapidly towards becoming a mass system. Between 1979 and 1999 the proportion of 18–19-year-olds in higher education (known as the age participation index, or **API**) more than doubled from 12 per cent to 32 per cent (HEFCE, 2001). Although since that time growth has slowed, widening participation has become a central plank of government policy with a target of a 50 per cent participation rate by the year 2010.

As a consequence of widening participation, higher education is no longer made up of exclusive, highly selective institutions but contains a range of institutions increasingly open to heterogeneous groups of students from diverse cultures who have a wide range of educational experiences behind them. As well as full-time students in the 18–21 age group, there are also more mature students, more part-time students – including those using distance learning (increasingly online) – more students with disabilities, more students from different ethnic, national, and religious groups. Although students from the lower social classes are significantly under-represented in higher education, their total numbers have increased. Students also enter the sector with many different educational qualifications and not only with A-level passes (HEFCE, 2001).

What are the implications of this massive change for higher education practices? We can no longer assume that there is a common understanding by students of the purposes of higher education or of the nature of studying at higher levels. Many students come from backgrounds in which there is not the cultural capital which enables them already to have an understanding of the key demands being made on them by their teachers. Another category of students who also require targeted learning support are students with disabilities. Recent changes in legislation (such as the Special Educational Needs and Disability Act – **SENDA** – 2002) are requiring universities to ensure that they do provide genuinely equal opportunities for students including those that have any disability.

Another dimension of the modern university in the UK is greater cultural and ethnic diversity. This derives from two sources – the increasingly multicultural nature of the UK population, and the growth of international students at UK universities. These national cultural and ethnic differences make particular demands on higher education institutions, but also provide opportunities, as we shall see later in this chapter.

Widening participation has brought increasing concern about the ultimate success of the students recruited. Questions about students progression and retention in higher education have become much more centre stage in recent years (DfES, 2001).

This chapter looks at how universities and colleges can effectively tackle ways of supporting the learning of students to ensure that they have a fair chance to stay until the end of the course on which they are registered and to succeed on that course. It will consider not only those things academic staff can do, but also the significant role of *all* staff across institutions who support student learning.

LEARNING NEEDS

In the changing context of higher education the need for a more systematic approach to supporting student learning becomes ever more important. A simple transmission model of teaching is even less adequate to meet the needs of students than it was in the past. In recent times, the sector has seen a significant change in emphasis from understanding teaching as a process in which academic staff simply lecture, to one in which students are supported in their learning. Higher education no longer operates entirely on a teacher-centred model of teaching and is shifting, albeit slowly and hesitantly, towards a more student-centred model (see Chapters 1 and 4).

Part of being 'student centred' is recognizing that, although there is a subject content which all students must learn in order to pass, each student approaches the subject from their own perspective, their own unique past experience and their own understanding of themselves and their aspirations. They have their own identity, or rather identities, influenced by factors such as gender, age, past educational experience and achievement, class, ethnicity, nationality, sexual orientation, self-perception, goals, abilities and disabilities, language skills and so on. These multiple identities inevitably shape their learning (see Chapter 2).

With increasing diversity among students comes increasing demands on universities to respond appropriately. A useful concept here is the idea of 'learning needs'. All students must undertake the journey from their existing level of knowledge to the level required to pass or achieve higher grades in their chosen courses. All students have their own learning needs that must be met sufficiently well for them to succeed. On this model supporting students' learning is not a remedial activity designed to bring a minority of students up to an acceptable level. Rather, it assumes that *all* students are engaged in a learning development process and structured learning support is designed to provide assistance to help students meet their goals. For some this means developing their IT skills, for others their language skills, for others their employability skills and so on (Cottrell, 2001). The object is for each student to build on and develop his or her existing skills.

Students need help to recognize their own learning needs and to find strategies to meet them. The university, or college, also has a responsibility for recognizing these needs and making provision to meet them. This happens through the interaction between teaching staff and students in lectures, seminars, the studio, laboratory, field trips and so on and through feedback provided to students informally or as part of the assessment process. Traditionally higher education relied on the opportunities provided in formal 'contact time' and other informal tutor–student interactions to meet the learning needs of students. How staff can support student learning through these processes will be discussed in the next section.

As staff student ratios have declined and modular schemes create a more fragmented student experience, these types of contact are not enough. Other forms of learning support, provided through central service departments, are also needed. It is important that tutors recognize the limitations of their expertise and know when it is better to refer students to others who have specialist expertise. These include, for example, library and IT staff, English language and study skills specialists, those with responsibility for supporting students with disabilities, student counsellors and academic advisors.

A useful distinction here is between services that support learners (students) and those that support learning development, and learning resources (Simpson, 1996). The services for students are designed to meet day-to-day needs for food, accommodation, healthcare, childcare, counselling, financial support, recreation and so on. Learning development services are about helping students to be more successful in their learning related to their programme of study. The role of institution-wide services which support learning and the methods for referral, integration, and communication to create a more holistic approach that brings together the role of departmental teaching staff and support staff are discussed later in this chapter. Learning resources are those facilities and materials which students make use of in their learning – books, learning packages, audio-visual aids, artefacts and online materials – and the infrastructure which makes these available – libraries, resource centres, laboratories, studios and IT services.

Supporting student learning is not simply the sum of the services and learning opportunities provided. It is also essentially about an ethos, which recognizes that:

- Students are individuals, each with their own learning needs.
- Support is available to all and is not stigmatized as 'remedial'.
- All tutors have a responsibility to provide support, not just specialists.
- Students need to be inspired and motivated.
- Successful support systems involve many departments and will require good communication between different parts of the institution.

Now let us look at various aspects of supporting student learning within teaching departments and higher education faculties or schools.

SKILL DEVELOPMENT

Skills are learnt mainly through practice, trial and error. Courses need to build in specific attention to skill development, where students can be allowed to fail and get feedback so that they can use the acquired skills in their assessed work.

Study skills

The skills and capabilities required of students in higher education are complex and vary to some extent between different subjects. Many of these skills are acquired over the whole period of study and cannot be learnt as separate and identifiable skills at the beginning of a course. However, help with some funda-mental study skills can be valuable to students, particularly if they are mature students who are unfamiliar with studying or those admitted to higher education on non-conventional entry routes. The study skills that are specific to higher education include conventions of academic writing, styles for references and bibliographies, searching for and selecting information in libraries and using the Internet, note taking from lectures, making presentations, revision and exam techniques.

Subject-specific skills

Each subject has its own set of specialist skills that students need to acquire. These need to be identified and students given the opportunity to develop and practise them. Subject-specific skills include laboratory skills, use of statistical methods, interpretation of texts, performance skills in the arts, investigative skills/methods of enquiry, field investigations, data and information processing/IT, professional skills (SEEC, 2002).

It is also important to recognize that academic writing is also a subject-specific skill. The types of writing demanded by academics reflect a variety of specialist genres. For example, essays required by each discipline have developed as part of the 'community of practice' of each subject and reflect subtle differences in the ways that arguments should be presented and authorities referenced, the extent to which personal opinion is acceptable or quotations are expected, the use of specialist terminology (or jargon?), and many other subtleties that are rarely made explicit to students. Other forms of English, like the laboratory report, legal writing, and research reports, are all context-specific forms of social practice.

All students need to be inducted into the writing skills that are an intrinsic part of learning the subject as an essential component of their study skills. No programme of study can take for granted that students understand what kinds of writing are expected of them, and students who are studying two principal subjects (as joint honours or major and minor subjects), or units from several disciplines from within a modular scheme, need particular guidance to ensure that they appreciate the differences required by each subject (or each tutor).

Higher level cognitive and analytical skills

Higher education distinguished by the demands it makes on students to operate at higher levels of thinking, creativity, problem-solving, autonomy and responsibility.

The QAA Qualification Descriptors states that 'typically, successful students at honours level will be able to critically evaluate arguments, assumptions, abstract concepts and data (that may be incomplete), to make judgements, and to frame appropriate questions to achieve a solution – or identify a range of solutions – to a problem' (QAA, 2001).

It is sometimes only too easy to take for granted that students know what is meant by terms like analysis, critical understanding, interpretation, evaluation, 'argument'. The meanings of these terms are quite subject-specific and tutors within the same discipline can have different expectations about what students need to do to demonstrate them in their work. Greater transparency can be achieved by using **learning outcomes** and **assessment** criteria (see Chapter 4), but it is essential that tutors take the time to discuss with students the meanings of the words used and give feedback using the same vocabulary.

Interrogating Practice

The SEEC Level descriptors use four categories of cognitive skills: analysis, synthesis, evaluation and application. For example, at Level 1 'synthesis' is defined as 'students can collect and categorize ideas and information in a predictable and standard format'.

In your subject think of a learning assignment for level one students which would enable them to practice and develop the skill of 'synthesizing'.

How would you introduce the categories or concepts students are expected to use in the synthesis of data?

How would you ensure that the exercise is set within a relatively predictable context?

How would you ensure that students understood what your subject requires as a standard format?

How would you provide feedback to reinforce students' learning?

Key, generic and employability skills

The key skills identified in Curriculum 2000 (www.qca.org.uk) apply equally to higher education, namely communication (written and oral), application of number, information technology, problem-solving, working with others, and improving own learning and performance. Another set of key skills is provided in the SEEC Level descriptors: group working, using learning resources, self-evaluation, management of information, autonomy, communications, problem-solving (SEEC, 2002).

It is not untypical for students to be assessed on group work skills without ever having had any learning support for this part of their work (see Chapter 7). Here are some ideas about how to develop group working skills:

- Make students aware of the phases of group formation.
- Discuss the different roles that individuals can take in groups (Jaques, 1992).
- Encourage students to keep a journal or log of their group work.
- Ensure there is an opportunity to reflect on the dynamics of the group.

LEARNING DEVELOPMENT

The process of supporting student learning begins as soon as students are recruited. Pre-entry guidance and support should provide students with some assistance in understanding the aims and structure of the course they have been accepted onto and some initial reading and enquiries which they can undertake before they arrive. Pre-entry guidance should also give students the opportunity to check that their choice of course, or chosen modules, is consistent with their career plans. If entering students are known to have special needs they should be referred to the disability service for their needs to be assessed as early as possible in order that support can be put in place – involving, for example, scribes, signers or a buddy to help with personal requirements. For some mature students, or those entering courses at levels 2 or 3, it is also necessary to agree the basis for any AP(E)L claim or credits being transferred, any course requirements that will need additional assessment and those which have already been met. Where there are identified language needs, eg, with students recruited from overseas, additional English classes can be agreed as part of the programme of study (see below for further details).

Student **induction** is normally thought of as being the first week of the first term, but some induction processes need to extend for the whole of the first semester or the first level of study, and new students transferring into levels 2, 3 or into postgraduate programmes also need induction. Induction serves four main purposes:

- Social: to provide a welcoming environment which facilitates students' social interaction between themselves and with the staff teaching on the programme of study on which they are embarking.
- Orientation to the university: to provide students with necessary information about the university, its facilities and regulations.
- Registration and enrolment: to carry out the necessary administrative procedures to ensure all students are correctly enrolled on their course of study.
- Supporting learning: to provide an introduction to a programme of study at the university and to lay the foundations for successful learning in higher education.

As we have argued above, it can no longer be assumed that students have a full understanding of the nature of higher education, the demands that tutors expect to make on them, and the requirements of the subject they are studying. It is therefore necessary to be explicit about all these matters and take nothing for granted. Furthermore, the importance of the emotional state that many students are in when they enter higher education needs to be recognized. Typically they are anxious, they lack confidence in their own ability to cope, they are full of uncertainty about what will be expected of them, and nervous about their relationships with other students as well as with staff. They will be asking themselves questions like 'What do I have to do?' 'Will I do it right?' 'How will I know if I'm doing OK?' 'Will tutors think I'm stupid?' 'Shouldn't I know this already?' Supporting student learning is about building students' self-esteem, enabling them to recognize their strengths (as well as identifying weaknesses), working from and valuing their existing knowledge, experience and cultures and providing opportunities to build confidence through becoming more competent, unlike the example offered in Case Study 1.

Case Study 1

This case study demonstrates the gap between a student's expectation and the reality she experienced on her entry to higher education. This student went on to become a Professor of Innovation Studies.

I chose an undergraduate course in social sciences. I had very little knowledge of what sociology was about, but I expected that it would help me to understand people and groups better, and perhaps to make sense of the tensions between the working-class culture of my family and the world of the grammar school (although I probably could not have expressed my expectations in that way at the time).

I soon discovered that sociology was taught consistently as if the experience of students and staff – those actually present in the classroom – was almost completely irrelevant. On a very small number of occasions I can recall when a lecture on a course in the sociology of religion encouraged us to do some undercover fieldwork by going out to visit church services organized by unfamiliar religious groups. Otherwise my studies were undisturbed by any need to reflect on my own direct experience. For the most part, I became alienated from formal study and concentrated my time and attention on gaining life experience through various youth subcultural activities and complex heterosexual entanglements.... (Nod Miller's story in Boud and Miller, 1996: 201)

Students typically ask themselves many questions when they enter higher education – 'How do I know what I'm supposed to do?' 'How do I know if I'm doing this right?' 'How do I know if I'm doing OK?' 'Am I on the right course?' 'What I am supposed to know?' 'Have I really learnt anything?' 'What is all this for?' – as illustrated in Figure 12.1. Rather than ignore these self-doubts and uncertainty it is better to begin to address these questions in induction, but they also need to be tackled throughout the first year, and some remain important throughout the students' programme of study.

Questions Students Ask Themselves	Learning Support
How do I know ...	Response
What to do?	Information to allow students to plan Clarification of expectations Skills development
If I'm doing it right?	Feedback on work in progress
How well I'm doing?	Feedback on assessed work
If I'm studying the right modules/courses?	Academic advice
What I've learnt?	Records of achievement
Where I'm going?	Career information and personal development planning (PDP)

Figure 12.1 Suggested institutional and departmental responses to students' anxieties

The specific topics required to achieve the transition to higher education may be tackled within a 'skills' module. Alternatively they may be integrated into core modules. The advantage of the former option is that it ensures that time is devoted to these topics and that student competences will be assessed. The disadvantage is that students do not always perceive the need or the relevance of such modules. The advantage of the integration model is that the skills can be learnt within a subject-specific context, but the disadvantage is that they may be squeezed out by the need to cover subject content and given insufficient attention.

Case Study: *Induction Policy*, University of East London

Supporting learning in induction: what to cover.

Aims and objectives of programme of study.
Academic calendar/programme; timetable of work.
Course structure – core, options, electives.

Assessment methods and assessment criteria.
Dates for submission of assessed work.
Progression requirements.
Credit accumulation, AP(E)L.
Introduction to learning resource centres (libraries), and IT facilities.
Explanation of plagiarism, why and how to avoid it.
Conventions for referencing and bibliographies.
Test that students meet English language threshold requirements – make use of referral opportunities.
Advice on study skills – identify support available.
Use and availability of ICT.
Reading lists and guidance on private study.
Identification of special needs – referral to disability and dyslexia services.
Health and Safety regulations – particularly for laboratory and studio-based courses.

(Adapted from Gosling, 1999)

How these topics can be tackled in more detail is described below.

Handbooks and Web sites

An important component of responding to students' anxieties about the course they are embarking on is having a good handbook. Much of this information can also be placed on the university's intranet or within a virtual learning environment (VLE, see below). The student handbook should be an important point of reference for students, containing all the essential information they need to pursue their studies. This will include a course structure diagram and descriptions of modules, their content and assessment methods – typically with learning outcomes and assessment criteria specified. It will also contain information about teaching staff, their availability and how to contact them; libraries and ICT facilities, location and opening times; bibliographic and referencing conventions; calendar for the year with significant dates and timetable for assessments; the course structure, with core modules and options identified; any special regulations relating to laboratories, studies, field trips; and support services which are available.

Diagnostic screening

Early in the first term, students should be set a piece of work that will act as a diagnostic tool to enable tutors to identify students with weaknesses that might justify referral to a service department. Such diagnostic tests can reveal students who may be suspected to have specific learning difficulties (eg, dyslexia), significant weaknesses in their use of English, problems with numeracy or early warning signs about their ability to meet deadlines and organize their work.

Personal development planning (PDP)

PDP is defined as 'a structured and supported process undertaken by an individual to reflect upon their own learning, performance and/or achievement and to plan for their personal, educational and career development' (Jackson, 2001). PDP is sometimes called student profiling (Assiter and Fenwick, 1993) or personal and academic record scheme (PARS) or similar (Gosling, 2002). Students are encouraged (or required, if it is a mandatory scheme) to keep a record of their learning achieved, both on-course and through their personal experience of work, voluntary activities, or other life experiences. They are also encouraged to reflect on how their learning matches the requirements that will be made on them in the future by employers. Jackson (2001) suggests that:

Personal Development Planning is intended to help students:

- become more effective, independent and confident self-directed learners;
- understand how they are learning and relate their learning to a wider context;
- improve their general skills for study and career management;
- articulate their personal goals and evaluate progress towards their achievement;
- and encourage a positive attitude to learning throughout life.

A criticism of modular schemes that are increasingly common in higher education is that they lead to a fragmented educational experience for students. PDP provides a vehicle for a more synoptic overview of what is being learnt and an opportunity to plan ahead to construct a programme of study that suits each student. It can also provide feedback to students on their progress and create a record of transferable and employability skills acquired which can aid career planning and CV writing. Such schemes can operate in dedicated skills modules or by regular meetings with a personal tutor or academic guidance tutor – say once a term or once a semester.

Providing formative feedback to students

One of the most important aspects of supporting student learning is the feedback that students receive on their work. A not uncommon fault, particularly within a semester system, is that students only find out how well, or how badly, they are doing when they receive their assessed work with a mark and comment. By that time, it is too late to take any remedial action. From the tutor's point of view it is difficult to give formative feedback to large classes in the short time available within a semester.

There is no easy answer to this problem, but some suggested solutions can include the following. Students submit a part of the final assessed work midway through the term, or they submit their planning work. Alternatively a short piece of assessed work can be set for early on in the semester with a return date before the final assessed work is completed. In some subjects multiple choice questions (MCQs) can be used and these can be marked electronically to provide feedback to students on their progress. Some forms of peer and self-assessment can be useful if these are well structured and use clear criteria.

Peer support

Supporting student learning is not only the province of tutors. Students can contribute through a variety of peer support mechanisms. Supplemental instruction (SI) is one such mechanism (Wallace, 1999). Another is the use of online discussion groups provided within **VLEs** (see below), which have the advantage that tutors can monitor what is being discussed. Peer mentoring schemes can operate well if students are motivated to support other students and there is a structure within which they can work. It helps if the student mentors can get some credit or recognition for their efforts.

Curriculum

The design of the curriculum is an essential aspect of supporting student learning. These are some of the key principles of course design that supports student learning:

- Begin where the students are – match course content to the knowledge and skills of the intake. Course content is sometimes regarded as sacrosanct but it is pointless teaching content that students are not ready to receive. Students need to be pushed and stretched, but the starting point needs to reflect their current level of understanding.
- Make skill development integral to the curriculum. Do not assume that skills already exist. Make space for skills to be acquired in a risk-free environment.

- Pay attention to learning processes and not simply content or products. Design in the steps that students need to be taken through to get them to the desired learning outcome.
- Demonstrate valuing of different cultures by building on students' own experience wherever possible. Knowledge and values cannot be taken for granted as higher education becomes more internationalized. Be on the lookout for cultural assumptions reflected in the curriculum and allow for alternative 'voices' to be heard.
- Avoid content and assessment overload which is liable to produce a surface approach to learning (see Chapter 2).

Teaching and learning methods

There are many opportunities for supporting student learning through teaching and learning. This is as much to do with creating an ethos between tutor and student as it is about using specific methods. Students should feel that they can admit to needing support without risking the tutor's disapproval, although this doesn't mean that it is appropriate for tutors to be available for their students all the time. Set aside specific times when you can be available and advertise these to the students. Support can also be given via e-mail or through discussion groups on the VLE.

Here are some ideas about things tutors can do to support student learning within the lecture room, seminar room, studio, or laboratory:

- Set regular, short, self-assessed tasks to check students' understanding of key concepts.
- Notice how students form into groups – ensure that all groups have your attention for equal time.
- Ensure that all groups have an opportunity to express their concerns.
- Collect formative feedback early in the term or semester to identify potential difficulties.
- Vary learning tasks to take account of students' different learning styles (see Chapter 15).
- Provide positive feedback, as well as comments which challenge or criticize.
- Encourage use of peer support within learning activities.
- Recognize and value students' constructive contributions to learning activities.

Useful texts that elaborate on these ideas are Ramsden (1992) and Biggs (1999).

CROSS-INSTITUTIONAL OR CAMPUS-BASED SERVICES

Library/resource centres

The role of library staff in supporting student learning is sometimes as important as the role of tutors themselves. This is because they are often more available at the time when students feel most in need of support and also because libraries are now far more than repositories of texts. While it remains the case that paper-based texts (books and journals) are the most important sources of information and knowledge, in this digital age libraries are also places where students can get online, access electronic databases and multimedia packages on CDs. Resource centres also provide services for students including materials for presentations, guide to the use of information technology (IT), study skills materials, learning aids for the disabled, and IT facilities.

Libraries are daunting places for many (perhaps all) students. Library staff have a special role in supporting students to help them understand not only the regulations about loans, fines and opening times, but more importantly about how to access information effectively, how to make judgements about relevance, currency and authority of the texts they access, and how to select what they need from the vast array of resources available on any topic. These skills are essential for the successful student and all students will need support not only at the introductory level, but also as they progress to more sophisticated literature searches for dissertations and theses.

IT

While a greater numbers of students now arrive in higher education with excellent IT skills, which can sometimes outstrip those of their tutors, a substantial number (particularly mature students) do not have these skills or the level of confidence in using IT that their course demands. All courses need to provide introductions to the use of basic word processing, spreadsheets, databases, presentation software, using e-mail and the Internet. Not all students will need introduction to all these. A diagnostic test can be used to determine which students need to develop their IT skills further to match the needs of the course. IT staff have an important role in supporting students throughout their studies, since the demands on students' IT skills typically rises as they progress to using more sophisticated subject-specific software.

Increasingly important are VLEs. These provide a vehicle for online learning by enabling tutors to make learning materials and assessments available via the Web (Internet) or an internal network (intranet). VLEs are also means by which students can communicate with each and with their tutors. Tutors can trace students' use of the VLE, while students have the advantage that they can access the course from any computer at any time. IT staff have a role in providing training, and supporting the use of VLEs for both staff and students (see Chapter 11).

Interrogating Practice

Consider how you could build into your course learning development in IT and library skills. For example:

- Using students self-assessment of relevant IT skills – with follow-up courses for those who need them.
- Requiring students to communicate using the VLE.
- Searching literature that tests information searching skills.
- Incorporating Web sites in your course handbook.
- Including discussion of library use within seminars.

English language and study skills support

Different subjects make different levels of demands on students' written and oral skills, but all programmes should make demands which require all students to develop their communication skills, both in writing and speaking. When students have difficulties meeting this demand, it can be for a variety of reasons. A common reason is the obvious one that English is not the students' first or home language. What is not so obvious is that this may be true of a substantial section of 'home' as well as international students. In universities which recruit from multi-ethnic communities in our large cities, these may constitute a significant number of students.

Second, there are students whose first or home language is English, but whose skills in the use of English do not match those required by their course. This is not just a matter of students whose spelling or grammar is idiosyncratic, since, as we noted above, writing is a subject-specific skill. Typically, when students exhibit poor writing skills this reflects a more general weakness in their approach to study. For this reason English language support is most effective when it is part of a holistic approach to developing students' study skills.

There is an important exception to this general rule, however, namely students who have specific learning difficulties, eg, 'dyslexia' as it is popularly called. Dyslexics have problems with writing which are the result of a disability rather than any reflection on their ability or grasp of the subject. Any student suspected of being dyslexic needs to be professionally diagnosed and assessed as we shall discuss in the next section.

The role of a central English languages service is to provide support for these students which goes beyond anything that subject specialists can provide. Teaching English for these special purposes is a skilled matter which is best tackled outside the normal classroom. Some materials may be made available online or through multimedia language packages, but face-to-face classes are also needed. However, this specialist support needs to be provided in close collaboration with subject departments to ensure that the subject-specific requirements are adequately met, as illustrated in Case Study 2.

Case Study

A Department of Cultural Studies at a new university was concerned that the failure rate of first-year students was increasing. The Year Tutor made contact with the English and Study Skills Unit (ESS) who discussed the issue in a meeting with all the tutors teaching first-year Cultural Studies. They agreed to refer to the unit students who were identified as having weak English as indicated by their performance in an early diagnostic writing assignment. The ESS Unit ran weekly classes aimed at the specific language needs of Cultural Studies students, incorporating attention to study skills. Cultural Studies lecturers monitored students use of this service through personal tutors and encouraged students to attend. The end of semester tests demonstrated that the mean score of students who attended this additional class was higher than that attained by those who were also referred but did not attend.

Supporting students with disabilities

The concept of a disability is slippery one. Many people have some disabilities, although they may be such that they rarely prevent them doing what they want to do, or it is relatively easy to compensate for the disability (eg, by wearing spectacles). Some have disabilities which are more significant because of the way so-called 'normal' life is organized. A simple example is the design of buildings. Steps and staircases constitute a barrier to those with mobility problems, whereas if there is a ramp or a lift the same person will no longer be disabled from getting where he or she wants to. Universities need to make provisions to remove the barriers which prevent students with disabilities having an equal chance as other students to succeed on their courses.

Recent governments have recognized the under-representation of students with disabilities in higher education. The reasons for this may be to do with under-achievement and low aspiration of children at school but we cannot rule out the possibility that a combination of prejudice and ignorance in admission procedures in higher education has also contributed. As a response to this situation special funding has been made available by HEFCE for projects intended to establish disability services or research the needs of disabled students.

The Disabled Students Allowance is now available in the UK to pay for equipment, tutorial support, personal helpers, scribes or whatever is determined to be necessary through the process of 'assessment of needs'. Universities also receive a funding 'premium' based on the estimated number of disabled students. A National Disability Team has also been created to lead a sector-wide initiative to improve provision for disabled students. From 2002 the Special Educational Needs and Disability Act (SENDA) places obligations on all higher education institutions. The Act opens up the possibility of students using litigation to ensure their rights to equal access and treatment are met. 'The best way to avoid claims under the Act is to achieve a change of culture regarding disability and ensure that disability issues are integrated into standard thinking by institution staff' (Ashcroft, 2001).

Although there may be some variations between different types of higher education institutions, the following would normally be expected to be found:

- a central service unit with responsibility for coordinating the support available to students with disabilities, monitoring institutional policy and compliance with legal requirements;
- carrying out assessment of needs (or making provision for assessment of needs at a regional Access Centre) and administrative support for students claiming the Disabled Students Allowance;
- a team of specialist tutors available to provide tutorial support – particularly for students with specific learning difficulties (eg, dyslexia);
- clearly understood and well-publicized referral by subject tutors;
- systematic procedure for identifying students with disabilities at enrolment and early diagnostic tests to identify unrecognized problems – particularly dyslexia;
- regular audit of accessibility to buildings, and safety procedures;
- provision of physical aids and facilities for students with disabilities, in libraries, for example.

A major issue faced by universities in supporting students with disabilities is the variation in support available to students and the lack of awareness by staff of the special needs of certain students. There can also be prejudice against disabled students and ignorance about what they are capable of, with appropriate support.

There is still a stigma attached to some illnesses and disabilities – to forms of mental illness, HIV and even to dyslexia. The result is that students are sometimes reluctant to reveal their disability or have anxieties about who knows about it. In the context of SENDA, all higher education institutions need to ensure that there is effective staff development as well as adequate provision made for students with disabilities.

Dyslexia typically accounts for about half of all students reporting a disability. For this reason alone it needs particular attention. Screening for students with dyslexia needs to be available for both students who think they may be dyslexic or those referred by their tutor. When screening suggests that a student may be dyslexic, a psychological assessment of the student should be conducted by a psychologist or appropriately trained person. If dyslexia is confirmed, an assessment of the student's study needs must be administered, so that an appropriate level of tutorial support and specialist equipment or software be provided. Adjustments to the student's assessment regime may also be necessary. This will need to be negotiated with the student's subject tutors. Raising tutors' awareness of the needs of dyslexic students is an important role for the central service.

The multicultural university

Universities in the UK are becoming more multicultural for two main reasons. First, the composition of the student body reflects the racial and ethnic diversity of multicultural Britain (although the distribution of students from so-called ethnic minority groups is not equal, but clustered in particular institutions). Second, higher education has become a global market and the UK attracts many international students from virtually every country in the world. Recent application of the Race Relations (Amendment) Act (2000) to higher education requires institutions to have an active policy to promote good race relations and ensure that no student is disadvantaged or suffers harassment or discrimination because of his or her race or ethnicity.

Responding to cultural and ethnic diversity requires a whole institution response which should:

- recognize cultural diversity in the curriculum;
- ensure that bibliographies reflect a range of perspectives;
- use teaching methods which encourage students from all cultures to participate;
- monitor assessment and results to check that fairness to all groups is demonstrated;
- consider the university calendar to ensure that major cultural and religious holidays are recognized;

- ensure that university publications do not contain assumptions about the ethnicity of the readers;
- develop proactive policies against discrimination and harassment;
- provide specialist counselling, advice and support services;
- provide places for all faiths to carry out acts of worship.

In these ways promoting equality of opportunity and good relations between multicultural groups contributes towards achieving a more supportive and enriched learning environment for *all* students.

CONCLUSION

Supporting student learning requires a multifaceted approach involving all parts of the university. Good liaison needs to exist to ensure that there are ways of referring students for additional help whether this be, for example, because of a disability, a need for study skills or English language support or to use the IT and library facilities. But supporting learning is primarily about having an ethos in all learning and teaching interactions which recognizes that all students have learning needs and that all students are undergoing learning development in relation to the skills that their courses demand of them.

REFERENCES

Ashcroft, R (2001) Presentation to a HEFCE seminar on SENDA, September

Assiter, A and Fenwick, A (1993), Profiling in Higher Education, in *Using Records of Achievement in Higher Education*, eds A Assiter and E Shaw, Kogan Page, London

Biggs, J (1999) *Teaching for Quality Learning at University: What the student does*, SRHE/Open University Press, Buckingham

Boud, D and Miller, N (1996) *Working with Experience: Animating learning*, Routledge, London

Cottrell, S (2001) *Teaching Study Skills and Supporting Learning*, Palgrave Study Guides, Basingstoke

DfES (2001) Higher education funding and delivery to 2003–04, Letter from the Secretary of State to the Higher Education Funding Council for England, 29 November

Gosling, D (1999) *Induction Policy*, University of East London

Gosling, D (2002) *Personal Development Planning*, SEDA Paper 115, Staff and Educational Development Association, Birmingham

HEFCE (2001) *Supply and Demand for Higher Education*, Paper 01/62, Higher Education Funding Council for England, Bristol

Jackson, N J (2001) *What is PDP?*, LTSN Working Paper 1, LTSN Generic Centre Web site: www.ilt.ac.uk

Jaques, D (1992) *Learning in Groups,* Kogan Page, London

QAA (2001) *The Higher Education Qualification Framework,* Quality Assurance Agency for Higher Education, Gloucester

Ramsden, P (1992) *Learning to Teach in Higher Education*, Routledge, London

SEEC (2002) *Credit Level Descriptors 2001*, Southern England Consortium for Credit Accumulation and Transfer, London

Simpson, R (1996) Learning Development: deficit or difference?, in *Opening Doors: Learning Support in Higher Education*, eds S Wolfendale and J Corbett, Cassell, London

Wallace, J (1999) Supporting and guiding students, in *A Handbook for Teaching and Learning in Higher Education,* 1st edn, eds H Fry, S Ketteridge and S Marshall, Kogan Page, London

FURTHER READING

www.qca.org.uk – Qualifications and Curriculum Authority

www.seec-office.org.uk – Southern England Consortium for Credit Accumulation and Transfer

www.hefce.ac.uk – Higher Education Funding Council for England

www.qaa.ac.uk – Quality Assurance Agency for Higher Education

<table>
<tr><td>13</td><td></td></tr>
</table>

13 Assuring quality and standards in teaching

Judy McKimm

INTRODUCTION

Managing and ensuring educational quality is one of the key responsibilities of all educational institutions and of those who work in them. Defining precisely what this experience comprises at any given time is not easy. Demands from external agencies define part of what is considered to be good practice and these demands combine with institutional culture and requirements to set the context for lecturers.

This chapter aims to offer an overview of current thinking about quality and standards from a national perspective. The intention is to provide a context within which lecturers can develop their understanding of quality issues in higher education, and hence of their possible roles and obligations in relation to quality and **standards**.

> **Interrogating Practice**
>
> What responsibility do you consider you have for maintaining and enhancing educational quality in your institution?

DEFINITIONS AND TERMINOLOGY

It is important to come to some agreement about terminology and definitions of quality and standards as these concepts underpin the thinking behind the design, delivery, assessment and review of educational provision. The development of shared language includes the adoption of a technical language drawn largely from industry that now determines how higher education institutions discuss and understand 'quality'.

Definitions and usage of the terms 'standards' and 'quality' vary and may depend on the aims and purposes of the educational provision or country and historical context. In the UK at present, 'standards' usually refers to expected or actual student attainment in terms of grading of performance. Quality is used in an even broader manner and with much variability in meaning, and may refer to a number of things, including individual student performance, the outputs of an educational programme, the student learning experience, the teaching provided, etc.

The concept of quality can be sub-divided into several categories, as Harvey, Burrows and Green (1992) demonstrated, including:

- Quality as excellence – the traditional (often implicit) academic view which aims to demonstrate high academic standards.
- Quality as 'zero errors' – most relevant in mass industry where detailed product specifications can be established and standardized measurements of uniform products can show conformity to them, but in higher education might be applied, eg, to learning materials.
- Quality as 'fitness for purposes' — focuses on 'customers' (or stakeholders) 'needs' (eg, of students, employers, the academic community, government, or society), and/or as defined by the stated aims and **learning outcomes** of a programme of study. In the last decade, in the UK, this has been the dominant usage of the word 'quality'.
- Quality as enhancement – emphasizes continuous improvement.
- Quality as transformation – applies either to students' behaviour and goals changing as a result of their studies or to socio-political transformation achieved through higher education.
- Quality as threshold – refers to meeting a minimum standard, as in **subject benchmarking**. Minimum standards are defined in most European higher education systems to enable a minimum, objective comparability of units or programmes. It is expected that minimum standards will be surpassed.

Interrogating Practice

Looking at the different definitions of 'quality', which of these best describe how teaching quality is talked about in your department?

The term **quality assurance** refers to the policies, processes and actions through which quality is maintained and developed. **Evaluation** is a key part of quality assurance. (Methods used to evaluate teaching are considered in Chapter 14.) Accountability and enhancement are important motives for quality assurance. Accountability in this context refers to assuring students, society and government that quality is well managed. **Quality enhancement** refers to the improvement of quality, eg, through dissemination of good practice or use of a continuous improvement cycle. The purpose of internally driven quality assurance is usually to effect an improvement in the functioning of a department or programme, whereas externally driven review is generally more about accountability. Quality assurance is not new in higher education, for example external examiners as part of assessment processes, and the peer review system for research publications, are quality assurance processes that have been present for many years.

Accreditation is recognition that provision meets certain standards, and may in some instances confer a licence to operate. The status may have consequences for the institution itself and/or its students (eg, eligibility for grants) and/or its graduates (eg, making them qualified for certain employment).

A set of performance indicators (PIs) generally form part of a quality assurance system. PIs are a numerical measure of outputs of a system or institution in terms of the unit's goals (eg, increasing employability of graduates, minimizing dropout) or the educational processes (eg, maximizing student satisfaction, minimizing cancelled lectures). Other indicators, not directly linked to performance, might include staff–student ratios and availability of learning resources for students. In developing a set of indicators, the aim is to find a balance between measurability (reliability), which is often the prime consideration in developing indicators, and relevance (validity). It is difficult to decide how to weight or combine indicators and indicators should be viewed as signals that show where strengths and weaknesses may be found, not as quality judgements in themselves.

The Bologna Declaration (1999) emphasizes the importance of a common framework for European higher education qualifications. In the UK a number of initiatives are being taken to help to ensure comparability between programmes in terms of standards, levels and credits (see 'The contemporary agenda' below).

Arrangements for quality assurance vary between countries, but many have created national agencies. Institutions offering higher education in England fall under the quality management system of the Quality Assurance Agency for Higher Education (**QAA**).

THE NATIONAL CONTEXT

Higher education in the UK is undergoing much rapid change. The massification of the system, widening participation, and the falling unit of resource have been among issues contributing to concern about maintaining and enhancing educational quality. This has contributed since the 1980s to government placing heavier emphasis on higher education being accountable for the public money it spends, on demonstrating quality, and on specification of outcomes. The evolution of the means by which government has required higher education to demonstrate and be assessed for quality in relation to education have been succinctly described by Middlehurst (1999), in the first edition of this handbook. It is convenient for the purposes of this chapter to take up that story in 1997.

The National Committee of Inquiry into Higher Education (**NCIHE**) reviewed UK higher education. The NCIHE published its findings and recommendations in the Dearing Report (1997). The report made wide-ranging recommendations including the framework for a new 'quality agenda', the establishment of a professional body for teachers in higher education and the formalizing of subject discipline networks. These resulted in the establishment of the Institute for Learning and Teaching in Higher Education (**ILT**) and the Learning and Teaching Support Network (**LTSN**) in 1999. The ILT, a professional membership body, has responsibility for accrediting individuals and programmes in teaching and learning in higher education against criteria that emphasize reflective practice and an understanding of the philosophy and learning methods appropriate to the sector. The subject centres of the LTSN are not involved in assuring the quality of programmes, but in quality enhancement through support of lecturers in their teaching role – by facilitating the sharing and dissemination of up-to-date information through conferences, Web sites and journals. Membership of the ILT and involvement in the work of LTSNs are quality indicators relating to teaching staff.

The QAA was formed in 1997. The QAA was contracted by the Funding Councils to carry out audits and assessments of the quality of education in publicly funded institutions on their behalf. Audit was concerned with verifying that academic procedures were as declared. Teaching assessment ('Teaching quality assessment' and then 'subject review') was concerned with provision at subject level and brought virtually all academics in England into contact with QAA processes. Over time the precise details of teaching assessment changed. Although slightly different methods were used in Scotland and Wales, the concept of using external review teams who were experts in their subject discipline was central to all teaching assessment processes. The teams of reviewers were selected from subject disciplines and led by a chair who was not a subject expert but whose role was to ensure adherence to the process and method.

Case Study 1 – Training subject reviewers

Between 1994 and 2002, some 4,500 academics, clinicians and professional practitioners have been trained to undertake subject level quality reviews across UK higher education. A mixed team of QAA officers, experienced review coordinators and senior staff from the **Higher Education Staff Development Agency**, delivers training, typically of two–three days' duration. Although each funding council has its own processes and emphases, the approach described below provides a general sense of the training and the significance attached to it.

Training is offered to potential reviewers after a rigorous selection process and it is a condition of appointment that all individuals undertake the training. This not only ensures effective induction to the role and initial consistency in briefing, but also provides an opportunity for prospective reviewers to be observed in simulated situations prior to work in the sector. The overall aim of training has been to produce individuals who understand and are committed to the review method and who are competent to undertake the range of duties required of them. Minimally, the reviewing role entails:

- a secure grasp of the processes and values underpinning the review method;
- familiarity with reference documentation, eg, the QAA Code of Practice, appropriate subject benchmarks;
- well-founded skills of analysis, information management and a capacity to make evidence-based judgements;
- effective communication and interpersonal skills to manage meetings with colleagues, peers, students and, possibly, employers;
- drafting and report writing skills necessary to contribute to the production of a report in the style and to the specification required by the QAA;
- a capacity to work accurately under pressure and to maintain a professional manner.

This particular amalgam of knowledge, understandings, skills and attitudes cannot be developed by a didactic approach; thus training is shaped by a strong philosophical commitment to use of a wide range of learning formats. The key vehicle for learning is an extensive simulation exercise. Reviewers are required to complete an initial personal analysis of preparatory materials before training commences. This preparation feeds into a simulated team meeting in which reviewers identify significant issues for further enquiry. Subsequently, reviewers are provided with opportunities to conduct meetings with 'staff' and 'students', to analyse samples of students' work, to revise their agenda in the light of cumulative evidence, to begin drafting a report and to engage with making judgements. These practical activities, undertaken on an individual and small group basis, are interspersed with brief informational inputs to highlight important issues, key processes, appropriate protocols and core values.

Every training event is evaluated and feedback is sought from participants on its perceived relevance and effectiveness in equipping them with the skills they need. Feedback has been consistently positive with 96 per cent of participants rating the training in the highest category. Participants indicate that reviewer training achieves its immediate objectives, but also provides an opportunity to think more generally about issues of curriculum design, approaches to assessment, the determination of standards of achievement, student support, mechanisms for quality improvement and the effective deployment of learning resources. As such, reviewer training produces individuals who are equipped to act as a resource with their immediate colleagues for local benefit, as well as contributing formally to a sector-wide system. In this sense, reviewer training is a powerful form of updating for experienced staff in mid to late career.

(Professor Gus Pennington)

Subject review examined six aspects of provision relating to learning and teaching:

- curriculum design and organization;
- teaching, learning and assessment;
- student progression and achievement;
- student support and guidance;
- learning resources;
- quality management and enhancement.

Visits normally took place over four days and in order to triangulate evidence (ie, obtain evidence from a range of sources) carried out a number of activities in reaching a judgement:

- documentary review, including a self-assessment document by the subject team and documents relating to the six aspects in a base room;

- formal meetings with staff and students covering the six aspects;
- meetings with senior managers and others;
- direct observation of teaching and learning events;
- visits to facilities and learning resources such as libraries, computer laboratories and other teaching rooms.

In England a numerical score for each aspect of provision was awarded. Written reports were produced for each visit, summarizing the main strengths and areas for improvement. These are publicly available (eg, on the QAA Web site http://www.qaa.ac.uk).

The last subject reviews are being conducted as this book goes to press, with the subsequent arrangements (see below) still being clarified, but the published outcomes of subject review and its predecessors will form the basis of many teaching quality league tables for several years to come.

THE CONTEMPORARY QUALITY AGENDA

During 2000–02 there was extensive debate about a replacement for subject review, with much discussion of reduction in external scrutiny and bureaucracy and an increase in institutional autonomy and quality as enhancement (rather than as inspection). New arrangements for 2002–03 onwards look likely to place greater emphasis on compliance with externally determined and audited standards and norms, but to have a lighter 'inspectorial' touch. The new agenda can be described as a 'jigsaw' comprising interdependent and interlocking processes that emphasize increasing transparency, accountability and specification.

The main elements of the quality framework will be a combination of institutional **audit** (at the level of the whole organization) and **academic review** (at the level of the subject discipline). Audit will have a 'lighter touch' and follow up areas of concern, consistent with the principle of intervention in inverse proportion to success. There will be an increased emphasis on public access to: 'easily understood, reliable and meaningful public information about the extent to which institutions are individually offering programmes of study, awards and qualifications that meet general national expectations in respect of academic standards and quality' (QAA, March 2002).

This will place considerable demands on lecturers and other staff. Examples of information likely to have to be provided include details of internal assurance processes, student evaluations, student satisfaction surveys, employers' evaluations and input to programme, examiners' reports (internal and external), intake and graduate data and more detailed information concerning programme content and assessment. There is also likely to be scrutiny of provision and take-up of staff development and training, particularly in the area of teaching and learning, including membership of a professional body such as the ILT, as these may be seen as quality indicators at institutional and departmental level.

QAA teams will consider how institutions have put into practice the new national requirements including:

- The publication of and adherence to a **Learning and Teaching Strategy** and use of the associated Teaching Quality Enhancement Funds.
- The use of external reference points including the **Code of Practice** for the assurance of academic quality and standards in higher education, the **Framework for Higher Education Qualifications** in England, Wales and Northern Ireland and subject benchmark statements.
- The development, use and publication of **programme specifications** and **progress files**.

Up-to-date information on QAA arrangements may be found on the QAA Web site.

Framework for Higher Education Qualifications (FHEQ)

The FHEQ was finalized in 2001 and aims to inform employers, students and other stakeholders about the levels that holders of a qualification have achieved and what skills they bring to a job. The framework simplifies the range of awards and describes five levels of achievement: three at Bachelor's degree level (Certificate in HE, Intermediate and Honours) which correspond to three years of study but incorporate the shorter 'foundation' degrees, one at Masters and one at Doctoral level. Generic statements indicate the levels of achievement expected within these awards, whatever the subject.

The FHEQ aims to assure the public that qualifications from different institutions and for different subjects represent similar levels of achievement. The levels are reference points to determine whether the intended learning outcomes for a programme are appropriate to the level of the qualification awarded. The external examiner system will become increasingly important as a means of comparison between programmes at different institutions. Lecturers and institutions will need to ensure their programmes match the appropriate level.

Programme specifications

In 1999 the QAA stated: 'programme specifications are an essential part of the strategy for helping higher education to make the outcomes of learning more explicit... and permit the programmes and awards to be related to the Qualifications Framework' (QAA, October 1999).

In a programme specification, teaching teams are expected to set out:

- The intended learning outcomes of a programme (specific, measurable intentions expressed in terms of what learners will be able to do (a) as knowledge and understanding and (b) as skills and other attributes).
- The teaching and learning methods that enable learners to do this.
- The assessment methods used to demonstrate the achievement of learning outcomes.
- The relationship of the programme and its study elements to the FHEQ.

Programme specifications affect the work of individual lecturers and course teams directly, as they must produce and amend them (often using an institution-wide format), and then expect judgements to be made against them by the university (through its quality assurance committees and boards), students, employers and external reviewers. Their production requires the essential elements of a programme to be synthesized into a short space, no matter what its complexity.

Subject benchmarking

Subject benchmarks describe general expectations about the standards, attributes and capabilities relating to the award of qualifications at a given level in a particular subject area. They were produced by groups of senior academics in each subject, in consultation with the sector. They are statements about 'threshold quality' or 'minimum standards'. For example, in medicine: 'the benchmarks for medical degrees have been defined in terms of the intellectual attributes, the knowledge and understanding, the clinical, interpersonal and practical skills, and the professional competencies which will allow the graduates to function effectively as pre-registration house officers and develop as professionals' (QAA, 2002).

Subject benchmark statements are used in conjunction with the FHEQ. For any given programme there should be compatibility between the intended learning outcomes and the relevant programme specification. The statements will be formally revised after 2005 to reflect developments in the subject and the experiences of institutions and others of working with them. Lecturers need to be aware of the benchmark statements for their own subjects, particularly if they are involved in curriculum design or the production of programme specifications. Statements can be used as a checklist when designing new programmes or when reviewing the content of existing curricula. The benchmark statements will be used by external bodies as reference points for checking purposes.

Interrogating Practice

How do/might the programme specification(s) and subject benchmark statements relevant to your teaching help you day to day, eg, in planning teaching sessions or designing assessments? What advantages and disadvantages can you see to an 'outcomes based approach'?

Progress files (PFs)

The PF has two elements. From 2002–03 the transcript or academic record element of the PF will be produced by institutions. It records student achievement according to a common format and contains details of the courses/modules taken by a student (including the results of assessment). The second part of the PF is owned and produced by the student and is termed personal development planning (PDP). PDP will facilitate students to monitor, build and reflect on their development. PDP should be fully implemented by 2005–06 and institutions must provide the opportunity for students to undertake PDP.

Staff will need to ensure that adequate, appropriate and timely assessment information is provided for the transcript. The precise degree of involvement and encouragement that academic or support staff may make to PDP is not yet clear, and may vary between institutions and disciplines. For example, it may be used as a means of structuring tutorials or meetings with individual students, and different types of PDP may be developed, ranging from a highly reflective 'journal' or diary to a more prosaic, descriptive record of development and skill acquisition. Issues of confidentiality and responsibility are likely to arise. In many institutions PDP will be electronic, but teachers will need to be aware of the format and process by which it is managed at their own institution.

Interrogating Practice

Has PDP been introduced into your institution? If so, how useful do students find it as a tool for developing a reflective approach to study and development? How do/might you as a teacher help students to use PDP for personal and professional development?

The external examiner system

The QAA plans to use external examining as a key element of ensuring quality and standards (QAA, March 2002). Work will be carried out to ensure that the external examiner system is operating so as to ensure public confidence in academic quality and standards. Summaries of external examiner reports will be published as part of the audit process.

Public information: student satisfaction surveys

A key plank of the new quality arrangements is the requirement for institutions to make a range of information (such as programme specifications) widely available to various types of 'customer' of higher education. Student ratings are one such area. At time of publication exact requirements in this area are still changing, but some form of student satisfaction data, broader than feedback on specific modules, is likely to be required.

Lecturers (and administrators) need to be aware that there may be national and institutional requirements on them to participate in the collection of data from students, to respond to the comments received, and to ensure that information is made available for public consumption.

Case Study 2: The student satisfaction approach at the University of Central England (UCE), Birmingham

The Satisfaction Approach has been developed at the Centre for Research into Quality over the last 15 years. The approach was designed to be an effective tool with which to obtain, analyse and report students' views of their total university experience in order to effect change and improvement. Student Satisfaction has evolved into a major quality and planning tool at UCE as part of a process of continuous quality improvement. It is a template for 'quality' information requirements in this area.

The Student Satisfaction Approach is a market leader and has been emulated and adapted by a number of higher and further education institutions both in the UK and overseas (including New Zealand, Sweden, Australia, South Africa, Hong Kong and Poland). The methodology is summarized briefly below. (Further information is available via http://www.uce.ac.uk/crq/satisfaction.htm or from Harvey et al (1997).

The methodology continues to evolve and allows the surveys to be flexible to address the pressing concerns of students. The methodology can be easily adapted to different situations. It has been used to explore the views of a variety of stakeholders: staff, postgraduate research students, employers, placement supervisors and even football supporters.

The Student Satisfaction approach is unique in combining the following four elements:

- Student-determined questions: the Student Satisfaction research focuses on the total learning experience as defined by students (via focus groups or in-depth interviews).
- Satisfaction *and* importance ratings: the research examines student satisfaction with aspects of provision and then identifies which of those areas are important for students.
- Management information for action: those areas which are important to students but where students are dissatisfied are priority areas for management intervention.
- A clear feedback and action cycle.

Management information

The items in the survey that are unsatisfactory but important for students become target items for action. Satisfaction data is also mapped longitudinally, which allows for benchmarking of improvement in student satisfaction year by year.

The survey results are reported to the Vice-Chancellor and, through him, to the Board of Governors and Senate. They are published in an annual report from the Centre, made available via the University Web site. A central feature of the report is the composite rating tables and trend graphs, which clearly identify areas for action and trends, without lots of impenetrable statistics.

Action and feedback

At the centre of the process is the action and feedback cycle (see Figure 13.1). The intention is that there is a process that identifies responsibility for action and subsequent follow-up to ensure action takes place.

The internal consultation process at UCE reviews action from previous years and prioritizes action based on student views, which is linked to budget allocation letters. The Vice-Chancellor interviews all the deans and heads of services about the outcomes of the report, who are required to

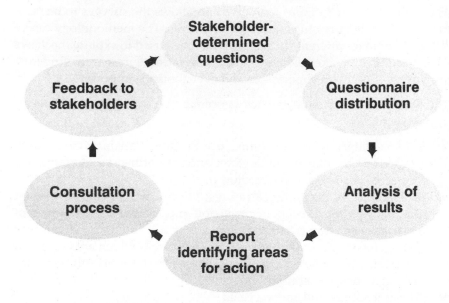

Figure 13.1 Satisfaction cycle

indicate what action they are intending to take and what has happened as a result of the previous year's agenda. The replies are made available to Senate for discussion and a summary of action taken is communicated back to students.

(Professor Lee Harvey, UCE)

Transitional arrangements

It is envisaged that in the transitional period from 2002–04 the QAA will engage with institutions to carry out institutional audits and to participate in discipline-based review or activity, which for most institutions will take the form of new, development-focused engagements intended to test internal procedures for assuring quality and standards. It is planned that by the end of 2005 all institutions will have participated in an audit. A limited number of academic reviews will also be carried out during the transition period.

Institutional audit

By the middle of the first decade of the 21st century national quality arrangements are likely to mean that there will normally be one institutional audit visit by an external review team on a five- or six-yearly cycle, focusing on the whole institution. The expectation is that the institution will be expected to produce a self-evaluation document (SED) approximately 13 weeks before the visit. Audits will consider several examples of the institution's quality assurance processes at work, at the level of the programme ('discipline audit trails' – approximately 10 per cent of programmes in terms of full-time equivalent student numbers – or across the whole organization –'thematic enquiries'). The audit team in consultation with the institution will select enquiries and trails. The capacity to 'drill down' through academic review at subject level in cases where the reviewers have concerns will remain, despite the main emphasis being at institutional rather than subject level. (Review by professional statutory bodies – PSBs – will continue alongside the audit process.)

Each audit is likely to comprise two visits, a short briefing visit, and five weeks later, the audit visit itself, normally five days. One of the main tasks of the audit team will be to consider the internal processes and outcomes of periodic quality assurance reviews of programmes/discipline areas (review panels in future will have to include external members). The audit team will seek to establish whether procedures are robust enough to ensure and enhance educational quality across all the provision that the institution manages. The audit will consider:

- the accuracy, completeness and reliability of published information (eg, on Web sites) about programmes and the standards of awards;
- the academic standards expected of and achieved by students;
- the experience of students as learners;
- the quality assurance of staff, including appointment criteria and the ways in which teaching effectiveness is appraised, improved and rewarded.

Audit teams will meet with staff and students, undertake documentary analysis (which will include samples of assessed student work and external examiner reports) in the course of discipline audit trails, and explore issues and procedures relating to internal quality assurance. Shortly after the visit, the audit team will summarize the main findings and recommendations, and produce a draft report. The final public report will state the level of confidence the audit team has in the provision. If the report contains positive statements of confidence and no recommendations for action then the audit will be formally 'signed off' on publication and there will be limited follow up with the QAA. If statements of confidence are qualified or recommendations suggest important weaknesses that should be urgently addressed, the report will be published but there will be a programme of follow-up action, including a revisit after one year to consider the institution's action plan and adherence to it. It is likely that in time, the audit process will have a 'lighter touch' for institutions that demonstrate they have sound quality assurance and enhancement mechanisms.

Interrogating Practice

How are the processes of institutional audit and academic review impacting on your work?

ENHANCING AND MANAGING QUALITY: THE ROLE OF THE LECTURER

It is often hard for individual academics to make connections between their fundamental concern to do a good job for their own and their students' satisfaction, and the mechanisms and requirements associated with the 'quality banner'. But educational quality can (and should) be seen as everyone's responsibility.

At institutional level, arrangements must be set in place for the formal management of quality and standards in accordance with the national agenda described above. External reviews by the QAA and PSBs (eg, in medicine or engineering) are often used by institutions as a framework for internal quality management and can provide a focus and milestone towards which many institutions work.

The institution will have a formal committee structure, part of whose function is to manage and monitor quality, including external examining. This is usually supported by an administrative function (often in Registry) to collect and collate data relating to academic quality, eg, student feedback questionnaires, annual course reviews, admissions or examination statistics. Structures and processes vary between institutions, but they should enable issues concerning educational quality to be identified in a timely and appropriate way and be dealt with. One of the senior management team (eg, a pro vice-chancellor) normally has an identified remit for ensuring educational quality and maintaining academic standards. Clear mechanisms for the approval of new programmes and a regular system of programme reviews should be in place. One of the fundamental elements of quality assurance is to enable feedback (from students, staff, employers and external reviewers) to be considered and issues addressed.

Additional formal mechanisms usually operate at faculty and departmental level in order to enable the consideration of more detailed issues and to address concerns more speedily. Committees (such as teaching and learning committees) include representatives from programmes. They act to promulgate, interpret and implement organizational strategy, policies and procedures; to develop and implement procedures for managing the monitoring and review of faculty/departmental programmes and procedures; and to respond to demands from review, accreditation or inspection bodies. Staff–student liaison committees are another example of committees operating at this (or programme) level.

It is at programme level where the individual teacher will be mainly involved in ensuring the quality of provision. All those who teach need to be committed to and understand the purposes and context of the programmes on offer, and be aware of the elements that may comprise a 'quality' learning experience for students. They will also need to be familiar with and understand the use of programme specifications, levels, benchmarking, etc. Those teaching on a programme will be required to have formal monitoring and review systems to consider all activity relating to learning and the learning environment, including administrative procedures (such as ensuring that assessment results are collected and analysed or that course materials are distributed in a timely fashion). Delivering a good 'student learning experience' requires a high level of competence and understanding: formal education about teaching and learning in higher education, the development of reflective practice (see Chapter 15) and peer review of teaching (see Chapter 16) all contribute to this.

Interrogating Practice

Do you know how the systems of feedback and quality management (eg, committee structures, external examining, and feedback loops) work in your department and institution?

Internal quality assurance procedures and development activities to enhance educational quality are likely to include the evaluation of individual staff members through systems such as student feedback questionnaires, peer review systems, mentoring for new staff or regular appraisals.

Interrogating Practice

Has your view of your responsibility for maintaining and enhancing educational quality changed while reading this chapter?

CONCLUSION AND OVERVIEW

Assuring and enhancing educational quality and academic standards can be seen as complex and multifaceted activities, but at the centre of these are the individual learner and lecturer. It often hard to maintain a balance between 'quality as inspection' and 'quality as enhancement'. Higher education in the UK is largely funded by public money and students as fee payers have a set of often ill-defined expectations relating to their programme of learning. The new quality agenda firmly sets out to make higher education more transparent and accountable and to define the outcomes of learning programmes more specifically. Awareness of the concepts, terminology and expectations of national agencies concerned with quality, coupled with increasing competence and understanding of teaching and learning processes, can help the individual teacher and course team member to contribute effectively towards the development and enhancement of a quality culture in higher education.

REFERENCES

Bologna Declaration (1999) at: http://www.unige.ch.cre/activities/Bologna

Harvey L, Burrows A and Green D (1992), *Criteria of Quality: Summary report of the QHE project*, University of Central Birmingham, Perry Barr, Birmingham

Harvey *et al* (1997) *Student Satisfaction Manual*, University of Central Birmingham, Perry Barr, Birmingham

Institute for Learning and Teaching in Higher Education: http://www.ilt.ac.uk

Middlehurst, R (1999) Quality and standards, in *A Handbook for Teaching and Learning in Higher Education*, 1st edn, H Fry, S Ketteridge and S Marshall, Kogan Page, London

National Committee of Inquiry into Higher Education (1997) (Dearing Report) *Higher Education in the Learning Society*, NCIHE, HMSO, London (also to be found at: http://www.leeds.ac.uk/educol/ncihe)

Quality Assurance Agency (QAA) (October 1999) Policy on programme specification, http://www.qaa.ac.uk/crntwork

QAA (March 2002) QAA external review process in Higher Education for England: operational description, http://www.qaa.ac.uk/crntwork/newmethod/fod.htm

QAA (2002) Subject Benchmark in Medicine, http://www.qaa.ac.uk/crntwork/benchmark/phase2/medicine.pdf

FURTHER READING

The Higher Education Funding Council for England's Web site contains some publications that relate to academic quality and standards: http://www.hefce.ac.uk

The LTSN Generic Centre have set up a Web resource area to support higher education in making effective use of QAA Policies at: http://www.ltsn.ac.uk/genericcentre/projects/qaa

Quality Assurance Agency home page: http://www.qaa.ac.uk

For code of practice; national qualifications frameworks; latest information on educational review and institutional audit (including handbook); programme specifications; progress files and subject benchmark statements see:
http://www.qaa.ac.uk/crntwork/currentwork.htm
Examples of learning and teaching quality manuals can be found on the Web site of the University of Southampton: http://www.clt.soton.ac.uk/qah

<table>
<tr><td>14</td><td># The evaluation of teaching</td></tr>
</table>

14 The evaluation of teaching

Dai Hounsell

INTRODUCTION

It is three decades since the first books on the **evaluation** of university and college teaching began to appear in the UK. At first the topic was highly controversial. It dumbfounded many academics while leaving some aghast at what they saw as an affront to their academic autonomy and an unwarranted deference to student opinion. Nowadays evaluation raises very few eyebrows. It has come to be seen not only as a necessary adjunct to accountability, but also as an integral part of good professional practice. And from this contemporary standpoint, expertise in teaching is viewed not simply as the product of experience: it also depends on the regular monitoring of teaching performance to pinpoint achievements and strengths, and to identify areas where there is scope for improvement.

Alongside this gradual acceptance of the indispensability of evaluation has come a greater methodological sophistication. In its infancy, evaluation in UK universities was strongly influenced by US practice, in which the use of standardized and centrally administered student ratings questionnaires had been the predominant approach (eg, Flood Page, 1974). Yet it was not widely understood by many who imported such questionnaires that they had been designed principally for **summative** purposes: that is, to yield quantitative data that could be used to compare the teaching performance of different individuals, and thus provide an ostensibly more objective basis for decisions about staffing contracts, tenure and promotion. They could not therefore be as readily adopted in systems of higher education such those in the UK or Australia, where teaching was commonly collaborative (Falk and Dow, 1971). Here the foremost concern was with the use of evaluation for developmental rather than judgemental purposes, and thus with contextualization rather than standardization

(Hounsell and Day, 1991). It was therefore necessary to develop more broadly based approaches to the collection and analysis of feedback (eg, Gibbs, Habeshaw and Habeshaw, 1988; O'Neil and Pennington, 1992; Hounsell, Tait and Day, 1997; Day, Grant and Hounsell, 1998; Harvey, 1998) and which are surveyed in this chapter.

Interrogating Practice

What recommendations or guidelines do you have in your institution or department on collection and analysis of feedback from students?

CONTEXTS AND FOCUS

There are many reasons for wishing to evaluate the impact and effectiveness of teaching. New lecturers are usually keen to find out whether they are 'doing OK', what their strengths and weaknesses are as novice teachers, and how their teaching compares with that of other colleagues. More experienced lecturers may want to find out how well a newly introduced course/module is running, and a programme coordinator may want to check that a fresh intake of first-year undergraduates is settling in reasonably well. To some extent, obtaining feedback can also have a cathartic function – an opportunity for the students to 'let off some steam' and 'to tell us what they really think about the course'. But the motives for seeking feedback to evaluate teaching may be extrinsic as well as intrinsic. The advent of **quality assurance**, for example, has brought with it the routine expectation that academic departments and faculties will regularly make use of feedback to investigate whether their curricula are succeeding in their **aims** and achieving appropriate **standards**. The quality assurance review process that will operate in England from 2002–03 (QAA, 2002) lists student feedback summaries as evidence that may be required for scrutiny as part of 'developmental engagement'. Likewise the Cooke Report on quality and standards (HEFCE, 2002) has recommended that the outcomes of surveys of student satisfaction should be made more readily available, both within institutions and more widely, via the Internet. Indeed, it is clear that the collection of such evaluative information and its accessibility to public scrutiny is receiving increased attention in the sector (see Chapter 13).

Similarly, providing documentary evidence to show that feedback has been sought (and has been constructively responded to) is emerging as an almost universal requirement in accredited professional development programmes for university teachers, while also being increasingly adopted as a basis for demonstrating teaching expertise in promotion procedures.

These differences in purposes are likely in turn to influence the nature of the feedback sought. The kinds of feedback evidence appropriate to a claim for promotion to a senior post (where excellence will need to be demonstrated) will be markedly different to those applying to someone approaching the end of their probationary period, where the prime concern will be to demonstrate competence at or above a given threshold (Elton, 1996; Hounsell, 1996). Such evidence may well be presented by means of a teaching **portfolio** (see Chapter 17). Generally speaking, feedback which is collected for extrinsic purposes has to fulfil a set of formal requirements, whereas someone collecting feedback for their own individual purposes usually has much greater scope over what kinds of feedback they collect and in what form. In either case careful consideration has to be given to what would be the most appropriate focus for feedback in any given instance. If, for example, the intention is to capture as full and rounded a picture as possible of teaching in its various guises, then the equivalent of a wide-angle lens will be needed. This can encompass questions of course design and structure, teaching–learning strategies, academic guidance and support, and approaches to assessment, together with interrelationships between these. But there may also be occasions when the overriding concern is with a specific aspect of teaching such as **computer-based learning** or the quantity and quality of comments on students' assignments, and where only a close-up will capture the kind of fine-grained information being sought.

These considerations will be influential in determining not only how and from whom feedback is to be sought (as will be apparent below) but also when it is to be elicited – a dimension of evaluation that is often overlooked. There is a widespread practice, for example, of waiting until the end of a course before canvassing student opinion, usually on the grounds that the students need to have experienced the whole course before they can effectively comment on it. But one consequence is that students often find it difficult to recall with much precision a series of practical classes, say, or a coursework assignment that took place several months previously. Another is that none of the issues or concerns that students raise will be addressed in time for them to derive any benefit – a situation which is not conducive to good teaching and likely to undermine students' interest in providing worthwhile feedback.

Interrogating Practice

At what points in your teaching do you gather feedback from students? Does this give you time to respond to issues they raise?

SOURCES OF FEEDBACK

In contemporary practice in higher education, there are three principal sources of feedback which are widely recognized. These are:

- feedback from students (by far the commonest source of feedback);
- feedback from teaching colleagues and professional peers (Chapter 17);
- self-generated feedback (the aim of which is not to enable university teachers to act as judge and jury in their own cause, but rather to cultivate **reflection** and promote self-scrutiny).

If it is to be considered appropriately systematic and robust, any feedback strategy is likely to make use of at least two – and preferably all three – of these sources, since each has its own distinctive advantages and limitations. Feedback from students, for instance, offers direct access to the 'learners' eye-view', and students are uniquely qualified to comment on matters such as clarity of presentation, pacing of material, access to computing or library facilities, 'bunching' of assignment deadlines and helpfulness of tutors' feedback on written work. There are some issues where departmental teaching colleagues may be better equipped to comment: for instance, on the appropriateness of course aims, content and structure; on the design of resource materials; or on alternatives in devising and marking assignments, tests and examinations. And third, self-generated feedback, which is grounded in the day-to-day teaching experiences, perceptions and reflections of the individuals concerned, opens up valuable opportunities to 'capitalize on the good things' and to 'repair mistakes quickly before they get out of hand' (Ramsden and Dodds, 1989: 54).

Over and above these three main sources of feedback, there is a fourth which, though readily available, is often under-exploited or goes unnoticed: the 'incidental feedback' which is to be found in the everyday routines of university teaching and course administration and therefore does not call for the use of specific survey techniques. It includes readily available information such as attendance levels; pass, fail, transfer and drop-out rates; patterns of distribution of marks or grades; the nature of the choices that students make in choosing between assignment topics or test and examination questions; and the reports of external examiners or subject reviewers. It can also encompass the kinds of unobtrusive observations which can be made in a teaching–learning situation, such as a lecture: how alert and responsive the students are; whether many of them seem tired, distracted or uninvolved; to what extent they react to what is said by looking at the teacher or avoiding his or her gaze (Bligh, 1998; Brown, 1978).

METHODS OF FEEDBACK

The question of the source from which feedback is to be obtained is closely related to the question of how it is to be sought (see Figure 14.1). Indeed, any such overview of sources and methods in combination helps to underscore the great wealth of possibilities that are currently available to university teachers in seeking and making use of feedback.

As far as methods of obtaining feedback from students are concerned, questionnaires remain extremely popular (see Case Study 1) – largely, one suspects, on two

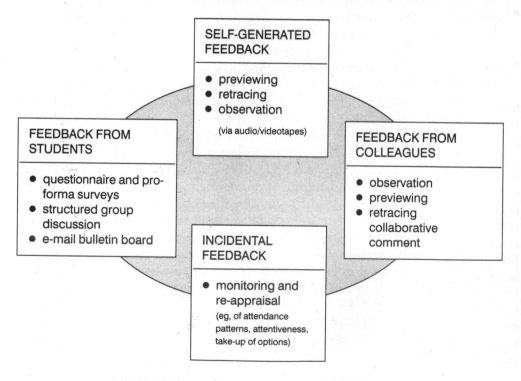

Figure 14.1 Sources and methods of feedback

grounds. First, there is the widespread availability of off-the-shelf questionnaires, which (though of widely varying quality) are to be found in abundance in the many books on teaching and learning in higher education (eg, Hounsell, Tait and Day, 1997), as well as being regularly bartered and cannibalized by course teams and individuals alike. And second, there are the signal attractions of a method that offers every student the chance to respond while at the same time generating data which are quantifiable. However, these easy virtues can trap the unwary. Over-intensive and indiscriminate use in some institutions has led to 'question-naire fatigue' on the part of students, while among staff there has been a growing awareness of the drawbacks of the questionnaire method. Concerns have been expressed about the considerable resources of time and expertise that are neces-sary both in designing questionnaires which are salient and to the point, and in systematically processing and analysing the resulting data. Happily, there is a growing range of alternative approaches to the canvassing of student opinion, including:

- 'instant' and 'one-minute' questionnaires together with a variety of pro-formas, the majority of which aim to side-step questionnaire fatigue by combining brevity with more ample opportunities for student comment;
- structured group discussion, student panels and **focus groups**, which offer less formal and relatively open-ended ways in which groups of students can constructively exchange and pool thoughts and reactions;
- electronic bulletin boards, to which students e-mail their comments and queries for open display.

Methods of obtaining feedback from colleagues and peers are equally diverse. Probably the best-known method is direct observation, where a colleague is invited to 'sit in' on a lecture, seminar or practical and subsequently offer comments as a knowledgeable third party (see Chapter 16). But there are likely to be situations – especially in small classes and in one-to-one tutorials or supervi-sory meetings – where the presence of a colleague would be obtrusive and inhibit-ing. It is here that the techniques of previewing and retracing come to the fore (Day, Grant and Hounsell, 1998: 8–9). Previewing involves looking ahead to a forthcoming class and trying to anticipate potential problem areas and explore how they might best be tackled. Retracing, on the other hand, is retrospective and is intended to review a specific teaching session, while it is still fresh in the mind, in order to pinpoint successes and areas of difficulty. Both techniques entail the use of a colleague as an interlocutor and critical friend, prompting reflection and the exploration of alternatives. Colleagues can also adopt a similar role in the crit-ical scrutiny of course documentation and teaching materials or in collaborative marking and commenting on students' written work.

Case Study 1: A questionnaire about practical classes

The University of Edinburgh

Many examples of end-of-course module questionnaires are readily available. Here is an example of a questionnaire used to collect feedback from practical/laboratory class teaching.

Questionnaire about practical classes

Please put a tick in the appropriate column to indicate your response to each of the following statements about the practicals you attended as part of the course.

	Strongly agree	Agree	Unsure	Disagree	Strongly disagree
The practicals:					
• covered key areas and ideas	☐	☐	☐	☐	☐
• were well linked to lectures	☐	☐	☐	☐	☐
• helped relate theory to practice	☐	☐	☐	☐	☐
• were well planned and structured	☐	☐	☐	☐	☐
• were lively and stimulating	☐	☐	☐	☐	☐
The demonstrator:					
• made clear what was expected of students	☐	☐	☐	☐	☐
• helped students with any difficulties they encountered	☐	☐	☐	☐	☐
• was interested in students and their progress	☐	☐	☐	☐	☐
As a student:					
• I looked forward to practicals	☐	☐	☐	☐	☐
• I enjoyed being in practicals	☐	☐	☐	☐	☐
• I learnt a lot from the practicals	☐	☐	☐	☐	☐

Please add below any comments about what would have made the practicals better for you:

Inevitably, the services of hard-pressed colleagues and peers can only be drawn on occasionally and judiciously, but many of the same techniques can also be adapted for use in compiling self-generated feedback. Video and audio recordings make it possible to observe one's own teaching, albeit indirectly, while previewing and retracing are equally feasible options for an individual, especially if good use is made of an appropriate checklist or pro-forma to provide a systematic focus for reflection and self-evaluation. Case Study 2 gives an example of a pro-forma which can be used in retracing a fieldwork exercise. Checklists can help to under-pin previewing, retracing, or direct or indirect observation, and aspects for consideration are reviewed in Chapter 16.

Case Study 2: A pro-forma that can be used for retracing fieldwork

The University of Edinburgh

Fieldwork is a typical case where feedback from direct observation or teaching is not usually feasible. Here the most appropriate way to obtain feedback is by retracing. This method readily lends itself to other teaching situations; for example, pro-formas can be adapted for one-to-one sessions in creative arts that may run for several hours in which a one-hour sample observation would not yield useful feedback.

A pro-forma for retracing fieldwork

Record by ticking in the appropriate column the comments which come closest to your opinion.

How well did I. . .?	Well	Satisfactory	Not very well
make sure that students had the necessary materials, instructions, equipment, etc			
get the fieldwork under way promptly			
try to ensure that all the set tasks were completed in the time available			
keep track of progress across the whole class			
handle students' questions and queries			
provide help when students encountered difficulties			
respond to students as individuals			
help sustain students' interest			
bring things to a close and indicate follow-up tasks			

ANALYSING AND INTERPRETING FEEDBACK

Any technique for obtaining feedback is going to yield data that need to be analysed and interpreted. Some techniques (eg, structured group discussion) can generate feedback in a form which is already categorized and prioritized, while questionnaires can be designed in a format which allows the data to be captured by an OMR (**optical mark reader**) or, in some institutions, processed by a central support service. Increasingly Web-based systems are being introduced which invite students to respond to multiple choice questions (**MCQs**) and enter comments in text boxes. From these, different types of report can be generated. Yet while possibilities such as these do save time and effort, there are little or no short-cuts to analysis and interpretation, for these are not processes that can be delegated to others. There is a body of thought, as Bligh has noted, which contends that the actions of a lecturer and the students' response to that lecturer (as represented in the feedback they provide) are not accessible to an outside observer or independent evaluator, but can only be properly understood 'in the light of their intentions, perceptions and the whole background of their knowledge and assumptions' (Bligh, 1998: 166). It is not necessary to endorse this view unreservedly. Put in uncompromising terms, no one is better placed than the teacher most directly concerned to make sense of feedback and to weigh its significance against a knowledge of the subject matter in question, the teaching aims and objectives, and the interests, aspirations and capabilities of the students who provided the feedback.

Equally crucially, it does not seem unreasonable to concede that there are occasions when involving others in the challenge of analysing and interpreting feedback has very particular and distinctive benefits. First, a sometimes uncertain path has to be steered between the twin snares of, on the one hand, dismissing unwelcome feedback too readily and, on the other, dwelling on less favourable comment to the neglect of those features of one's teaching which have attracted praise and commendation. In circumstances such as these, calling on the 'second opinion' of a seasoned teaching colleague makes good sense. Second, specialist help may often be required in analysing and interpreting findings – and especially so when a standardized student questionnaire has been used and results for different individuals are being compared. Studies undertaken at the London School of Economics (Husbands, 1996, 1998) draw attention to the complexity of the issues raised. Third, the interrelationship of information and action is far from unproblematic. Good feedback does not in itself result in better teaching, as US experience has suggested (McKeachie, 1987). Improvements in teaching were found to be much more likely when university teachers not only received feedback but could draw on expert help in exploring how they might best capitalize upon strengths and address weaknesses.

Interrogating Practice

In your department, what happens to feedback data from student questionnaires? Is it made public to the students involved? How do staff analyse, review and act upon the findings from this source? How are students informed about changes made in response to their views?

ACTING ON FEEDBACK

This last point is a crucial one, especially given that many university teachers will not have easy access to a teaching–learning centre or educational development unit offering specialist guidance and support. It is therefore important to acknowledge that acting on feedback constructively entails a recognition of its practical limitations. Sometimes feedback produces unclear results which only further investigation might help to resolve, or it may be necessary to explore a variety of possible ways both of interpreting and responding to a given issue or difficulty.

Two examples may help to illustrate this. In the first of these, feedback on a series of lectures has indicated that many students experienced difficulties with audibility. But where exactly might the problem lie? Was it attributable to poor acoustics in the lecture theatre, or because many of the students were reluctant to sit in the front rows, or because the lecturer spoke too softly or too rapidly? And what would be the most appropriate response: installing a microphone and speakers, encouraging the students to sit nearer the front, better voice projection and clearer diction by the lecturer, or greater use of handouts and audio-visual aids, so that students were less reliant on the spoken voice?

The second example is one in which pressures on resources have led to larger tutorial groups, and feedback has revealed that students are dissatisfied with the limited opportunities they have to contribute actively to the discussion. One way forward might be to halve the size of tutorial groups by scheduling each student to attend tutorials at fortnightly rather than weekly intervals. Another might be to experiment with new strategies to maximize tutorial interaction and debate. And a third might be to reconfigure teaching–learning strategies, enabling fuller opportunities for tutorial interaction through greater reliance on self-study materials.

As these two examples make clear, in many teaching–learning situations there is no one obvious or ideal response to feedback, but rather an array of options from which a choice has to be made as to what is appropriate and feasible. Some options may have resource implications; some may necessitate consulting with colleagues; and some (the second example above is a case in point) may best be resolved by giving the students concerned an opportunity to express their views on the various options under consideration.

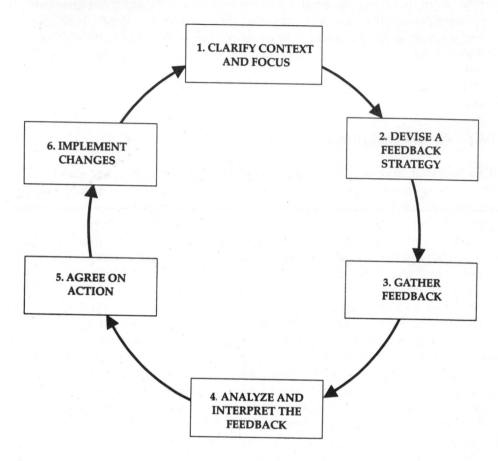

Figure 14.2   The evaluation cycle

OVERVIEW

This chapter has looked at the principal factors to be considered in evaluating teaching. The sequence followed was not fortuitous, as Figure 14.2 suggests, for the processes involved, when viewed collectively, can be seen as a series of inter-locking steps which together comprise a cycle of evaluation. Overlooking any one of these steps is likely to be dysfunctional. Neglecting to clarify focus and purposes, for example, may result in feedback which is unhelpful or of marginal relevance, while failing to respond to issues which have arisen by not implementing agreed changes risks alienating those who have taken the trouble to provide feedback.

It would be misleading, nonetheless, to see this cyclical perspective on evaluation as a counsel of perfection. No university teacher can realistically subject every aspect of his or her day-to-day practice to constant review, nor can workable evaluation strategies be devised in isolation from careful consideration of the resources of time, effort and expertise which would be called for. Effective evaluation may be less a matter of technique than of the exercise of personal and professional judgement.

REFERENCES

Bligh, D (1998) *What's the Use of Lectures?*, 5th edn, Intellect, Exeter

Brown, G (1978) *Lecturing and Explaining*, Methuen, London

Day, K, Grant, R and Hounsell, D (1998) *Reviewing your Teaching*, Edinburgh and Sheffield: University of Edinburgh, TLA Centre/CVCP Universities' and Colleges' Staff Development Agency

Elton, L (1996) Criteria for teaching competence and teaching excellence in higher education, in *Evaluating Teacher Quality in Higher Education*, eds R Aylett and K Gregory, Falmer, London

Falk, B and Dow, K L (1971) *The Assessment of University Teaching*, Society for Research into Higher Education, London

Flood Page, C (1974) *Student Evaluation of Teaching: The American experience*, Society for Research into Higher Education, London

Gibbs, G, Habeshaw, S and Habeshaw, T (1988) *53 Interesting Ways to Appraise your Teaching*, Technical and Educational Services, Bristol

Harvey, J (ed) (1998) *Evaluation Cookbook*, Learning Technology Dissemination Initiative, Heriot-Watt University, Edinburgh

Higher Education Funding Council for England (HEFC) (2002) *Information on Quality and Standards in Higher Education*. Final report of the Task Group chaired by Sir Ron Cooke. (HEFCE Report 02/15).

Hounsell, D (1996) Documenting and assessing teaching excellence, in *Evaluating Teacher Quality in Higher Education*, eds R Aylett and K Gregory, Falmer, London

Hounsell, D and Day, K (1991) Feedback, evaluation and quality in teaching in higher education, in *Managing the Higher Education Environment*, ed M Wright, Napier Polytechnic/EAIR, Edinburgh (proceedings of the 13th International Forum of the European Association for Institutional Research, Edinburgh, 1–4 September)

Hounsell, D, Tait, H and Day, K (1997) *Feedback on Courses and Programmes of Study*, University of Edinburgh, TLA Centre/Universities' and Colleges' Staff Development Agency/Institute for Higher Education Development in South Africa, Edinburgh, Sheffield and Johannesburg

Husbands, C T (1996) Variations in students' evaluations of teachers' lecturing and small-group teaching: a study at the London School of Economics, *Studies in Higher Education*, **21** (2), pp 187–206

Husbands, C T (1998) Implications for the assessment of the teaching competence of staff in higher education of some correlates of students' evaluations of different teaching styles, *Assessment and Evaluation in Higher Education*, **23** (2), pp 117–39

McKeachie, W J (1987) Instructional evaluation: current issues and possible improvements, *Journal of Higher Education*, **58** (3), pp 344–50

O'Neil, M and Pennington, R C (1992) *Evaluating Teaching and Courses from an Active Learning Perspective*, Universities' and Colleges' Staff Development Agency, Sheffield

Quality Assurance Agency for Higher Education (QAA) (2002) *QAA External Review Process for Higher Education in England: Operational description*, 019 03/02

Ramsden, P and Dodds, A (1989) *Improving Teaching and Courses: A guide to evaluation*, 2nd edn, University of Melbourne, Melbourne

FURTHER READING

The following are practical guides, each approaching evaluation in a distinctive and contrasting way.

Day, K, Grant, R and Hounsell, D (1998) See above (http://www.tla.ed.ac.uk/ryt.html)

Gibbs, G, Habeshaw, S and Habeshaw, T (1988) See above One of two handbooks mentioned above that provide a range of practical examples of checklists, questions and pro-formas.

Harvey, J (ed) (1998) See above (http://www.icbl.hw.ac.uk/ltdi). Of particular interest to anyone wishing to evaluate the use of **C&IT** in university teaching.

Part 2
Development of the academic for teaching and learning

Reflective practice

Margot Brown, Heather Fry and Stephanie Marshall

INTRODUCTION

We are frequently exhorted to encourage our students to be **reflective** and to adopt reflective practices. These concepts are as relevant to ourselves in relation to our progress as teachers as to our students. This chapter focuses on how (new) academics can develop reflective practice in respect of their teaching.

REFLECTION

Reflection is a valuable but much abused concept (Boud and Walker, 1998). It has a central part to play in transforming and integrating new experiences and understanding with previous/existing knowledge (see Chapters 2 and 10). It has gained most currency as a key part of learning from experience (Kolb, 1984). However, it is often viewed as a very passive and overly 'naval-gazing' activity. In reality, it is something which works best with engagement and proactivity on the part of the learner. As teachers, we seek to build situations for our students in which they will be forced to reflect. We do this through strategies such as asking them questions, encouraging self-assessment (Boud, 1995), encouraging them to write diaries (Boud, Keogh and Walker, 1985), using **critical incident analysis**, and asking them to analyse and critique ideas and practice in less structured ways. By so doing we are seeking to bring about learning by changing previous knowledge, and to inculcate habits which will build reflection into learning, thus ensuring that learning will not end the minute the student graduates from university. Reflection can be used in the context of cognitive, psychomotor, affective and interpersonal domains. It can be used to help learners construct new schemata in relation to theories and concepts and in relation practice (see Chapters 2 and 10). Furthermore, this chapter argues that as teachers we should be seeking to become active, purposeful, reflective practitioners. Biggs suggests that reflective activity, through a process of interpretation and integration, translates lower-order inputs to higher-order knowledge (Biggs, 1988: 190). However, in the mid- to late 1990s the notion of reflective practice most regularly promoted via various professional development programmes came under attack due to its uncritical application. For example, Harvey and Knight (1996) suggest that reflective practice had become the 'fashionable solution' to professional development, with Barnett (1997) taking this stance further, proposing that reflective practice may mask the hidden agenda of instrumentalism. While acknowledging the validity of these arguments, this chapter seeks to explore the benefits to be gained from conscious reflective practice as a means of promoting critically reflective learning.

NOVICE TO EXPERT

There have been many studies in the professions tracing the development of practitioners from **novice** to **expert** (for an overview, see Eraut, 1994). Professions in which such work has taken place include the police, nursing, and school teaching. One of the original classifications of the stages of progression is that of the Dreyfus brothers (1986). Level 1, the novice stage, is characterized by adherence to taught rules and little discretionary judgement; level 2, the advanced beginner, takes more account of the global characteristics of situations but tends to treat all aspects and attributes as having equal importance. At level 3 the practitioner is considered competent and is beginning to see actions as part of longer-term goals, and is able to undertake conscious and deliberate planning and perform standardized or routine procedures. At level 4, that of proficiency, situations are seen more holistically, important aspects are more readily recognized, decision making is less laboured and guiding axioms can be interpreted differently according to situation. The expert, the level 5 practitioner, no longer relies on rules and guidelines and has an intuitive grasp of situations based on deep understanding, knows what is possible, and only uses analytic approaches in novel situations or when new problems occur. Thus the expert stage is characterized by implicit and unconscious practice. For the experienced teacher in higher education, much practice will be at the expert level. For the new lecturer (and every occasion on which a lecturer tries out a new technique) practice will not have reached this implicit and almost instinctive state. Reflection is something which helps us to continuously examine practice and move it on to higher levels; it facilitates maintenance and improvement of practice.

BECOMING A REFLECTIVE PRACTITIONER

The notion of 'becoming a reflective practitioner' is one referred to regularly in induction programmes for new academic staff. However, the various components of such practice are rarely unpacked, either in general terms or in relation to specific activities.

When we are expert practitioners, if we wish our practice to continuously move on, we will have become 'unconscious reflectors', the state all teachers in higher education are in with respect to their discipline – specific knowledge where they constantly meet, challenge, innovate, create and incorporate new knowledge and understanding.

How can teachers become more self-aware of how they teach, the implications this has for learning, how this links to appropriate assessment and how one can be discriminating in the choice of method (within time and resource constraints) which will be most appropriate in any given situation? The rest of this chapter attempts to indicate some approaches which may help the practitioner to progress along this road.

When looking at the range of activities that a teacher in higher education might be involved in, it is appropriate to consider reflective practice as an activity which will take place continuously, but noticeably, first, on or during an individual teaching and learning activity; second, on completion of a course module; and third, on completion of a programme of study (those interested in how reflection can be used in portfolios should read Chapter 17). To assist the 'novice' to become an 'expert', reflective practice must be linked to action (Kolb, 1984; Freire, 1985). Such a concept is explored below.

An individual teaching and learning activity

Using the classification of novice to expert referred to earlier, the individual teaching and learning activity would appear to be the logical starting point for developing the skills of reflective practice for practitioners new to teaching or engaged in a new area of teaching. For example, further to the delivery of a lecture, consideration of the success or otherwise of the activity could lead the teacher to focus on one or two areas about which they have concern: eg, pacing of delivery and gauging student engagement. Reaching a conclusion – in this case, 'the pacing was too fast' – further to such 'contemplation' (Jarvis, Holford and Griffin, 1998), is what distinguishes reflective practice from the process of thinking. Repeated practice, and focusing on different aspects of delivery of the lecture, will assist the practitioner to move along the continuum beyond level 1 – or novice – towards level 5 – or expert. Furthermore, such an approach will assist the practitioner in moving from reflection-on-practice at one end of the continuum to reflection-in-practice at the other end (Schon, 1987).

Completion of a course module

There is a range of opportunities for reflective practice at the completion of a course module, opportunities which include weighing up feedback from individual learning activities. Continued reflective practice should assist the process of offering a balanced and meaningful analysis of student feedback questionnaires, module **assessment**, feedback via staff–student committees or board of study student representation. For example, are student feedback questionnaires to be considered solely on their numerical analysis – contrary to all the best advice (see Chapter 14), or are other factors, such as diverse learning needs and styles, to be taken into account? Is module assessment reflected on purely in terms of degree classification, or is a more diagnostic approach adopted whereby the teacher is asked to reflect on points at which students may have been better assisted in their learning? Brown and McCartney (1999) assert that reflection aids the transformation of experience into knowledge, and, in the examples just provided, it would follow that not only will reflective practice benefit the individual practitioner, but all involved in the department's teaching and learning activities, assisting teachers to move along the novice–expert continuum.

Completion of programme of study

Further to teaching, learning and assessment across all aspects of a study programme, the practitioner will have reflected on a range of different activities. Through an iterative process, the skills of reflecting 'on', and reflecting 'for' action, should lead to the ability to reflect 'in' action. This ability to reflect while in action, adapting and changing one's behaviour further to this reflection, is what distinguishes the expert from the novice. It is what Schon (1983) suggests is the mark of a professional, in that professionals are capable of thinking on their feet, responding to unique situations, and producing new skills. Further to Boud and Walker's (1998) assertion that reflection is both a cognitive and affective process, reflection 'in' action will also, in many instances, need to take account of other factors including sociological, environmental, technical and political processes.

Recording and using reflective practice

As with students' recording of reflection, the most commonly accepted means of recording reflective practice is to retain a 'learning log' or diary. Clearly from the above it follows that mere recording is not sufficient, for without reflection informing future behaviour or action, in this context, it is meaningless. Thus, on conclusion of a teaching and learning activity, one might make notes such as 'next time I will...'. This diary will serve as a useful *aide-memoire* in planning teaching activities, allowing the teacher the benefit of recorded hindsight and points of detail to which he or she should pay attention to improve subsequent teaching activities.

CONCEPTIONS OF TEACHING

Ramsden (1992) draws together the work of several researchers (notably Margaret Balla, Gloria Dall'Alba, Elaine Martin and John Biggs) to develop a typology of 'higher education teachers' theories of teaching' (1992: 111–19). Other similar typologies exist (see Chapter 22). Three broad theories were identified (it is not suggested that all aspects of one practitioner's teaching will only fall within one of the theories; they are 'ideal' types). Theory one centres on the notion of teaching as telling or transmission, theory two typifies teaching as organizing student activity, while theory three centres on teaching being an activity which makes learning possible.

Interrogating Practice

List up to five statements which describe what you consider teaching in your discipline to be about. For each statement decide into which of the three conceptions of teaching it fits. Does your overall conception of teaching (as represented by your statements) fall mainly into one of the three groups?

Teaching and learning styles

As suggested, the more experienced reflective practitioners will be able to adapt their approach to assist the bringing about of successful outcomes in their students. Unpacking of the factors contributing to successful learning requires an awareness of one's own conception of, and style of, teaching.

There have been several attempts to classify particular styles or types of teaching by linking a number of teaching practices or behaviours into sets (eg Butler, 1987; Entwistle, 1988). This work is useful to practitioners who may wish to identify their favoured approaches; however, it is not suggested that teachers only ever exhibit behaviour from one set or style of teaching.

The more aware teachers are of the characteristics of different styles, the more effective they will be in supporting effective learning for students. We all have to undertake a range of tasks, for example, the request to return marked scripts by a particular time on a particular day (Style 2); keeping a steady line of positive communication between personal supervisor, module tutors, examination boards, pastoral or counselling services, students (Style 3); ensuring students are prepared for assignments and examinations (Style 4); developing a variety of teaching strategies to meet the different learning needs in student groups (Style 1). The more flexible teachers are in respect of tasks which require different approaches, the more effective they will be. This same flexibility of approach is required of students.

Interrogating Practice

What different strategies for teaching have you used over the past month (eg, role-play, small group work, teaching a skill through demonstration, lecture)? Which did you feel most comfortable with? Do the method(s) you felt most comfortable with map onto your conceptions of teaching and/or any one of the four teaching styles?

Table 15.1 Four postulated styles of teaching and their suggested behaviours

Style 1: Do I...	Style 2: Do I...
challenge students to move beyond existing knowledge; value students' originality; foster creativity by introducing new resources and activities; provide a 'stimulus rich' environment; work with big ideas with no standard structure or format; set open-ended tasks?	emphasize practical learning; provide structured tasks with detailed directions; encourage concise, ordered formats and outcomes; foster creativity through phototypes and replicas; cover content in detail; set clear tasks; finish on time?

Style 3: Do I...	Style 4: Do I...
encourage students' personal expression and imagination; give praise generously; enjoy change and variety; promote cooperative tasks; create an unstructured, friendly environment; develop content through a variety of media including artistic, aesthetic or literary?	emphasize ideas, concepts, theories; analyse and evaluate ideas; want students to have a bank of knowledge; have consistent and reliable rules and procedures; dislike distraction; rely on logical reasoning; need time to think through ideas and organize programmes?

(Adapted from Entwistle, 1988)

As teachers, one way we can reflect on practice is to consider the implications and effects of our actions on different learners. A way of doing this is in relation to learning styles. Butler (1987) has shown that failure of a student to learn can be attributed not only to matters such as motivation and prior learning, but also to a mismatch between the lecturer's teaching style and the students' learning style.

Learning styles

An understanding of learning styles and their characteristics is part of a teacher's 'tool box' of analytical and reflective skills. Observing and analysing learning characteristics has led to definitions of learning style (see also Chapter 2), which includes the axiom that the way in which an individual typically approaches a learning situation derives from a mix between their cognitive process and personality. It can be argued that there are basic differences in personality which affect styles or approaches to learning and the way thinking is organized (Briggs Myers, 1987).

Although learning style theorists have developed different terminology to describe learning characteristics, there is broad agreement that in any group of learners there will be at least four bands of learning styles represented, though not in equal proportion. The characteristics of these styles have been identified to include those listed in Table 15.2.

No learning (or teaching) style is judged better or worse than another. Each style is valid for that learner. Many learners will share characteristics from more than one group but will feel most comfortable when taught in ways that correspond to their 'dominant' style. Learners who are more strongly 'C' in their learning style, for example, will respond well in situations where a variety of teaching strategies are the norm but will be less responsive to an undiluted diet of didactic approaches. However, while each style may be valid for the individual learner, inevitably that learner will encounter situations, individuals or tasks which do not match his or her preferred learning style. Some of these tasks will prove more challenging and extra support from the tutor will be required. For example, if a task requires reading for attention to detail, then those who more naturally skim read may need guidance to unlock the text – eg, structured questions based on small sections.

Avoiding pitfalls

Learning style deals with only a limited, though important, number of variables which affect the learning process. Students bring with them a wide variety of other characteristics which influence their learning experiences. These include existing content knowledge, abilities and skills; personal background including

Table 15.2 Four postulated styles of learning and their characteristics

Style A

works well alone;

plans work effectively;

is good at meeting deadlines;

reads instructions carefully;

is wary of open-ended tasks;

takes good notes;

is impatient of other ways of working;

can be preoccupied by detail – misses the 'big picture';

not always able to work well with others.

Style B

organizes material well;

enjoys problem solving;

works things out well on paper;

is precise and thorough;

sees links between ideas;

may want too much information before beginning work;

may be overcautious;

may not necessarily be a creative thinker;

learns well through formal lectures.

Style C

can come up with creative solutions;

can see the whole picture – but may ignore detail;

will often pinpoint new questions;

can be uncritical of ideas;

finds categorizing difficult;

may work in bursts of energy;

is easily distracted;

responds to varied stimuli – video, music, etc, which generate responses.

Style D

works well with others;

is willing to try new ideas;

is intuitive – can't always explain 'why';

enjoys variety and change;

prefers skim reading;

does not tend to plan in advance;

may leave things until the last minute;

does not always attend to detail;

may have problems organizing time;

is a divergent thinker.

(Adapted from Butler, 1995)

socio-economic status, gender, ethnicity and language; and motivation to learn (see Chapters 5 and 10). It would not be helpful to use an understanding of learning style to identify or 'label' students, to ignore the other variables – temporary or permanent – which influence learning, or to use them as a self-fulfilling prophecy.

Learning styles can help teachers understand more comprehensively problems which students may encounter, and identify appropriate teaching strategies to provide support. Teachers can plan to address different learning styles in two main ways. One is to structure contact time with students to encompass a variety of styles. Another way is to ensure that all styles are addressed over the whole of module delivery, as outlined in the Case Study 1.

Case Study 1: Undergraduate Module – Education for a Culturally Diverse Society, Educational Studies, University of York

This module, offered to first- and second-year undergraduates in the Department of Educational Studies, comprised nine two-hour sessions. The group size ranged from 10–16 students who are not necessarily planning to go into teaching. Over the nine weeks, learning styles were addressed in different ways.

Teaching/Learning Activity Undertaken	Learning Style Addressed
Seminar preparation – involved working individually, using library resources and set reading	A, B
Lecture	A, B
Requiring students to be out of their seats and moving around the room	D, C
Identifying analysis of key theories in selected texts	B, A
Using personal testimony through video, poetry, literature, autobiography	C, D, A
Preparation of a presentation on a topic of choice related to the course	A, B, C, D
Analysing incidents as reported (as part of a problem-solving task) using cue sheets and role cards to show perspectives	D, C, B
Reviewing National Curriculum documentation in the light of theories of cultural pluralism	B, A
Working in a small group setting on a task set with focus on cooperation and communicating results to the whole group	A, B, C
Using photographs, text and video, developing questions to highlight analysis	C, D, A

Students also write an extended essay of 5,000 words on a topic of their choice which requires analysis, evidence of wide reading and linking of ideas and theories.

(Margot Brown)

To promote effective teaching and learning requires a range of teaching strategies, and individual teachers may be uncomfortable using some of the strategies. However, reflecting on practice and revisiting the concept of teaching and learning styles can assist the practitioner in devising a range of teaching strategies which, with practice, will become part of the repertoire in the varied delivery of a course module.

OVERVIEW

This chapter has considered factors which could assist teachers to become effective and reflective practitioners. Effective practitioners are likely to be those who reflect on their teaching, update their skills and think of teaching from the perspective of its impact on learners rather than from the perspective of 'covering content'. Ramsden identified six key principles of effective teaching in higher education (1992: 96–102). Subsequent formulations have not substantively changed the items he identified:

- making the teaching session interesting and giving clear explanations;
- showing concern and respect for students and student learning;
- giving appropriate assessment and feedback;
- providing clear goals and intellectual challenge;
- ensuring independence, control and active engagement of learners;
- learning from students.

All these are clearly important considerations to the reflective practitioner, but added to this should be included the need for confronting one's own conceptions of teaching. Through a focus on teaching and learning styles, it is hoped that practitioners will have gained some additional tools which will assist in the deconstruction of their own conceptions of teaching, leading to reflection on the most appropriate and effective teaching and learning strategies for both teacher and student.

REFERENCES

Barnett, R (1997) *Higher Education: A critical business*, SRHE/Open University Press, Buckingham

Biggs, J (1988) Approaches to Learning and to Essay Writing, in *Learning Strategies and Learning Styles*, ed R Schmeck, Plenum Press, London

Boud, D (1995) *Enhancing Learning through Self Assessment*, Kogan Page, London

Boud, D, Keogh, R and Walker, D (eds) (1985) *Reflection: Turning experience into learning*, Kogan Page, London

Boud, D and Walker D (1998) Promoting Reflection in Professional Courses: the Challenge of Context, *Studies in Higher Education*, **23** (2), pp 191–206

Briggs Myers, I (1987) *Introduction to Type: A description of the theory and application of the Myers-Briggs Type Indicator*, Consulting Psychologists Press, Palo Alto, California

Brown, R and McCartney, S (1999) Multiple mirrors: reflecting on reflections, in *Developing the Capable Practitioner*, eds D O'Reilly, L Cunningham and S Lester, Kogan Page, London

Butler, K (1987) *Learning and Teaching Style in Theory and Practice*, The Learner's Dimension, Columbia, Connecticut

Dreyfus, H and Dreyfus, S (1986) *Mind over Machine: The power of human intuition and expertise in the era of the computer*, Basil Blackwell, Oxford

Entwistle, N (1988) *Styles of Learning and Teaching*, David Fulton Publishers, London

Eraut, M (1994) *Developing Professional Knowledge and Competence*, Falmer, London

Freire, P (1985) *The Politics of Education*, Macmillan, London

Harvey, L and Knight, P (1996) *Transforming Higher Education*, SRHE/Open University Press, Buckingham

Jarvis, P, Holford, J, and Griffin, C (1998) *The Theory and Practice of Learning*, Kogan Page, London

Kolb, D A (1984) *Experiential Learning*, Prentice-Hall, Englewood Cliffs, New Jersey

Ramsden, P (1992) *Learning to Teach in Higher Education*, Routledge, London

Schon, D (1983) *The Reflective Practitioner*, Jossey-Bass, San Francisco

Schon, D (1987) *Educating the Reflective Practitioner*, Jossey-Bass, San Francisco

FURTHER READING

Brookfield, S (1995) *Becoming a Critically Reflective Teacher*, Jossey-Bass, San Francisco. Written specifically for teachers in higher education. Guides readers through many processes for becoming critically reflective about teaching.

Eraut, M (1994) See above. Most useful in exploring the nature of professional knowledge and theories of professional expertise.

O'Reilly, D, Cunningham, L and Lester, S (1999) *Developing the Capable Practitioner*, Kogan Page, London. The focus of this book is on developing the capable practitioner, with one of its five sections devoted to the reflective practitioner.

Schon, D (1987) See above. A must for any professional taking reflective practice seriously. Focuses particularly on reflection-in-action.

16 Observation of teaching

Hazel Fullerton

INTRODUCTION

Observation of teaching, as a means of enhancing the quality of teaching and learning, is now commonplace in the UK higher education sector. However, until the early 1990s there was little of this taking place, except as part of the training of teachers for the school sector. The practice has since increased steadily as many universities and colleges have come to recognize the value of observation schemes. For others, the impetus to adopt direct observation was driven by the Teaching Quality Assessment methodology (**QAA Subject Review**). Although this is not continuing in the same way, the process has become embedded and most institutions have built teaching observation into their quality assurance mechanisms. Many staff now regard direct observation as an integral part of their own professional development as teachers and value the process, both in their roles as the observer and the observed. This gradual acceptance of observation has helped to break down some of the 'no-go' areas previously associated with colleagues observing each other's teaching. Many have been supported by a collection of papers (Brown, Jones and Rawnsley, 1993), outlining a range of approaches and models of observing teaching.

Teaching observation is an integral part of development programmes for new lecturers and for established staff, and peer observation has become increasingly common in departments. It aims to develop and enhance effective practice and to provide a springboard for further development through shared reflection and in some cases through action research.

The LTSN Generic Centre (www.ltsn.ac.uk/genericcentre/projects/peer-ob/) has built up an extensive set of Web-based resources about past experience of observation of teaching and also explores potential directions for the future.

RATIONALE

It is axiomatic that every lecturer strives to be competent in all facets of his or her duties, but it is not so obvious how to achieve this in all aspects of teaching. In exploring and developing approaches to teaching, staff may be tempted to revert to their related experience of the delivery of research papers. However, that approach may mean that the lecture is almost certainly pitched too fast, too high and too impersonally. Previous experience also comes into play, with new lecturers frequently relying upon a style in which they themselves were taught. Most can remember inspirational lecturers who made learning exciting and meaningful and whom they would like to emulate. It is unlikely however that they observed and reflected on that sufficiently analytically to be able to identify the elements that constituted the real magic.

BENEFITS

The observation process benefits both the observer and the observed. It is also a rare opportunity for an observer to see and analyse what students are actually doing. Participants on courses for new lecturers consistently rate feedback from teaching observations as the most valuable aspect of their learning and development of practice. For them it is an opportunity to validate what is working well, to exchange practical ideas, to solve problems and to explore and align practice with a developing understanding of theory, as well as to learn from the practice of others. It is an opportunity to gain confidence and competence. For both inexperienced and experienced staff, observation is a process that prompts them to question what they do and to apply an analytical approach to the development of their own teaching practice.

Observation offers:

- insight into what helps learners to learn and what happens in effective teaching sessions;
- feedback on individual teaching skills and style;
- discussion, collaboration and exchange of ideas;
- mutual support between colleagues;
- earmarked 'quality time' to talk about learning and teaching;
- feedback on piloting a new idea, method or solution to a problem;
- triangulation with other evaluative procedures, eg, student perception questionnaires, module and programme evaluations;
- focused reflection on specific teaching sessions;

- the opportunity in departments to broaden understanding of teaching in the discipline and the student learning experience;
- the opportunity to see exemplary practitioners at work.

Interrogating Practice

Who is regarded as a good teacher in your department? Ask that person if you can come and observe. (If you explain why, he or she will be flattered).

WHEN AND WITH WHOM

The right time to start having one's teaching observed is now. At any stage of a career there are things to be learnt, but this is especially true for the new lecturer who needs feedback, reassurance, tips, help and a chance to reflect on how reality is relating to theory. No one expects a new lecturer at the start of a career to be proficient immediately. New lecturers may find that as part of their probation, there is a requirement for them to have a number of teaching sessions observed and that systems are set up for observation by a **mentor**, staff/educational developer or course tutor from a training programme. It is also beneficial to set up a reciprocal arrangement for mutual observation with another new lecturer to share experience of teaching and learning in a less formal way. Observers should be selected to include those who can discuss and offer expertise in teaching the discipline, as well as comment on the communication with and engagement of the learners.

Interrogating Practice

You may wish to check the requirements for observation of teaching in your own department and, if you are on probation, as part of any initial training programme run by your college or university.

WHAT TO OBSERVE

There are as many answers to this question as there is variety in the role of the modern lecturer. Observation may take in lectures, tutorials, seminars, laboratory classes, fieldwork, creative workshops and teaching with patients. Commonly it is lectures that are observed, as much store is set on making them effective, especially as the size of lecture groups has increased. They offer a relatively short, contained, learning experience with specific **objectives** or **learning outcomes**, requiring a clear structure as well as clear communication and explanation.

ASPECTS FOR OBSERVATION

The features to be observed will vary according to the type of session and for the discipline concerned. For a typical lecture session (see Chapter 6), observers will note:

- the appropriateness and achievement of objectives / learning outcomes;
- communication of objectives to learners and links to prior knowledge;
- structure of the session, eg, an introduction, organization into sections and a summary;
- delivery – including pace, audibility, visibility;
- communication with students – including interaction, questioning and activities;
- the engagement of students in the learning process.

For most types of small group teaching activities, such as tutorials and seminars (see Chapter 7) an observer might note the:

- relationship of the session to the articulated objectives / learning outcomes;
- interaction of students with the tutor and each other;
- facilitation skills of the tutor, including engaging students, managing the group activity, questioning, listening, responding, prompting of critical and analytical thinking;
- involvement of all members of the group;
- encouragement of students;
- use of the teaching space;
- quality of formative feedback to students;
- provision for summing up and consolidating what has been learnt;
- ways in which students are helped to become aware of their own learning.

Interrogating Practice

When you next engage in an observation of a teaching activity in your discipline, either as the observed or the observer, what features of teaching that do not appear in the above list would you want to discuss?

PROCESS

At the University of Plymouth observation involves a four-stage process (ie, an initial discussion, the observation itself, a follow-up discussion meeting, production of a written record that may include a reflective response from the observed).

Stage 1: initial discussion

The discussion in advance of the session (in person, by phone or e-mail) provides the observer with:

- an understanding of the context of the session;
- information on the background of the students;
- the purpose and objectives of the session and how it relates to the rest of the student learning experience;
- any aspects on which the observed wants specific feedback;
- any relevant documents for the session, such as handout or case study material.

New lecturers often say they want feedback on 'anything and everything'. As they develop an awareness of their own practice, they become more specific.

Stage 2: observation

When undertaking an observation, the observer will normally arrive early and place him- or herself unobtrusively in the room, not becoming involved in the session. Unless it is a very large group, the observer's presence should be explained to the group. The observer will probably make notes, either chronologically or related to specific agreed criteria, or using a departmental or institutional pro forma (checklist) for the purpose. Many institutions have developed their own pro-formas for observation based upon the framework used in the former QAA Subject Review (QAA, 1997). An observational pro-forma from the

University of Plymouth is given in the appendix to this chapter. For other examples, see the Web pages at Centre for Academic Practice at Nottingham Trent University (www.celt.ntu.ac.uk/pages/pot.htm) and a SEDA paper on observation (Brown, Jones and Rawnsley, 1993).

It is helpful if the observer records some actual phrases or actions that can demonstrate what affected the learning or interaction in the session. The observer will watch both what the students do as well as what the lecturer does. It is sometimes feared that the presence of the observer influences the behaviour of the group. In the author's own institution, students have never reacted by playing up as is sometimes feared. On the contrary, groups may behave too well and not respond in as lively and interactive a way as normal.

Stage 3: follow-up discussion

Up to one hour may be required for the follow-up discussion, ideally immediately after the session (if impossible do it within 24 hours). This is probably the most valuable part of the process for both the observed and the observer. Almost regardless of their experience, the sharing of beliefs, values, approaches, interpretations, ideas, experiences and relationship to theory can create a rich and creative dialogue. However, if the discussion is not handled with sensitivity, it can be counter-productive, as will be discussed later.

Stage 4: record of the observation

A written record of the observation is usually given to the observed as a summary of the main points arising from the session, and might also include action points from the feedback discussion. The departmental or institutional pro-forma may commonly form the basis of this record. Observers should produce this record of the observation as soon as possible while their recall is still clear. The report writer should make specific notes of strengths so that the lecturer will continue to embody them, but also indicate what development needs would be worth focusing on next. At the University of Plymouth, the observed is then expected to make a written response to the observer's record, to comment on what he or she will do as a result and note any implications for his or her own continuing professional development. An alternative practice is to have the observed write his or her own summary record and development plan.

Confidentiality of records of observation can be a contentious issue and, in general, the record should be kept confidential to the observed and the observer. The observed may wish to include the record in his or her teaching portfolio (see Chapter 17). In some institutions, heads of departments may want to see records of their staffs' teaching observations, or at least an assurance that it has taken place. Also such records may become part of the agenda for **appraisal** discussions.

Practice in institutions will vary across the sector and local guidelines may place different amounts of emphasis on the stages, often combining the final two. The University of Bradford, for example, operates a three-stage scheme (Martin and Double, 1998).

Interrogating Practice

A great deal can be learnt from watching a selection of teaching sessions on video or DVD. Make observation notes for yourself using an approved pro-forma or checklist from your department or institution. If you can, borrow materials from your staff or educational development unit. The 1996 resource pack from the former **UCoSDA** (now **HESDA**) entitled 'Making the Grade' contains useful video clips and observational notes by experienced observers.

FEEDBACK

It is good practice to give the feedback as soon as possible after the observation. The observed is usually asked to comment on the session, to identify what went well and why, and reflect upon what went less well and why. It is important that the observer highlights the things that worked effectively.

There is always an element of nervousness about the giving and receiving of feedback. No matter how experienced one is, the feelings associated with feedback cannot be ignored. They become less of a concern when the purpose is clearly recognized as contributing to the development of both participants. There should be a shared intent and an awareness that it may also be a creative process leading to personal development by both sides. Embarrassment when working with colleagues can be reduced by agreeing ground rules for giving feedback and by the use of standard pro-formas for observational schedules.

Guidelines for giving feedback

Giving feedback to colleagues is a skill needed throughout an academic's professional life:

- Having got the observed to reflect first, the observer should start with the positive points – there are always positive elements. End on a positive note too.

- Focus on the behaviour that can be changed rather than the person. (This is where specific examples of what is said can help).
- Tailor the amount of feedback to what the observed can make use of at that time.
- Less effective aspects can be dealt with by factual objective comments, eg, 'When you turned to write on the board, I couldn't hear you at the back'. Alternatively, aspects could be posed as problems to solve, eg, 'There was a problem when you realized that time was running out and there were still things you wanted to cover. Have you any thoughts about how to deal with that?'
- Be constructive by making positive suggestions for improvement: there is no point giving feedback on something the observed can do nothing about, eg, to say, ' If you were to spend less time behind the lectern, it would be easier for the students to relate to you', is preferable to 'You're too short and no one can see you'.
- Avoid making value judgements, eg, reporting that, 'After the first 20 minutes of your main section, the students seemed to drift and become restless', is going to lead to more useful discussion than saying, 'You were really rather boring and went on in the same way for too long'.
- Use questions to guide the discussion and encourage the observed to reflect on practice and help develop an action plan, eg, 'What effect did you feel it had when you said that?', 'How do you think you could have involved them more in this?', 'How do you know if they achieved this objective?', 'What were you trying to achieve at this particular point?', 'How did you feel about this part?', 'How can you address this concern?'

Guidelines for receiving feedback

Receiving feedback is never easy:

- clarify what kind of feedback is going to be helpful to you;
- be prepared to accept honest and constructive criticism;
- explore ways to address any areas of less effective practice identified;
- ask for examples or ideas for other approaches;
- good feedback will lead naturally to the development of an action plan which may include observing another practitioner with known expertise in a particular area of teaching, further reading or a staff development session.

The University of Wisconsin has a Web site (www.wisc.edu/MOO/index.html) with useful information on peer observation of teaching as a means or developing teaching and it includes a list of characteristics of reflective feedback (www.wisc.edu/MOO/listfb.html).

OTHER MODELS AND INNOVATIONS

This chapter has so far concentrated on observation as it will affect new lecturers who may be involved in some initial formal training. However, in the case of established staff, 'peer observation' of teaching has become more prevalent across the sector, with self-selecting colleagues undertaking one or more observations on each other per year. Observation in pairs is the most common form, although staff may also work in triads, in which A observes B, who observes C, who observes A.

Alternatively, two members may observe a third, or one may observe the two others **team-teaching**. Jarzabkowski and Bone (1998) give some useful guidelines and checklists for peer observation. At Anglia Polytechnic University, a form has been specially developed to help the observer reap the full self-development potential from peer observation (Cosh, 1998). Clusters involve groups of four or five, each undertaking observations of at least one other member of the group. Smith (1998) describes a system whereby peer clusters come together to share and identify issues which have resulted in significant curricular change.

For some academic staff, video recording is the ultimate objective record of a teaching session. Despite fears that this may be intrusive in teaching, lecturers usually forget about the presence of a video camera in a teaching session within 10 minutes. It can be used as a self-appraisal process or shared with others in teaching process recall (Claydon and McDowell, 1993). Using this approach, the observed is very much in control of the replay initially, choosing the parts to show and seek comment on. With time and confidence, the lecturer invites more comprehensive feedback. This scheme is illustrated and demonstrated in a video pack produced by the University of Northumbria at Newcastle (Claydon and Edwards, 1995).

Case Study 1: Routine observation of teaching with a new lecturer

With a Probationary Lecturer in the School of Electronic and Electrical Communication Engineering, University of Plymouth

Context

The mentor was undertaking a third observation using a standard University pro-forma (see Appendix, page 237). The lecturer was incorporating aspects arising from previous observations, ie, to specify learning objectives at the start and to incorporate an in-class exercise. He had also requested feedback on interaction with students and on the use of an exercise.

From the observer's comments:

- Good 'route map' to the session but be careful about assumptions about how much the students actually know.
- You could be more positive in your responses to students. If you compliment them when they raise a good point or question, you will maintain good interaction.
- Your strengths include a clear voice (no need to shout), and a good sense of humour. The group activities worked very well, reinforcing the learning process. Don't be afraid to move around the group, checking their understanding and how they're getting on. The screen in this room is not good, so your overhead transparencies have to be very clear.

From the observed's reflective notes:

- I was pleased that aims, objectives and 'route-map' came over as sensible and I was glad to get positive feedback on the handouts and exercise. I hadn't been at all sure it would work with a group of 50.
- I'll try to remember to compliment students for asking their own questions as well as for answering mine.
- I hadn't realized the problem with the screen; it's good to be made aware of it. I'll watch the time more carefully to allow for questions at the end.
- There were a lot of suggestions on general factors that will help my overall performance, as opposed to simply enhancing the future delivery of this particular lecture.

OVERVIEW

The use of observation of teaching has become an established part of practice in teaching and learning in higher education. Observation is common in initial training programmes for new lecturers. Observing, being observed and reflecting offers a fast track to confidence and improved performance. Peer observation is becoming embedded into institution's systems for quality enhancement through quality review processes. For many staff it is a standard item for discussion on their appraisal agenda. Observation of teaching is more acceptable and useful when it is used for formative development and leads to dialogue and lively debate rather than in summative assessment. Paying attention to how to give and receive feedback is crucial. As observation becomes more widely established, a greater range of models and means of recording practice is emerging. The more common the practice becomes, the less self-conscious staff feel about their teaching being observed and the sooner all parties will benefit from the dialogue, reflection and enhanced practice generated. There is now a growing body of experience gained in peer observation from across the sector which can be shared between institutions. For example, Gosling (2001) discusses advantages and principles and Cove and Lisewski (2001) put forward a code of conduct.

REFERENCES

Brown, S, Jones, G and Rawnsley, S (1993) *Observing Teaching* (SEDA Paper 79), Staff and Educational Development Association, Birmingham

Claydon, A and Edwards, A (1995) *Teaching Process Recall: A user's guide*, Educational Development Service, University of Northumbria at Newcastle

Claydon, T and McDowell, L (1993) *Watching Yourself Teach and Learning from it*, Paper in *Observing Teaching*, (SEDA Paper 79), Staff and Educational Development Association, Birmingham

Cosh, J, (1998) Peer observation in higher education: a reflective approach, *Innovations in Education and Training International*, 35, pp 171–76

Cove, G and Lisewski, B (2001) *Peer Observation for Teaching: Code of conduct in peer observation of teaching: taking it beyond surveillance*, University of Salford, Salford

Gosling, D. (2001) *Guidelines for Peer Observation of Learning and Teaching*, www.escalate.ac.uk/briefing/briefing 01

Jarzabkowski, P and Bone, Z (1998) A 'how-to' guide and checklist for peer appraisal of teaching, *Innovations in Education and Training International*, 35, pp 177–82

Martin, G A and Double, J M (1998) Developing higher education teaching skills through peer observation and collaborative reflection, *Innovations in Education and Training International*, 35, pp 161–70

Quality Assurance Agency for Higher Education (QAA) (1997) *Subject Review Handbook, October 1998 to September 2000*, QAA, Gloucester

Smith, B (1998) Adopting a strategic approach to managing change in learning and teaching, in *To Improve the Academy*, ed M Kaplan, 17, pp 225–42, New Forum Press and the Professional and Organizational Development Network in Higher Education, Stillwater, Oklahoma

FURTHER READING AND VIEWING

Brown, S, Jones, G and Rawnsley, S (1993). See above. A particularly good source of advice on setting up the process; establishing ground rules and examples of different pro-formas and checklists, including self-assessment forms.

Claydon, A and Edwards, A (1995) See above. An illustrative video with a booklet explaining the TPR procedure. This would be particularly useful for a small group of new lecturers working together on observing practice. Online at www.ltsn.genericcentre.projects/cpd/london/pres%20-%20June(BL).ppt.

Gosling, D. (2001) See above. This site discusses groupings, principles, structure, advice and proofreads for observation and departmental action plans.

UCoSDA (1996) *Making the Grade: Achieving high quality assessment profiles, video and use guidebook,* Universities' and Colleges' Staff Development Agency, Sheffield. This very useful package includes two videotapes containing 10 recorded examples of teaching in a range of disciplines. The accompanying book includes examples of forms formerly used in teaching quality assessment for observation and comments by assessors.

USEFUL URLS

www.celt.ntu.ac.uk/se/observ/html – Peer observation of teaching: a range of forms for observation.

www.ltsn.genericcentre.projects/peer-ob/ – Peer observation of teaching: general overview including general updates and national and international perspectives.

www.wisc.edu/MOO/index.html – Peer review of teaching at University of Wisconsin, Madison.

APPENDIX: OBSERVATION FORM FROM THE UNIVERSITY OF PLYMOUTH

This form is designed primarily for working with new lecturers. The person to be observed completes the front sheet, the observer completes the middle two sheets after the follow-up discussion and the lecturer completes the final page, after reflection.

Observation of Teaching and Learning

Please complete this side before the session commences

Name	Date
Observer	Venue
Group	Start time
Number of students	Length of observation
Type of session	Time of feedback

Aim
*In terms of **your** aims and relationship to module descriptor*

Objectives
*What are the specific learning objectives planned for the **students** (eg knowledge and understanding, key skills, cognitive skills, and subject-specific, including practical/ professional skills)?*

Outcomes
*How **students** will benefit in the longer term from this and the related learning experiences*

Any particular factors/problems taken into account when planning the session?

Any aspects of the session which are new to you?

How have you incorporated suggestions made previously (if applicable) from any recent development?

Are there any particular aspects you would like feedback on?

Observer's comments

The breakdown of each category (in italics) is a guide to the observer as to aspects for comment and discussion. They are not intended to be comprehensive, and not all need be covered every time. Different disciplines will have additional aspects to consider.

Teaching characteristics -- Comments

1 Planning and start of session

Appropriateness of aims, objectives and outcomes. Communication of these to students. Orientation eg aims, objectives, 'route map'. Continuity with other sessions and students' prior knowledge.

2 Presentation

Structure. Relevance and organization of content. Attitude to subject matter. Clarity of presentation. Emphasis of key points. Pace of session. Summary (end and/or interim). Student follow-up work etc.

3 Student participation

Question and answer technique. Exercisers/activities. Class management. Instructions to students. General class atmosphere. Level of participation and interaction between students. Attention and interest. Attitude to students. Awareness of individual needs. Evaluative procedures. Student–teacher rapport.

Observer's comments (continued)

Teaching characteristics -- comments

---

4 Methods and approaches
Choice/variety of teaching/learning methods. Use of OHP and/or other technologies, board, handouts, real examples and other linked materials etc. Use of appropriate reinforcement. Examples and analogies. Emphasis of key points. References and links to research.

5 General
Were the objectives achieved? Appropriateness of teaching/learning methods. Was effective communication achieved? Awareness of needs of learners and differences in approach? Any accommodation problems?

6 Future areas of focus

7 Strengths

Course member's notes about observation

Name:
Please complete and return this page to your observer after your post-session discussion

What have you found helpful about the observation process?

In the light of comments are you likely to adapt any approaches? What further reading or formal or informal staff development would help?

Any further comments about the session and observation?

Teaching portfolios

Heather Fry and Steve Ketteridge

DEFINITION

A teaching portfolio (sometimes referred to in this chapter as a '**portfolio**') is a personal record of achievement and professional development as a university teacher. It is a carefully selected and structured collection of material that may demonstrate a level of attainment, a range of skills and activity, and/or progression.

Portfolios can be assembled for different purposes, generally: for use in summative assessment, as part of a qualification or programme of study; and/or to demonstrate achievement for purposes such as passing through probation, promotion and continuing professional development (CPD).The distinction between these two types of portfolios can sometimes be blurred, but it is a helpful aid to discussion of construction and related issues.

It is usual for portfolios to conform to a structure specified by an institution or external professional body. Many readers of this chapter may be involved in preparing a portfolio that may directly or indirectly lead to becoming a member or associate of the Institute for Learning and Teaching (ILT). Ideally portfolio material should be purposefully collected over a period of time, but in other circumstances may be assembled immediately prior to submission. Increasingly a portfolio is expected to include some form of specially prepared commentary – this is especially so for a portfolio created for summative assessment.

BACKGROUND

Teaching portfolios are nothing new. One of the pioneers of the teaching portfolio was Queen's University, Canada, where they were introduced in the 1970s (Kappa, 1995). Since then their use has spread across the United States, where it has been estimated that by the mid-1990s some 500 colleges and universities were experimenting with the use of teaching portfolios or 'dossiers' (Seldin, Annis and Zubizarreta, 1995). Their usage has extended to other English speaking countries, notably Australia (Weeks, 1996). In the UK the work of Gibbs, while he was at Oxford Brookes University, focused attention on the value of portfolios (Gibbs, 1988). For a comprehensive review on portfolios with an emphasis on the development of practice and their use in promotion and probation decisions, see Seldin (1997).

The teaching portfolio provides a means of illustrating the experience and expertise of a university teacher. It is comparable with the types of portfolio that are produced by many professions, for example the professional development records assembled by those seeking membership of the Institution of Electrical Engineers or Royal Institution of Chartered Surveyors. We are all familiar with the concept of demonstrating achievement in research, typically through publication and securing successful grant funding, coupled with subsequent listing in the curriculum vitae. The portfolio provides a comparable means of documenting activity for supporting student learning, which can also be subjected to feedback and review by colleagues. Nicholls (2001) provides an interesting overview of the contemporary approach to developing professionalism in teaching and research, including a discussion of the nature of scholarship and the role of professional bodies, such at the ILT.

The portfolio has come to prominence in the UK in recent years as competence in teaching has risen up the policy agenda. The portfolio is not a confidential document, and it is usually open to scrutiny by panels, assessors and peers. Portfolios may contain sensitive information (eg, about the learning support provided to a particular student, or, in the case of practice-based learning, about patient care, or the requirements of a professional client) that requires data to be anonymized and infringement of data protection rights to be avoided.

PORTFOLIO CONTENTS

Guidelines on the precise structure and contents of a portfolio are usually provided by an institution or professional body. It is vital in construction to follow these, whether for summative assessment or other purposes. There may be requirements to submit materials in different categories and/or of different types in order to ensure spread, comprehensiveness and comparability. Typically a portfolio will have three components:

- an index or map of the portfolio;
- a collection of selected, illustrative material drawn from practice and providing evidence of it;
- a commentary discussing the evidence.

The balance between the three elements may vary considerably depending upon the purpose of the portfolio, its requirements and the nature and concerns of different disciplines. Typically the second and third components listed above will be sub-divided to reflect the purpose and/or required structure of the portfolio. The requirements for passing probation, achieving success on an ILT accredited programme and for promotion (eg, to a higher lecturer grade) are likely to involve different portfolio structures.

Map of the portfolio

A 'map' is provided to enable the reader to find the things they are looking for in the portfolio. Typically they will be looking to see that the portfolio supports a claim that is being made. This claim may be that certain specified outcomes or values are demonstrated in the portfolio (eg, on a programme accredited by the ILT), or that certain things have been included (eg, in a portfolio being used for promotion purposes). A 'map' may be a separate document or table that guides the reader through all or part of the portfolio, pointing out where the required things can be found. Alternatively, the reader may be guided by means of sign-posts or comments placed within the evidence and/or commentary.

Materials drawn from practice

A teaching portfolio requires the inclusion of authentic pieces of evidence about the teaching and support for learning of the practitioner. This evidence is not created just for the portfolio, but is a part of everyday practice. It is useful to put the evidence into context for the reader, for example by mentioning the courses, modules and units taught. Types of materials which might comprise 'the evidence' include, in no particular order:

- self-authored documents such as study guides or **programme specifications**;
- module descriptions including aims and **objectives/outcomes**;
- session plans, or planning notes;
- records of supervisory meetings;
- Web-based learning resources;
- **problem-based learning** triggers;
- AV materials, eg, handouts from PowerPoint presentations;
- student handouts or workbooks;
- documentation to support practical teaching;
- instruments for assessment of student learning;
- summary of examination results;

- student evaluations – instruments, views and results;
- quality assurance reports;
- external examiners' reports;
- examples of student work;
- video, audio, DVD and photographic material;
- self-authored **C&IT** materials;
- self-created learning resources such as models;
- printouts of electronic communications;
- written evidence of observed teaching sessions;
- details of courses and workshops attended on teaching and learning;
- educational publications;
- list of recent professional development activities undertaken.

Interrogating Practice

Using the above list, and thinking of your own teaching, identify six specific pieces of evidence you could present to illustrate your own practice. How will you keep a record of this and make sure you will have the evidence to hand in the future?

Commentary

The commentary part of a portfolio may take many forms and it is this section which is must likely to differ according to purpose and institution. For those using a portfolio as part of summative assessment, the commentary has to elaborate on the evidence, by placing it, linking it to specific themes, referring to literature and showing that practice is a product of informed and considered thought. The latter aspect is often called **reflection**.

Reflection involves looking back on practice, justifying methods and approaches, formulating amendments, and taking action to enhance practice. It has not been a tradition in academia for thoughts, arguments and reasoned actions to be articulated in this way and it is for this reason that this part of the portfolio presents a particular challenge. However, in reality this process is one that professionals use all the time when they make a discriminating choice about a course of action – even if it means not making a change, whether in teaching or research. The challenge is to tease out the reasons and present them in a scholarly, written format. Lyons (1998) surveys some experiences of staff developing as reflective practitioners.

Reflection in its fullest sense is more than description; it involves self-evaluation and analysis, making it a higher level cognitive skill. As a result of reflection, action is taken to enhance personal practice and to demonstrate a response to feedback from students and peers. Reflection is an integral part of enhancement of the quality of learning and teaching.

It is important in a portfolio to ensure that written reflection goes beyond the level of simple description. Mezirow (1992) makes this point by talking about three different ways of reflecting:

- content reflection will show evidence of discriminating thought that distinguishes between beliefs and evidence in reasoning about change;
- process reflection will show consideration of success of the strategies (routes/changes/etc) adopted to solve a problem;
- premise reflection will show questioning of the underlying relevance or validity of the problem itself.

Such categorizations offer pointers towards the types or levels of things that assessors will be seeking in a Masters level portfolio. In this context the demonstration of reflection is one way of showing the exercise of higher level thinking skills in relation to practice, by displaying powers of discrimination, evaluation and synthesis and thereby the exercise of professional judgement.

Interrogating Practice

As a start towards getting into a reflective frame, think about the last piece of teaching you did. List: (i) the aspects that seemed to go well; (ii) the things that didn't seem to work quite as well as expected; (iii) how you might change the latter and why.

In the commentary authors should demonstrate familiarity with common educational concepts and principles and with an understanding of the norms and best practice of teaching and learning within their discipline. (Much good practice is illustrated in Part 3 of this book.)

A commentary can be organized in a number of different ways. These may include detailed discussion of one particular course from a number of perspectives, consideration of a number of themes, organization around the outcomes that are required to be demonstrated, a story to be told, or simply commentary on the pieces of evidence. Commentaries may also include or even be based upon a critical incident analysis. Another common inclusion is extracts from a reflective diary or log, or reflection on the process of feedback from observation of teaching. Sometimes a commentary might include reports of action research.

The commentary will often need to include a statement setting out your CPD needs, arising from an analysis of your own strengths and weaknesses.

PORTFOLIO BUILDING

The key action in building a portfolio is starting to collect the material for the evidence section. Selective and discriminating choice from this material may come at a later stage. All universities will have preferred or required guidelines for the portfolio and these have to be another starting point for portfolio work. Another key step is thinking about how you will organize the commentary – will it be around themes, for example, or around any outcomes you may be demonstrating. Another factor to consider is how you will handle material that may have been jointly written by yourself and a colleague; again, consulting institutional guidelines will be vital.

In most cases where a portfolio is being produced for a summative purpose there will be some support provided by the institution; this may be through a 'critical friend', through receiving feedback on a draft, through learning sets, etc. Other key points to take into account are as follows:

- Be clear about the requirements and criteria pertaining in your institution.
- Check the deadlines for submission.
- Start collecting representative documents from your first day as a university teacher.
- Look at existing portfolio examples where they are available.
- Participate in any preparatory workshops your institution may offer.
- Discuss your portfolio with your mentor/adviser/tutor.
- Acknowledge any joint contributions.
- Be discriminating in final selection – the issue is quality, not quantity.
- Do not include 'time expired' material.
- Ensure the commentary takes an analytical and scholarly approach.
- Comply with any requirements to prove authenticity of material.
- Present the portfolio and its contents professionally.

Case Study 1: Reflections upon the writing of a teaching portfolio

The case study sets out the reflections of a lecturer in law on her experience of having created a portfolio as part of a postgraduate certificate in teaching at South Bank University.

A portfolio is a rare form of assessment in that the product is a genuine illustration of the learning process achieved. I found myself experiencing satisfaction in being able to see what I had learnt about teaching and learning while I was preparing the portfolio. Now it is one of the few pieces of work upon which I have been assessed and enjoy reading again.

For me, one of the most difficult points was in knowing how to start the portfolio. The other was deciding when the work was ended.

So, how to begin? Some words of advice that I had been given rang impatiently in my ears: 'Don't leave your portfolio until the last minute!' The hunt for some positive ideas on how to begin led me to consider writing a reflective diary. This would be my personal record of the main events occurring in each week's teaching and learning, and my reflections upon them.

Shunning technology for once, I requisitioned a large stationery book from the stationery cupboard and started writing, adding to the diary every week or so. At the end of the first semester, I researched through the diary for proof that I have achieved each of the learning outcomes for the unit before writing up my thoughts for the assessors. This part of the process was not so much writing (although there was plenty of that) but of thinking about what it was important to write.

I did not know when the task was finished, but I soon realized that a portfolio is never completed as long as you are developing as a teacher, so that any ending must be self-imposed. I stopped writing the portfolio in time for the deadline for its submission.

(Penny White)

NON-PAPER-BASED PORTFOLIOS

Recent years have seen a proliferation of the media used to deliver teaching: DVDs, CD ROMs, video, Web- or audio-based materials are increasingly common. Some portfolio evidence will therefore not be suited to paper-based format, and portfolios will need to include evidence in various media. Indeed, some portfolio authors may be so comfortable with C&IT that they will wish to present their entire portfolio over the Web or on a CD. Case Study 2 considers the advantages and difficulties of online portfolios and concludes with guidelines for authors of electronic portfolios developed at one institution.

Case Study 2: Online portfolios at Queen Mary, University of London

Staff, particularly those who use the Web in their teaching, may want to produce and submit a portfolio online.

The advantages of online portfolios:

- If authors already use the Web in teaching, they can easily link to existing Web materials as evidence.
- A portfolio is a cross-referential document, and so is suited to the flexible, non-linear structure of hyperlinked pages.
- An online portfolio is accessible from different locations.
- An online portfolio is adaptable to other needs as candidates continues their career; as a portable professional record it can remain 'live' longer than a paper copy.

Some issues to be overcome are listed below, with possible solutions suggested after each point:

- Submission date. If candidates have access to their portfolio's Web space, they may be tempted to change content after submission, which may lead to discrepancies between versions seen by various assessors. (Require CD copies of online portfolio, or set up a temporary ftp account for the candidate, access to which closes after submission date.)
- Privacy. If the portfolio is on the Web any sensitive personal information is theoretically open to the world. (Allow candidates to submit confidential information on supplementary CD, or create a secure, password-protected area for the portfolio to reside.)
- Access. If the portfolio is on an institution's intranet, there will be access problems for external assessors. (Require candidates to supply an additional CD, or assessing department burns a CD.)

- Permanence. The portfolio may be hosted on the author's Web space, and liable to be changed, moved or removed, making it difficult to keep a permanent record as may be required. (CD copy, as above.)
- Readers' Web skills. The Web may be unfamiliar territory for some readers, and still others may be used to annotating documents as they read them. (Prepare a basic 'Web skills' training document.)

A workable solution?

Educational and Staff Development at Queen Mary, University of London considered the practical possibilities of the above factors and arrived at the following guidelines for those offering portfolios for the Postgraduate Certificate in Academic Practice:

Guidelines for electronic portfolios

Candidates may submit their portfolio in electronic format, either on a CD or online. If the portfolio is delivered online, candidates must also provide two copies of the portfolio in its finished form on CD. The CD or CD case must display the name of the candidate, the date of submission, and, if it is online, the URL where the portfolio may be found. Online portfolios should not be altered after they have been submitted, and before the assessment is complete; ie, during the assessment period they should bear the same content as the CD copy marked with the submission date. There must be clear instructions about how to access the first page of the portfolio from the CD.

Evidential material that is on the WWW and hyperlinked does not need to appear on the CD, but should do so if it is liable to move or change over the assessment period. If such material is maintained by the author (eg, course material he or she has put on the Web) the author is responsible for ensuring that it does not change or move during the assessment period. Evidential material on the College intranet must be included on the CD.

The candidate may include confidential material on a supplementary CD or on paper.

(Sam Brenton)

ASSESSMENT BY PORTFOLIO

Portfolios generally have reasonably high **validity**; however, because they are so individual and may only be examined by two or three assessors, they generally have poor **reliability**. Generally, universities are still getting to grips with portfolio assessment procedures that would be entirely defensible. Some of the tensions and unresolved issues associated with portfolio assessment have been reviewed elsewhere (Fry and Ketteridge, 1999). This is an area of ongoing research. One of the studies published to date (Baume and Yorke, 2002) describes an investigation of the reliability of assessors of teaching portfolios at an Open University programme to accredit teachers in higher education. One useful message from this work is the need to train assessors, building up a shared understanding of the task in hand and applying the assessment criteria.

The provision of clear and open specifications, criteria for assessment and a specified structure help to make portfolios a fairer method of assessment. Criteria may include requirements for minimum and maximum lengths or word counts relating to specific sections. Criteria may also specify the outcomes to be met by the author. There may also be descriptors of levels of attainment, for example as relating to pass/fail. Many institutions, at present, when making summative decisions, will opt for a threshold judgement of either satisfactory completion or referral, rather than attempt finer grades of judgement.

As with all assessment decisions, there is an element of balance to be struck between the form of the assessment, its purpose and how it will be judged. With the university teaching portfolio, the **formative** educational value of producing a portfolio, its relative feasibility and the validity of its content may overshadow issues of reliability.

Interrogating Practice

If you do not know, find out the points in your career at which your institution may require you to present a teaching portfolio. Does your institution have guidelines on the structure and nature of portfolios for different purposes?

OVERVIEW

Teaching portfolios are becoming commonplace, as they represent a tangible means of demonstrating competence and professionalism. Producing a portfolio has become a normal activity, with most institutions providing frameworks for the portfolio. The most difficult aspects of portfolio building are writing the reflective commentary and discriminating choice of evidence. Institutions are rapidly gaining experience in the summative assessment of portfolios. Experience gained in producing a portfolio early in one's career is good preparation for later usage in connection with applications for promotion, or to present to prospective employers to demonstrate evidence of one's teaching expertise. Increasingly portfolios are becoming used to document CPD.

REFERENCES

Baume, D and Yorke, M (2002) The reliability of assessment by portfolio on a course to develop and accredit teachers in higher education, *Studies in Higher Education*, **27** (1), pp 7–25

Fry, H and Ketteridge, S W (1999) Developing teaching in undergraduate medical and dental schools: introduction of teaching portfolios in the context of a national requirement programme, in *Selected Proceedings*, 8th Ottawa Conference on Medical Education, Philadelphia

Gibbs, G (1988) *Creating a Teaching Portfolio*, Technical and Educational Services Ltd, Bristol

Lyons, N (1998) Portfolios and their consequences: developing as a reflective practitioner, in *With Portfolio in Hand: Validating the new teacher professionalism*, ed N Lyons, pp 247–64, Teachers College Press, Columbia University, New York

Kappa, C (1995) The origins of teaching portfolios, *Journal of Excellence in College Teaching*, **6** (1), pp 5–56

Mezirow, J (1992) *Transformative Dimensions of Adult Learning*, Jossey-Bass, San Francisco

Nicholls, G (2001) *Professional Development in Higher Education*, Kogan Page, London

Seldin, P (1997) *The Teaching Portfolio*, 2nd edn, Anker Publishing Company, Bolton, Massachusetts

Seldin, P, Annis, I, Zubizarreta, J (1995) Answers to common questions about the teaching portfolio, *Journal of Excellence in College Teaching*, **6** (1), pp 57–64

Weeks, P (1996) The teaching portfolio: a professional development tool, *International Journal for Academic Development*, **1** (1), pp 70–74

FURTHER READING

Newble, D and Cannon, R (1994) *A Handbook for Medical Teachers*, Kluwer Publishers, London. Contains a useful appendix on constructing a portfolio that can easily be used in many disciplines.

Seldin, P (1997) See above. Contains many examples of portfolio material from different disciplines, but embedded in the US system.

Part 3
Working in
discipline-specific areas

<table>
<tr><td>18</td></tr>
</table>

Key aspects of teaching and learning in experimental sciences and engineering

Tina Overton

INTRODUCTION

The aim of this chapter is to explore the distinctive features of learning and teaching in the experimental sciences and engineering. Staff working in chemistry, physics, biological sciences, environmental sciences, materials and all branches of engineering should find this chapter useful.

This chapter will review the context, issues and methods that are particularly relevant in science and engineering. It extends and updates the review by Kate Exley (1999) in the first edition of this Handbook, which is still of relevance to readers in these disciplines.

CONTEXT

While in many disciplines curricula may be developed entirely by academic staff, within experimental sciences and engineering the curricula, and even learning and teaching methods, may often be determined to some extent by professional bodies. Some professional bodies accredit or recognize undergraduate programmes in a fairly liberal way, **accreditation** indicating that the **programme of study** meets certain minimum standards. Other professional bodies are much more active in their interaction with higher education and their accreditation of programmes may be vital for the future professional practice of graduates. In these cases, professional bodies may determine entry standards to undergraduate programmes, may lay down detailed curricula, may insist on certain methods of assessment and may even specify minimum requirements for practical work or projects. Clearly, some of these issues can have an impact on what and how we teach. In addition to such professional requirements are the **QAA Subject Benchmarking** statements (QAA 2000–02), which may or may not co-exist easily alongside accreditation requirements.

Interrogating practice

Do you work in a discipline in which curricula are influenced by the requirements of a professional body? What is the attitude of that relevant professional body to the accreditation of undergraduate programmes? What specific requirements must be in place for your programmes to be accredited? How does this affect your teaching?

A major challenge for science and engineering departments is the recruitment of undergraduate students. Science and engineering subjects are increasingly seen as 'difficult' and 'unattractive' to young people. At present, many branches of science and engineering may look unfashionable alongside the plethora of emerging new disciplines. Accordingly the rise in student numbers during the last two decades has not been matched by a proportionate rise in numbers within these disciplines (Institute of Physics, 2001). The proportion of students studying science AS and A2 courses is decreasing and unless this issue is addressed, institutions will be recruiting from an ever-decreasing pool of potential applicants. In many cases, inevitably, this means that entry grades are falling and less well-prepared students are studying these demanding subjects. This has serious implications for curriculum design, approaches to learning and teaching, systems for student support and retention, especially in the early stages of study.

Another important issue which directly affects teaching and learning in the sciences and engineering is the mathematical preparedness of undergraduates. The decline in the mathematical ability of young people is well researched and documented (eg, The Engineering Council, 2000). Even students with good A2 grades may struggle with the mathematical aspects of physics and engineering. The recruitment pressures mentioned above mean that increasingly departments have to accept students who have not achieved AS or A2 mathematics. To remedy this, supplementary mathematics courses have to be offered to students. This presents its own problems, as students can become disillusioned by being presented with a demanding mathematics course in their first few weeks in the institution, when this is not their chosen discipline. The provision of mathematics support for undergraduates is itself an important topic and is beyond the scope of this chapter (but see also Chapter 12). Useful ideas and resources on mathematics support for students can be obtained from the Learning and Teaching Support Network (LTSN) Subject Centres.

During the 1990s, science and engineering disciplines, with support from professional bodies, developed the 'enhanced' undergraduate degree, sometimes referred to as an 'undergraduate Masters' programme. These M level courses grew out of a need for more time at undergraduate level to produce scientists and engineers who can compete on the international stage. Arguments for these new programmes were variously based upon the need to include more 'cutting edge' engagement in the later stages of the programme and the need to address the weaker science base of new entrants to higher education. These M level programmes, eg, MChem, MPhys, MEng, MSci, etc, have grown rapidly and have developed in variety of ways. Many remain similar to the BSc/BEng with a substantial project and some **transferable skills** development in the final year. Other departments have adopted a '2 plus 2' approach, with a common first and second year for all students and then quite distinctive routes for year 3 of the BSc and years 3 and 4 of the M level programme. Many departments only offer the M level undergraduate programme. In other institutions, the M programme is offered alongside a traditional BSc/BEng. In this case there are issues related to the distinctiveness of the Bachelors and Masters routes and the need to avoid portraying the BSc as a second-rate degree. Where both Bachelors and Masters programmes co-exist, they should have distinctive outcomes, thereby having implications for curriculum design and learning, teaching and assessment methods.

Consequently, the environment faced by many new academics coming into the teaching of science and engineering disciplines in higher education is one in which there are challenges in the recruitment of well-qualified students, erosion of mathematical skills and, in some cases, curricula influenced to a large extent by external bodies.

LEARNING AND TEACHING

Some learning and teaching methods are particularly important to sciences and engineering and are discussed in some detail here. Others, such as the lecture, tutorial or seminar, are well covered in generic terms in earlier chapters (see Chapters 6 and 7). A particular feature of the disciplines represented in this chapter is that they are heavily content driven which has led to overloaded curricula as the knowledge base has expanded without any material being removed

The lecture

The lecture is still the main way of delivering 'content' in science and engineering. The lecture format in sciences and engineering has changed in recent years, as many lecturers have introduced more opportunities for student interaction, participation and activities.

Curricula in sciences and engineering are also predominantly linear in nature. Commonly there are basic underpinning concepts that have to be mastered before further study can be considered. This is not always the case in other disciplines where modules and courses can be placed in almost any year, the level being determined by how the topic is approached rather than the 'level' of the content itself.

Interrogating practice

What are the aims and objectives of your next lecture? What do want your students to learn? Design one short activity in which your students can participate during the lecture.

Small group teaching

The **tutorial** is still much in evidence within science and engineering disciplines, although it is increasingly under pressure as group sizes grow. This can be a difficult form of teaching for new staff and suggestions on how to promote engagement and participation in tutorials is given in Chapter 7. Small group teaching can be particularly challenging in sciences where the discipline itself does not always present obvious points for discussion and students often think there is a single correct answer to a given problem. If problem-solving is an aspect of small group work, then it is worth designing open-ended or 'fuzzy' problems to which there may not be a single correct answer. This provides opportunities for students to discuss multiple responses rather than simply working out where they 'went wrong'. It is worth trying to identify problems and topics that provide such opportunities. This is not always easy and there are several publications related to this issue which may be of interest (eg, Garratt, Overton and Threlfall, 1999).

Interrogating Practice

List the aims of your next tutorial. What do you hope your students will learn? What strategies will you use to promote active participation by your students?

Problem-based learning

Whilst much teaching in science and engineering is fairly conventional in approach, there are some significant new developments, such as **problem-based learning** (PBL), notably in engineering. PBL is a style of learning in which the problems act as the context and driving force for learning (Boud and Feletti, 1998). All learning of new knowledge is done within the context of the problems. PBL differs from 'problem solving' in that in PBL the problems are encountered before all the relevant knowledge has been acquired and solving problems results in the acquisition of knowledge and problem-solving skills. In problem-solving, the knowledge acquisition has usually already taken place and the problems serve as a means to explore or enhance that knowledge.

PBL is well established in medical education (Chapter 23). It has spread across other practice-based, health-related disciplines and is now being adopted in other 'professional' disciplines such as engineering. It has also extended to other science-based disciplines.

It is claimed that a PBL approach:

- produces better-motivated students;
- develops a deeper understanding of the subject;
- encourages independent and collaborative learning;
- develops higher order cognitive skills;
- develops a range of skills including problem-solving, group working, critical analysis and communication.

The curriculum is organized around the problems. So problems have to be carefully matched to the desired learning outcomes. In PBL, students work in groups to solve the problems. There are no lectures, instead students engage in self-directed learning and the tutor acts as a **facilitator**, mentor or guide.

There are some disadvantages of using a wholly PBL approach. The content covered in this way is reduced, compared to the amount that can be covered in lecture-based courses. In terms of staff input, PBL takes more staff time than traditional methods because the group sizes have to be restricted. A PBL session with 200 students in a lecture theatre doesn't work! Many institutions may be short of the sort of space that helps PBL to work well – flat seminar rooms with movable furniture. Such group work may suffer from non-participation or personality clashes and strategies have to be put in place to ensure effective group working.

Problems that are used for PBL should address curriculum objectives, be real and engaging, be 'fuzzy' and place the group in a professional role, ie, as scientists or engineers. Students should be required to: develop a problem-solving strategy, acquire new knowledge and make judgements, approximations and deal with omitted/excess information. It is not a trivial task to develop effective 'problems' for PBL, but many academics think the initial investment is worth the effort (Overton, 2001). Case Study 1 describes the introduction of PBL into engineering programmes at the University of Manchester.

Case Study 1: The advent of PBL in engineering

University of Manchester

From September 2001, the Manchester School of Engineering (MSE) adopted PBL as the primary teaching method in its undergraduate programmes. While PBL itself is not innovative, its application to engineering and in particular to the first year of an engineering degree course is. MSE is the first School of Engineering in the UK to adopt this radical approach, which has involved a transformational cultural change.

Students progress through the programme by solving simple, contextual problems. In the first year of the course these problems are designed to reinforce the learning process, rather than to ensure total coverage of material. Later in the course, when students have developed their learning skills, problems typically become more knowledge focused.

Within a PBL activity, students work systematically on problem scenarios in groups of eight. Each group has a base room containing a computer and printer, lockable filing cabinet and flip chart. Typical problem scenarios can range from one day to two weeks in duration. The group appoints a chairperson and a scribe and then begins to analyse the problem and works towards defining a problem statement.

The students are monitored by an academic facilitator whose role is to guide the group towards achieving the intended learning outcomes for the problem, as determined by the PBL designers. In addition, the facilitator will also deal with any group issues that cannot be resolved by the group themselves. During the early PBL activities in the first year, students are required to adapt to the method and there is a great deal of intensive contact with the facilitator at the beginning, However, as time progresses the students begin to work more independently, eventually becoming less aware of the facilitator in most cases.

The students attend facilitated meetings a minimum of three times a week, but the timetable also incorporates expert forums and workshop sessions, which provide extra guidance. During meetings, the students present the findings of their research to the rest of the group and pool their knowledge. Here they take on the role of teaching one another, helping colleagues and at the same time reinforcing their own learning. Everybody is under pressure to contribute since the students are mutually dependent on each other's information. This approach requires students to plan, and reach agreement through negotiation and self-discipline. Continual self-evaluation is encouraged, and the students keep a reflective log known as a learning journal as part of their Personal and Academic Development Plan (PADP). For the duration of the PBL exercise, students keeps a record of their own notes, teaching materials received from other group members, and a reflective commentary on their own progress. This commentary includes personal skills acquired through team working and may also include the roles played by individuals in the group, how well the group stuck to the task, time management, and how the group resolved differences.

Assessment is managed using a range of group and individual tasks. These include a multiple choice test (MCQ), presentations, Web-page design, report writing test and demonstrations. The students' PADP forms part of the assessment as a record of process, reflection and peer assessment, and of the knowledge acquired during the PBL period and the application of that knowledge.

Since the move to PBL has brought with it a culture change for staff as well as students, facilitators have met once a week to share experience and best practice, and to provide a rapid response to problems that arise in sessions. An outcome of PBL is that staff are working much more in teams than in the more traditional lecture-based system. Members of academic staff also have the opportunity to act as advisors during the development of new PBL exercises, and are aware of the material being developed by their colleagues.

(Beverley Hopping)

Industrial work experience

Embedded, credit-bearing, **work-based learning** is increasingly a feature of many science and engineering programmes, especially in year 4 of Masters programmes (see also Chapter 10). The period of work experience can vary from a few months, or a whole semester to a full year. Employers value work experience very highly and students who return from industrial placement are generally highly motivated and have developed a range of transferable and personal skills. However, industrial experience has to be meaningful if it is to be credit bearing and employers have to be chosen carefully and partnerships developed between the institution and the employer. Many academic departments have identified members of staff who are responsible for building partnerships with employers, placing students and supporting them during their work placement. The aims of the work experience have to be clear to both parties. If the placement is credit bearing, then there have to be tangible outcomes that can be assessed (Murray and Wallace, 2000).

Key stages in a successful work placement scheme include the following.

Finding the placement

A departmental system in which an industrial training tutor makes initial contact with industry, and maintains a coordinating role, will provide the best service to students and companies, and will encourage a partnership approach.

The partnership – the company, the university, the student

A successful partnership will develop if there is a clear basis in terms of statements of responsibilities, set out in a handbook, sectionalized for student, visiting tutor and industrial supervisor. Prompt attention to approaches from industry by the industrial training tutor and a continuance of this liaison by the visiting tutor will encourage the partnership to thrive.

Preparing the student

Students need to be informed of the benefits of work placements, the timescale and methods of application and the normal requirements of the workplace (such as dress code). Courses on writing CVs, application forms and interview techniques are important. Presentations about industry, by industrialists or students returning from industry, are useful.

Maintaining contact with the student

Students should be encouraged to contact the university to discuss problems and successes. In the workplace students are best supported by a visit by an academic member of staff. Students on placements might be further supported by electronic means, either between staff and students, or between peer groups of students.

Assessment

Students will gain most benefit from the placement if the formal assessment of process is clear. Students need to be conscious of their development and to be encouraged to assess their own progress. This may be assessed via a **portfolio** or personal development diary. Students may be expected to support their placement work and prepare for their return to university with some academic study. This may be assessed via written assignments or examination on return to the institution. Many students in industry carry out project work and the project report may also form a major part of the assessment process.

Practical work

Laboratory/practical classes and workshops plays a major role in the education of scientists and engineers (Boud, 1986). It is in this environment that students learn to be scientists or engineers and develop professional skills. Sciences and engineering are practical subjects and academics see this practical experience as vital and non-negotiable. Students in these disciplines will have high class-contact time compared with arts and humanity students. Such learning experiences are very expensive in terms of staff time, support staff, consumable materials and equipment. Consequently, it is important to ensure that the learning experience is as effective as possible. This experience is vital for the development of practical, discipline-specific skills, but it also provides rich opportunities for the development of intellectual and transferable skills.

Although students are carrying out an investigation, producing a design, etc, the learning objectives for sessions are usually much broader. The aims for a practical session might include to:

- gain practical skills;
- gain experience of particular pieces of equipment/tools;

- produce a design;
- plan an experiment;
- make links between theory and practice;
- gather data;
- manipulate and interpret data;
- make observations;
- form and test hypotheses;
- use judgement;
- develop problem-solving skills;
- communicate data and concepts;
- develop personal skills;
- develop ICT skills;
- develop safe working practices;
- motivate and enthuse students;
- simulate professional practice.

This list could be extended as practical work is a complex interaction between theory and practice, student and tutor. Practical work may be very constrained and confined, in which students follow detailed instructions with little scope for independent thinking. These experiences have their place in developing basic practical skills and giving students confidence, especially early in a course. Practical activities may take a more open-ended approach, requiring students to be involved in some aspects of experimental design or real investigation. These experiences further develop practical and technical skills, but also develop design skills and problem solving, and require application of theory to practice. Such activities may be more applicable in the later stages of a course.

The module teacher does not always plan a laboratory class from scratch. Most inherit activities and are constrained by available resources and equipment. When planning a practical session it is vital to ensure that you are clear what the intended learning outcomes are and that the learning experience can deliver those outcomes. Ensure that the assessment method assesses all the skills that are important and that this is reflected in the marking scheme. Can a written report and discussion of theoretical concepts really assess technical skills? Can your students gain a good mark for practical work for being 'good' at writing the report, rather than having good practical skills? If the answer to this last question is 'yes' then the assessment method or marking scheme may need some attention.

Students should come to a laboratory, workshop or **field trip** familiar with the activity they are about to perform and any relevant background theory or information that they will need. Unless this requirement is made explicit students will turn up not having read through their schedule or manual. The easiest way to ensure that students think about the practical before they arrive is to use a pre-practical exercise. This exercise may be fairly short and consist of a few questions, based on the manual or handout they will use, or require students to carry out some background reading. The students should be required to complete the exercise before starting the session. Such 'pre-pracs' or 'pre-labs' may be paper-based or automated via the Web or a **VLE**. They are very effective in ensuring that students are well prepared and get the most out of the session. Case Study 2 looks at a way of preparing students for fieldwork, which is usually an expensive form of teaching and therefore one in which the students need to be particularly well prepared.

Case Study 2: Preparing for fieldwork in environmental sciences

University of Plymouth

Fieldwork plays a central role in most modern environmental science courses. In its various forms, fieldwork can be employed to enhance theory covered elsewhere. It provides students with opportunities to develop their discipline-specific and transferable skills, including not only the techniques and methods for sampling and data analysis, but also invaluable training in problem solving, especially within 'real life' scenarios.

There remains, however, a challenge in teaching fieldwork to undergraduate students, especially in the early stages of their degree courses. The reasons for this are not simply limited to the subject material that needs to be covered, which often demands some subject interdisciplinarity. The *process* of fieldwork is unfamiliar to most students, and as a result, an appreciation of demands and expectations is often lacking.

In order to address this issue, a number of methods can be useful, including introductory lectures and supporting documentation. Unfortunately, student feedback suggests that such methods are often inadequate at delivering the most valuable 'message' and there can be a risk of information overload. As an alternative, Web-based materials offer the possibility of combining various elements of preparative fieldwork in a flexible and interactive format.

The BSc Environmental Science degree at the University of Plymouth includes weekly local fieldwork, together with an integrated, week-long study of the Teign catchment of south-east Devon. This involves an assessment of land use (both ancient and modern) on water quality in the Teign district, and takes in several regions of managed woodland, agricultural, extraction industries, and tourism. In order to better prepare students for the expectations and learning outcomes of this activity, we have developed an interactive Web site (www.science.plym.ac.uk/departments/learn/teign/teign_home.htm) which features all of the individual site visits throughout the week-long period of study. The content of the Web site is far from being a substitute for the hands-on nature of the fieldwork, but focuses more on the preparative components that are required in order for the fieldwork to be effective. Along with suitable graphics and links between the different site visits, each section has an interactive self-assessment section that enables students to evaluate their own level of understanding. Thus, by using the Web site, students are made more aware of their own learning and are encouraged to develop independence. The Web site is accessible at all times and a scheduled session, approximately one week before the fieldwork, replaces introductory lectures.

Evidence to show the effectiveness of this approach is largely anecdotal, from teaching staff who comment that students generally suffer from less downtime at the beginning of each site visit. In terms of student feedback, and in particular their responses to the question, 'How effective was the introductory talk/session in preparing you for the field week?', the percentage of returns scoring 'Very high' has risen from 50 per cent (introductory lecture) to 90 per cent (Web site session). Students also use some of the content of the Web site in their presentations that constitute part of the formal assessment. The accessibility of the site together with its interactive style almost certainly contributes to its success.

(Simon Belt)

Another issue vital to an effective practical session is the quality of support from demonstrators. Many departments use postgraduate students or postdoctoral workers as demonstrators in the laboratory, workshop or on a field trip. As student–staff ratios inevitably grow, postgraduate demonstrators are becoming essential members of the team and the quality of the support they provide is becoming much more crucial. In order to be effective they have to be familiar with the activity, well briefed in terms of what is expected from them, have a good rapport with the students and be willing and able to deal with any problems. Most universities organize training sessions for demonstrators, either at departmental or institutional levels, to ensure that those who work as demonstrators have the necessary skills, knowledge and attitude to teaching. As a lecturer in charge of a practical class you are well advised to hold a briefing session immediately before the activity to ensure that demonstrators are familiar with the purpose of the class, familiar with equipment and have sufficient background knowledge to deal with any queries. Ensure that both you and the demonstrators are clear what their role is and what is expected of them. If demonstrators are involved in marking students' work, then ensure that they all have a detailed marking scheme to ensure consistent standards across the team. Many university departments use questionnaires to seek undergraduate student views of the quality of support provided by demonstrators in laboratory and practical classes and fieldwork.

Interrogating Practice

Write down a list of the qualities of an ideal postgraduate demonstrator. Ask the demonstrators assigned to your next practical session to do the same.
How do the two lists compare? If there are major differences, discuss these with your demonstrator.
Find out how your department/institution trains postgraduate demonstrators.

Another key aspect of learning how to 'be' an engineer or scientist is project work. Project work may take various forms (see also Chapter 8). It may involve original research alongside research staff in the department. Alternatively, it may be based on fieldwork, or may involve an investigative literature review or be computer based. Students may undertake individual or group research projects and projects may extended over part or all of the final academic year,

SKILLS AND EMPLOYABILITY

All Subject Benchmark statements (QAA, 2000–02) include statements about transferable skills acquisition. The Dearing Report (NCIHE, 1997) argued that there are four skills which are key to the future success of graduates whatever they intend to do in later life and these are communication skills, the use of information technology, numeracy and learning how to learn. In one study of skills required by employers of science and engineering graduates, it was found that employers highly valued the 'soft' personal skills and they commonly noted failure in one of more aspects of communication and presentation (Ketteridge and Fry, 1999). There is no escaping the fact that we have to make a concerted and real effort to provide our undergraduates with the opportunity to develop a range of these skills – (this is considered in more detail in Chapter 9). In the case of science and engineering undergraduates, often the best way to 'sell' skills is to embed them within a discipline context in a module. Thus, the development of, for example, communications skills, might take place within a context of giving a presentation about a scientific topic. Such a model of skills integration is described in Case Study 3. Practical work, projects and open-ended problem-solving activities offer many opportunities for personal and transferable skills development, but the opportunities and skills must be made explicit to undergraduates if they are to recognize and value them. The advent of **progress files** may do much to encourage staff and students to pay attention to skills development and to make time for development and reflection within the curriculum.

Case Study 4 provides an interesting glimpse of a different type of skills development. It outlines a module in Physics at the University of Leicester that additionally raises students' awareness of business and entrepreneurial skills.

Case Study 3: A communication course for chemists

University of Manchester Institute of Science and Technology

Our Communicating Chemistry module is one way in which a range of communication skills can be covered in an integrated way, using tasks that the students generally enjoy, and providing reasonable opportunities for the skills to be developed. An essential feature of the module is that the students *use* their subject-specific skills in (fairly) realistic settings, and that they have sufficient time to try, assess, and re-try their newly learnt skills. The primary aim of the module is not to produce brilliant communicators, but to show each student where his or her strengths lie, and to enable each to improve his or her communication skills. While these skills are learnt within a subject-specific environment, the skills are of course generic, and can be transferred easily to other situations.

We identified the following skills that we wished to address:

- information retrieval;
- oral, written and visual communication;
- problem solving and critical thinking;
- team working.

Most of the exercises are designed to address two or more skills. We aimed to achieve a fairly balanced coverage overall, using 10 exercises that required 100 student-effort-hours during an eight-week module. Concerning the nature of written, visual and oral delivery, the exercises involved concise reports or articles, poster presentations, and short talks. The content of the module is summarized in Table 18.3.

Table 18.3 Development Skills in Communicating Chemistry module

Exercise	Description	Length (Hours)	Information Retrieval	Written Delivery	Visual Delivery	Oral Delivery	Team Work	Problem Solving
The Fluorofen Project	Exercise to solve a chemical problem (teams)	1					✓	✓
Scientific paper	Exercise to dissect a chemical paper (teams)	3	✓				✓	✓
Keyboard skills	Basic skills with Word and ChemDraw (individuals)	10		✓	✓			
New Scientist article	A short paper is turned into a *New Scientist* article (pairs)	18	✓	✓	✓		✓	
WWW treasure hunt	Introduction to the Net, BIDS, and e-mail (individuals)	8	✓	✓				✓
Dictionary of Interesting Chemistry	Write brief entry for a *Dictionary of Interesting Chemistry* (pairs)	20	✓	✓	✓		✓	
Research poster	Produce a poster on a new area of research (teams)	12	✓	✓	✓		✓	
Annual review talk	Give a five-minute talk to 10–12 peers on any interesting chemistry (individual)	12	✓		✓	✓		
Interview	All students are interviewed by another company (CV required)	8		✓		✓	✓	
Hwuche-Hwuche bark	Business game with real chemical problems	8	✓			✓	✓	✓

This module is based on the premise that these communication skills are best taught within subject-specific intensive exercises (as well as being reinforced elsewhere in the mainstream course) and that the exercises are most effective when they are built around a relevant scenario, and involve plausible problems and tasks. Student feedback has been extremely positive, and the skills that are developed are ones that recent graduates feel are insufficiently developed in most chemistry courses (Bailey and Shinton, 1999).

(Pat Bailey)

Interrogating Practice

Find out the strategy for skills development in your department. You could also look at your institutional Learning and Teaching Strategy. List the transferable skills development opportunities available in the courses you teach.

Are your students aware of these opportunities? Are the transferable skills developed reflected within the assessment?

Case Study 4: Developing business and entrepreneurial skills for physics students

University of Leicester

This module in the Physics Department aims to:

- provide a vehicle for introducing basic awareness of business skills;
- enable students to begin to learn about business by experience;
- teach high-level group skills and use group work to motivate student interest and engagement;
- exploit Internet technology.

Students are introduced to aspects of running a business including: researching the market, market sectors, making a business plan, financial control, quality matters. They then run an Internet training company for six weeks providing training courses to students in the Faculty of Science. Finally they produce a company report with groups of students responsible for individual sections, including marketing, finance and customer satisfaction.

The Management Centre at the University of Leicester teaches the business skills aspects of the course. Participating students organize the signing up of customers and delivery of the classes. While the business aspect is simulated, the training and/or other services provided by the company is real and evaluated in terms of customer satisfaction.

The first session is a briefing explaining the course structure, learning outcomes and assessment. The initial part of the course is six lectures delivered by two staff from the Management Centre. In the second part of the course the students organize a company to deliver a Web-training course. The company Web site, marketing strategy and teaching materials are produced by the students and the course is delivered to registered students who provide feedback for the evaluation. The company report is prepared jointly and assessed by the lecturers according to the extent to which it showed that the lecture material had been understood and applied.

The students adopt roles within the company. They are Director of Operations, Director of Strategy, Marketing Director, Customer Relations Officer and Finance Director. They deliver three class training sessions and produce follow-up tutorial material on their Web site. There was no student drop-out during the student-led course and the tutorial materials were felt to be of great value.

(Derek Raine)

ASSESSMENT OF STUDENT LEARNING

The main assessment tools encountered in science and engineering disciplines are:

- unseen written examinations;
- written assignments or essays;
- MCQs (especially at lower levels);
- laboratory/practical/fieldtrip reports;
- project reports and software developed;
- portfolios and personal development plans;
- poster presentations;
- oral presentations.

Richard Wakeford discusses the first five of these methods of assessment elsewhere in this book (see Chapter 4). Of the methods listed here, unseen written examinations still remain the principal means of summative assessment within science and engineering disciplines. For a new lecturer, one of the most daunting tasks is being asked to write his or her first examination questions and this is often made all the more difficult by the fact that the questions will, more than likely, be required before the course has been taught. Many academics consider unseen written examinations to be the only rigorous form of assessment, even though they cannot easily assess the range of qualities and skills demanded of a professional scientist or engineer.

One distinctive feature of experimental sciences and engineering is the assessment of large numbers of written laboratory or practical reports, usually to assess understanding and application of knowledge, written communication skills, reasoning, etc. Students in these disciplines often produce such written reports for, perhaps, one or two sessions per week over a module or during the course of a year and these are assessed by academic staff, often assisted by postgraduate demonstrators. The value of repeating this skill so many times is not always questioned. There are alternative ways of assessing practical skills and the outcomes of experiments, such as computer-marked results, summary reports, entries on answer sheets, MCQs, etc, and these are reviewed elsewhere (eg, Gibbs, Gregory and Moore, 1997).

Interrogating Practice

List the objectives of your next laboratory/practical class or workshop. How will you assess the knowledge and skills developed in this work? Check that your assessment protocol is valid and that it measures what it is supposed to measure.

THE USE OF COMMUNICATION AND INFORMATION TECHNOLOGY (C&IT)

Apart from the generic use of C&IT in word-processing, using spreadsheets, etc, increasing use is being made of electronic resources to support learning and teaching in experimental sciences and engineering. This includes the use of software packages, managed or virtual learning environments (VLEs) or Web-based resources. In many cases the use of C&IT does not extend beyond placing conventional lecture notes on a server. While this may be useful for students, especially absent ones, it is sometimes no more than an opportunity to shift printing costs from a department to the students and, in itself, cannot be considered particularly good practice.

One of the common uses of software is for mathematics support where a software or Web-based resource can be accessed as needed by the students. There are many professionally produced mathematics support packages which, while of very high quality, may be prohibitively expensive. There are also a growing number of home-grown mathematics support resources, many of which are tailored to a particular discipline's needs and which may be available over the Internet or for a small cost from the author. See any of the relevant LTSN Subject Centre Web sites for further details.

Simulations of experiments are another area where the use of C&IT can be beneficial. Laboratory use of expensive equipment is not always available to all students and so a simulation can provide large numbers of students with some limited experience of a specialized technique. An example is provided in Case Study 5. Another use of simulations is in enabling students to generate a large number of results in a fraction of the time it would take to generate them in a laboratory, thereby enabling extended experiments to be carried out. The LTSN Subject Centres can provide details of simulations available in your discipline.

Case Study 5: Developing an online experiment in chemistry

Oxford University

In an ideal world, the content of a university science practical course would be determined entirely by what is academically desirable. In reality, we are restricted to what is physically and financially achievable. Limitations imposed by space, by the availability of appropriate demonstrating skills or by finance are much more fundamental than those imposed by the need to seek out (or create) suitable experiments.

The practical course in Physical Chemistry at Oxford University exemplifies this. Chemistry has a large student intake – some 190 per year. The cost of providing multiple sets of experiments is significant. In our first year, every student performs two compulsory exercises on experimental error. These exercises are much more effective when students use real equipment to create the data required for statistical analysis, rather than relying upon a computer to do this for them, but this requires that suitable equipment be available.

When, several years ago, the equipment used in this experiment required replacement, we decided that the limited funds available could be used most effectively if wide access to a single experimental rig could be offered, and we decided to create an experiment which could be accessed and controlled through the Internet. One instrument could then be used virtually simultaneously by several groups of students, minimizing the total cost.

A number of practical difficulties arise when real equipment is to be controlled through the Web. There may be contention between different users who are trying to access equipment simultaneously; malicious or inexperienced users might cause damage to the equipment; if chemicals are required, over-zealous online users might consume large quantities of chemicals, thus negating any initial cost benefits. Various options exist to deal with such difficulties. We have chosen, for the first experiment we have placed online, to work with equipment which has no moving parts and consumes no chemicals. The running costs are therefore minimal, and the chance of mechanical failure is reduced. Through a hidden queuing system we can ensure that users' requests cannot clash, and can also prioritize requests for experiments if several users are online. Since a Web request automatically comes tagged with the user's IP address, it is straightforward to give high priority to users within defined institutions, while giving unrestricted access to other users at times of low demand.

Although the aim was initially to provide an updated experiment for our own course, there is much to be gained by the creation of a network of many (perhaps 20 or more) different Web-based experiments shared among institutions. Advantages of such an arrangement include reduced cost in the provision of practical experiments, broadening of the curriculum, access to real (as opposed to simulated) experiments for those who suffer from disabilities or who are pursuing a remote-learning course, access to expensive or unusual equipment and so on.

The Web was not designed as a medium for running experiments, so practical difficulties remain. However, the advantages of the creation of a pool of experiments, widely accessible through the Internet, are very substantial. We expect that, within a few years, a portion of the practical work performed by many science students will be carried out using Web-based experiments.

(Hugh Cartwright)

WHERE TO FIND MORE SUPPORT

All academics practice their teaching skills within the context of their discipline and all students learn within the context of a discipline. So, some of the most useful support should be available to academic staff from within their own discipline. Many professional bodies provide some professional updating in teaching related areas or organize conferences on teaching and learning and these can be very useful. The Learning and Teaching Support Network (LTSN) Subject Centres provide discipline-specific support for all teachers in higher education. Their services are free and they act as repositories of good practice and providers of continuing professional development, organizing meetings and workshops, producing a variety of useful publications and maintaining substantial Web sites which pull together examples of good practice from across the disciplines. Many of them also provide services specifically for new academics and those on initial programmes in teaching and learning. If you are interested in drawing on the expertise of the LTSN Subject Centres, then start by looking at their Web sites to get a flavour of their services. Here are contact details for the Subject Centres relevant to this chapter:

The Learning and Teaching Support Network, www.ltsn.ac.uk/
LTSN Bioscience, http://bio.ltsn.ac.uk/
LTSN Engineering, http://www.ltsneng.ac.uk/
LTSN Geography, Environmental and Earth Science, http://www.gees.ac.uk/
LTSN Maths, Stats and OR, http://ltsn.mathstore.ac.uk/
LTSN Materials, http://www.materials.ac.uk/
LTSN Physical Sciences, http://www.physsci.ltsn.ac.uk/

OVERVIEW

This chapter provides an essential overview of teaching and learning in experimental science and engineering disciplines. It draws attention to the distinctive features of teaching and learning in the various subjects and how this has developed in the light of changing demand from students, changes in how well students are prepared for higher education and the requirements of external stakeholders. This chapter is richly illustrated with case study materials from a range of different universities, which showcase exemplary practices in teaching and learning across the subject areas it represents.

REFERENCES

Bailey, P D and Shinton, S E (1999) *Communicating Chemistry: A teaching manual for university teachers*, Royal Society of Chemistry, London

Boud, D (1986) *Teaching in Laboratories*, SRHE/Open University Press, Buckingham

Boud, D and Feletti, G (1998) *The Challenge of Problem-Based Learning*, Kogan Page, London

The Engineering Council (2000) *Measuring the Maths Problem*, Engineering Council, London

Exley, K (1999) Key aspects of teaching and learning in science and engineering, in *A Handbook for Teaching and Learning in Higher Education*, 1st edn, eds H Fry, S Ketteridge and S Marshall, Kogan Page, London

Garratt, J, Overton, T and Threlfall, T (1999) *A Question of Chemistry*, Longman, London

Gibbs, G, Gregory, R and Moore, I (1997) *Labs and Practicals with More Students and Fewer Resources, Teaching More Students 7*, Oxford Centre for Staff Development, Oxford

Institute of Physics (2001) *Report of the Inquiry into Undergraduate Physics*, Institute of Physics, London

Ketteridge, S and Fry, H (1999) *Skills Development in Science and Engineering*, Final Project Report to the Department for Education and Employment, URL: http://www.innovations.ac.uk/btg/projects/theme2/digests/project9.htm

Murray, R and Wallace, R (2000) *Good Practice in Industrial Work Placement*, LTSN Physical Sciences

National Comittee of Inquiry into Higher Education (NCIHE) (1997) (Dearing Report) *Higher Education in the Learning Society*, NCIHE, HMSO, London (also to be found at: http://www.leeds.ac.uk/educol/ncihe)

Overton, T (2001) *Web Resources for Problem Based Learning*, LTSN Physical Sciences

Quality Assurance Agency for Higher Education (QAA) (2000–02) *Benchmarking Academic Standards*, QAA, URL: http://www.qaa.ac.uk/crntwork/benchmark/index.htm

FURTHER READING

Barrett, J (1996) *Teaching University Students Chemistry*, Technical and Educational Services, Bristol

Moore, I and Exley, K (eds) (1999) *Innovations in Science Teaching*, SEDA Paper 107, Staff and Educational Development Association, Birmingham

Habershaw, S and Steeds, D (1993) *53 Interesting Communication Exercises for Science Students*, Technical and Educational Services, Bristol

Planet Special Edition 2 (2001) *Case Studies in Problem-based Learning (PBL) from Geography, Earth and Environmental Sciences*, LTSN GEES

Planet Special Edition 1 (2001) *Embedding Careers Education in the Curricula of Geography, Earth and Environmental Sciences*, LTSN GEES

Race, P (2000) *Designing Assessment to Improve Physical Sciences Learning*, LTSN Physical Sciences, Hull

Savin-Baden, M (2000) *Problem-Based Learning in Higher Education: Untold stories*, SRHE/Open University Press, Milton Keynes

Smith, R A (1991) *Innovative Teaching in Engineering*, Ellis Horwood, Chichester

Wankat, P and Oreovicz, F (1993) *Teaching Engineering*, McGraw-Hill, London

<table>
<tr><td>19</td></tr>
</table>

Key aspects of teaching and learning in information and computer sciences

Gerry McAllister and Sylvia Alexander

CONTEXT

Information and computing skills are an essential component of all undergraduate programmes and the wider process of **lifelong learning**. In addressing the key issues of teaching and learning in the information and computing sciences (ICS) it is useful to have an insight into the short history of the subject in order to put it in context. Certainly no other subject community can claim that their industry or interest has had a greater impact on the everyday life of so many in the developed sector of our world. Likewise, no other subject discipline has been exposed to the rate of change that has occurred within computer science.

The computing industry itself has grown since the 1940s and was initially dominated by technology which provided large number-crunching and data-processing solutions within large commercial organizations or university research departments. The evolution of the technology progressed through a phase of lesser machines called minicomputers in the 1960s and 1970s, which both economically and physically facilitated functions such as industrial control and smaller commercial administrative operations, and were within the budgets of academic research projects. Thanks largely to the development of the single microprocessor chip, today we have desktop computers on practically every desk in every office and through the merger of the computer and communications industries a worldwide interconnection of computers.

University departments, particularly in science and engineering, are more and more being tasked with being in step with the needs of industry. Furthermore, they are expected to be ahead of the game and to teach about tomorrow's technology. Predicting the future, however, is littered with disastrously wrong statements. In the 1940s the then chairman of IBM predicted that the world needed 'a maximum of five computers' and later standards were set of a maximum speed of 10 MHz for networks which were considered would meet any future demand. Clearly no one had accurately foreseen the impact that new technology would have and the concurrent demand for more and faster services. Current Internet address space of 10^{32} is now all but absorbed and the proposed new version of 10^{128} addresses will accommodate 7×10^{23} devices on every square metre of the earth's surface – including the water. At present, one can possibly predict a trend towards mobile computing and access to computing resources from wireless devices. Advances in the profession, unlike those in other disciplines, are very much driven by large multinational corporations seeking to create greater profits. Thus academics within the discipline must strive to ensure the value they contribute is not merely specialized training in commercial products but that it is recognized as an intellectual academic subject.

The last national report on computing science education was produced as a result of the then TQA in 1994 (NISS), although Information Science has had more recent assessment. This chapter reflects on many of the comments in the 1994 report and highlights changes in this rapidly changing discipline in the intervening years.

CURRICULUM DESIGN

Computer science degrees in higher education institutions (HEIs) are little more than 30 years old. The academic perspective of the profession evolved from other disciplines such as electronic engineering, mathematics, aspects of business and to a lesser extent other scientific-based subjects. As such, many of the academic subject community teaching in HEIs received third-level qualifications and background experience in these other disciplines. The early computing curriculum focused on machine and assembly language programming and other languages such as Algol, basic operating systems, a study of compilers and assemblers and a mathematical approach to theory.

Today, practically all UK universities have a Computing Science or Informatics department/school or faculty. The curriculum has evolved beyond recognition to concentrate on 'Internet friendly' and object-oriented languages such as Java, graphical user interfaces (GUIs), Web technologies, scripting languages, artificial intelligence, distributed systems, computer network protocols and application oriented topics such as multimedia. Many more experienced practitioners have witnessed this complete transformation, through the intermediate stages encompassing languages such as Pascal and Modula. Computer science education is characterized by its rapid rate of change – it is unlikely that any other discipline has to deal with a curriculum which has such a short shelf life.

The continuously evolving curriculum

In comparison with many subjects in higher education, computer science is relatively new. Departments have sprung up and been located in different faculties within the higher education structure and as a result different approaches to teaching are employed. Whatever the approach, a good balance needs to be maintained between the theoretical material and research that underpins modern curricula, and vocational experiences which prepare students for the world of work.

Computing skills and competencies have, in recent years, become more deeply embedded within all academic disciplines. This convergence has resulted in a host of new interdisciplinary topics (eg, multimedia, medical informatics, computer ethics, etc). As a result, it is difficult to provide a precise definition of 'computer science' due to the continuous development of new specialisms.

There is no national consensus for what constitutes a syllabus in computer science – a view echoed by the computing benchmark statement (www.QAA). The subject benchmarks define a conceptual framework which serves to provide coherence and identity for the discipline. They define the intellectual capability and understanding which should be assimilated together with the skills and competencies which should be developed through the study of computing. However, as the subject benchmarks for computing indicate, the content of a course can include a wide spectrum of subject material. Individual departments must decide what their courses should contain, with consideration for the key professional needs and other needs such as the local and national commercial software community. As a result curriculum are often planned and influenced by a broad range of research interests, industrial experiences and the professions.

Both the British Computer Society (BCS) and the Institution for Electrical Engineers (IEE) are concerned that educational institutions maintain standards appropriate for those wishing to follow a career in computing. Both professional bodies offer systems of exemption and accreditation for appropriate courses, providing a route to membership. These schemes are valuable forms of recognition by professional bodies that courses offer appropriate curricula to meet the needs of industry and commerce. In considering courses for exemption or accreditation, evidence is required to show that course content aims to provide students with sufficient breadth of coverage in appropriate computing topics to provide sound academic grounding in the discipline. The curricular guidelines produced by the validating bodies are not prescriptive with respect to core course content, thus enabling institutions to develop specialisms and provide a distinctive flavour to their course provision.

Despite the flexibility in programme design there are certain core elements which remain common, most notably the teaching of programming. Problems associated with the teaching (and more importantly the learning) of programming, have generated considerable debate within the profession.

Teaching programming

Programming is a core skill in computing science. The teaching of programming is perceived to be problematic and programming modules are identified as having a detrimental effect on retention rates within degree programmes. The cognitive difficulties in learning to program and the skills that make a good programmer are difficult to identify. Probably more time is invested in teaching programming than any other area of the discipline, yet students struggle as they try to master the skill. Many graduates of computing science are deemed to be deficient in the topic and will indeed seek employment where the need for the skill is minimal. Academics must consider carefully how best to deal with the problems associated with programming in order to provide better student support.

Case Study 1: Teaching programming

University of Leeds

Teaching computer programming is indeed a problem. At the heart of the problem lies the very nature of the skill itself; programming is something that is best learnt over a long time and with a great deal of practice. This is not a learning model that fits happily in today's still prevailingly lecture-based and often semesterized higher education system.

There is a danger in any lecture setting that students can become little more than passive recipients of information conveyed by the lecturer. The old cliché has this information passing from the notes of the lecturer into the notes of the student, passing through the minds of neither. This scenario might be acceptable, or even effective, in some disciplines, but it is absolutely fatal when programming is being taught or learnt.

The key to making lectures on programming more effective is for the 'lecturer' to make the students participate. The students should be *active participants* rather than *passive recipients*. There are many ways in which this can be done – the only limitation is the imagination of the lecturer. Some examples:

Parameter Passing
There are usually two forms of parameter passing supported in a programming language, and the difference is subtle, especially for novices. The essential difference between parameters passed as *values* and those passed as *references* can be illustrated with a simple demonstration.

Armed with some sample functions, accepting a variety of parameters, the instructor can record the values of variables on the back of a collection of Frisbees. Different colours of Frisbee, or different sizes, can be used to indicate different variable types. The sample functions can be 'walked through', and a student (or group) is nominated to carry out this process; they are *passed* the appropriate parameters by the instructor. Where a value parameter is required, the instructor simply reads out the value. But if a reference parameter is used, the value (the Frisbee) must itself be *passed* to the students representing the function. If the function changes the value of the variable, the students must change the value recorded on the Frisbee, which is returned when they reach the end of the function call.

This simple strategy graphically illustrates the difference. An extension is to attach a piece of string to each passed Frisbee so that a swift tug can precipitate the return; this provides a further neat illustration of pointers!

Data structures
When they have mastered the basics of programming students often move on to implementing simple data structures such as linked lists or stacks. A significant part of the battle in teaching these structures is to explain to the students what such a structure is and how pointers are usually used to implement and eventually traverse one.

The students in a lecture room can be turned into a linked list. One student is nominated as the head of the list (effectively a pointer to the first item) and is equipped with a large ball of wool. The student throws this to another in the room, who forms the second element, and so on. When a suitable structure has been created, the instructor can show how to traverse the list to find certain values, and can show how it is vital not to lose the first element.

It is straightforward to extend this idea to explain more complex operations with these structures, such as the deletion of an element. This requires some temporary pointers (and scissors!) as the wool forming the list is cut and then tied back together.

A word of caution
The effectiveness of these techniques lies in their novelty. Lectures using ideas such as these will hopefully be memorable, and the subject of much discussion afterwards. That is important.

It is probably possible to devise demonstrations to illustrate most parts of an introductory programming course, but if they are over-used, they can lose the crucial novelty value.

(Tony Jenkins)

TEACHING METHODS

Courses in ICS provide a mix of both theory and practice, thus enabling transfer of knowledge and the development of skills. Individual institutions adopt a variety of curricular styles and a range of learning and teaching practices including lectures, tutorials, seminars and laboratory work, with increasing emphasis being placed on the learning experiences gained through **industrial placement**, group and individual projects. These new patterns of learning facilitate the need to inculcate **transferable** skills as well as develop subject specialist skills. However, this transfer requires the exploitation of new approaches to facilitate and manage the learning and support of students who spend a significant proportion of their time remote from the university and in isolation from their peers. There is therefore an increasing need to apply technologically-based solutions, which will be discussed later.

Computing science is funded as a laboratory subject and as such practical sessions are a key aspect of all courses. Scheduled laboratory classes are most often supervised by academic staff or **graduate demonstrators** who encourage and support students in making independent progress without heavy supervision. In addition to supervised sessions, students also have opportunities to access equipment for personal study and independent learning outside formal class times. This issue will be further discussed in the section on student support where issues relating to resources to support student learning will be explored.

Interrogating Practice

Reflect on your current teaching methodologies. What is the rationale for their use? Does your current approach maximize learning opportunities for the student? What new methods might you try?

ICS is a major growth area within the national economic scene and the demand for skilled graduates continues to grow. The future demand for computing science education is therefore unlikely to be fully satisfied by conventional courses. Furthermore, qualified practitioners require access to short professional development courses in order to maintain currency, expand their skills base and keep abreast of new developments in the field. E-learning is viewed by many as an opportunity to support access to curricula and learning materials and providing short top-up courses covering areas of perceived need. Virtual learning environments (**VLEs**) are central to the delivery and management of e-learning programs providing an exciting and intellectually challenging environment for teaching and learning which stimulates students and encourages academics to vary their teaching style (see Chapter 11).

Interrogating Practice

Consider how you might introduce a VLE to support a module which you teach. Would the communication/collaboration tools provide opportunities to extend and build upon the classroom-based teaching? Would this enhance the student experience?

Teaching large groups

Nowhere has the increasing student numbers in higher education been more acute than within ICS. The growth in recent years has been such that computing is now the largest single discipline (in terms of staff and student numbers) within the domains of engineering and the physical sciences. In contrast, conventional support for academic lecturers in ICS is declining, due to decreasing per capita student funding and a difficulty in attracting computing science research students, whose skills are generously rewarded in industry and commerce. The growth and diversification of the student population is producing an increasingly complex higher education structure (advancing in both size and scope), which challenges traditional delivery methods. At the same time technology is developing to a stage where it can provide sophisticated support for such complexity.

Interrogating Practice

How does your department deal with the diverse range of experience of incoming students? Do you take into account their differing learning styles and requirements when planning your teaching and assessment (see Chapters 12 and 15)?

Presenting lecture material to large numbers (often in excess of 300) frequently results in a pedestrian, didactic style; the main purpose of which is to impart information. Tutorials and seminars have always been an important component of course delivery – they provide effective reinforcement to large group teaching and present opportunities for academic staff to emphasize the impact of research activity on curricular content. While the conventional classroom lecture can accommodate numbers limited only by physical space provision, in many cases small group tutorials have been abandoned, largely due to resource constraints. Academics must therefore identify other teaching methods that stretch students intellectually, challenging and stimulating them to consider facts and principles beyond the content delivered in the lecture theatre.

Groupwork

Today's employers have expressed a need for graduates to improve their group-working and communication skills. Group working forms an integral part of ICS programmes. With increasing student numbers, the ability to coordinate and manage group projects is a laborious task. The system is fraught with problems, including allocation of members to groups, delegation of tasks within the group, motivation of team members and attributing appropriate marks for individual effort. The problem is further exacerbated where a course is offered in mixed mode with part-time students/distance learners finding it difficult to engage in activities with their full-time counterparts. Furthermore, the pedagogic shift from the traditional teacher-centred to a student-centred approach requires a fundamental change in the role of the educator, from that of information provider to a facilitator of learning (see Chapter 2).

Team exercises and small group work enhance both the personal and professional skills of students and are often employed to inculcate transferable skills. Group projects are particularly useful for sharing ideas (and concerns), debating issues of mutual interest and learning to work to an agreed schedule. They can also help to promote confidence among quieter members of the team.

Collaboration is not easy but can provide added value in a number of areas, most notably the stimulation and motivation of students, who take responsibility for planning, and the generation of ideas. There are a number of examples of good practice in team working, especially where they have been used to develop both transferable and specialist skills. At Durham, second-year students undertake a group project in software engineering (see Case Study 2). The organization of this project is based on a tutor, supported by research students trained specifically for the purpose of acting as facilitators at group meetings. The students run the meetings and keep **log books** and minutes, all of which are signed off weekly by the facilitator. This organization is simple but effective.

There are a number of examples of good practice in team working, especially where they have been used to develop both transferable and specialist skills.

Case Study 2: Group working

University of Durham

Within Computer Science at Durham the organization of the Software Engineering Group project is based on a customer who acts as the driver and academic overseer of the group. Since each group has different requirements there are substantial differences between the work of individual groups thus there are no issues of plagiarism. On the management side the students run the group work coordination meetings and keep log books and minutes, all of which are reviewed by the academic facilitator. Thus a careful watch is taken of the contributions of members and the progress of the group as a whole.

Unfortunately however, group work practices are not without their difficulties. Typical problems include the accurate assessment of group work products, the evaluation of individual's contributions within the group which is usually not equal and thus should be reflected in the assessment marks, and finally controlling the project so that a good learning environment can be made available to all students. Solutions to three of the main issues that are adopted within the Durham system are now described.

Assessment
Assessment of group work projects is often made difficult by the freedom placed upon the group. In order to maximize the learning potential it is beneficial to minimize the control placed upon the group. The outcome of this is that frequently groups produce very varied products. Thus the assessment of such a varied field is difficult. Furthermore, since within Durham the assessment is conducted by the customer, who sets the requirements, there is also a need to ensure that the approaches and criteria for the marking process are consistently applied across each of the groups. Clearly what is required are detailed marking criteria that are relevant for all group work. This is aided in Durham by the setting of a basic specification upon which each customer sets each of the requirements. Since no individual supervisor has the power to modify the basic specification a common set of marking criteria or tests can then be applied at some levels to all of the groups final systems.

Evaluating individual contributions
There are a number of strategies possible for arriving at an individual mark for the assessment of group work. Some institutions give all students within a group an equal grade for their group work activities. Within Durham individual contributions are assessed, which ultimately results in a specific mark being attributed to an individual student. The approach adopted involves a process of tutor, peer and self-assessment of the contribution that each member has made to specific phases of the group work project. Based on the individual's contribution then the group mark is modified for individual members but not changed. Thus for a group of three (students: A, B, C) with a group mark of 60 per cent, individuals within the group may receive marks based on their contributions of A=55, B=60 and C=65 per cent. From research conducted at Durham the best approach identified to establish such a mark is to ask the students and staff to rank students' contributions where the ranking positions is significantly greater than the number of a group. Thus if a potential ranking set of 15 slots (Slot_1 showing highest potential contribution, slot_15 the lowest) is available, in the above example the slots may be used A=slot_12, B=slot_7, C=slot_3. In this way the relative positioning of the students are demonstrated along with the potential to show the significance of the differences between each student.

Controlling the project
Experience at Durham has shown the importance of having someone to drive and control the process. Problems do occur with group work practices and are often associated with personality clashes between group

members. It is important to deal with these problems quickly before they begin to affect the academic work of the group members. At present it has always been possible to provide resolutions to problems within groups without the necessity to modify the group structure. In most instances this is solved by greater involvement of the group's tutor within the decision-making processes.

The other significant issue that experience has shown is often attributed to group work project within computing is that of the over-enthusiasm of the students involved. While in most instances student enthusiasm is considered desirable, when taken to the extreme it may mean that students start to forsake their other modules. Within Durham, experience has shown that this issue is mainly concerned within the implementation phase where the students actually implement their ideas. Over the last couple of years steps have been put into place to ensure that students work in a controlled manner via the issuing of tokens. When planning their implementation students identify a phased implementation approach. This phased approach is then applied during the implementation phase, and in order to be able to move on the next phase students must apply for a token. The basis of receipt of the token rests on the students' ability to show that the next proposed implementation phase has been adequately planned for.

A final word of encouragement
Many of the problems associated with group work may lead the reader to wonder if setting up group work activities is worth the bother. However, experience in Durham is that the skills and enjoyment that the students gain from this work far exceeds additional considerations such an approach requires. Furthermore, from responses from past students it seems that for computing at least the skills that they acquire are those that they perceive are most frequently used within industry.

(Liz Burd)

Interrogating Practice

What are the specific learning outcomes of your group work exercises? Do you assess transferable skills and what assessment criteria do you use? How will you know if the learning outcomes have been achieved? How do you resource and manage groupwork? What training did those providing the management/facilitation role receive?

ASSESSMENT

As students become increasingly strategic in their study habits, there is much evidence (Brown, Bull and Pendlebury, 1997) to show that assessment is the driving force behind student learning (Kneale and Collins, 1996). Students are motivated by regular assessment (and feedback), which is shown to have a marked improvement on students' overall performance (Schmidt, Norman and Boshuizen, 1990).

The issue of assessment is one of the areas of greatest concern for ICS academics. The problems of assessing group work projects has already been alluded to. Similarly, the increase in student numbers has resulted in large numbers of individual final year and MSc projects which need to be supervised and examined. The increase in staff numbers has not grown proportionately, resulting in academics being burdened with increased loads at already busy times (examination periods). As final year projects are a universal requirement, some innovative approaches to the management and assessment of student projects, including the use of formative peer assessment and poster-based presentations, have already been adopted. ICS programmes are challenged by resource constraints. As such, there is great demand for demonstration of exemplar practices that can be tailored to local needs.

With large student numbers, the task of setting regular assignments and providing timely, **formative feedback** is an onerous one.

Interrogating Practice

What assessment methods do you use? Which are used for formative and which for summative purposes?

Staff–student relationships can be significantly enhanced by the efficient collection and marking of assessed coursework. It is therefore no surprise that interest in automated methods to support the process of testing and assessment continues to grow.

Assessing practical work with large groups

Many departments operate informal mechanisms for offering extra assistance to students, thus placing responsibility on students to assess their own progress and judge when to seek assistance. Staff–student communication can be enhanced by employing technology-based solutions which facilitate efficient collection of some forms of coursework. Such systems have the potential to greatly assist learning and provide early warning of potential problems.

As mentioned, programming is a core component of all computing programmes. Assessing the practical skills associated with programming is a time-consuming activity which is exacerbated by the need for regular submission and quick turnaround time. A further problem is the prevalence of plagiarism which can often go undetected due to the large numbers involved. The vast array of materials readily available via the Internet makes it difficult to detect the work of others, submitted by students and passed off as their own. ICS academics have long been concerned with issues relating to plagiarism detection and most departments have drawn up proactive anti-plagiarism policies. A JISC commissioned study of source code plagiarism detection outlines the issues surrounding this problem together with the tools and methods available to assist the busy academic in uncovering and dealing with issues relating to plagiarism.

Interrogating Practice

Are you familiar with your institutional policy on plagiarism? Do your students realize the implications of plagiarizing work? How do you deal with issues relating to plagiarism within your particular course/module?

Systems to assist in the administration of courses, assignment marking and resource management all have a part to play in increasing the leverage of the human resource investment. At Warwick, a system has been developed facilitating online assessment methods to address the pressing problems associated with the management and assessment of large student numbers. The BOSS system, explored in Case Study 3, provides students with 'instant' detailed feedback on their submitted coursework while enabling staff to monitor the students, automate assessment of their work, and generate reports about plagiarism possibilities. Using BOSS, students are able to complete more coursework with more efficient feedback.

Case Study 3: Managing the assessment of large groups

University of Warwick

Automated tools for the submission and assessment of programming assignments have been developed in the Department of Computer Science at the University of Warwick since 1994. The original motivation was the need to streamline the process of marking assignments, ensure accuracy, and facilitate timely feedback.

Known as BOSS ('The BOSS Online Submission System'), the package began as a UNIX text-based utility, targeted specifically at two large Pascal programming modules. Since then, it has developed into a large platform-independent networked tool, and is used in over a dozen modules delivered by Computer Science and by other academic departments. Modules include introductory programming (Pascal, Java, SML, C++, UNIX Shell) and advanced software modules (Software Engineering, Concurrent Programming), with class sizes up to 300.

BOSS allows any piece of work stored on a computer to be submitted online. A student's identity is verified against data held on the University's student database, and an electronic receipt for the assignment is returned to the student as an e-mail. Security measures are employed, such as the inclusion in each receipt of a hash code (which can be thought of as a digital signature) for each file submitted, in order to ensure the integrity of submitted work should a student later claim the system had corrupted his or her files.

If an assignment is a computer program, or is suitable for running automatic checks on (for example, a style analyser in the case of an essay), then BOSS will run automatic tests in a secure environment, to prevent over-enthusiastic students accidentally – or deliberately – corrupting system data. Tests can be made available to students prior to submission in order for them to check that their assignment meets the criteria set. One or more markers are given access to an intuitive interface to allocate marks to various marking categories (including, but not restricted to, the automatic tests) set by the module leader, who subsequently moderates prior to feedback being e-mailed to the students. The use of slider bars, buttons, and other graphical devices in the user interfaces speeds up the process as much as possible. Finally, BOSS contains a tool called 'Sherlock' which assists the module leader in detecting assignment submissions that have degrees of similarity, and are possible instances of plagiarism.

The response, both of staff and of students, has been generally very favourable. The overall time taken to manage an assessment has been substantially reduced, and the consistency of marking is invariably high. The number of successful appeals against errors in marking has been reduced to almost zero. Regular use of a plagiarism detection tool has reduced the identifiable number of disciplinary offences to very small numbers. In situations where no tests are to be performed, and where BOSS is simply a device to facilitate assignment submission, it has proved to be a highly effective administrative tool.

The successful use of such a tool should not be a surprise to a computer scientist. What is of particular interest is the process of developing the tool, and the issues, both technical and pedagogic, encountered during its development and deployment.

BOSS was developed 'in-house' since no comparable tool was available to purchase (and even now there is none that would satisfy our current needs), and general issues about developing large-scale software are therefore relevant. For example, initial coding, maintenance and development of the software require suitably skilled programmers who are seldom willing to work for the remuneration which UK universities are willing to afford. The software is 'mission-critical', and staff and students must have full confidence in it. Security is paramount (and must be demonstrably so), and thorough testing is crucial.

Automatic tests on computer programs are notoriously difficult to write, and even small programs yield unexpected surprises. Early versions of BOSS allowed such tests to be specified so that text output of programs was compared to the expected output. Variations in punctuation, whitespace, number presentation, and even spelling, could cause tests unexpectedly to fail for individual students. Tight specification of a program's behaviour gives rise to student criticism that the software is too 'picky', whereas the alternative reduces the effectiveness of the testing harness. The specification of tests in the context of graphical output or input is difficult (although the use of Java objects can be helpful).

If an assignment carries a significant proportion of a module's marks, it is undesirable for all of the marks to be awarded for automatic tests. Furthermore, there must be a manual check of any automatically awarded marks to ensure that no unforeseen system problem has accidentally penalized any students (and this is now a requirement of the University).

Perhaps the major lesson we have learnt is that computer systems are invariably much less reliable than we would desire. When 200 students are attempting to use a network application at the same time, and five minutes before a deadline, then the possibilities for system failure are immense. Computer crashes and network failures are common, and the scalability of the software is tested to the limit. Departmental processes, such as deadline enforcement, must be flexible to accommodate this, and it is prudent to have competent staff available at crucial times to deal with the unexpected. The software has been made open source, and documentation and software downloads are available at sourceforge.net/projects/cobalt/

(Mike Joy)

STUDENT SUPPORT

Computing is a major growth area within the national economic scene and the demand for skilled graduates in the subject continues to grow. Recruitment to ICS courses in most institutions has risen steadily in recent years. Computing science now receives a larger group of applicants than engineering sciences, mathematics or physical sciences (Wand, 2001) although difficulties related to female participation remain. The rapid expansion in the IT industry and the attractive salaries offered to ICS professionals has resulted in a similar growth in the number of mature and non-traditional applicants wishing to convert to computing from another discipline. With this comes a requirement to accredit prior experiential learning. These students tend to be highly motivated and many have some form of industrial experience (although diverse in nature). Nevertheless, the condensed nature of such courses (typically one year) presents academics with a considerable challenge to ensure that all students have both the necessary skills base and the breadth and depth of knowledge required to equip them for a future career in the industry.

All ICS departments are therefore challenged with factors that include rising student numbers and associated increased expectations, overburdened faculty resources, and increased competition. These impose great demands within the subject discipline and present a significant challenge to the ICS higher education community.

The sharp rise in student recruitment has inevitably led to problems in providing and sustaining adequate student resources and support. While recruitment is currently not a problem within the ICS disciplines, retaining large student numbers (with limited resource) is a widespread problem. Associated with large student numbers is the issue of intake standards that have the potential to threaten the quality of teaching and learning. Well-thought-out admissions procedures and good induction programmes are essential in order to facilitate the transition to university life (see Chapter 12). The content of courses must be properly explained to prospective students to ensure there is adequate identification of the extent of their prior learning. Personal tutorial systems provide an effective and desirable mechanism for providing academic and pastoral care. However, rapid increases in student numbers and overstretched resources mean that it is not always possible to implement such a scheme, resulting in a lack of individual academic support.

ICS programmes attract entrants from a wide variety of traditional and vocational educational backgrounds, resulting in a diverse student population. Support mechanisms need to be in place to ensure that all students reach the recognized and accepted standards of attainment.

Widening participation

Widening participation takes two main forms, a general trend towards relaxing entry requirements and an increasing number of access course arrangements with further education colleges and foreign institutions, thereby facilitating transfer and progression from one course to another. The problems associated with widening participation are most acute in the further education sector. Higher education provision in further education is already an area of substantial growth within the ICS disciplines, further exacerbated by the introduction of foundation degree programmes. The associated problems of work-based learning and transfer routes into higher education are a cause for growing concern. Providers in further education find difficulty in maintaining currency due to their heavy teaching loads.

Despite differences in institutional structure and curriculum development, most departments are aware of the need to widen student access and are committed to increasing flexibility of both curriculum delivery and student choice within their courses. Most departments have already adopted flexible modular programmes which support credit accumulation and transfer schemes and enable students to transfer between different modes of study. Increased flexibility can however lead to complex teaching programmes and students embarking on the course may lack the ability and prior experience required to achieve the objectives set by the programme of study. Academic staff must be careful to monitor individual progress and ensure that students are able to make the necessary links between discrete units or modules.

While the demands faced by ICS departments are daunting, technology-supported learning provides both possible solutions and new opportunities. Many departments are currently developing an e-learning strategy, which will incorporate advanced pedagogical tools into a technological framework, thus enabling departments to:

- continually improve the quality of course/programme provision;
- attract and retain students;
- widen participation by expanding campus boundaries;
- improve graduate employability.

However, it is widely acknowledged that academic staff need to learn new skills to move from traditional to e-tutoring mode. In order to take full advantage of these emerging technologies, ICS academics must keep abreast of current good practice which will inform local developments and ensure effective exploitation of existing resources.

Learning resources

The current rate of growth within the ICS disciplines is unsustainable without additional resources. As a result, academics are now looking for innovative approaches to address this pressing problem. With an increase in the number of part-time, distance and lifelong learners in the ICS disciplines, the interest in technology to support this expanding group of students with diverse learning needs is growing rapidly. In recent years, technology has helped to improve communication between staff and students, providing a platform for online learning support together with reference materials that are greatly appreciated by students. When used to complement and enhance traditional teaching activities, technology-based support can be of demonstrable benefit, resulting in new learning opportunities and increased scope for independent learning.

ICS education promotes independent learning as an important feature. Computer science is funded as a laboratory subject and as such classroom and laboratory teaching are both important and integral parts of the educational provision. There is heavy reliance on equipment, which is expensive to purchase and subject to continual and rapid development. As discussed in the second section of this chapter, developing the practical skills associated with programming can be particularly time and resource intensive: it is therefore important that there is access to adequate and appropriate resources for this purpose.

The special relationship which exists between the computer as an educational tool and the subject of computing itself provides opportunities for enhancing the learning process which are peculiar to this discipline alone. The core business of computing requires students to have access to high quality facilities. These facilities can also be used to provide access to appropriate tools and practices to support the learning process. Conversely, the same close relationship has on occasion fostered a myopic tendency to overlook the power of technology to support the teaching of ICS. Technology still awaits a willingness to grasp its full potential although recent moves towards increased learning efficiency has raised interest. Resource constraints brought about by the rapid increase in student numbers and exacerbated by the need to continuously update both curriculum and equipment, inhibit enhancement of the quality of teaching and learning. Appropriate use of technology can promote innovative and effective teaching, providing extensive opportunities for independent learning by students.

ICS is a diverse and highly dynamic discipline area, the shelf life of computing curricula and learning materials is extremely limited by the rapidly changing nature of the subject, making computing science and technology-related areas of information science very volatile in terms of resources. Traditionally, this has deterred authors and publishers from committing resources to media production that will age. The now universal platform independent route to materials via the WWW means that courseware is now easily upgradeable and has resulted in a rapid growth in the quantity of information available. However, much of this information is unclassified and unstructured making the search for useful and relevant material particularly difficult. Users in the academic community find great difficulty in locating relevant and up-to-date resources and a great deal of effort is required in order to conduct successful research. The quantity of materials available means that the process of discovery, evaluation and selection of materials and products that reach the required standard is an onerous one.

Information and communication technologies services and networks are rapidly transforming the way people live, work and learn. Preparing individuals with the knowledge and skills they need for the emerging 'Information Society' and for continued lifelong learning is becoming a priority task for educators at all levels. Competence in ICT is rapidly becoming a 'life skill' that ranks alongside basic literacy and numeracy. ICS graduates clearly have the necessary IT skills. However, it is the 'communication' dimension which is assuming increasing importance in the sense of equipping young people to transfer their thoughts and ideas. ICS educators need to develop awareness of how online teaching technologies can become an integral part of the process and management of all teaching and learning; to enhance and enrich education; to provide access to electronic information sources and interactive learning resources; and to encourage flexible and effective patterns of learning.

THE ICS PROFESSION

New developments in the ICS curriculum planning process must recognize the importance of distance and lifelong learning in terms of meeting the skills shortage, employability and professional development. In order to ensure skills development for employability and professional development, departments must adopt a culture of innovative responsiveness to economic, social and cultural needs. New employment-related higher education qualifications (in the form of foundation degrees) provide students with the specialist technical knowledge and skills needed for jobs at the associate professional and higher technician level and as such require a fresh approach to interaction with business, community and public sector organizations. Departments are increasingly exploiting partnerships between their institutions and local business. Industrial input to teaching and learning is common – many departments have established good local links with employers which have led to successful student placements, industry-based projects, research collaboration and curricular development through joint academic/industrial appointments, thus providing a means of exposing students to current industrial practice. Such partnerships clearly provide opportunities to disseminate knowledge from research into the community and have a further advantage in so much as industrial collaborations can significantly shape research and curriculum.

According to EU Enterprise Commissioner Erkki Liikanen, 'Innovation is the key to competitiveness' (CORDIS, 2001). Business operations have changed as a result of competition and globalization, with increasing emphasis being placed upon the generation and adoption of new and innovative ideas. In order to be successful in the workplace, ICS graduates must be equipped with the entrepreneurial skills necessary for new product development.

There is clearly a need for well-trained entrepreneurial thinkers. The dot.com market is heavily laden with recent graduates whose probability of success when embarking on entrepreneurial ventures is greatly enhanced by some underpinning university-based study of entrepreneurship. Through the Science Enterprise Challenge, 12 Science Enterprise Centres have been established in universities around the UK. These Centres focus on the incorporation of entrepreneurial skills into programmes of study in science and engineering and must therefore combine a focus on developing a culture of entrepreneurship with the development of critical personal and team skills. To accommodate the introduction of these evolving professional topics, already crowded ICS curricula are being squeezed still further, further exacerbating some of the problems associated with retention.

The development of an entrepreneurial culture among students is underpinned by work experience. In the 1997 UK Inquiry into Higher Education (NCIHE, 1997), Lord Dearing recommended that institutions should 'identify opportunities to increase the extent to which programmes help students to become familiar with work, and help them to reflect on such experience'. Work-based learning helps students to develop towards professional maturity and gain a broad understanding of industrial requirements and how the industry is developing. Furthermore, students returning from industrial placement often bring knowledge and expertise that enhances the teaching and learning experience of the whole class.

> ## Interrogating Practice
>
> What unique experiences do students returning from placement bring with them? How can you best harness these experiences in order to enhance classroom practice?

Many departments have a strong vocational element with a significant work-based learning (placement) component and as such have excellent industrial links. Industrial placements, which typically last one academic year, are intended to provide experience of, and the skills needed for, commercial practice. Such schemes are regarded as beneficial by both students and employers – effective sandwich placements often lead to permanent employment. **Work-based learning** has played an integral role in ICS programmes for many years, however, the acute rise in student numbers has brought about a corresponding increase in the administration and monitoring of this process. Innovative approaches to the management, monitoring and assessment of industrial placement include the use of VLEs to support aspects of the placement process.

Students on placement prepare reports covering not only their technical role but also details relating to the management and market position of the employing organization. Students find difficulty in preparing such reports in isolation as they have little practical knowledge of other comparable organizations. By using the communication facilities offered by a VLE, students can work collaboratively to resolve issues and achieve common aims, without reducing individual responsibility. In addition students have access to necessary support materials that define essential information, emphasize principles and concepts and incorporate selected publications which aid understanding. Students value the opportunity to communicate with both tutors and peers, seek assistance with problems and share concerns.

The strong vocational element in many ICS courses, together with an emphasis on personal and transferable skills, has ensured the production of employable graduates with skills appropriate to industry and commerce. Many departments have initiated a programme of professional skills training as an integral part of taught programmes. Furthermore, personal development planning (and the scheduled introduction of progress files) will require students to track and record skills and competencies gained throughout their academic lifespan. Assessing personal and professional skills normally requires production of a personal portfolio, providing a continuing audit and documented evidence of work carried out and skills acquired. Such a process must be highly structured and has a substantial mentoring requirement in terms of identifying and reviewing the knowledge, skills and understanding that needs to be acquired and developed and deciding actions to be taken together with responsibilities and timescales. Being able to understand, reflect upon and plan for personal development are important life skills which help students to develop and equip themselves with the skills to survive and thrive in the ever-changing world of employment. ICS graduates seeking membership of relevant professional bodies need to maintain a portfolio as part of their continuing professional development (CPD) and find this process useful in preparation for membership.

ICS graduates are a highly prized commodity in the employment market – a fact that is reflected in the high rates of employment and associated salaries. In comparison with many other subjects, the employment record of ICS graduates is still good. Students who are successful in ICS-related courses at all levels normally find ready employment in industry and commerce. The majority of those seeking permanent, relevant employment normally secure posts shortly after completion of their course. Currently the IT industry both nationally and globally is in a consolidation phase with reduced demand for new recruits. It is, however, expected that demand for computing courses will remain high and will grow steadily, matching demand for staff from an ever-increasing range of application areas in which computing is relevant.

In conclusion, within the discipline of computing and information science, the higher education sector faces a dual challenge: first, that of attracting new staff, with experience and knowledge of current practice, and second, ensuring continuing professional development of existing lecturing staff in order to provide a workforce with the appropriate knowledge and skills for employment and entrepreneurial venture. National initiatives such as establishment of the LTSN centres, with their role for sharing and disseminating best practice as illustrated in this chapter, are particularly relevant to the information and computing science disciplines, as academics endeavour to address the problems discussed.

REFERENCES

Brown, G, Bull, J and Pendlebury, M (1997) *Assessing Student Learning in Higher Education*, Routledge, London

CORDIS (2001) *Focus*, **186**, 3 December (ISSN 1022–6559)

Kneale, P and Collins C (1996) *Study Skills for Psychology*, Edward Arnold, London

National Committee of Inquiry into Higher Education (NCIHE) (1997) *Higher Education in the Learning Society*, NCIHE, HMSO, London (also to be found at: http://www.ncl.ac.uk/ncihe/index.htm)

NISS, Quality Assurance Agency Overview reports: www.qaa.ac.uk

QAA Subject Benchmark for Computing http://www.qaa.ac.uk/crntwork/benchmark/benchmarking.htm

Schmidt, H, Norman, G and Boshuizen, H (1990) A cognitive perspective on medical expertise: theory and implications, *Academic Medicine*, **65**, pp 611–21

Wand, I (2001) *Research Assessment Exercise 2001: Overview Report from the Computer Science Panel*, UoA, **25**

FURTHER READING

See Ltsn-ics@ulst.ac.uk for a comprehensive overview of the work of the Learning and Teaching Support Network for Information and Computing Sciences, to include hyperlinks to other relevant sites

20 Key aspects of teaching and learning in arts, humanities and social sciences

Philip W Martin

INTRODUCTION

The purpose of this chapter is not to provide a catalogue of classroom techniques, but to ask a series of questions about what it is that we do in the classroom, and why we do it. Two axioms provide the basis for this chapter. First, at the centre is placed the student as active subject. That is to say that there is no presumption here, at any point, that passive learning, or the consumption of knowledge, is at all possible within the arts and humanities. No colleague teaching in these areas would demur from the legitimacy of this axiom, yet at the same time, some would also see it as an ideal proposition. Second, arts, humanities and social sciences are disciplinary fields which are heavily value-laden. That all education may be value-laden is doubtless a contention to be taken seriously (see Rowland, 2000: 112–14) but the point to be stressed is that the academic subject areas addressed in this chapter are cored through and through with ethical issues, social concerns, judgement, and the recognition of human agency, in a way that hotel and catering management, for example, cannot be, and in a way that physics, for example, may not be. So, discussion of teaching and learning in these subject areas consistently acknowledges the high degree of volatility that derives from a rich constitutional chemistry: in these classrooms the validity of personal opinion, subjectivity, individual experience and creative scepticism mix with judgements about right and wrong, truth and untruth, order and chaos. Our task as teachers is to ensure that such judgements as emerge are best provided for by being well informed, and that this threshold of information is also served by a schooling in argument, the careful presentation and interpretation of evidence, and the identification of the valuable questions that need to be asked.

CONCEPTS

Broadly the Arts and Humanities have this in common: they do not understand themselves to be an education primarily structured around the imparting of skills and competences, but one primarily structured around a series of engagements with a body of knowledge, or (in the case of the practical arts) a body of practice. Although these 'bodies' are very difficult to define or delimit in precise terms, and are continuously disputed by academics and practitioners, this wide definition holds true.

Of course, a distinction such as this is to an extent artificial. Engaging with knowledge, or practice, requires the acquisition of methods of understanding, and those in turn require technical comprehension (in the analysis of language or data for instance, or in the understanding of the processes whereby artefacts are made). A student cannot 'naturally' engage. He or she must learn the disciplines that govern, or make sense of, the ways in which we can approach and negotiate knowledge, and this learning could indeed legitimately be described as accomplishment in 'skills'. But it is not the imparting of this accomplishment, primarily, which governs the concept of the educational experience.

And here we discover a major paradox. For just as we cannot fix the centre of the education in skills, or the range of abilities needed to acquire and negotiate knowledge, neither – surprisingly – can it be fixed in the other quantity of my definition, the body of knowledge or practice. This is awkward, frustrating even, but it is essential to understand this if we are then to comprehend the key aspects of teaching and learning in the arts, humanities and social sciences. For across the whole spectrum, these subjects are concerned with *acts of continuous reinterpretation and revision*. Hence the use of the word 'engagement'. These subjects break up the bifurcation, or the conventional grammar, of knowledge and understanding, just as they break up the equivalent relations between teaching and learning. Let us explore this for a moment, beginning with the latter pairing.

It was not so long ago that our understanding of classroom practice in higher education was dominated by notions of teaching. Then the term 'teaching and learning' came into being as a means of acknowledging the student experience both within and beyond the classroom, and this, commonly, is now inverted (with a somewhat overbearing political correctness) to become 'learning and teaching', in order to give emphasis to the most powerful armature of the educational experience. Yet whichever way round this phrase is put, it is an awkward instrument, implying a division between the two elements that is uncomfortable. At its crudest, this division implies (for instance) an active projection (teaching) and a passive consumption (learning); or, less crude, synthesis and assimilation (learning) related to, or deriving from, an activity directed at, or to, or between, the two primary subjects (teaching the student, teaching the subject). It is clear that these linguistic structures, or even simply the vocabularies, are forcing awkward divisions. The term 'teaching and learning' can of course refer to an undivided practice involving both tutor and student: in such cases the force of the conjunction ('and') has to be read very strongly as a unifying force, rather than a yoking together of discrete elements. But even when this is the intention, the terms are still sufficiently powerful to imply their separate functions.

Similarly, understanding and knowledge operate within a charged semantic field. 'Knowledge' we could say, is out there to be 'understood'. It exists as a primary subject to be understood by a secondary practice. But of course we would dispute this: understanding, we would argue (since knowledge is not raw data), constructs knowledge; it does not simply operate in a purely interpretative function. Knowledge, or more precisely the division of knowledge, is an historical construct.

Interrogating Practice

Is it possible to divide work in your discipline into categories of knowledge and categories of skills of analysis and understanding? Are such skills modes of knowing in themselves, and therefore a form of knowledge? In planning your classes what do you want students to *know*, and what do you want them to be able to *do*?

So 'teaching and learning' and 'knowledge and understanding' are awkward terms for the arts and humanities, which is not to say that we cannot use them, but that they will be used in a qualified way. For an arts and humanities education is not understood primarily as the imparting of knowledge, nor as the imparting of skills. Rather, student and tutor alike are involved in the revision and making of knowledge. As part of this process, 'skills' are to be seen also as constructs, as powerful determining agents in the making and unmaking of knowledge. In short, teachers in these areas do not tell their students what to think or how to think it; they try to encourage their students to think for themselves, and to understand this process as something operating within a broad academic rationale. And in this way, tutor and student alike are engaged with the construction and revision of bodies of knowledge, and in the arts, in a strongly parallel way, bodies of practice. To those involved in these subjects this may seem like stating the obvious: if opinions and ideas did not change, for instance, we would still be teaching history through Macaulay; if literary interests were always to remain the same, then English departments up and down the country would not be teaching half the writers now featuring on curricula.

Unlike the sciences, wherein change in the subject is driven most strongly by discoveries altering underlying paradigms; or the technological subjects, in which such change derives from technological advances; or some vocational subjects wherein change derives from changes in professional practice in response to commercial or legislative shifts, the arts and humanities change continuously by virtue of their being elements of a culture always in a condition of transition. Thus they transform through internal dispute, contestation, revision of tastes and methods, discovery or recuperative research, politics and philosophies. These subjects are continuously in debate and discussion: as new writers or artists emerge (or are discovered) to challenge existing norms, a field of discursive activity is stimulated; as new historical theories, evidence or discoveries are made, different and challenging historical narratives follow which will then be tested in debate. All these subjects operate in these ways for student and tutor alike: they require active, participating students, for discussion and argument are fundamental to their practice but this, in itself, can present difficulties, as illustrated in Case Study 1. In such dynamic fields, where new areas of work are continuously evolving, it is therefore vital to consider carefully how students are to be adequately supported.

Case Study 1: Teaching contemporary literature

English Subject Centre, LTSN, Royal Holloway

When students encounter contemporary fiction they often feel that they are being asked to let go of the handrails that have guided them through their programmes thus far. If they are preparing to comment on or write about Dickens' *Bleak House* or Jane Austen's *Pride and Prejudice* they can draw on their prior encounters with the author's work through novels, films and TV adaptations. Such classic texts and authors have, oddly, a kind of cultural currency which students can make use of in seminars and assignments. This familiarity often needs to be decentred by the tutor, as anyone who has tried to encourage readings of Jane Austen that reach beyond romance will know. Nevertheless, in many courses in English departments there is cultural capital there to draw on and experiment with when the module begins.

Contemporary Irish prose is under-researched, compared with English fiction or even Irish poetry. While students generally enjoy reading it, studying it often produces a crisis of voice as students realize they will be required to comment on a text without the opportunity to weave their comments into a prior conversation about a novel conducted among critics, a conversation which is normally ratified as acceptable through its publication and presence in the library. Students often see their encounter with contemporary fiction as one which requires them to develop an unmediated response to the text in question. When the fiction also invites them to investigate a culture different from their own this sense of vulnerability and the perceived risk of saying 'the wrong thing' can be acute.

There is a balance to be struck in these circumstances between giving students the sense of security they feel is lacking and encouraging the risk-taking that enables original work. I try to achieve this balance first by being clear about expectations. In a detailed handbook, I acknowledge anxiety and aim for clarity about what students are and are *not* expected to know. I then provide a glossary for dialect words and references to public figures or political acts that the texts refer to, in addition to a bibliography, and students can propose additions to both as the course develops. I also provide brief seminar preparation exercises which give the students some guidelines about issues to look out for and possible reading strategies. Students have responded particularly well, for example, when they have been asked in advance to read Eavan Boland's passionate arguments about women in Irish writing 'against the grain', reflecting on rather than acquiescing to the poet's arguments in *Object Lessons* (London: Vintage: 2000). These exercises help students to navigate their way through unfamiliar texts. They are in turn built into a course which is divided into three sections. The sections encourage the students to think of the course in terms of plateaux and progress so that they can develop a sense of achievement and development as the course proceeds.

In lectures and seminars, comparisons with texts students are already familiar with, through prior or synchronous modules, is helpful. If they are using Eve Kosofsky Sedgewick's ideas about sexuality elsewhere, they can be invited to summarize their understanding of her ideas for the benefit of other students. As in all seminars, students rely on the known to get to the unknown but it is important for the tutor not to become the only guide in this process: the sole authority on interpretation when other direct sources of commentary on the texts in question are not available. Locating the students as fellow critics through the use of primary sources in the seminar can help you to concentrate on developing students' independence. For instance, *Bunreacht na hÉireann*, the Irish Constitution, is available online and students can be asked to read it as a paratext for Colm Tóibín's *The Heather Blazing*, which focuses on a Supreme Court judge and his rulings on it. Short essays on Irish culture, like those to be found in the Attic Press series of 'LIP pamphlets', can form the basis for staged debates in the classroom, with groups of students adopting the position of one of the authors of the secondary texts. The advantage of this kind of approach is that it stages critical strategies for students and allows them to rehearse their critical voices before they have to prepare their readings of the fiction they have studied. Simple strategies, such as asking students to produce questions rather than answers in seminars, and asking them to answer each other's questions in small groups can help to raise students' awareness of the critical skills they already possess and those they need to develop.

I find it is crucial to stress that learning how to operate as an independent critic is as much the focus of a module as the fiction we are studying itself. This dual focus on the fiction and the student-critics is enabled in part by the theoretical issues with which my module on contemporary Irish fiction is concerned. The students are being asked to reflect on the different ways in which Irish authors draw on and move away from discourses associated with Irish nationalism. As students make their first attempts to respond to texts independently they are reflecting critically on how, and with what effects, the authors they are studying and they themselves are moving away from what John McGahern calls 'those small blessed ordinary handrails of speech' (1990: 52).

(Siobhán Holland)

The description of active and engaged students involved in the contestation of knowledge may sound rather too much like a highly idealized notion of a community of learning without hierarchies or differentiations, in which a liberal, or postmodern philosophy denies the validity of knowledge, because it can only ever be provisional, or relative. And perhaps in its most abstract sense, the concepts described amount to something of the kind. But we do not live in an abstract universe. We live in a material one, and the materialization of these concepts, most obviously in the construction of a curriculum, in classroom practice, in the three or four years of a conventional undergraduate education, require a good pragmatic response that is still capable of acknowledging the intellectual underpinning of our subjects. In this sense, perhaps, we can distinguish between the subject (as a concept) and the discipline (as a practice). Our first task, therefore, is to decide on strategies that are fit for purpose, and to consider curriculum design, and the context that such a design provides for the teaching which brings it to life.

CURRICULA AND CURRICULUM DESIGN

Designing curricula is in itself a predicate of change, since it offers the opportunity to reflect on past practice and assumptions, usually through the stimuli of student and staff feedback on the one hand, and research-generated change on the other. At the same time, because it is essential to conceive of the student as active participant, curricula need to be designed with the *desiderata* that the students following the curriculum should be stimulated by it. For some, or perhaps now only a benighted few, curriculum design is an odd, new concept. Believing that the values of the subject are sacrosanct, and should therefore remain undisturbed, they might prefer, therefore, to teach the subject as a reified object (rather than a field of human activity), regardless of its context (an insistence, in other words, on teaching the subject rather than the students). Quite apart from this being an indefensible stance in the face of cultural and intellectual change, it is pedagogically irresponsible in its denial of the need to recognize the student and the contextualization of student learning. Curricula in the arts, humanities and social sciences have a wide variation, for the scope of study is enormous. First, there are the conventional sub-divisions within the conventional disciplines, which include cultural and period divisions, there are also sub-disciplines (eg, within language and linguistics), and in the practical arts, divisions of genre (drawing, performance, painting, printmaking, sculpture, ceramics, etc.). Second, there are inter-disciplinary areas, some growing out of marriages between subjects (eg, literature and history); others the result of relatively recent political, social, or technological/cultural developments (gender studies on the one hand, media studies on the other); yet more that derive from theoretical challenges to conventionally conceived areas (there are, for example, many people working within the broad province of 'English' that will see themselves, primarily, as cultural historians, or cultural critics). Third, there are new, distinct areas growing out of more conventional regions of practice: thus visual culture is developing out of media and cultural studies on the one hand, and art history on the other; creative writing is developing out of English, and even as it does so, is cross-fertilizing with journalism, and script-writing from performance or film studies programmes. Although change is a constant condition of arts, humanities and social sciences, the pace of change is faster than ever before in this growing fluidity, this proliferation of cusps between subjects, as well as in the emergence of powerful new areas. Alternatively, the current context of change can be read less positively as a dissolution of the disciplines (Barnett, 1994: 126–39).

Interrogating Practice

To what extent do you understand your subject as a practice whose borders are defined by particular disciplinary procedures? What do you think students expect of the subject, and how would you explain to them its coherence and/or its interdisciplinary connections?

The first question confronting us when we begin curriculum design is that of situating our programme within this intellectual ferment, and although the prospect of marking out such territory is exciting, it also has to be done with the utmost care, to ensure that our own enthusiasm for exploration does not result in chaos or confusion for the students. Potentially good programmes can be easily marred by the unconscious displacement of academics' intellectual enthusiasms, or crises, into the student experience.

So, marking out the territory is an essential first stage, but this must be done concurrently with an understanding of the student body, and a conceptualization of what the whole programme might add up to. This, again, is challenging. There is a huge diversity in student intake nationally in these areas, and in some cases, this diversity has almost as great a range in individual institutions. Academics now teach mixed ability classes more than they ever used to, and all the signs are that this will continue and spread – even to institutions long accustomed to accepting only very highly qualified A level candidates. The implications for teaching and learning in general are considerable, but there are also very particular implications for curriculum design. Without a doubt, it is most usually the first level of a programme that deservedly receives the most attention in all curriculum design activities. Most academics have a clear idea about where they want their students to be upon completion of the degree, and their understanding of their discipline is such that they are confident about how a graduate in that discipline should be defined. Much less certainty now attends the understanding of how undergraduates should begin their degrees, and the reasons for this are manifold. First, the threshold of students' knowledge and abilities is no longer assumed to be stable or held in common (Haslem, 1998: 117–18). Second, every department will have its own understanding of the foundational experience required by the students. Third, institutional infrastructures and structures – and particularly those determined by modular schemes – would exert a strong logistical influence over what is possible. Each of these is addressed in turn below.

Interrogating Practice

How can the curriculum be designed so as to serve the needs of students and tutors in monitoring progress in the early stages? What are the best practical means of providing feedback to students that will allow them to identify strengths and weaknesses?

Students' threshold knowledge and ability

The majority of students in these disciplines will be coming from a school or college experience with a highly structured learning environment, which apportions tasks and assessments in a phased programme of learning. Others will be coming from **access courses**, or the equivalent, which are traditionally more intimate learning environments in which peer and tutor support are key elements. In addition, most of them will be impelled to follow disciplines in the arts, humanities and social sciences not as a means to a specific end, but because they have elected for an education of personal development which marks them out as an individual, and not simply as a consumer of knowledge and skills. In this education, pleasure and satisfaction, those orphans of a utilitarian educational policy, are essential motivators, and they will have been developed in, and practised by, the students in many different curriculum contexts. Here then, is a series of challenges for the curriculum designer: the students will find themselves in a learning environment that treats them as independent learners expected to construct, for the most part, their own particular interests and responses within the broad remit of their modules; they will find themselves less supported by peers or schooling; they will be seeking, amidst this, to sustain and develop further the pleasures and satisfaction that probably governed their choice of degree. All the time, during the first year, they will want to know how they are doing; their lecturers, in the meantime, will be concerned to know much the same thing, perhaps from another perspective. Feedback, therefore, is all-important, and is a vital agency to be used in the complex acculturation of the student in the early stages of higher education, where the new cultural forces at play are particularly volatile (see Barnett, 1990: 95–109).

Each department, ideally, will be agreed on how their students should develop in the first level of their study. Most will want to be assured, that whatever the students' prior experience, they will be well prepared for the second and third levels of their degrees, and able to choose an appropriate and coherent pattern of study where choice is an option. For most academics in these disciplines, the design of the early stages of the curriculum should be governed by the need to achieve an optimum balance between a grounding in knowledge, and the establishment of the necessary tools of analysis, including the acquisition of a critical, theoretical or analytical vocabulary.

Grounding is important for the students' future location of their own work within the broad map; tools of analysis provide the essential means by which students can define themselves confidently as active learners, for the primary materials (texts, documents, data) are converted from an inert condition into the constituents of new meanings and ideas through the students' own work. Precisely how either area is designed will be determined by the particular programme's character and purpose, which may range from the highly theoretical through to the pragmatic. What is essential here is that this character, or philosophy, should be clearly visible to the student, and not something that he or she is left to work out through arbitrary encounters with tutors of different preferences.

Most universities and colleges now work under the pressure of a system in which space in their buildings and infrastructure is measured and accounted in relation to student numbers and activities. In addition, a great many universities and colleges run modular schemes which offer student choice both within and across discipline areas. These common features have large and different effects on the teaching and learning of subject disciplines that should be acknowledged, and taken into account at the point of curriculum design: what it is that can be studied cannot be divorced from how it will be taught, and that, in turn depends on the availability of resources and time. A curriculum designer may, for excellent reasons, require four-hour blocks of time only to discover that a modular timetable prohibits this; similarly, rooms for small groups of students to work in pairs or fours with adequate facilities may not be available. A further complication for the disciplines is that that many degree structures now require or encourage students to explore a wide discipline base in their first year, thus minimizing the time available for the foundational phase. Such structures have (probably unbeknown to themselves) produced a graphic template for curriculum design within the disciplines that is an inverted pyramid, with students' subject experience growing from a narrow base to a broad tip across the three years of their degree.

Foundational experience

Having explored these three critical elements impacting upon the start of students' studies, we can recombine them into a composite picture, and then develop this across the extent of the degree programme. Where students are studying a combination of subjects (and very large numbers of students are in these disciplines, particularly during the first year, or level) then the inverted pyramid, or its near equivalent, is the key factor to be addressed, for it means that there is only a small proportion of the students' total study time available for the foundational phase in each subject. And in the arts, humanities and social sciences this foundational phase is commonly understood to be, of necessity, rich in content. Students studying English will usually be introduced to a range of genre, and some historical context, as well as methods of understanding; students of history will explore a range of periods and locations, or one rich period in depth, so as to maximize understanding of the different kinds of historical analysis, as well as comprehending the nature of sources, and historiography. Students of the practical arts will have an equivalent need to understand such breadth through their own practice (although the nature of such programmes usually means that their students have progressed somewhat further with this experience because of the benefit of the extra year provided by their foundation year, or its equivalent in access courses). Since this foundation is already compressed by the need to maximize feedback and concurrently build both knowledge and tools of analysis, curriculum designers are commonly forced into some hard, discretionary thinking that will focus on identifying essential components. In these subjects, such a phase is likely to have a broad and representative content rather than a narrow one, in order to allow the student sufficient introduction to the variety and kinds of materials to be discovered later in more depth. At the same time, a broad content will also provide sufficient range for the introduction of the different modes of analysis that will be refined as the students progress.

Interrogating Practice

If the foundational phase of the programme is broad based, what are the implications for work at the subsequent levels in your discipline? Conversely, if it is narrow (part of the inverted pyramid), what are the implications?

For a great many departments, discretionary thinking comes down to difficult and practical choices. What can be achieved within the established resource? Can the resource (between the three levels of the student experience) be redistributed? Should first-year students receive more, intensive teaching, since so little time is available in which so much needs to be established?

These questions have an added urgency for those departments that are offering an undifferentiated second stage (that is to say where modules are not designated by progression at levels two and three, but are offered to all students at both levels). Here, even more pressure is exerted on the first stage, since students will progress into classes in which the expectations attached to second-year full-time students will be the same as those in their third year. Where the curriculum designer is faced with a differentiated system at levels two and three however, there is an opportunity, and in the case of a steeply angled inverted pyramid structure, possibly an imperative, to push introductory work up into the second level.

Institutional infrastructure and levels

Levels are therefore useful devices for curriculum designers attempting to plot carefully student progression. Three levels will reduce the intense pressure of the first level experience; they may also allow a steady gradient of assessment tasks to be plotted similarly, to allow, for instance, the nurturing of independent research skills, or the training required for oral assessments and presentations. Without levels, such diversity is not always possible, for there can be no acknowledgement of a stage in which some carefully accounted risk can be attached to the development of new techniques, which will then, in turn, be assessed when the student is properly prepared. Although there are, doubtless, imaginative ways around this, undifferentiated systems tend to be conservative in assessment styles, honing very high levels of abilities in specific areas, and founded upon a homogeneous student body, usually very highly qualified.

There is resistance to progressive level structures in these disciplines in some quarters that stems from the essential nature of learning that they share, described at the beginning of this chapter. Since we are dealing here with content-laden bodies of knowledge, whose division into manageable portions is to a certain extent arbitrary, or conceptual, and not based on a linear knowledge pattern in which one stage necessarily predicates another, then levels are not, specifically, appropriate. Once a foundation has been established, there is no reason to suppose (for example) that the study of Picasso is intrinsically any more difficult than the study of Turner, or that the study of post-colonial ideologies is any more difficult than the study of medieval theology. While some credence would be attributed to the notion that some primary materials are more difficult, or less accessible than some others, this does not immediately convert into the assumption that they might be, intrinsically, third-level subjects. Academics in these subjects therefore have strong intellectual grounds for their resistance to models of learning which derive from content rigidly ordered by standard prerequisites.

Interrogating Practice

What is the rationale for progression in the programmes with which you are familiar? Is there, in your discipline, a convention or an understanding of the order of topics for study?

TEACHING AND LEARNING

Over the last decade or so, those teaching in the arts, humanities and social sciences have found their student numbers increasing at a high rate. Most of this increase occurred in the early 1990s, mirroring expansion within the sector as a whole. One effect of this was to stimulate reflection on student learning, as tutors discovered that the traditional techniques on which they had hitherto relied, predominantly the lecture, the seminar and the tutorial, were proving less effective. The prime reason for this, of course, was the group size: as tutors struggled to maintain high levels of participative discussion with their students, they discovered, unsurprisingly, that the seminar was not to be indefinitely distended, and that whole group discussion around a nominated theme of topic became more and more difficult. In subjects where the principle of learning itself relies so heavily on participation in discussion, and the exchange of ideas between peers, the advent of high student numbers, combining with the erosion of the unit of resource, produced something close to a crisis in the understanding of how students were to be best taught.

A whole stream of new techniques began to be adopted in the face of this difficulty, and these are perhaps best described as regenerative rather than revolutionary, since most were concerned not to alter radically the aim of the learning experience, but to sustain and continue to develop its best aspects. As a result, most subjects are now still operating within a framework of teaching delineated by the lecture, the seminar, and the workshop (supplemented by tutorials in specific cases). These terms are capable between them of classifying most of the formal teaching contact, but, in reality, they cover a wide repertoire of teaching techniques. It is also the case that in themselves, lectures and seminars do not adequately describe the current learning environment, which, in practice, is made up of a much wider range of elements, many of which have developed as a response to harnessing technology to enhance the learning process. Disciplines such as history and archaeology were early advocates of the benefits to be accrued from use of IT, and are discussed at length in the first edition of this Handbook (Cowman and Grace, 1999). Case Study 2, which follows, looks at the harnessing of technology to support the teaching of philosophy.

Case Study 2: Teaching the history of modern philosophy

University of Leeds

I tell my students that philosophy is an *activity* that they can learn only by *doing*. This applies as much to its history as to any other aspect of the subject. Struggling through a difficult primary text is like climbing a mountain – and if I were teaching them mountaineering, they would feel cheated if all I did was to show them pictures of the view from the summit, and describe the wrong routes taken by other mountaineers. They need to get their boots on, and work up a sweat.

In teaching the history of philosophy, the easiest method (for teachers and student alike) is for teachers to give the students their own interpretation of the text. But then the students have no need or motive to read the text itself, and they are left cheated. It isn't reasonable to expect them to plough through page after page of material which they don't have the background knowledge to understand. So how can they be helped? As with mountaineering, one can help by removing unnecessary obstacles, and by guiding them through the difficulties that remain.

One unnecessary obstacle for philosophy students (though not necessarily for students in other humanities disciplines) is *linguistic*. When I first gave a course comparing Descartes and Hobbes, students complained that they couldn't understand Hobbes's English. 'Why couldn't Hobbes write decent modern English like Descartes?', as one student put it. So I translated the Hobbes texts into modern English, and ever since, most students report more satisfaction from reading Hobbes than Descartes.

As for guidance, students need to be led by the hand at the precise point where there are difficulties. It's not much use having a dense text on one part of the desk, and a running commentary beside it, if there's no easy way of relating the commentary to the text. The simplest solution is to provide all the material electronically, with a split screen. The text, broken up into short paragraphs, is presented in the upper frame, with a running commentary in the lower frame. Hyperlinks enable the student to summon up the relevant commentary from the text, or the relevant text from the commentary.

In order to make the students' learning experience more active, I encourage them to digest the material by creating a dossier of course notes. By splitting the screen vertically, they can have two portrait windows, one with text and commentary, and one with a word-processing package; and they can copy and paste from the former to the latter. They are guided in their note taking by a series of questions, which are also discussed in face-to-face seminars.

Needless to say, there are serious problems in getting students to participate actively in this approach to enhancing student learning. Too many students simply print out the documents (at considerable cost to themselves), and they lose the benefits of hyperlinking. The module is under continuous development, and my hope is that by adding more and more features that are available online only, future students will take full advantage of this mode of delivery.

(George MacDonald Ross)

Lectures

Commonly denigrated by many educationalists as an inefficient technique for student learning, the lecture nevertheless continues to occupy an eminent position in many of these disciplines, but perhaps no longer as a theatrical experience, the dramatization of the great mind at work. The arguments against lectures are powerful ones: they produce, potentially, an awkward relationship of an active teacher and a passive, consuming student; they make unreasonable demands upon the concentration span; they have the liability of being implicitly monological, and thereby, construct alienating models of knowledge; they privilege a first-order discourse of speech, while initiating second-order recording devices through the writing of notes; they do not require, ostensibly, student participation. All of these objections have some validity, and moreover, they are underpinned by the certain knowledge that the bad lecture is surely, irrevocably, the very worst of all bad teaching experiences.

However, there are counter-arguments to be made on the lecture's behalf. None of them are strong enough to rescue the bad lecture, or to remove the risk of its occurrence, and none of them can be defended without being carefully related to the aims of such teaching. In this respect, it is not possible to defend the lecture as an aggregated mode of teaching; it is only possible to defend the different kinds of lectures in relation to the purposes for which they might be fit. For this reason, more space is dedicated to a taxonomy of lecturing here than to any other teaching modes, since the different kinds of seminars, tutorials or workshops are probably familiar enough.

Lectures are adopted or retained partly because of the pressurized unit of resource which has encouraged departments to move towards large group sessions. At the simplest level, lectures offer an efficient mode of teaching large numbers of students all at once. Even so, the question must be asked: what is it that the lecture can offer? In turn, this can only be answered sensibly by stating first that there are many different kinds of lectures; the first principle here is to analyse what it is that we wish the lecture to achieve. The **exemplification lecture** is a lecture designed around a series of analytical examples. It will take, in the case of literature students, for example, a literary text with which the student is familiar, and demonstrate different modes of interpretation. It will show the advantages and disadvantages of these modes, thereby calling on the students to be arbitrators of a kind, seeking simultaneously, to explore the distinct intellectual or theoretical positions which underpin the different modes. The **thesis lecture**, is, in contrast, a piece of argumentation, frequently contentious, possibly provocative, but always building a case. This mode of lecturing is designed to provoke a response, or deliver a surprising perspective on a familiar subject. Closely related to this is the **explicatory lecture**, a lecture which seeks to mediate and make more comprehensible a difficult area, the value of which depends almost wholly on the opportunities therein for the lecturer to demonstrate how such concepts and ideas can be better understood, while simultaneously periodically checking on the students' progress.

Lectures can also be arranged around the provision, or definition of *context*: the consolidation of relevant materials through which the object of study may be illuminated in different ways. 'The lecture' may be a broad category, but it is constituted by several sub-genre, each of which is characterized by specific aims and objectives. In each case, the lecture provides that which cannot be provided by other means: it offers the dramatization of intellectual processes, by which I do not mean an extravagant performance, but the living exploration of questions, ideas, theories and counter-arguments.

Further, lectures not only come in a variety of forms deriving from their purpose, their styles or modes are various too. They can be informally interactive, inviting unscheduled interruptions and questions; formally interactive, with such slots built in – usually with predetermined lines of enquiry, and including discussion between the students as well; they can be 'dialogues' in which two lectures present contrasting arguments; they can be one, or a series, of 'mini-lectures' where several lecturers may present for only 5 or 10 minutes, in a carefully coordinated series.

Seminars

In their purest form, seminars are, of course, very different. Deriving from the Latin term for seed-bed, ideally the seminar is precisely this, a place wherein students' ideas and intellectual development will be nurtured by way of discussion and reflection. Conceived in this way, the seminar should not be a place for tutor 'input', so much as a place for his or her guidance. In practice, seminars are not just this: the student group size frequently exceeds the sensible limit for discursive activity (around 10), and the term 'seminar' is used commonly to describe a one- to three-hour group event that may well include some formal input from the tutor, followed by general or structured discussion. 'Workshop' is an alternative name for such activity. Seminars and workshops, of course, may be further divided into sub-categories.

The rationale for choice of teaching mode here is almost always guided by the principle of student engagement. Will students be best served by the structuring of group discussions within the seminar, by presentations from groups or individuals, or by a series of structuring questions set by the tutor? There is no single mode of teaching that is likely to prove intrinsically more effective than another: the essential question is whether it is fit for purpose.

A seminar itself (as the inert form) is just as likely to stifle discussion and exchange as promote it. Teaching forms are loose structures that need to be made taut around their purposes: if the aim of the seminar is to promote discussion between students on a given text or topic, then preparation for the seminar must be given proper priority, and the subsequent arrangement of the seminar requires careful planning to ensure proper interchange. Large groups, for example, need to be more orchestrated and structured than smaller ones.

If, on the other hand, the purpose of the seminar is to get students to explore a given topic, text or document together, then it is important to ensure that they will be in sufficiently small groupings to ensure that their collective explorations are truly beneficial. There are no slick rules to be adopted here, but there are optima to bear in mind: a cryptic two-line poem by e e cummings, for example, may be under-served by discussion in pairs; an extended passage of literary theory, or a complex historical primary document, however, may be more effectively examined by just two people working together.

Today's higher education classrooms, with a wider range of mixed ability students, many of whom are also from different educational backgrounds, require a far higher degree of organization and preparation. Most tutors find that seminars are best served by a greater structuring of student time outside the classroom, and requirements for specific forms of preparation. Increasingly, tutors are discovering the advantages of supplementary forms, such as the **virtual seminar**, which provides the opportunity for students to reflect on points in the discussion, read, research and think, before replying. These synthetic processes, so important in these subjects, can be very well supported by the new technology. In addition, the virtual seminar can provide confidence-building for students uncertain of their oral abilities, reducing the performative anxiety that afflicts the large seminar group. In both respects, virtual seminars can bring benefits to live seminars, providing a structure for preparation, and an opportunity for shy students to discover the authenticity and acceptance of their own voices.

Interrogating Practice

Bearing specific examples in mind, what might be the group size optima for particular seminar topics in your discipline, and how might these change in a typical programme from week to week? How can seminars be organized to provide sufficient flexibility?

ASSESSMENT

There is perhaps no more contentious area in teaching the arts, humanities and social sciences than the assessment of students, and no single area, perhaps, that has seen so much innovation of practice over the last decade (innovations that are being pulled back at the time of writing, in some universities, by an insistence on a proportion of assessment by examination driven by fears of student plagiarism). Assessments now take a wide variety of forms, ranging from creative or practical work, through illustrative and design work, discursive essays and theses, social science style surveys and interpretation of data, performance and oral presentations done in groups or individually, online assessments, and so on. Such forms of assessment also transform in their various modes, such as examinations, course work, and formative or summative assessments. An interesting approach to assessment, and an interesting approach to consideration of gendered space, is illustrated in Case Study 3.

No attempt will be made here to summarize this almost endless variety, since assessment catalogues in themselves are probably not particularly useful in these subjects. It is essential, nevertheless, for there to be a rationale for the assessment diet in any given programme, and for practitioners and tutors to reflect upon the purpose of the assessments set.

Case Study 3: Teaching social geography

University of Gloucestershire

For most of my students, the level 2 module in Social Geography is their first taste of the subject. The aim of the module is to explore the significance of space to social life, and I select topics from current events debated in the media, or from areas of students' own experience, to engage their interest and to encourage them to feel that they have something valid to contribute. Mindful of the fact that they will need to start work on their dissertation at the end of the year, the module must develop research skills, including presenting and analysing social patterns via (carto)graphical and statistical techniques. Beyond this, I try to elicit an awareness of alternative ways of explaining such patterns, to question the 'taken-for-grantedness' of popular and other accounts of issues such as minority ethnic segregation, homelessness, or crime.

This range of intended outcomes calls for a fairly imaginative mix of teaching modes. The usual format for my two-hour classes is a loose structure of lecture 'bites' interspersed with different activities. These activities might involve a practical exercise with maps or calculators. More frequently, I ask students to reflect on some material stimulus which I've brought to class – a video or audio tape, a newspaper article, or a set of questions. They jot down ideas, then share them in a plenary session which leads into a mini-lecture.

To give an example: because of the limited opportunities to develop the topic in level 1, most students are barely aware that gender has any relevance to geography. So the session on gender and environment starts by asking students to work in small (mixed) groups to identify places where they feel 'out of place' because they are male or female, and (an idea I adapted from a recent student text), to think of the kinds of images typically used on birthday cards for 'Mum' and 'Dad'. By using their own diverse experiences to demonstrate how space might be gendered, students' own knowledge is both legitimized and, gently, challenged.

To explore how different theories are constructed, I present students with brief written accounts from semi-academic pieces. They must read these quickly, focusing not on the details of the argument, but on the language: 'underline those words or phrases which you find particularly striking'. For instance, one piece on urban gentrification might be couched in the language of 'urban pioneers' while another highlights flows of capital. I ask each student to call out one word or phrase which I write up on the board; later, this rather distinctive selection of words will be the vehicle for examining how knowledge is constructed in each written account. Similarly, in investigating how environment might contribute to crime, I focus on the case made in a influential book of the 1980s which has had a significant impact on public policy. After a brief introduction, students read (condensed versions of) a critical review of the book published in a geography journal, the rejoinder from the book's author, and the reviewer's response in return (each of these is written in a pretty vigorous style, which helps to spark their interest). Working in pairs, students identify two positive points and two negative points concerning the claims of the original book, and they write these on overhead transparencies; I collect these transparencies, cut them into strips, rearrange and present them on the OHP. These then become my visual aid for a mini-lecture on the debate over how environmental design determines social behaviour. In a linked session, we debate the alternative strategies deployed to control street crime and urban incivilities in the context of their own experiences of the local nightlife, considering how these strategies reflect different underlying assumptions about the structure of social life (including prejudices about students), as well as different political agendas.

Students' learning is assessed in two ways. The seen examination is a conventional summative assessment of their capacity to engage with ideas. The other element of assessment is a project on the social geography of a selected social group in a particular locality, to be written up in the form of a journal article. Each student negotiates the choice of topic with me early in the module (at which stage I head off anything that sounds like a reworked A-level project). Progress is checked in individual tutorials which direct them to sources of information they need to collect (statistics, field observations, interviews), and the books or articles to contextualize their primary research. Students' achievement on the project element is usually high, and they evaluate the task as challenging but fulfilling. I encourage them to think about expanding this topic for their dissertation, so that the summative assessment in this module becomes formative for the next level of study.

(Caroline Mills)

A key factor in Case Study 3 is that of skills. This chapter has not emphasized the teaching of skills as something distinct from content, but in the area of assessment, due consideration must be given to student training in the mode of assessment. This is particularly so in these areas where an enthusiasm for diversification on the one hand, and the breaking down of discipline divisions on the other, can compound to produce potentially damaging effects on the students, and indeed, on standards.

Nowhere is this more obvious than on joint degrees or in modular schemes where students move across two or three subjects. Drama students, for example, may be highly competent in oral and presentational skills (having received practice and training) where other students may not be; design or media students may be particularly skilled in Web site exercises, where English students, for example, have had little prior support. Thus diversifying assessment in more traditional subject areas is a complex matter requiring sensitivity: setting a Web site design task may be an exercise underpinned by a set of criteria that other subject areas may deem to be well short of an undergraduate standard. Similarly, tutors will need to satisfy themselves that they have adequate skills to advise and support the students in their assessment tasks, while simultaneously being sure that the new mode of assessment has the integrity to support the level of content required. Innovation is not intrinsically virtuous (Hannan and Silver, 2000: 1–13), and innovative or diversified assessment tasks should be achieved within a scale that pays due attention to training, support and the extent of the assessment tasks required of students, for too much variety will give insufficient practice and too little opportunity for students to refine their competences.

Essentially, my point here is an argument strongly in favour of a coherent assessment strategy focused *around* a broad agreement of the range of skills to be assessed. Once established, such a strategy provides a safe and well-mapped territory in which diversification can take place.

Interrogating Practice

What are the advantages and disadvantages of the predominant modes of assessment in your discipline? If you were to design an assessment strategy for your department, what would be the chief factors to consider?

OVERVIEW AND OUTCOMES

This chapter has acknowledged the great diversity of practice and kinds of learning undertaken in these disciplinary fields, and attempted to stress the need to be sensitive to context while focusing on the prime aim of engaging the students as active participants. In these respects, it has argued for the importance of a rationale for all that we do, a rationale that is sufficiently broad and flexible to deal with – in most cases – the current student constitution of mixed ability.

It remains to make some cautionary remarks about rigidity in such a rationale or strategy. That teaching and learning should be carefully planned, and conceptualized within a framework that acknowledges pedagogical styles and preferences, and further, that it should be understood to be moving towards specific kinds of developments in understanding, is incontrovertible. At the same time, the disciplines covered in this chapter are not constructed as linear or accumulative patterns of knowledge, each stage predicated by a former stage, and it does not follow therefore, that planning and structure map neatly onto the notion of specified 'outcomes' (see Ecclestone, 1999). Indeed, a strong feature of these areas is that of unpredictability: there is a sense in which the very best teaching session is the one which usurps and transforms the tutor's anticipated outcome (Rowland, 2000: 1–2). In such instances the students, individually or otherwise, bring a form of analysis to bear on the object of study which radically transforms the knowledge produced; alternatively, they may recast it through modes of understanding shaped in another discipline, or indeed, through forms of prior knowledge which have not been anticipated by the tutor. And even without these forms of intervention, anticipated outcomes can be subverted in other ways. The anticipated level of student understanding, for instance, may have been overestimated, or homogenized to an excessive extent. Such instances sometimes give rise to a series of fundamental questions at a basic level, which even so, are of radical potential in terms of their ability to challenge received views (Seitz, 2002). The mixed ability classroom is also a classroom in which casual assumptions about cultural knowledge, so prevalent in these disciplines, can no longer be made.

REFERENCES

Barnett, R (1990) *The Idea of Higher Education*, SRHE/Open University Press, Buckingham

Barnett, R (1994) *The Limits of Competence: Knowledge, higher education and society*, SRHE/Open University Press, Buckingham

Cowman, K and Grace, S (1999) Key aspects of teaching and learning in arts and humanities, in *A Handbook for Teaching and Learning in Higher Education*, 1st edn, eds H Fry, S Ketteridge and S Marshall, Kogan Page, London

Ecclestone, K (1999) Empowering or ensnaring?: the implications of outcome-based assessment in higher education, *Higher Education Quarterly*, **53** (1), January, pp 29–48

Hannan, A, and Silver, H (2000) *Innovating in Higher Education*, SRHE/Open University Press, Buckingham

Haslem, L S (1998) Is teaching the literature of Western culture inconsistent with diversity?, *Profession*, pp 117–30

McGahern, J (1990) *The Pornographer*, Faber, London

Rowland, S (2000) *The Enquiring University Teacher*, SRHE/Open University Press, Buckingham
Seitz, D (2002) Hard lessons learned since the first generation of critical pedagogy, *College English*, **64** (4) March, pp 503–12

FURTHER READING

Learning and Teaching Support Network (LTSN): http://www.ltsn.ac.uk. Click on 'subject centres' for all Subject Centre addresses, where subject specific materials relating to the enhancement of teaching and learning will be found.
http://www.hca.ltsn.ac.uk/
http://www.gees.ac.uk/
http://www.english.ltsn.ac.uk/
http://www.lancs.ac.uk/palatine/
Brown, S and Knight, P (1994) *Assessing Learners in Higher Education*, Kogan Page, London
Davies, S, Lubelska, C, and Quinn, J (eds) (1994) *Changing the Subject: Women in higher education*, Taylor and Francis, London
Downing, D B, Hurlbert, C M and Mathieu, P (eds) (2002) *Beyond English Inc.: Curricular reform in a global economy*, Heinemann, Portsmouth, New Hampshire
Gibbs, G, Habeshaw, S and Habeshaw, T (1988) *53 Interesting Things to do in your Seminars and Tutorials*, 3rd edn, Technical and Educational Services, Bristol

Key aspects of teaching and learning in nursing and midwifery

Della Freeth and Pam Parker

INTRODUCTION AND AIMS

This chapter aims to assist relatively inexperienced educators by exploring key issues for teaching and learning in nursing and midwifery. It is anticipated that educators from other disciplines will also find some aspects of the chapter helpful.

It begins by discussing the ever-changing context of healthcare and its implications for the knowledge, skill and attitudes that education for nurses, midwives and other healthcare practitioners seeks to develop. Recent curricula changes are outlined before turning to teaching, learning and assessment. A variety of teacher/facilitator roles that have evolved to support student learning are described. But first, we should acknowledge our own context and its inevitable influence on the chapter.

The authors work in a large, inner city school of nursing and midwifery in England. The local population is extremely diverse: ethnically, linguistically, economically and socially. Pre- and post-registration education for nurses and midwives is focused mainly upon preparing practitioners for work within the NHS, with an emphasis on meeting the particular healthcare needs of the local population. The School is also particularly committed to interprofessional education. Naturally, this context influences our perceptions.

CONTEXT

In recent decades the agenda for healthcare has changed rapidly. Students in the healthcare professions must acquire skills and attitudes that will enable them to respond positively to the opportunities and challenges of continual change.

Changes in the context of healthcare have caused changes in service delivery, requiring new or adapted professional expertise and, hence, a review of approaches to learning, teaching and assessment. The drivers for change include: an aging population, smaller households and dispersed families, changed patterns of disease, new technologies, political intervention, changed expectations of patients/clients and their families, increased engagement with complementary therapies, increased participation in higher education, workforce shortages and changed patterns of employment. Government and professional bodies have discussed many of these issues, and the responses that they require from the health service and higher education, for example in the landmark documents *Making a difference* (DoH, 1999), *Fitness for Practice* (UKCC, 1999) and *A health service of all the talents* (DoH, 2000).

Nurses and midwives have developed expanded roles (UKCC, 1992, 1997, 2002). They are increasingly likely to act as the lead professional for particular groups of patients/clients; a role previously reserved for doctors. The need for higher-level technical, professional and managerial skills has increased the demand for continuing professional development.

In recent years the student population has become more diverse in a number of ways including: age, cultural diversity, prior educational preparation, prior work and life experience. This has implications for teaching and learning, as do the increased demand for return-to-practice programmes and 'stepping-on/stepping-off points' (DoH, 1999; UKCC, 1999).

Essential though it is to respond to these changes in context as curricula are reviewed, this is not sufficient. There is a need to be proactive, to anticipate the future, to prepare students to deliver the healthcare that is required today *and* participate in shaping tomorrow's healthcare services.

Interrogating Practice

For the courses to which you contribute, do you know when and how they are reviewed to ensure they remain appropriate for current and predicted service needs? How might you make effective contributions to this process?

KNOWLEDGE, SKILLS AND ATTITUDES

The climate of continual change in healthcare requires a flexible, adaptable practitioner, committed to **lifelong learning** (DoH, 2001). Skills that facilitate lifelong learning include the recognition of learning needs and the ability to plan means of addressing identified needs, ie: information seeking and information management skills, critique, synthesis, evaluation, and experience in applying knowledge to professional practice in locally adapted ways. In addition to engagement with lifelong learning for themselves, students will need to facilitate the learning of others (peers, junior colleagues, service users): they must prepare to become educators.

Across the wide range of healthcare settings, nurses and midwives assess individual patients'/clients' needs and problems in order to identify appropriate and effective care. To achieve this they engage in clinical reasoning founded on theoretical knowledge and experience of clinical practice. Within resource constraints, nurses and midwives plan, coordinate, deliver and evaluate care that should be informed by the best available evidence. These core professional activities dictate most of the content of nursing and midwifery curricula, although there is scope for variety of learning, teaching and assessment strategies to achieve these outcomes.

Healthcare professionals need to spend much of their time listening, informing and negotiating, all of which must be conducted sensitively and respectfully. Good communication skills are essential, along with attention to diversity and ethics. The complex needs of clients are best met through effective interprofessional collaboration, which requires knowledge of professional roles and responsibilities in addition to good communication. Students should learn to practice in a range of settings, learn to be effective members of multidisciplinary teams, learn to educate and support relatives or volunteers that provide care.

The increased use of technology has affected all aspects of our lives but has particularly impacted upon health. Effective interventions can now be made where previously none were possible. Interventions can be quicker, at or near home, and often less invasive. Expectations are higher and professionals must learn new skills to exploit new technologies competently and humanely. In addition, service users and professionals can now access (and need to evaluate) a wide range of information from the Internet (eg, the National Electronic Library for Health (NeLH) www.nelh.nhs.uk) or a plethora of telephone and e-mail advice services, including the nurse-led service for England and Wales 'NHS Direct'. Better-informed patients/clients expect to be more involved in the planning of their care, and students must be prepared for the possibilities and tensions of this process.

Quality initiatives such as evidence-based healthcare (Trinder and Reynolds, 2000) and clinical governance (NHS Executive, 1999; Swage, 2000) have added to the responsibilities and educational needs of healthcare staff.

Widening access to nursing and midwifery education has increased the need for student support in relation to personal and academic matters. Much of this support is directed at developing or reawakening effective approaches to learning and meeting the demands of academic assessment (see Chapter 12).

In summary, practitioners require all the competencies incorporated in the provisional model of professional **competence** offered by Cheetham and Chivers (1999):

- metacompetencies of communication, self-development, creativity, analysis, problem solving;
- knowledge/cognitive competences (tacit/practical, technical/theoretical, procedural, contextual);
- functional competences, including occupation-specific organizational, cerebral and psychomotor skills;
- personal or behavioural competence, including communication skills and collaborative working;
- values/ethical competencies, eg, adherence to the law and professional codes, sensitivity, patient-centredness, confidentiality.

Development of this range of knowledge, skills and attitudes requires a broad and challenging education programme. Nursing and midwifery programmes lead to academic qualifications and registration with the professional body: that is, they offer a licence to practice. Therefore, it is particularly important that the assessment of students is **reliable**, **valid** and safeguards the public.

Interrogating Practice

In the light of the knowledge, skills and attitudes desired in the health care professions, which approaches to learning, teaching and assessment are likely to be most effective? How does your programme seek to help students achieve the required knowledge, skills and attitudes?

RECENT CURRICULA CHANGES

The incorporation of schools of nursing and midwifery within universities in the 1980s and 1990s saw an increased emphasis on theory and research. However, in recent years there has been criticism of practical skills of newly qualified nurses and midwives (NBS, 1998; UKCC, 1999). In addition, although flexibility to meet local need was thought necessary, there was felt to be an undesirable level of variation in programme content and standards: a particular problem for a course leading to a licence to practise. In response, the professional body published **learning outcomes** and competencies for pre-registration midwifery and nursing curricula (UKCC, 2000a, 2001).

A new pre-registration nursing curriculum was introduced at 16 pilot sites in September 2000 with all other schools introducing this within 2001. This curriculum uses a one-year foundation period, common to all branches of nursing, and a 'branch programme' of two years, which permits a greater focus on the speciality (adult, children's, learning disability, mental health nursing). This curriculum also emphasizes the development and assessment of clinical skills, and longer placements in practice settings. A requirement for placement experience to form 50 per cent of the programme remained unchanged, but there is new emphasis on a reduced range of placements. It was hoped that fewer, longer placements would aid skills development and provide a more authentic experience of patient care, from problem identification to problem solving or alleviation, and including the variations in demands on nurses over the 24-hour and seven-day cycles. There is also an emphasis upon linking students to a 'Home Trust' for the majority of their clinical experience, with the aim of encouraging a sense of belonging and, ultimately, recruitment to Home Trusts. Additionally, there is emphasis on interprofessional learning and collaboration (UKCC, 1999). The new curricula were almost immediately subject to review (although generally needed little change) following the publication of **subject benchmark** statements (QAA, 2001a, b). Ongoing review includes the intention of the Nursing and Midwifery Council (www.nmc-uk.org) to conduct a consultation on the four branch structure.

Criticism has not been restricted to pre-registration curricula. At all levels, the Department of Health (1999) proposed more flexible approaches to the provision of education; more use of **work-based learning** and learning focused upon the interprofessional team; and increased use of strategies that promote **reflection**.

In common with other disciplines, as the knowledge and skills demanded of nurses and midwives has increased, curricula have become overcrowded and there is concern about over-teaching students. As a means to address this problem some programmes have turned to problem-based learning (**PBL**), which is sometimes known as enquiry-based learning (EBL) (see Chapter 23 for a fuller description and discussion).

Staff shortages in healthcare have resulted in continual increases in student numbers for both pre-registration education and return to practice programmes.

This has resulted in very large number of students requiring supervision in clinical placements. In addition, the trend towards community-based care presents real challenges for supporting students' learning in practice placements (ENB, 2001; Hodgson, 2000).

LEARNING, TEACHING AND ASSESSMENT

Nursing and midwifery, in common with medicine, dentistry and the allied health professions, are practice-based disciplines. 'Hands-on' practical skills are key to professional competence. However, this is not simply craft knowledge, gradually acquired through peripheral participation, demonstration, practice, feedback and coaching. A number of key aspects are examined below and their relevant teaching, learning and assessment strategies are discussed. More general approaches to teaching can be found in Chapters 6–8, to assessment in Chapter 4 and consideration of some of the types of assessment mentioned below in Chapter 23.

Developing clinical reasoning

Theoretical perspectives, empirical knowledge and reflection all underpin the clinical reasoning that leads to clinical decision making. Higgs and Jones (2000) is an excellent edited collection exploring the nature of clinical reasoning in the health professions and strategies for assisting learners. The image they offer (Higgs and Jones, 2000: 11) is an 'upward and outward spiral' to demonstrate a cyclical and developing process, triggered by a client encounter. This notion has resonance with Bruner's enduringly popular model of a spiral curriculum (Bruner, 1966 – see Chapter 2).

It is good practice to begin with a client encounter (a real encounter or a PBL trigger, case study, or patient management scenario). This capitalizes on the intrinsic motivation to provide appropriate care to be found among healthcare students. The learning trigger should be suited to students' prior knowledge and experience in order that an appropriate level of disjuncture is created. Disjuncture is the gap between what you know and understand (consciously or unconsciously), and what you feel you need to know and understand (see Jarvis, 1987 for an elaborated discussion). Moderate disjuncture creates a readiness to learn and thereby close the gap; excessive disjuncture leads to learners giving up – a 'miseducative experience' (Dewey, 1938).

Providing appropriate learning triggers is made more difficult by heterogeneous groups, or poor knowledge about the learners for whom the trigger is intended. It therefore follows that writing or selecting good triggers for interprofessional groups presents special challenges. Experience in writing triggers is often key. It may be possible to work with a more experienced colleague, or colleagues whose knowledge of the student group or field of practice exceeds yours.

The assessment of clinical reasoning also presents challenges. The dilemma is that this skill is practice orientated but based upon theoretical or empirical knowledge. The usual assessment division of the theoretical and the practical is not helpful. Assessment approaches that can probe the various facets of clinical reasoning are required. Practice-based assessments (PBAs) conducted by clinical staff who act as mentors (the final part of this chapter elaborates on the role of mentors) can be effective: as can the simulated version of this, an Objective Structured Clinical Examination (**OSCE**).

Theory and underpinning knowledge

The theoretical perspectives and empirical knowledge underpinning practice for nursing and midwifery are drawn from many disciplines, including the biological sciences, psychology, sociology, ethics and philosophy, management, education and informatics. These are synthesized or complemented by research and theoretical perspectives originating directly from nursing and midwifery. To suit the subject matter and **learning objectives,** varied approaches to learning and teaching are necessary in such wide-ranging curricula. There is a place for the traditional lecture, for seminars, tutorials or supervision; for laboratory work, practical skills classes, **experiential learning,** individual and group projects; for simulation, **self-directed learning,** Web-based learning and portfolios; for problem solving and PBL/EBL.

A range of approaches to facilitating learning should strengthen the learning experience by capitalizing on the strengths and minimizing the weaknesses of each approach. For example, lectures accommodate large numbers and often prove useful for introducing new topics or concepts, providing an 'advance organizer' (Ausubel, 1978) for subsequent smaller group or individual learning. Lectures can also ensure uniformity of exposure. A good quality lecture is well structured and paced, providing opportunities for interaction and active engagement. It takes account of students' prior knowledge and experience, in addition to the place of the topic in the contexts of the wider educational programme and professional practice. Each teaching method can be similarly analysed. For example, see Part 1 of this book or Quinn (2000). Light and Cox (2001) also provide scholarly, insightful analysis and practical advice.

Assessing students' grasp of theory, recall of knowledge, and the synthesis and application of both, is best achieved through a range of approaches. Recall can be tested through unseen, written examinations or online tests via, for example: multiple choice questions, annotation of diagrams, or short structured answers.

Longer written responses are required to demonstrate reflection, synthesis, application and creativity. Examinations requiring essay responses have their place but should be augmented with assignments completed over a period of weeks, for example: coursework essays, portfolios, learning journals, project reports. Presentations might also be employed.

With each mode of assessment it is important to ensure that the process is, so far as is possible, transparent, fair, ethical, valid and reliable. The face validity of an assessment is important for maintaining student motivation. The assessment of the higher level skills listed in the previous paragraph should encourage students to apply theories and empirical knowledge to client care scenarios. The integration of theory and practice is returned to later in this chapter. For a more detailed discussion of assessment see Rowntree (1988) whose text is seen as an essential reader for those who need to understand and grapple with the many issues associated with the process of assessment.

Interrogating Practice

What are the strengths and weaknesses of the approaches to learning, teaching and assessment employed in your courses? Is each approach used to best effect?

Practical skills and professional judgement

Pre-registration nursing and midwifery curricula must allocate 50 per cent of the programme hours to learning through supervised experience in practice settings (ENB/DoH, 2001a). Supervised experience in clinical placements typically lasts from four weeks to just over three months. The focus of learning is different for each placement and should relate to the student's level and identified learning needs. Each student is allocated a mentor from within the clinical team to provide support and facilitate learning. Students should both observe care and participate in giving care. Their placements should be in a range of settings, including hospital wards, health centres and patients' homes, thus providing opportunities for developing a broad spectrum of skills and giving exposure to a variety of professional specializations. This requires schools of nursing and midwifery to have access to a broad spectrum of clinical placements (ENB/DoH, 2001a).

As noted earlier, providing sufficient suitable clinical placements is a difficult task. In many areas, nursing and midwifery students compete with students from other disciplines for practice experience. Continual effort is required to identify new placements; to prepare these for students; support the clinical staff in their roles of supervising, mentoring, educating and assessing students; and regularly audit all clinical learning environments.

The large numbers of students now in clinical placements, the shortage of clinical supervisors and the busy nature of health practice, make it desirable that students acquire some basic skills before entering clinical areas. This protects both students and patients. Teaching these skills is best conducted in the simulated ward settings of traditional practical rooms or more sophisticated clinical skills centres.

In a spiral curriculum, higher-level skills and more complex professional judgements are gradually mastered through repeated experiences of a variety of episodes of care. Experiential learning in clinical or simulated environments should be designed and supported so that the full learning cycle is completed: concrete experience, observations and reflections, formation of abstract concepts and generalizations, testing implications of concepts in new situations (Kolb, 1984).

The assessment of practical skills, clinical reasoning and professional judgement in the practice area usually takes the form of a practice-based assessment of clinical and communication skills, conducted by the mentor. Alternatively the student and mentor may complete a skills schedule: a booklet of skills that a student has to practice over a period of time in a variety of clinical settings. The mentor identifies, via reference to level descriptors, the student's level of achievement in each skill that is relevant to that placement. Students revisit skills in subsequent placements, improving their recorded level of attainment. The curriculum lays down threshold requirements for the number, range and level of skills acquired at milestones within the programme. Practice-based assessments (PBAs) vary between schools but usually require students to demonstrate achievement of specified learning outcomes at key points in the programme. For nursing students this may mean demonstrating competence in certain core skills at the end of the foundation year, before progressing to the branch programme.

PBAs and skills schedules are widely used in a broad spectrum of health professions, practitioners generally taking a positive view of their face validity, authenticity and practicality. However, there is some disquiet in relation to reliability, objectivity and the equality of opportunity. The concerns arise largely because of the large number of students on programmes and the consequent number (usually several hundred) and the range of placements, offering variable learning opportunities. Several hundred mentors involved in assessing students present challenges in relation to education and updating to promote consistency and accuracy in both interpretation of the learning outcomes, and application of the assessment tool. Schools strive to overcome these concerns by moderating at least a sample of mentors' assessments, or by augmenting mentors' assessments with more easily controlled, tutor-led assessments in simulated practice settings.

Simulation

Learning through simulation has been an established part of nursing and midwifery education for decades. Role play is discussed in the next section. Simulated environments such as traditional practical rooms or more modern clinical skills centres (Nicol and Glen, 1999) create some of the conditions of a clinical environment (eg, ward, outpatient clinic, or client's home) and permit the practice of psychomotor skills, experiential learning, discussion and reflection. Advances in technology have brought increasingly sophisticated mannequins and other simulators, permitting practice of psychomotor skills such as venepuncture and suturing. Computer-based simulation enables students to, for example, listen to heart sounds and arrhythmias, or to respond to emergency situations via an interactive CD ROM.

Simulation has many advantages. Learning can occur without risk to patients. Students can be allowed to make mistakes and learn from these. Practical skills can be developed in a systematic, supported manner, which can be difficult to achieve in busy clinical environments (for a description of one approach to doing this see the case study by Nicol in Fry and Marshall, 2002). Group sizes of 16–20 are common and manageable in a skills centre, but could not be accommodated in clinical practice. Discussion of theoretical and ethical matters can occur in parallel with developing practical skills in a simulated setting. This would normally be inappropriate in the presence of a patient and may be forgotten later in a clinically-based learning and teaching interaction.

The development of a key set of basic skills is possible in the early weeks of the pre-registration programme, prior to experiences in clinical settings. The most important skills are those that make clinical placement experiences safer, not only for patients but also for students and their colleagues: moving and handling, prevention of cross-infection, checking and recording patient information, etc. Other important skills are those that will allow students to feel and be viewed by qualified staff as useful members of the team, for example, taking basic observations. This will improve the learning experience of students.

Later in programmes, simulated practice environments such as clinical skills centres are useful for reflection upon experience in clinical areas and drawing out learning points, many of which can be addressed through simulated practice. Thus simulation contributes to the development of clinical reasoning and to the integration of theory and practice, both of which are addressed elsewhere in this chapter.

Assessment of practical skills in this environment is usually undertaken using an OSCE. Some nursing/midwifery OSCEs follow the short format developed in medicine (see Chapter 23), however, in nursing and midwifery a series of short assessment tasks raises some concerns. The behaviour encouraged runs counter to holistic care founded on knowledge, good communication, reflection and professional judgement. Therefore some schools have modified the OSCE format, particularly by lengthening the duration of each 'station' and assessing several skills in relation to one simulated patient (Nicol and Freeth, 1998). Objectivity may be reduced, but authenticity is improved.

Communication skills

It is almost impossible to name an aspect of clinical practice or educational practice that does not have communication as a key element. Therefore, it seems somewhat artificial to separate communication skills from the activities in which they are embedded. However, good communication is so important to promoting the well being of patients/clients, and for effective service delivery, that healthcare curricula will always contain learning outcomes related to communication in order to highlight this professional skill.

There may be teaching sessions labelled as 'communication skills', addressing such topics as: the psychology of communication, verbal and non-verbal communication; cultural diversity, language barriers and working through interpreters or advocates; communication with relatives, breaking bad news, etc. Ideally, most sessions are conducted with small groups in an undisturbed environment, with a supportive facilitator, and opportunities to experiment and practise this core skill.

Discussion and role-play are the dominant teaching strategies in this area of the curriculum, each requiring participants to be **active learners**. Such 'props' as telephones or one-way mirrors may support role-play; or where resources permit, input from specially trained, professional actors. The actors simulate patients and then come out of role to provide feedback to the students. A communications suite permits video recording for later self-analysis or tutor feedback.

The presence of timetabled slots for the development of communication skills does not obviate the need for attention to communication issues to be integral to other teaching and learning activities. For example, it is essential to discuss and practise appropriate communication while teaching junior students the practical skills of washing and feeding patients. Some teaching sessions concern psychomotor skills that are inevitably uncomfortable or embarrassing procedures. Supportive verbal and non-verbal communication is an important part of nursing and midwifery practice in these circumstances and should be considered alongside the development of the psychomotor skill. Furthermore, tutors who support students in their clinical placements are well placed to discuss communication challenges, to observe student performance and provide formative feedback.

Communication skills are rarely the sole focus of an assessment. Since communication is integral to other activities it is entirely appropriate to assess communication skills in parallel with knowledge or psychomotor skills. The main assessment vehicles are essays, reports and practical examinations such as an OSCE (see above). Presentations and posters are more closely focused on assessing communication skills. Whatever the mode of assessment it is important to develop clear assessment criteria; without these communication assessment may be downgraded. This can occur because of the complex and nuanced nature of communication, and because assessment in a manner that can be defended as reliable and valid presents challenges.

Interprofessional collaboration

Students need to appreciate that multidisciplinary teams deliver care, possibly spanning the NHS, social services, the private sector and the voluntary sector. Effective, efficient, client-centred care requires interprofessional and inter-agency collaboration. Each team member must understand his or her own role and its boundaries, and seek to understand the contribution of other team members. Good communication, other skills for team working, and a commitment to helping the client through productive collaboration must be developed during educational programmes. Appropriate skills and attitudes *could* be developed within learning experiences confined to one profession, but multidisciplinary and interprofessional learning are often seen as key to enhancing collaborative practice (DoH, 2000; GMC, 2002; UKCC, 1999).

Implementing interprofessional learning within pre-registration education is fraught with difficulties. These include coping with the large numbers of students, differing programme lengths and academic levels, timetable and other resource constraints, meeting the requirements of professional bodies, organizational problems, and geographical dispersion of related disciplines across universities. Despite these problems, enthusiasts regularly pioneer shared learning initiatives. A range of examples can be found within Barr et al (2000) and Glen and Leiba (2002).

While many shared learning initiatives have been classroom or skills centre based, there is increasing interest in capitalizing upon opportunities for shared learning within practice placements. After all, this is where interprofessional collaboration matters most. The task for educators is, in collaboration with their practitioner colleagues in the clinical setting, to coordinate the activities of the students from various professions that are placed within the same clinical environment. Facilitation for learning *with and from* each other should be provided. Case Study 1 outlines one approach to this.

> ## Case Study 1: Interprofessional training ward placement
>
> Senior students from four professions worked together in teams on an orthopaedic/rheumatology ward. Under supervision, they planned and provided care for a group of 12 patients. The aim of this project was that the students would develop an understanding of each other's roles and contributions, thus learning to collaborate more effectively.
>
> The teams consisted of at least one member of each profession involved in the pilot study (medicine, nursing, occupational therapy, physiotherapy) and they worked together for two weeks. The teams covered the seven-day week and worked the nurses' shift pattern of 'earlys' (07.30–15.30) and 'lates' (12.30–21.00) but no night shifts. They conducted interprofessional handovers at the beginning and end of each shift. Patient care was planned and delivered jointly by the interprofessional team. After a late shift the team would remain for an hour-long, facilitated period of reflection on their practice and learning.
>
> Evaluation of the pilot study found that the interprofessional training ward placement was highly valued by participants, but that some aspects of the original design needed modification before the interprofessional placement became a core component of several health professions programmes. More details can be found in Freeth *et al* (2001) and Reeves and Freeth (2002).
>
> This project has undergone substantial revision. It is now located within a range of clinical settings concerned with the care of the elderly and involves nine professions. A new format for the student learning experience will be piloted from September 2002.
>
> (Della Freeth and Pam Parker)

Integrating theory and practice

It is necessary for students to study underpinning theories and empirical knowledge in parallel with developing their practical skills. They must undertake care, knowing the rationale for their actions. Undertaking care also provides motivation for learning theory. There is a symbiotic relationship.

Approaches to learning and teaching and assessment that enhance the integration of theory and practice, include:

- PBL/EBL employing triggers that focus on the needs of an individual and any relative or friend assisting with care. This can also be used in practice settings with patients as the triggers. The emphasis is on active learning and critical enquiry; the analysis of needs, possible responses, choices and their implications. PBL also develops communication skills and is a suitable vehicle for interprofessional collaboration.
- Portfolios containing reflective analyses of experiences and learning, identification of strengths and weaknesses, consideration of future professional and personal development needs. The aim of this is to maximize learning through continual monitoring (Gannon *et al*, 2001). Reflective writing, while difficult at first, does provide a means through which students may develop critical analytical skills (Jasper, 1999).
- Simulated professional practice using patient/client situations where students have to undertake practical skills and also provide some discussion of the rationale underpinning their actions. For example, Lyons, Miller and Milton (1998) describe a 'pregnancy simulator' consisting of both physical simulations and multimedia computer simulations designed to develop abdominal assessment skills. This educational development was underpinned by Laurillard's (2002) 'conversational framework' for learning and teaching.
- Many schools assess students' knowledge and understanding of the links between theory and practice through reflective accounts of experiences from practice placements. Students describe and critique an anonymized clinical case or incident, analysing the care and its underpinning theory.

Interrogating Practice

Are there separate elements of theory and practice in your educational programme? If so, how do you integrate them?

Large and heterogeneous student cohorts

Earlier, we identified increasing diversity within student cohorts (age, culture, language, educational background and life experience, etc) and pressure to educate more nurses and midwives in order to meet workforce development requirements within the NHS. Case Study 2 illustrates the magnitude of the educational enterprise within our own School. It is essential to sub-divide cohorts, provide good academic and pastoral tutorial systems, provide learning support where needed, make good use of technology, and resist the temptation to over-lecture and over-assess.

> ## Case Study 2: Creating groups for learning – St Bartholomew School of Nursing and Midwifery, City University, London

The post-registration provision is very large and complex. The School has pre-registration intakes of 150–200 nursing students three times per year and an annual intake of 40–60 midwifery students. The student population is extremely diverse. For example, one of the 2001 pre-registration nursing intakes has 146 students, 88 per cent female, 12 per cent male. The age and self-reported ethnic composition of the cohort is as follows:

Age Range of Intake		Self-Reported Ethnic Composition	
17–24	37%	Bangladeshi	1%
25–30	27%	Black African	58%
31–35	14%	Black Caribbean	11%
36+	22%	Black Other	1%
		Indian	1%
		White	20%
		Other	8%

These students have a wide variety of entry qualifications from the UK and beyond, including university degrees and diplomas, school-leaving examinations, vocational qualifications and access courses. Some students have previously worked as healthcare support workers.

Pre-registration cohorts are divided into groups of no more than 23 students. Group membership is subject to as few changes as possible to enable the group to develop an identity and an environment in which students feel safe to discuss and debate issues.

(Della Freeth and Pam Parker)

ROLES AND ORGANIZATIONS THAT SUPPORT LEARNING

There is a wide range of roles that support student learning in the UK. There are prescribed professional and educational requirements for most of these roles

(ENB/DoH, 2001b; UKCC, 2001). This ensures that professionals who guide students' learning and assess students' performance have appropriate experience as nurses or midwives, and have studied the relevant educational principles. Mentor preparation is at degree level, while practice facilitators, practice educators, lecturers and tutors undertake postgraduate studies.

The new nurse or midwife lecturer/tutor should aim to understand the contributions of each of the roles that support learning in their local context.

Mentors

Within practice areas each student must be allocated a mentor (UKCC, 1999). Mentors facilitate students' learning by providing or highlighting appropriate learning opportunities. In addition the mentor assesses the student's practice, taking responsibility for identifying whether prescribed or negotiated outcomes have been achieved. The mentor must indicate whether he or she considers the student fit to practise. It is expected that all qualified practitioners who meet the educational requirements for the role will act as mentors in areas where students are placed.

Practice facilitators/educators

Practice educators are practitioners employed by NHS trusts rather than the university. Several drivers influenced the development of this role, including: the increased number of students now in clinical placements; the demise of the clinical teacher role; and increased demands upon lecturers' time, curtailing their ability to spend extended time in practice areas. The role is evolving rapidly but the intention is that the practice educator is both clinically competent and familiar with the students' educational programmes. The practice educator's role is focused upon the theory–practice link and learning from practice experiences. Practice educators support both students and mentors. They maintain close contact with the university staff responsible for managing and developing practice placements.

Lecturer practitioner

Lecturer practitioner roles are a combination of the practice educator and traditional lecturer role. They were developed as a link between trusts and universities so that practitioners could undertake a practice role with students and mentors for part of their time, and also develop a university teaching role. They were seen as a useful 'stepping stone' for those who wished to move from practice into education. It can be difficult to manage the demands of two employers and these positions are less popular than they once were.

Lecturers/tutors

University lecturers have multifaceted roles. For example, they deliver the theory-based teaching and assessment in students' programmes and relate this to practice. They link with service delivery settings, supporting students, mentors and their line mangers, and supporting practice development. Lecturers act as personal tutors to students. They also engage in curriculum development, scholarship and research. Most lecturers in schools of nursing and midwifery are nurses or midwives, but lecturers from other health professions may also be employed. Sometimes, lecturers without a health professions background are selected because of their ability to provide complementary disciplinary expertise and alternative perspectives.

University-based specialist learning services

An increasing range of specialist posts that support student learning are emerging (see Chapter 12). These include library staff with expertise to support PBL/EBL, technology (IT) and media resources staff who help students harness the power of newer technologies, and tutors offering language and learning skills support. Artists, poets or writers in residence are also increasingly employed to improve the quality of student learning.

Organizations that support learning

The Institute for Learning and Teaching in Higher Education (**ILT** – www.ilt.ac.uk) is a professional body for those who teach and support learning in higher education in the UK. It accredits programmes of training in learning and teaching, organizes events and produces publications. The ILT works closely with the Learning and Teaching Support Network (LTSN – www.ltsn.ac.uk). The **LTSN** comprises a 'Generic Centre', offering expertise and information on learning and teaching issues that cross subject boundaries, and 24 'Subject Centres'. The Subject Centre most relevant to those engaged in education for nursing, midwifery and the allied health professions is the Centre for Health Sciences and Practice (www.health.ltsn.ac.uk).

For those interested in researching their educational practice, in addition to the ILT and LTSN, useful information and contacts may be obtained from the British Educational Research Association (BERA – www.bera.ac.uk). BERA contains a number of special interest groups (SIGs), including one for learning in the professions.

Interprofessional learning has a particular champion in CAIPE (UK Centre for the Advancement of Interprofessional Education – www.caipe.org.uk).

Interrogating Practice

Which roles support student learning in your educational programmes? How are people prepared for their roles? How does your role complement the role of others?

OVERVIEW

This chapter has discussed key aspects of teaching, learning and assessment in nursing and midwifery. It considered the context of education, the required knowledge, skills and attitudes, strategies used to develop professional expertise and the range of roles that support learning. In a single chapter it is not possible to provide more than a glimpse of these issues; those who are interested are directed to the suggestions for further reading.

REFERENCES

Ausubel, D (1978) *Educational Psychology: A cognitive view*, Holt, Rinehart and Winston, New York

Barr, H et al (2000) *Evaluations of Interprofessional Education: A United Kingdom review for health and social care*, CAIPE/BERA, London

Brunner, J (1966) *Towards a Theory of Instruction*, Oxford University Press, Oxford

Cheetham, G and Chivers, G (1999) Professional competence: harmonising reflective practitioner and competence-based approaches, in *Developing the Capable Practitioner: Professional capability through higher education*, eds D O'Reilly, L Cuningham and S Lester, Kogan Page, London

Department of Health (DoH) (1999) *Making a Difference: Strengthening the nursing, midwifery, and health visiting contribution to health and healthcare*, DoH, London

DoH (2000) *A Health Service of All the Talents*, DoH, London

DoH (2001) *A Framework for Lifelong Learning for the NHS*, DoH, London

Dewey, J (1938) *Experience and Education*, Macmillan, New York

English National Board for Nursing, Midwifery and Health Visiting and Department of Health (ENB) (2001) *Report on the Quality of Students' Practice Experience in the Community in Pre-registration Nursing Programmes*, ENB/DoH, London

ENB and DoH (2001a) *Placements in Focus: Guidance for education in practice for Healthcare Professions*, ENB/DoH, London

ENB and DoH (2001b) *Preparation of Mentors and Teachers: A new framework of guidance*, DoH, London

Freeth, D *et al* (2001) 'Real life' clinical learning on an interprofessional training ward, *Nurse Education Today*, **21**, pp 366–72

Fry, H and Marshall, S (2002) Revitalizing and renewing the curriculum, in *The Effective Academic*, eds H Fry, S Ketteridge and S Marshall, Chapter 10, pp 182–99, Kogan Page, London

Gannon, F T *et al* (2001) Putting portfolios in place, *Nurse Education Today*, **21**, pp 534–40

General Medical Council (GMC) (2002) *Tomorrow's Doctors*, GMC, London

Glen, S and Leiba, T (eds) (2002) *Multi-professional Learning for Nurses: Breaking the boundaries*, Palgrave, Basingstoke

Higgs, J and Jones, M (eds) (2000) *Clinical Reasoning in the Health Professions*, 2nd edn, Butterworth-Heinemann, Oxford

Hodgson, P (2000) *Clinical Placements in Primary and Community Care Project*, NHSE, Leeds

Jarvis, P (1987) *Adult Learning in the Social Context*, Croom Helm, London

Jasper, M A (1999) Nurses' perceptions of the value of written reflection, *Nurse Education Today*, **19**, pp 452–63

Kolb, D A (1984) *Experiential learning*, Prentice-Hall, Englewood Cliffs, New Jersey

Laurillard, D (2002) *Rethinking university teaching: a conversational framework for the effective use of learning technologies*, Routledge/Falmer, London

Light, G and Cox, R (2001) *Learning and teaching in higher education: the reflective professional*, Paul Chapman Publishing, London

Lyons, J, Miller, M and Milton, J (1998) Learning with technology: the use of case-based physical and computer simulations in professional education, *Contemporary Nurse*, 7, pp 98–102

National Board for Nursing, Midwifery and Health Visiting for Scotland (NBS) (1998) *Information Base on Arrangements which Support the Development of Clinical Practice in Pre-registration Nursing Programmes in Scotland*, NBS, Edinburgh

National Health Service Executive (1999) *Clinical Governance: Quality in the new NHS*, NHSE, Leeds

Nicol, M and Freeth, D (1998) Assessment of clinical skills: a new approach to an old problem, *Nurse Education Today*, **18**, pp 601–09

Nicol, M, and Glen, S (eds) (1999) *Clinical Skills in Nursing: The return of the practical room?* Macmillan, Basingstoke

Quality Assurance Agency for Higher Education (QAA) (2001a) *Subject Benchmark Statements: Healthcare programmes – Nursing*, QAA, Gloucester

QAA (2001b) *Subject Benchmark Statements: Healthcare programmes – Midwifery*, QAA, Gloucester

Quinn, F M, (2000) *Principles and Practice of Nurse Education*, 4th edn, Stanley Thornes, Cheltenham

Reeves, S and Freeth, D (2002) The London training ward: an innovative interprofessional initiative, *Journal of Interprofessional Care*, **16**, pp 41–52

Rowntree, D (1988) *Assessing Students: How shall we know them?* 3rd edn, Kogan Page, London

Swage, T (2000) *Clinical Governance in Healthcare Practice*, Butterworth-Heinemann, Oxford

Trinder, L and Reynolds, S, (2000) *Evidence-based Practice: A critical appraisal*, Blackwell Science, Oxford

United Kingdom Central Council for Nursing, Midwifery and Health Visiting (UKCC) (1992) *Scope of Professional Practice*, UKCC, London

UKCC (1997) *Scope in Practice*, UKCC, London

UKCC (1999) *Fitness for Practice: The UKCC Commission for Nursing and Midwifery Education*, UKCC, London

UKCC (2000a) *Requirements for pre-registration midwifery programmes*, UKCC, London

UKCC (2000b) *Standards for the Preparation of Teachers of Nursing, Midwifery and Health Visiting*, UKCC, London

UKCC (2001) *Requirements for pre-registration nursing programmes*, UKCC, London

UKCC (2002) *Report of the higher level of practice pilot and project*, UKCC, London. (Executive summary available in printed form; full report available only from Web site www.ukcc.org.uk)

FURTHER READING

English National Board for Nursing, Midwifery and Health Visiting and Department of Health (2001) See above: available for download from the Internet: www.doh.gov.uk

Higgs J, and Jones M (eds) (2000) See above.

Light, G and Cox, R (2001) See above.

O'Reilly, D, Cuningham, L and Lester, S (eds) (1999) See above.

Quinn, F M (2000) See above.

Rowntree, D (1988) See above.

22 Key aspects of teaching and learning in languages

Carol Gray and John Klapper

INTRODUCTION

This chapter will discuss issues relevant to the effective learning and teaching of modern languages in higher education. The first sections will consider:

- the changing face of language study in higher education;
- the implications for higher education language learning of changed school curricula and examinations;
- insights from second language acquisition research;
- communicative approaches to language teaching;
- autonomous learning;
- communication and information technology (C&IT);
- translation.

Following this is a case study of a first-year post-advanced language course which illustrates many of the recent developments in language learning and teaching and demonstrates how these can be integrated into a coherent whole. The focus throughout will be on language learning rather than the non-language elements of degree courses since the latter are covered elsewhere in this book, in particular in Chapters 9 and 10.

LANGUAGES IN HIGHER EDUCATION

Developments in the teaching of foreign languages over the past 40 years have resulted partly from new methodological perceptions but also from the changing role of the higher education institution as language provider. Higher education language courses were once characterized by a predominantly post-A level intake, by translation into and out of the target language, academic essay writing, the study of phonetics and 'conversation classes'. Nowadays languages are frequently offered *ab initio*; there is considerably less emphasis on translation, especially in the early stages of the undergraduate degree; there have been moves in several institutions towards increased use of the target language as the medium of instruction and towards broadening the range of learning activities to include oral presentations, group discussions, debates, précis, summaries, letters, reviews and reports.

'Non-language' components have also changed, with less study of pre-20th century literature, more of writing by women, and the addition of sociocultural, political and media studies and film. The extent to which the foreign language is used here as the medium of tuition is variable; in some cases because modularization has mixed language and non-language students on Area Studies courses, in others because staff fear a 'watering down' of intellectual content.

There is increasing employment of part-time staff, postgraduate research students and 'colloquial assistants' – now usually called foreign language assistants – in the delivery of key course components. The extent to which these categories of staff receive training and support for this vital role is variable (see Klapper, 2001).

The total number of students studying languages increased dramatically in the early 1990s but Thomas's survey (1993) suggested that well over 60 per cent of these were 'non-specialist' linguists. Marshall's more recent survey (2001) suggests a 51/49 per cent split in favour of non-specialists or, as he more correctly labels them, 'less specialist' learners. Drawing on the HESA modular record he puts their number at 63,000. This represents another major agent of change; the mushrooming of language courses for non-specialists, so-called institution-wide language programmes, or IWLPs, usually delivered by language centres. These range from one-semester modules to full four-year degrees with a year abroad, and account for anything between 10 per cent and 25 per cent of course credits. One of the features of provision for non-specialists, in contrast to much language teaching in academic departments, is the use of trained 'dedicated', full- or, more likely, part-time language teachers, often operating on non-academic contracts.

THE INCOMING STUDENT

One of the most widely accepted tenets of teaching is 'meet the students on their own ground and build on their strengths and their weaknesses' (Saunders, 1996: 32). This, along with insights into the acquisition cf both first and second languages (L1 and L2) as discussed below, has been the driving force behind curricular and examination changes in secondary education over recent decades. Examples of such changes are:

- the spread of comprehensive education;
- the development of the GCSE examination catering for a greater range of ability than the O level;
- the introduction of national curriculum orders outlining what and how pupils should learn during their compulsory school years;
- legislation requiring all pupils of compulsory school age to study a modern foreign language as part of their national curriculum entitlement;
- a 'bottom-up' rather than 'top-down' reform in education, whereby changes introduced in the early years of secondary education are determining the format of GCSE and ultimately A-level examinations, and thus the nature of entrants to higher education.

These are both causes and symptoms of a drive to make language learning accessible and useful to all, rather than to a small academic élite.

Such developments have far-reaching consequences for teaching in higher education. Methodologies and assessment procedures used in schools are no longer designed to prepare pupils for an academic career in linguistics and literature, rather to convince a wider clientèle that language learning is both feasible and worthwhile, and to equip pupils for their potential and widely differing needs.

The challenge is not easy. The original GCSE examination which attempted to modernize attitudes and skills is often attacked nowadays for shifting the balance too far from accuracy to fluency and for improving neither. In an education system judged by league tables a topic-led syllabus has inevitably led to a focus on 'getting through the topics' rather than facilitating true language learning. While there is thus some justification for complaints about incoming students' lack of grammatical awareness, higher education language teachers must not underestimate the contribution which GCSE has made to increasing access to languages. Without it, numbers studying languages in higher education would probably be even lower. The task of higher education is to find imaginative and effective ways to tackle this potential deficiency while simultaneously building upon the skills of incoming students.

The National Curriculum Programme of Study defines pupils' entitlement; it is a process- rather than content-based programme which emphasizes enjoyment, spontaneity in use of language for real purposes and the development of positive attitudes towards other cultures. This reflects the principles of a **communicative approach** to language learning which sees language as a means of communication rather than an object of academic study. There is also, however, a recognition of the crucial role of 'pre-communicative' work and the need to re-establish the relationship between communicative skills and more formal language-learning skills. The National Literacy Strategy is likely to support this. (There *have* been difficulties implementing the national curriculum in modern foreign languages – see Dobson, 1998.)

In practice, pupils' learning is largely determined by public examinations and the numerous but essentially similar textbooks which have been produced to support study towards them. GCSE and A-level examinations must conform to the principles of the national curriculum as interpreted through their various codes of practice. The major changes at GCSE level have been the increased use of target language both for examination rubrics and for testing purposes and the associated move towards mixed- rather than discrete-skill testing. Positive marking is also a key feature, ie, giving candidates credit for meeting criteria rather than deducting marks for mistakes.

Beyond 16, many young people now pursue GNVQs, and sixth-form colleges offer a range of syllabuses and examinations accredited by RSA and City and Guilds among others. Nevertheless, many of the students continuing their language study into higher education are likely to have followed a more traditional route of A-level qualifications, though these too are undergoing constant reform. In particular, they are changing in response to the skills and interests of potential learners and current thinking on teaching and assessment methodologies. There is an emphasis on **mixed-skill** teaching and testing, on the use of the target language as the main medium of communication and upon encouraging the development of real-life language learning skills by provision for the use of texts in examinations as well as individual student control of tapes in listening components. In addition, the 'modular' nature of courses allows for students to follow different pathways, academic, literary, or vocational; it is also possible to 'bank' modules over a limited period of time. Perhaps the most radical recent development at A level has been the encouragement of a broader curriculum base through the introduction of A1 qualifications to reward a shorter period of study in a greater number of subjects, which can stand alone or be developed into fully fledged A2 awards. The long-term results of these changes are yet to be seen.

INSIGHTS FROM WORK ON SECOND LANGUAGE ACQUISITION

Second language acquisition (SLA) has been the focus of considerable research in recent years (see Mitchell and Myles, 1998, for an overview). There is still no coherent agreed model owing to the difficulties involved in separating out and evaluating the diverse elements which contribute to second or foreign language (**L2**) acquisition and disagreements over the role of a learner's mother tongue (**L1**) in this process.

Nevertheless, all language teachers need a basic understanding of the principle aspects of SLA. Towell and Hawkins (1994: 7–16) list these as:

- 'transfer': learners' unconscious application of L1 grammatical features to their L2 grammar;
- 'staged development': learners progress through a series of intermediate stages towards L2 acquisition;
- 'systematicity': the broadly similar way L2 learners develop their ability in the target language; the majority of L2 learners go through the same developmental stages regardless of their L1 or the type of input they receive;
- 'variability': during the developmental stages, learners' 'mental grammars of L2' allow alternative forms which may co-exist for a long period;
- 'incompleteness': the failure of most L2 learners to attain a level of automatic grammatical knowledge of L2 comparable to that of native speakers.

One of the implications of these features of SLA is that error and inaccuracy are both inevitable and necessary. The traditional assumptions of language teaching that learners must master new forms in a conscious manner when they are first presented to them, that error should not be tolerated and indeed should be avoided at all costs, are misguided. SLA research reveals, on the contrary, that L2 competence both generally and in specific grammatical instances is *by its very nature* developmental, that it grows as a function of both conscious and unconscious learning and that error plays a major part at all stages of this process.

L1 acquisition depends on learners interacting with other L1 speakers and engaging with increasing amounts of new information which steadily builds on previous knowledge. It therefore seems reasonable to suggest L2 acquisition will similarly be furthered by interaction with authentic language. While **immersion learning** (eg, in Canada) and bilingual programmes in several countries have highlighted the dangers of 'fossilization' if no formal learning takes place, they have also crucially demonstrated that learners need repeatedly to focus on meaning while being exposed for extended periods to L2. For this reason **target language** use in the classroom and the deployment of a wide range of authentic texts are now both recognized as crucial to the language-learning process at advanced levels. The real benefit of authentic texts is that they help shift the focus on interaction along the continuum of L1/L2 medium-orientated communication towards L2 message-orientated communication (see Dodson, 1985). That is to say, authentic texts and realistic tasks (eg, preparing an address in a mock French election based on some aspect of a political party's programme) provide learners with an explicit, content-based learning purpose in which the focus is on the message and the achievement of the task. While not sufficient in themselves, such tasks do encourage *implicit* learning of syntactical, morphological and lexical features of the target language.

The above suggests L2 acquisition resembles L1 acquisition in a number of important ways. However, most L2 learners clearly approach the target language with a degree of proficiency and literacy in their L1. This means that they can use reading and writing to help promote their L2 learning. Furthermore, they bring to the L2 learning process a capacity for exploring grammatical forms in a conscious and explicit manner, and are able to talk *about* language. These facts make L2 learning in a formal educational setting a much more deliberate and intentional process.

The difficulty is that knowing formal rules does not by itself guarantee the ability to formulate language which obeys these rules. This is a real problem for many learners, especially those combining languages with other disciplines in higher education: in language learning, **inductive learning** processes are just as important as the more cognitive, **deductive approaches** typical of many other academic disciplines, in which it often *is* possible to learn things as a result of explicit rule teaching and error correction. Language learning, however, is not always a conscious activity dependent on the availability of explicit knowledge about the language and the way it functions, but rather the product of a complex process of both conscious learning and the gradual, unconscious development of an internal ability to use language naturally and spontaneously without reference to the conscious mind.

It is the challenge of the language classroom to develop learners' internalized linguistic competence, that is their implicit knowledge of and capacity for appropriate language use, *in tandem and interactively with* explicit knowledge of grammatical and phonological rules. This requires the development of an expanding body of interlocking skills through imitation, repetition, drilling and frequent practice in extended contexts to the point where these skills become automatic and unconscious. Little and Ushioda's analogy with piano playing seems most apposite in this context: 'Just as the novice pianist must consciously learn finger placements and pedalling, so the language learner must consciously learn bits of language – words and phrases, pronunciation and patterns of intonation – that become embedded in memory and can be accessed spontaneously' (Little and Ushioda, 1998: 15).

TOWARDS A COMMUNICATIVE APPROACH TO LANGUAGE TEACHING

These insights have contributed to the development of a communicative approach to the teaching of modern foreign languages which is nowadays to be found in various guises in all educational sectors. The past 40 years have seen a number of different approaches to modern language teaching. Grammar-based language teaching, such as **grammar-translation** and **audio-visual/audio-lingual** methodology, all adopted a rigid, graded approach to structures. Textbooks written in these traditions (and there are still a lot of them about) present items in what is considered a logical sequence (eg, present tense before past, nominative case before dative), which is intended to teach learners to acquire certain items before progressing to other, supposedly more complex ones. Such an approach fails to take account of the insights from SLA outlined above. It precludes, for example, the teaching of such central communicative expressions as 'je voudrais' or 'ich möchte' until learners have covered the conditional and the subjunctive respectively.

An approach to language based on communicative need, on the other hand, starts from a consideration of what learners are likely to have to do in the foreign language and then builds in the vocabulary, expressions and grammar needed to perform these 'functions' (see Wilkins, 1976, for an introduction to functional-notional syllabuses). As a result, the same grammar points are revisited again and again throughout a language course. This acknowledges that grammar is not acquired in a linear fashion or in discrete chunks digested one at a time, but that it is rather a staged developmental process which cannot be regimented or rushed.

The principal aim of the communicative approach is to facilitate independent communication by the learner (Pachler and Field, 1997: 70). The communicative classroom is therefore characterized by the following:

- grammar as a facilitator of communication;
- phased development from pre-communicative to free communicative exercises;
- inductive learning of grammar;
- maximum use of the target language;
- a focus on meaning;
- language used for a purpose;
- the foregrounding of learners' needs;
- personalization of language;
- the creative use of language;
- learner interaction;
- the use of authentic language and materials;
- a mixed-skill approach to teaching and assessment.

This means in practice that instead of being based on a purely structural syllabus which works its way in sequence through a range of grammar points with the aim of building up linguistic knowledge and accuracy, a communication-based course sees form as a necessary tool for expressing and exchanging meaning. This does not preclude or diminish the role of grammar. On the contrary, advanced and skilful communication can only take place when learners have assimilated a range of complex structures together with understanding of their application and potential effects within a wide range of situations. However, grammar and knowledge 'about' language are no longer seen as ends in themselves.

Furthermore, grammar is not taught deductively by artificial isolation and presentation of a series of rules, but inductively by the identification of useful patterns within content-focused language. Attention is drawn to recurrent structures, with subsequent clarification and drilling exercises. However, the emphasis is firmly on the context in which such structures occur and hence the meanings which they have the potential to convey. It is a question of identifying rules from examples rather than creating examples on the basis of a presented rule.

Interrogating Practice

Think of a point of grammar you have taught recently. Did your students learn it successfully? Did they learn it deductively or inductively? Can you think how you might have presented it more effectively?

One of the major tenets of a communicative approach is that of maximum use of the target language for instruction and interaction. If the language is not used whenever viable within the learning process, then not only is its status as a means of communication severely undermined, but learners are also denied their only genuine stimulus for developing coping strategies and learning to negotiate meaning. In addition, being surrounded by examples of the language in real situations exposes them to a far wider range of patterns and vocabulary than they would otherwise experience.

The focus of classroom interaction must be the expression of meaning, for where nothing new or meaningful is being said, communication ceases. Consequently, especially at advanced level, the meanings which learners themselves wish to express should form the core of the learning process. Content, materials and the sequence in which grammatical patterns are introduced therefore need to reflect students' needs and interests, so that they can be encouraged to engage with them and to assimilate language through use.

This also underlines another important aspect of the communicative approach, a personalization of the language taught and learnt so that it becomes the learner's own. Inherent in this is unpredictability about language use, whereby learners are encouraged to create their own meanings with language rather than simply repeat what they have heard or seen. The social context of the seminar room itself provides a rare genuine focus for this communication.

Essential to the development of such a course is the use of real, or 'authentic' materials which reflect the social and cultural context of the language. At early stages of the learning process texts may need to be adapted to make them accessible; after all, we learn our first language to a large extent through adapted exposure by means of specially written books and carefully tailored adult speech.

Finally, communicative language teaching involves the integration of the four language skills of listening, speaking, reading and writing. Real-life language usage incorporates a mixture of skills: we engage in conversations which require both listening and speaking; we respond to written stimuli by filling in forms, writing letters, or discussing the content of our reading with others. Modern methods of teaching and assessment recognize this interdependence of skills and incorporate it into tasks for learners rather than creating artificial distinctions.

AUTONOMOUS LEARNING

If, as suggested above, the learner is to take increasing responsibility for progress and the teacher aims to facilitate, not control, the language learning process, then autonomous learning becomes crucial. Autonomous learning does not mean self-instruction or learning without a teacher. Rather it is a way of complementing face-to-face tuition which makes learning more productive and develops independence. Educational research has long recognized that learning is less effective the more learners depend on the teacher and the less they take responsibility for their own learning. Therefore the emphasis currently being placed on the role of the learner in the pedagogical process is to be welcomed.

In a world which is changing so rapidly students need not so much to accumulate a set body of knowledge as to learn how to acquire knowledge both now and in the future. Language teaching thus implies the development of transferable language learning skills based on an understanding of what makes an effective language learner.

There are three essential parts to this: first, students need to discover how languages are learnt; second, they need to identify their own strengths and weaknesses as language learners; and third, they need some involvement in shaping their course.

Providing students with an insight into the nature of language learning means explaining to them the reasons for engaging in particular classroom activities. It also means teaching them techniques and strategies for:

- learning vocabulary: eg, grouping words semantically or grammatically; using colour coding or word cards, recognizing cognates, using imagery, mind maps or word association;
- learning grammar: colour-coding structures, using mnemonics for rules;
- reading: activating background knowledge, making use of titles or illustrations, skimming and scanning of texts, spotting cohesive and coherence markers (Nuttall, 1982: 110–11);
- listening: listening with a purpose, practising gist listening by using background knowledge, listening with and without a text;
- writing: producing drafts, checking written work, spotting errors;
- speaking: reading and repeating after a tape for pronunciation, phrases and techniques for seeking repetition/explanation, etc, ideas for increasing oral interaction outside the classroom;
- making the most of CALL: working in pairs/individually, focusing on personal weaknesses, using FL spell-checkers, using the Internet as a source of information and means of communication.

Such techniques can usefully be listed in a course or module guide at the start of the year but should also be integrated into language learning tasks themselves in order to demonstrate their relevance and applicability and to encourage their transfer to similar tasks beyond the classroom.

Students need to establish how they learn most effectively. A distinction is frequently made between 'field dependent' and 'field independent' learners (Skehan, 1989: 111–13). The latter are thought to be able to structure information more easily and therefore to be more deductive in their learning style and more concerned with accuracy. The former are inductive learners, more sociable and therefore more likely to be good communicators in L2, with a greater concern for fluency than accuracy. Learners' preferred strategies are influenced by their cognitive learning styles and it is important both that they become aware of how they learn and that they be encouraged to practise strategies which depend on their less dominant, natural or 'instinctive' cognitive style.

Important though learning styles are, students' motivation is ultimately *the* major factor in successful language learning (Dörnyei and Csizer, 1998; see also Chapter 5). Lambert and Gardner (1972) distinguish between 'integrative' and 'instrumental' motivation; the former indicates a genuine interest in the foreign country and the speakers of L2, while the latter denotes greater concern for the practical benefits of learning the language, such as gaining a qualification or using it to further one's career. Integrative motivation and close identification with the target culture seem to be more successful in motivating learners to persist with the long, demanding process of L2 learning. The further students move towards the integrative end of this continuum, the more likely they are to succeed. It should moreover be remembered that, unlike other disciplines, language learning requires students to forsake part of their own identity: their sense of self as defined by their relation to a particular language community. They also have to adopt once more the uncertain role of the imperfect speaker with its inevitable sense of insecurity. Success will depend to a considerable extent on how they cope with these two factors. Teachers need to be sensitive to these motivational issues both in the image they present of the foreign country and its people, and in the way they structure classroom activities to handle students' uncertainties.

Involving students in the organization of the course implies some or all of the following:

- seeking student preferences as to topics;
- allowing students some say in the choice of materials;
- engaging students in independent information-gathering;
- involving them in individually chosen project work;
- linking tuition to a range of activities in open learning facilities.

In summary, learners need to accept responsibility for their language learning, to develop the capacity to reflect on their individual learning style and to use that reflection to shape the content and process of subsequent learning.

USING C&IT IN MODERN LANGUAGES

Communication and information technology (C&IT) can be a useful tool in the development of autonomous learning. Language teachers often argue that language means interpersonal communication and interaction, requiring face-to-face contact which allows language support mechanisms such as facial and body language to contribute to meaning. However, the growth of e-mail as a means of interpersonal communication, the expansion of the Internet as a source of information, and the increasing use of Intranets within institutions as a means of dissemination and interaction cannot be ignored. The computer has many valuable assets as one of a range of potential learning tools, and it is the teacher's duty to encourage learners to make full use of any appropriate tool.

The key question is: 'What is appropriate?' Any computer-based learning or teaching activity must be assessed according to its contribution to the learner's language skills and to how well it promotes learner independence. The development of C&IT skills is important but usage needs to be language- rather than C&IT-driven. One also needs to be certain of the specific advantages brought by the use of the computer to ensure that valuable time is not wasted in the development and execution of activities which would be more effective using paper and pen.

There are ways in which appropriate software, both generic and language-specific, can make a unique and valuable contribution to the learning process; for example:

- With tutorial guidance, students can make use of grammar-based programmes to improve their accuracy by drill and test exercises (see the use of SAF in Case Study 2).
- Multimedia CD ROMs can be used to develop pronunciation and fluency.
- Standard CD ROMs can be a valuable source of research material for project work.
- With appropriate guidance on where to look and how to evaluate the reliability and validity of information, the Internet can be a useful source of authentic and interesting material (see WELL, 2002).
- Institutional Intranets can be used as a means of communication and support for learners within a guided self-study scheme;
- E-mail and video-conferencing can be used to enhance the language learning environment.

The list is far from complete, and many accounts of innovative usage can be found in language learning journals (see, for example, LLJ, 1998). Although in many cases the technological revolution has been thrust upon higher education staff rather than being the result of organic growth within institutions, language teachers need to harness its clear potential for enhancing the teaching and learning environment. Case Study 1 describes an ILT-funded project to assist staff develop the requisite skills to harness technology. This is particularly important when, in a climate of diminishing resources, higher education institutions are investing large amounts of money to comply with government C&IT directives. Linguists must ensure they are in a position to reap their share of benefits from this development.

Case Study 1: Funding a staff development project with the National Teaching Fellowship Scheme (NTFS)

London School of Economics

Departments in higher education have often had the problem of receiving one-off funding for technical equipment, but no access to funding for training staff how to use it effectively. This results in only a few key people being able to maximize its use, with the consequence that many staff members, particularly hourly paid staff, feeling alienated from new technology. This is particularly serious for Language Centres, as all rely on a high proportion of hourly paid staff. These teachers find themselves in the position of not being able to use new equipment, and consequently are not able to help students to use it effectively, despite the demands that are now made on all teachers to do so. I decided to use my NTFS prize to fund a project we named Communitec (Communicating technology), focusing on how technology is communicated to teachers, helping them develop at their own pace. In short, to help technophobes become technophiles! We have over this year implemented a far-reaching training programme that is designed to cater for the differing needs of teachers, and which gave permanent staff relief of teaching hours to train, and hourly paid staff money for their time and trouble. The training programme is delivered in stages over the academic year to enable all to reach an acceptable knowledge base, and then allows further opportunities for those who want or are able to acquire more expertise in creating teaching materials. Those teachers with greater expertise will be able to act as mentors to new staff, or to existing colleagues who want to progress at a later stage. Our aims are:

- to train all staff members in the use of digital technology;
- to enable all staff to feel at ease with new technology;
- to create an in-house team of teachers capable of mentoring new staff members;
- to make full use of bought-in technical expertise;
- to create subject-specific Web-based materials for face-to-face and independent learning;
- to engender an atmosphere of creativity;
- to encourage teamwork in a disparate workforce.

For further information: www.lse.ac.uk/depts/language

(Nick Byrne, Director, Language Centre)

TRANSLATION

In many universities, 'prose' and 'unseen' translation, ie, translation into and out of the foreign language, are still very common teaching and testing techniques. (Note that in this section we use L1 to denote English, although in view of the increasing numbers of overseas students studying languages in UK higher education, English may not always be students' mother tongue.) It is difficult to prove whether translation helps students to learn language. Many now have doubts but still argue for the retention of L2 to L1 translation, at least with final year students, as a **key skill**. Others see some residual benefits; for example: '… it would seem likely that, because the exercise involves scrutinising bits of language and evaluating equivalents in the target language, there is some increase in the students' mastery of both languages' (Sewell, 1996: 142).

Reservations about the continued use of translation relate particularly to many departments' traditional approach: students write a translation in their own time, hand it in for marking by the lecturer who then spends most of the class hour going over the piece, highlighting problems and possibly offering a 'fair' version. Such an approach fails to make clear how students are to learn *about*, or indeed *from* translation. Instead, it treats translation simply as a vague support to general language learning, and the process becomes in effect little more than repeated testing. An alternative approach, offered in Case Study 2, aims to encourage students to learn about translation.

Case Study 2 : Making translation a more effective learning process

Fourth-year German–English translation class for non-specialist learners of German, University of Birmingham

One of the basic principles of this course for students of Law, Politics or Economics, is that if they are to be able to approach the text in an effective manner, students must first be told the context of the extract being used, ie, its significance within the whole work, the purpose for which it was written and its intended audience.

At the start of the module, students are shown that translation is not about simply transposing items from one language to another at the level of lexis and syntax, but that it is about conveying meaning. In order to take this first step in reconstructing meaning, short exercises are employed to encourage students to read the whole text thoroughly, actively and critically, addressing such questions as:

- Why has this been written in this way?
- Why does this sentence or paragraph come first?
- Is there any reason for having this long sentence in the first paragraph or these very short sentences?
- Does it matter if I merge sentences in my translation and what would be the effect of this?

The novice translator needs to see him- or herself as a mediator between cultural worlds, ie, as someone who helps those unfamiliar with a culture to understand and appreciate.all the cultural nuances of the original text. Translation is therefore a communicative act. Far more than a test of ability to de-code, it is a process of en-coding.

Students on the course are encouraged to use a translation dossier, to make a systematic note of possible translations of or strategies for coping with expressions/phrases which recur frequently and are often forgotten in the flurry of translating week after week. This can be arranged under alphabetical, structural or key word headings. Students are also required to produce an occasional annotated translation, giving their reasons for the choices made. This forces them to focus consciously on the act of translation, thus helping to make them more reflective. Repeated translation without focus on the process provides no evidence of learning or progress.

In addition to the strategies outlined above, the course tutor repeatedly seeks to focus students' minds away from grammar and lexis towards whole-text and translation-task issues in order to avoid literal and 'safe' translations. The following ideas are useful for this purpose:

- Students provide an L1 summary of an L2 text as a briefing to someone visiting the foreign country for a specific purpose; this helps to focus attention on relevance and appropriateness of material, on the information needs of the target audience as well as on the style of students' English versions.
- The teacher supplies a specific brief (eg, to translate an article for inclusion in a particular quality UK daily newspaper) which requires clear explication of cultural references, foreign figures or events.
- Students translate a passage for inclusion in a specialist English-language journal and adapt their translation to the particular 'house style' (Fraser, 1996: 128–29).
- Students correct an inaccurate translation which, depending on their proficiency, can be at a simple factual level or may include idiom, collocation, metaphor, etc.

Translation into L2 poses particular problems and can be both very demotivating and a poor learning experience for many students. Often learners are asked to perform too many simultaneous tasks and there is insufficient focus on individual weaknesses. There are three alternatives as follows.

Demonstration

A basic pedagogical principle is to demonstrate how to do something before asking learners to do it themselves. In translation this can be achieved by giving students a parallel text which allows contrastive analysis of the two languages. It reveals how the translator has set about the task and highlights interesting discrepancies and even mistakes which are a source of fascination to learners. Students can then move beyond lexical and grammatical points to look for differences in tone, style and register. At the end of a class spent working on the parallel texts the L2 text can be withdrawn and students required to translate the L1. Marking then involves a lot less correction and the process is less demotivating for everyone. Feedback using the original L2 text can focus on students' alternative renderings, thus emphasizing that there is always more than one correct version and reinforcing the message that it is *meaning* that translators should be seeking to convey.

Comparison

Two L2 versions could be used and students asked to compare the two translations, focusing on, for example, lexis, grammar or even idiom. This is a demanding task but carries much potential for learning in the form of more sophisticated contrastive analysis. Setting up these tasks is not easy, but a bank can be built up based on versions produced by two different language assistants or Erasmus/Socrates students. It is also sometimes possible to find two L2 translations of English literary texts. (This exercise can, of course, work well the other way, comparing and contrasting two L1 versions of an L2 text.)

Collaboration

As an alternative to 'cold' translation, students can be asked to prepare a text in pairs by underlining any potentially problematic structures and circling any unknown vocabulary. Ideas are then pooled in fours, and groups subsequently brought together for plenary discussion. Vocabulary and structures can be shared on an overhead with all acceptable ways of translating a particular expression being listed and dictionaries being consulted collectively to further good reference skills. The text is then set for homework. The advantages of this approach are that the weaker benefit from collaboration with more able peers and marking time is reduced as less correction of common difficulties is required. The diagnosis of individual errors with ensuing provision of targeted advice thus becomes much easier.

These approaches to translation focus attention on process, on learning *how* to translate and avoid using translation as a continual testing mechanism.

Case Study 3: First-year language course for single and joint honours students of French

University of Birmingham

Many of the above points are illustrated in the following description of a newly developed language course aimed at bridging the gap between the skills of school leavers and the needs of university language studies. The course has not yet been formally evaluated and is not therefore held up as a model to emulate in its entirety, but shows how one department is moving towards meeting the changing needs of the post-advanced student. It has been positively received by students, and staff are enthusiastic about its progress and hopeful of the eventual outcomes.

Developed as part of a comprehensive review of all four years of the Single and Joint Honours language curriculum, the course addresses the needs and skill profile of first-year students and takes account of contemporary views on SLA and student-centred learning. In particular, it seeks to provide a balance between, on the one hand, advanced interpersonal communicative skills and, on the other, familiarity with key areas of French grammar and the ability to apply them in written work.

The old

The previous language programme consisted of a highly cognitive, knowledge-based grammar syllabus, featuring elements of grammar-translation methodology, linked to traditional 'conversation' classes with largely untrained *lecteurs/lectrices*. Very challenging paraphrase exercises figured quite prominently, while both oral-based work and free writing in French played a relatively minor role.

The new

By contrast, the objectives of the new programme are:

- to retain and foster students' enjoyment of language learning and their motivation;
- to build on experience and skills acquired at A level by developing the use of oral and written language in 'real-life' communicative situations;
- to foster a greater awareness of the need for accuracy by encouraging the development of learning strategies which enable students to increase and apply their grammatical competence;

- to extend knowledge of grammatical structures via a carefully graded programme, mixing basic analytical presentation and individual and group research with repeated opportunities for reinforcement and re-use;
- to promote autonomous learning, especially the use of CALL in consolidating basic grammatical competence;
- to promote French as the normal language of classroom instruction;
- to develop the ability to use dictionaries effectively and to take notes in French;
- to extend students' vocabulary acquisition and their awareness of register by systematic exposure to authentic texts.

Structure
The programme is built around three contact hours per week:
a) 'Le cours de langue': conducted largely in French with groups of 16 and organized around the advanced communicative text *Le Nouveau Sans Frontières 3* (CLE, 1990), it features a range of oral and written exercises, often conducted in small groups, and is also used for feedback on and discussion of a weekly written task.

b) 'Le cours d'expression orale': groups of eight or nine students are taught by a *lecteur/lectrice* who has attended the University's part-time teacher training course (attendance at this five-day course is compulsory for all new foreign language assistants – see Gray, 2001); it is run entirely in French and features exercises aimed at promoting comprehension and oral skills; students' participation is reflected in the continuous assess-ment mark awarded for oral work.

c) 'Le cours de grammaire': a lecture which assumes that grammar *knowledge* does not necessarily equate with accuracy in oral and written tasks and that grammar is not learnt in a linear, 'once-and-for-all' fashion. In contrast to the old grammar lecture which laid considerable emphasis on the 'what' and the 'why' of the grammar syllabus, this new one stresses much more the 'how'. It is interactive, taught initially in English and then increasingly in French, covers a much reduced and simplified grammar syllabus, and employs formal presentation linked to practical worksheet adaptation in small groups of the material presented. It also features an extensive scheme of autonomous learning, whereby students are required to research grammar rules, check on usage and apply their findings to suggested tasks and exercises; keys to all exercises and worksheets are available in the self-access resources centre.

Grammar: identifying weakness

All students sit an initial **diagnostic test** designed to indicate grammatical weaknesses. On the basis of this test they are responsible for devising a remedial programme of study in preparation for two subsequent progress checks. The aim is to instil in them from the very beginning good language learning habits, training them to find things out for themselves and to use their own initiative. More able students are also encouraged to move beyond the basic programme.

Grammar: self-assessment

The University's Student Assessment Facility (SAF) enables staff to create computerized assessments using a simple mark-up language which are then mounted on the open learning server and can be accessed from a number of different computer clusters around campus:

- There are 24 French tests each of between 100 and 250 gapped sentences.
- Each assessment consists of 20 such gaps.
- Students complete at least three tests on each of eight grammar points by a series of cut-off dates.
- Feedback is provided at the end of each test with remedial help if required.
- Students can do up to five tests on each grammar point and receive a different selection of items on each occasion since the programme selects new items from the database every time a student logs in.
- Results are stored centrally, and following each assessment deadline a report is produced and delivered to the course coordinator who records as a formal coursework mark the average of each student's best three scores for that particular test.

Autonomous learning

Besides the SAF materials students are given a clearly defined programme of autonomous learning based on:

- reference books, dictionaries, grammars;
- newspapers and magazines;
- satellite TV, audio and video tapes;
- CD ROMs and commercial CALL programmes.

Linked to this autonomous learning strand is the Study Diary which all students are expected to maintain and in which are kept notes on all work done outside the course that has contributed to their language learning. This includes an initial work plan to revise grammar following the diagnostic test, which students discuss individually with their language tutor. The whole Study Diary forms the basis of a discussion with the student's personal tutor at the end of the first semester.

Assessment
Coursework: two written tests, one oral task, six written tasks, eight SAF tests (25 per cent).
Oral/aural examination (25 per cent)
Three-hour written examination (50 per cent).

OVERVIEW

Language teachers in higher education need to respond to recent changes in the understanding of how languages are learnt as well as in the secondary education system which provides its raw material. Perhaps the most significant change of focus in recent years has been towards content-based, meaning-driven language learning within which students are encouraged to explore topics relevant to their needs and interests via mixed-skill activities. This is in contrast to the traditional grammar-led approach focusing on the written language which is now out of step with the prior learning experiences of many incoming students. The strengths and weaknesses of these students need to be addressed within a flexible learning package, which encourages language acquisition, develops transferable learning skills and identifies and tackles individual formal weaknesses. As Case Study 3 shows, C&IT can be a valuable tool in providing individual support for learners in this process, encouraging an independent approach to the all-important grammar drilling. Where translation remains part of the language curriculum, attention needs to be paid as much to the process as the product.

REFERENCES

CLE (1990) *Le Nouveau Sans Frontières*, Paris
Dobson, A (1998) *MFL Inspected: Reflections on inspection 1996/7*, CILT, London
Dodson, C J (1985) Second language acquisition and bilingual development: a theoretical framework, *Journal of Multilingual and Multicultural Development*, 6, pp 325–46
Dörnyei, Z and Csizer, K (1998) Ten commandments for motivating language learners: results of an empirical study, *Language Teaching Research*, 2, pp 203–29
Fraser, J (1996) 'I understand the French, but I don't know how to put it into English': developing undergraduates' awareness of and confidence in the translation process, in *Teaching Translation in Universities*, eds P Sewell and I Higgins, pp 121–34, AFLS/CILT, London

Gray, C (2001) Training postgraduate and foreign language assistants: the DOPLA approach, in *Teaching Languages in Higher Education*, ed J Klapper, pp 56–74, CILT, London

Klapper, J (2001) *Teaching Languages in Higher Education: Issues in training and continuing professional development*, CILT, London

Lambert, W and Gardner, R (1972) *Attitudes and Motivation in Second Language Learning*, Newbury House, Rowley, Massachusetts

LLJ (1998) *Language Learning Journal*, **18**

Little, D (ed) (1989) *Self-Access Systems for Language Learning*, Authentik, Dublin

Little, D and Ushioda, E (1998) *Institution-wide Language Programmes*, CILT/Centre for Language and Communication Studies, Trinity College Dublin, London/Dublin

Marshall, K (2001) Survey of Less Specialist Language Learning in UK Universities (1998–99), unpublished report of the University Council for Modern Languages

Mitchell, R and Myles, F (1998) *Second Language Learning Theories*, Arnold, London

Nuttall, C (1982) *Teaching Reading Skills in a Foreign Language*, Heinemann Education, London

Pachler, N and Field, K (1997) *Learning to Teach Modern Foreign Languages in the Secondary School*, Routledge, London

Saunders, K (1996) Grammatical accuracy: a response to Derek McCulloch, *German Teaching*, **13**, pp 30–32

Sewell, P (1996) Translation in the curriculum, in *Teaching Translation in Universities*, eds P Sewell and I Higgins, pp 135–60, AFLS/CILT, London

Skehan, P (1989) *Individual Differences in Second-Language Learning*, Edward Arnold, London/New York

Thomas, G (1993) *A Survey of European Languages in the United Kingdom*, CNAA

Towell, R and Hawkins, R (1994) *Approaches to Second Language Acquisition*, Multilingual Matters, Clevedon/Philadelphia

WELL (2002) Web-enhanced language learning, FDTL project Web site, www.well.ac.uk

Wilkins, D A (1976) *Notional Syllabuses*, Oxford University Press, Oxford

FURTHER READING

Broady, E (ed) (2000), *Second Language Writing in a Computer Environment*, AFLS/CILT, London. A varied collection of case studies of innovative ways to teach L2 writing.

Bygate, M, Tonkyn, A and Williams, E (eds) (1994) *Grammar and the Language Teacher*, Prentice-Hall, Hemel Hempstead. A collection of articles on different views of the role of grammar in language teaching.

Coleman, J A (1996) *Studying languages. A survey of British and European students*, CILT, London. A key study of British undergraduate language learners, their proficiency, skills, motivation and background.

Engel, D and Myles, F (eds) (1996) *Teaching Grammar: Perspectives in higher education*, AFLS/CILT, London. Contains a number of suggestions for integrating grammar into the modern languages curriculum.

Hervey, S and Higgins, I (1992) *Thinking Translation: A course in translation method*, Routledge, London. Available in French (1992), German (1995), Spanish (1995) and Italian (1999).

Lewis, T and Rouxeville, A (eds) (2000) *Technology and the Advanced Language Learner*, AFLS/CILT, London. A set of articles that look at innovative uses of technology such as video, CALL, e-mail tandem partnerships, bulletin boards and discussion lists.

Parker, G and Rouxeville, A (eds) (1995) *'The Year Abroad'. Preparation, monitoring, evaluation, current research and development*, AFLS/CILT, London. A thorough and practical introduction to all aspects of this central element of the undergraduate degree.

Towell, R and Hawkins, R (1994) *Approaches to Second Language Acquisition*, Multilingual Matters, Clevedon/Philadelphia. One of the more readable surveys of the theoretical principles of SLA.

CILT produces a useful 'Pathfinder' series on all aspects of language learning. Although often written with a secondary audience in mind, the very practical issues discussed in these slim volumes are relevant to all educational sectors.

23 Key aspects of teaching and learning in medicine and dentistry

Adam Feather and Heather Fry

AIMS, SCOPE AND INTRODUCTION

This chapter builds on earlier generic chapters, including those on student learning, assessment, lecturing and small group teaching. Chapters 3, 4, 11, 12, 18 and 21 also contain much of relevance. Here, the distinctive aspects of teaching and learning in medicine and dentistry are reviewed with the intention of elucidating them for the relatively inexperienced teacher, in the context of undergraduate education in UK-style universities.

This chapter focuses on:

- patient-centred teaching and learning;
- teaching skills in simulated settings;
- **experiential learning**;
- **problem-based learning** (PBL);
- assessment.

It is a truism to say that educating doctors and dentists is a complex business. Medical and dental education involves:

- Remembering a large amount of factual material.
- Understanding complex mechanisms.
- Competence in a wide range of technical skills.
- Understanding and use of the scientific method.
- Developing socially responsible attitudes and ethical practice.
- Promoting interpersonal skills for working with colleagues and patients.
- Developing sophisticated problem-solving and reasoning skills.
- Personal skills, including self-evaluation.

Few medical and dental educators teach all of these aspects, but all need to be aware of the spectrum, and discriminating in their choice of appropriate methods. Medical and dental education share many overlapping concerns but also have areas of variation. One of the key differences in the training needs of the two professions is that, at undergraduate level, dental students are more involved in invasive work with patients than their medical counterparts. Another is that, on graduation, the dentist has to be capable of independent practice without supervision.

Context and background

The education of dentists and doctors is embedded in the practices and mores of two large service activities, namely, education and healthcare provision. These dual strands are present at all levels (pre- and post-registration, specialist training, and continuing professional development) and are not always compatible. Since the early 1990s the UK health service and the practice of medical and dental care have undergone major changes that have shifted the emphasis away from hospitals towards primary care. This has an impact on how, and for what, dentists and doctors need to be trained (Turner, Collinson and Fry, 2001).

The General Dental Council (GDC) and General Medical Council (GMC) have statutory responsibility for approving undergraduate courses and publish curriculum guidelines and recommendations. The Quality Assurance Agency **subject benchmarking** is compatible with GMC and GDC guidelines and also having an impact on curricula (QAA, 2002a and 2002b).

In 1993 the GMC set out radical and extensive requirements for undergraduate curricula; these were updated in 2002 (GMC, 2002). *Tomorrow's Doctors* (1993) emphasized the global expansion of knowledge and the rate at which it becomes obsolete. Like several earlier documents, it criticized factual overload in curricula. Among new expectations for undergraduate education in the 21st century are encouraging innovation around a core of skills and knowledge, interprofessional training, and a greater emphasis on self-assessment and ethical practice. The GMC emphasizes learning and study skills, being curious and critical in approaching knowledge and acquiring understanding of underlying principles, concepts and mechanisms rather than the teaching and regurgitation of enormous amounts of material. This is in line with contemporary understanding of how students and professionals learn (see Chapter 2). Major outcomes of the recommendations have been the moves by UK medical schools to a 'core plus options' approach to curricula, and more problem-based methods of delivery. Core skills and knowledge are now often taught with other interprofessional undergraduates, including nurses, therapists and radiographers. Assessment has generally lagged a little behind other curricular reforms.

As a result of government recommendations, including those on the expansion of medical student numbers (Medical Workforce Standing Advisory Committee, 1997), further change in undergraduate medical education has been initiated, with implications for curricula, assessment, student support, teaching and learning. The desire to change the demographics of medical student entry has led to the emergence of graduate entry programmes. These, pioneered in the UK by St George's Hospital Medical School, London, attract graduates from higher education. With more mature learning skills these students pass through an accelerated, four-year programme. New medical schools have also been created. The uniting of the London medical schools has led to several 'super-schools', taking 300–400 medical students each year. This has taxed the imaginations of many curriculum leaders, in terms of space, facilitation of small group learning, clinical rotation and other facilities, and given new meaning to 'lecturing to large groups'.

The publication of the GDC undergraduate curriculum recommendations (1997) brought considerable change. The GDC emphasized its desire to see educationally progressive ideas and improved methods of study incorporated into curricula that exhibited reduced congestion and earlier patient contact. The GDC recommendations are more prescriptive of 'essential elements' than the medical equivalent.

Postgraduate training has also been examined closely and there is growing concern for a more holistic view of undergraduate and postgraduate training, including of the post-registration year vis-à-vis undergraduate training, and for a continuum of learning and updating extending until retirement. The Calman Report (1993) made specialty training shorter and more structured, introducing greater formality in appraisal and assessment. In 1997 the GMC set out professional and educational requirements for pre-registration house officers. The vocational year for newly qualified dentists has now become a requirement prior to independent National Health Service (NHS) practice and specialty registers have been established.

It is likely that the role of dentists and doctors will change further as nurses and dental therapists take on more clinical responsibility and interprofessional practice develops. It is also likely that training for tomorrow's dentists and doctors will include greater preparation for an evidence-based approach to practice, and more training in the use of information technology. The trend to formalize post-graduate education and continuing medical/dental education will continue. All these developments have implications for undergraduate curriculum design, teaching, workplace learning and assessment.

Interrogating Practice

Are you familiar with national recommendations for undergraduate and postgraduate training operating in your country and specialty?

PATIENT-CENTRED TEACHING AND LEARNING

Clinical teaching is a three-way dynamic between teacher, patient and student. It occurs in the workplace environment. As the controlling factor, the teacher is obliged to maximize the situation from all perspectives. With earlier clinical exposure, students may be forced to develop a more balanced approach to the acquisition of knowledge, technical skills and professional attitudes and behaviours.

Interrogating Practice

If you are a clinician:
Think back to your first days as a student in the clinical environment. What types of things did you learn in, and from, that environment? What can you do to help students learn those types of things?

The patient

Whether in the clinic, surgery or ward setting, or even the lecture theatre of the clinical demonstration, the patient is the most vulnerable of the three parties. Most medical patients find clinical teaching extremely rewarding, often commenting that they feel students 'have to learn'. In dentistry there is a slightly different relationship. The patient receives treatment from a novice under instruction. Their vulnerability is magnified and the teacher has added (statutory) responsibilities. The patient must be reassured that a watchful eye is being cast. In both cases, the patient's attitude towards being used in teaching should always be respected and it should be reinforced that, whatever their decision, it will not affect their treatment and care. Within teaching hospitals and surgeries, patients should be made aware that the facility is a teaching environment and that students may be present, or in the case of dental students, carrying out the required treatment. This allows the patient to prepare for the initial encounter and to raise any anxieties they may have. At all times one needs to keep the patient informed, reach mutual agreement about the session, and most importantly, ensure that patient privacy and dignity are maintained. One should explain to the medical patient the number and level of the students who will be in attendance and the patient's proposed role. Common questions include, will they be asked to undress, will the students be performing a procedure on them, will there be a discussion about them or the case? Verbal agreement should be obtained. Dental sessions differ in that the patient is being treated and followed up by the student under the supervision of the teacher. The dental supervisor must approve the proposed treatment, ensure it has been explained correctly to the patient and review its course and outcomes.

The student

With new curricula in the UK, students from a very early stage of their training will meet the challenges of the clinical environment. As with the patient, good preparation reduces anxieties, and sets out a clear level of professional conduct.

Before students are ready to interact with patients they need to practice basic clinical and communication skills. This should occur in a safe, supportive environment such as that of a clinical skills centre (see next section). For dental students, competence in core skills will have to be demonstrated prior to their introduction to the clinical arena.

Students should be encouraged to attend clinical sessions in the right frame of mind. The dental student is immediately faced with professional obligations, and the teacher must stress their responsibility to their patients. Punctuality, appearance, background reading and practice of skills need to be emphasized. Experiential learning is key in clinical settings. The teacher should make provision for teaching and learning when patients are unable to attend; **self-directed learning (SDL)** and **computer-assisted learning (CAL)** will allow students time to test knowledge and skills at their own pace.

For medical students, their clinical experience is all too often a rather less demanding time. However, they too should demonstrate similar professional obligation and be in possession of basic equipment such as a stethoscope. (It may be necessary for the teacher to provide additional equipment such as a patella hammer, ophthalmoscope or auriscope.) Before they go on the ward, or into the clinic, students should be well briefed.

Students should not be placed in an unsupported environment or pressured into performing tasks that are beyond their level of training or conflict with cultural beliefs. Students may encounter ethical dilemmas, but they should not be asked to face them without guidance.

The teacher

For the clinician, the clinical environment will be one in which they feel comfortable. They will be familiar with the setting, the staff, and hopefully aware of the potential problems that may be encountered while teaching.

Full-time members of university staff perform the majority of dental undergraduate teaching and this removes many hazards familiar to the 'part-time' medical teacher. Bedside teaching often involves the teacher, patient and several students. In contrast, teaching in the dental clinic involves several students, each with their own patient, being overseen by one teacher. A teacher–student ratio of about 1:8 is common. Dental students work closely with other healthcare professionals from an early stage of their training and the supervisor should be aware of this relationship and its development. The teacher's role is one of supervision, guidance and ensuring safety of all participants.

On the wards it may be necessary to check that the patient(s) you wish to use in teaching are not going to be 'employed' in procedures or investigations. Check that your session does not encroach into ward routines. Locations and times may suddenly need to be changed, but the onus is firmly on the teacher to try to be punctual and prepared, or at least inform students and patients of unavoidable changes. (Medical students often quote lack of information and disregard by the clinical staff as reasons for recurrent non-attendance.)

Whatever the setting, the teacher should not use the patient session to lecture, or use the patient as a 'chalkboard' or living text. The guiding principle in medicine should be one of demonstration and observation, with opportunities for practice as far as it is safe and ethical. Feedback on practice (from tutor, peers, self and patient where appropriate) is key, but often neglected. In dentistry the chairside role is primarily that of advice and supervision. For the teacher, student–patient interactions may appear routine but for the other parties they are often complex and require a great deal of guidance, particularly in the early stages of training. Opportunistic teaching may present itself in both contexts and should never be overlooked; indeed in medicine detailed and advanced planning of much patient-based teaching is often impossible. In the medical setting clinicians need to be aware of the overall goals (**learning outcomes**) of the rotation of the undergraduate student and have thought about how patient encounters may contribute to their being achieved. Questioning, from teacher to students and student to teacher is an important skill in clinical teaching (see the relevant section in Chapter 7), but again respect for the patient needs to be considered. Good preparation and time for student **reflection** and **feedback** should be built into sessions.

Clinical teaching and learning is exciting and rewarding, but lack of essentials within the modern NHS, such as appropriate lighting, routine equipment and even patients, make teaching challenging. Within the outpatient, community and dental settings, the potential to regulate, plan and control this environment is very much greater than on the wards.

Points to consider when teaching in a patient-centred environment:

- Patient, student and teacher safety and anxieties.
- Introduction of students to the clinical environment.
- Skills acquisition, practice, feedback and assessment.
- Observation and practice of professional behaviour.
- Teaching versus treatment.

SKILLS AND SIMULATION IN TEACHING AND LEARNING

For many years clinical medicine and dentistry were taught by the principle of 'see one, do one, teach one'. The inception and use of simulation within clinical teaching and learning has allowed students to confront their anxieties within a safe environment, while providing the teacher with a regulated, reproducible teaching arena. The simulated element will most commonly refer to materials, actors and **role play**.

A clinical skills centre or laboratory, where practical procedures and communication skills may be demonstrated and practised, is now incorporated into the infrastructure of most medical and dental schools. The form that this centre takes, and the equipment within it, vary between institutions, from single rooms to multipurpose 'laboratories' and from latex and plastic manikins to high fidelity and virtual reality simulators. The centre may be used for teaching by clinical staff and for SDL and CAL. We found (at a medical school at which we both worked) that the employment of a dedicated skills teacher revolutionized the use and potential of the centre, as have others, eg, at Leeds University Medical School (Stark, Delmotte and Howdle, 1998). While dental schools have commonly abandoned rooms of phantom heads, more sophisticated models and partial operatories fulfil similar functions (Suvinen, Messer and Franco, 1998).

Peyton (1998), a general surgeon, describes an excellent, and widely advocated, model for teaching skills, in simulated settings and otherwise, known as the 'four stage approach'.

Stage 1

Demonstration of the skill at normal speed, with little or no explanation.

Stage 2

Repetition of the skill with full explanation, encouraging the learner to ask questions.

Stage 3

The demonstrator performs the skill for a third time, with the learner providing the explanation of each step and being questioned on key issues. The demonstrator provides necessary corrections. This step may need to be repeated several times until the demonstrator is satisfied that the learner fully understands the skill.

Stage 4

The learner now carries out the skill under close supervision describing each step before it is taken (adapted from Peyton 1998: 174–77).

This model may be expanded or reduced depending on the background skills of the learner. Video may be used in Stages 1 and 2. As with all teaching, the learner must be given constructive feedback and allowed time for practice of the skills. Within the medical clinical skills centre, particularly in SDL, we have found the use of itemized checklists useful adjuncts to learning.

Interrogating Practice

If you are not already using it, how could you use/adapt Peyton's four-stage approach to your own (simulated/non-simulated) clinical teaching?

Simulation

Through the lead of communication skills teachers, simulation of clinical scenarios has become increasingly sophisticated, now employing professional actors. Within the safety of this setting, students can express themselves more freely, while investigating the patient perspective through the eyes of the actors. The teacher must provide a clear brief for both actor and student, including detailed background scripts for the actors. Real patients may also be trained and used in clinical training and assessment. It is important that students feel reasonably comfortable within their given role and that the scenario is within their expected capabilities. Clear student learning **objectives** are required at all stages, but excessive demands and expectations are often counterproductive.

Simulated patients (SPs) were first used in the 1960s with their use in dental and medical undergraduate and postgraduate education expanding rapidly since the 1980s (Barrows, 1993). They may be used instead of real patients in difficult clinical scenarios, eg, breaking bad news and in the reproduction of acute problems that would not be assessable in traditional clinical examinations. In the United States, SPs are also used for training and assessing potentially embarrassing clinical procedures such as vaginal speculum examination. In dentistry, SPs are principally used for communication skills training and in assessment (Davenport *et al*, 1998). Despite many advantages, simulation has its limitations and should be additional, usually as a preliminary to, and not a substitute for, clinical opportunities with real patients.

Role play is another extremely useful teaching and learning tool. Students are able to investigate, practice and explore both sides of a clinical interaction through their adopted roles; these advantages may need to be pointed out to the student. Criticisms of this technique are usually a product of poorly prepared sessions. Clear roles, with demonstration by teachers, or using pre-prepared videos, are useful ways of directing student learning. Encouraging a supportive but quite formal environment during the sessions also encourages students to maintain their role. Pre-warned, with adequate debriefing and reflection, the students usually find this a useful technique.

Videotaping has long been used in general practice, particularly for postgraduate learners. It is, however, an area that has not been so fully exploited in dentistry. It is a useful tool, particularly for reflection, self-assessment and feedback, and may be employed in simulation, role play and the recording of 'real-life' interactions.

Questions to think about in relation to skills and simulation:

- How does the learning environment of the clinical skills centre differ from that of the clinical arena?
- What are the positive and negative attributes of simulation?
- How far can and should patients be used in training?
- What should be the role of simulation in assessment?
- What is the potential for greater IT usage?

EXPERIENTIAL LEARNING

Once students has been introduced to the clinical environment, much of their learning is, born from opportunity, experiential in nature. Experiential learning is introduced in Chapter 2. Figure 23.1 is a possible representation of experiential learning in the medical and dental context.

As students meet a new concept or change in practice, eg, presenting a student clerking on a business ward round, they must learn to adapt their previous model (understanding) of this activity. This will involve reflection on their teachers and other role models, on peer group experiences, their own behaviour/performance and the function fulfilled by the activity or meaning of the concept. Such models are in continual evolution throughout the undergraduate and postgraduate periods; the skill for the learner being to recognize valuable recommendations and adaptations, to re-shape their own understanding, behaviour, skills and attitudes and to disregard the unhelpful. The teacher should encourage learners to question practice and not to be afraid of their own uncertainties. There is much

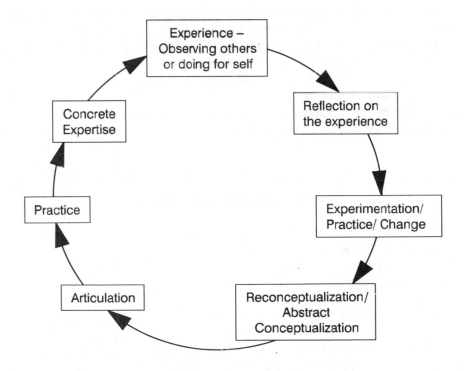

Figure 23.1   Student experiential learning (adapted from Peyton, 1998 and Kolb, 1984)

that the teacher and course designer can do to harness experiential learning, (see Stanton and Grant (1999) for some useful ideas).

PROBLEM-BASED LEARNING

Problem-based learning is an idea that has had currency since the 1960s (Neufeld and Barrows, 1974), but was not widely used in medical and dental education in the UK until the mid-1990s. It is now an element in many UK medical and dental undergraduate curricula, in some cases being the main organizing principle and pedagogical method.

There are many variants of PBL; Boud and Feletti (1996) review the range. However, there are some elements that are usually present, including:

- learning and teaching stemming from, and coming after, exposure to a scenario or trigger (the 'problem') which is presented without prior detailed teaching of all the material involved;
- a trigger in written, videotaped or patient 'format';
- small interactive groups of students exploring the problem in a structured manner and subsequently sharing knowledge and understanding;
- students, not the teacher, making the immediate decisions about what they will research/learn in relation to the scenario;
- a student 'scribe' recording the deliberations of the group;
- a non-didactic facilitator;
- integration of disciplinary and clinical and non-clinical subject matter;
- students reporting back their findings.

Interrogating Practice

To check if you understand how PBL differs from problem solving, examine the list above and reject any item that would not generally be a feature of a course using problem solving. The rejected item(s) are what distinguish PBL.

The University of Maastricht version of PBL is probably the most widely known. Each problem or scenario is investigated by students following the 'seven-jump' model, in which they:

1. Clarify terms and concepts in the problem – students pick out words and phrases not understood and see if any group member can explain them.
2. Define the problem – students set out/restate the terms and ideas that need to be explained or understood.
3. Analyse the problem – students generate possible explanations (usually some are incorrect).
4. Make a systematic inventory of the explanations in Step 3 – students do this by linking ideas, showing relationships, etc.
5. Formulate learning questions – these are the things students think they need to learn/answer to be able to understand or explain the problem.
6. Collect information – students do this before the next session, attempting to find the answers to the learning questions.
7. Synthesize and test the information – students report back and discuss their findings. (Adapted from Bouhuijs, Schmidt and van Berkel, 1987.)

A typical PBL curriculum has problems sharing a common theme arranged into blocks. Each block has overall objectives and a title indicating the area of study. Short PBL problems typically run over two sessions, with Steps 1–5 being covered in session 1, Step 6 occurring and then Step 7 taking place within a week, in session 2. Alternative approaches use longer and more complex problems, requiring longer study periods, and/or more sessions per problem and gradual revelation of more case-related information. In all instances the ideal is to timetable appropriate clinical demonstrations, laboratory work, etc, to coincide with relevant triggers.

Case Study 1: A scenario for problem-based learning

Faculty of Medicine and Health Sciences, University of Newcastle, Australia

Trigger
Peter Fraser, age 47, is brought to the accident and emergency department at the Mater Hospital, by a friend. They had been driving home from a business dinner at a local club when Peter said he felt sick and asked the taxi driver to pull over to the kerb. Peter got out of the car and a minute or so later he vomited food mixed with fresh blood into the gutter. His friend wasn't sure how much blood he had vomited, but thought it was probably about a cupful. Peter had told him he felt a bit shaky and sweaty, so his friend asked the taxi driver to bring them to the hospital.

This problem is used in the third term of the first year of the Bachelor of Medicine curriculum at the Newcastle Medical School, Australia. Clinical reasoning is regarded as central to student learning; the process is explicit in the tutor guides and groups learn to approach problems through an hypothesis-based enquiry. Hypotheses are based on basic science mechanisms, rather than 'diseases', as their aim is to achieve learning of basic and clinical science in a clinical context. The process is assessed **formatively** and **summatively** in year one of the course.

The focus of the trigger is acute upper gastrointestinal blood loss, and hypotheses will be based on the likely site of blood loss and the likely nature of the lesion. The observation of the patient felt 'shaky and sweaty' leads to consideration of the effects of acute blood loss (previously studied in the first term in relation to blood loss after trauma).

(Dr Jean McPherson)

Teachers starting to use PBL often find they need to develop new skills. The following generic guidelines are useful pointers. The facilitator:

- Is not there to lecture. The facilitator keeps the process on time, on track, ensures students do not go away from a problem with misinformation, asks non-leading questions when appropriate, and (in many versions) assesses performance.
- Establishes or reiterates group ground rules when taking a new group.
- Assists the student 'officers' to fulfil their roles, but does not usurp their positions.
- Assists in creating an exploratory and non-threatening *learning* environment.
- Makes sure students feel able to question and query each other, using an appropriate manner.
- Encourages students to use and formally evaluate a wide variety of information sources.
- Assists students to present cogently and avoid rambling 'lectures'.
- Encourages the involvement of all students.
- Asks students periodically to summarize a case or aspects of it.
- At the end of each problem asks students to summarize their findings, evaluate how they tackled the problem and suggest how the process could have been more effective.
- Gives feedback to students about their performance in a specific, constructive manner (generally within the group setting).

Given that the introduction of PBL into an established school requires a substantial change, why is the effort made? Several meta-analyses reported in review articles examine evidence of the effectiveness of PBL (Schmidt, Dauphinee and Patel, 1987; Norman and Schmidt, 1992; Vernon and Blake, 1993; Albanese and Mitchell, 1993; Berkson, 1993). The five studies cover a wide range of arguments and attributes, although, as with many aspects of education, it has proved hard to produce definitive evidence. However, all five studies find evidence to suggest that PBL students are better able to take a **deep approach** to learning (see Chapter 2). Another well-substantiated aspect is that while students on traditional curricula tend to score slightly higher on conventional tests of knowledge, PBL students retain their knowledge longer. Some of the meta-analyses also show that students seem to perceive PBL as more clinically relevant and to rate their programmes more positively. There is less consensus on the efficacy of PBL in continuing medical education, although even here doctors report being more satisfied with it as a mode of learning than with other methods (Smits, Verbeek and Buisonjé, 2002).

Issues to consider when introducing PBL

Variable aspects of PBL include: at what stage students are provided with tutor-determined learning objectives; whether each student follows up all the learning questions/objectives; if there are supporting layers of information that can be revealed to students. There is also debate about the extent of tutor intervention, how far PBL is usable in the more clinical parts of courses and whether the expert or non-expert makes the best type of PBL tutor. No matter what version is used, it is important to train staff and students in its usage, provide adequate tutorial and study rooms and ensure learning resources are available. The Internet is a frequently used source for student learning, but brings with it issues about reliability. PBL requires assessment methods appropriate to the expected learning outcomes and suitable evaluation (see Chapter 14). Time is needed for curriculum planning, writing problems, and developing supporting tutorial material.

ASSESSMENT

The challenge is to use appropriate assessment methods, following the basic guidelines of assessment (see Chapter 4 and Crosby, 2002). Assessment should be **valid, reliable, fair,** feasible, defendable and well conceived from the perspective of impact on learning.

Cynics may point to the emergence of examination litigation, notably within the United States, as a reason for change in assessment methods, but there are other more cogent reasons, especially needing surety that we assess the main things we want students to know, do and understand. The principal problem with the older forms of clinical assessments (eg, the short and long case) is relatively strong validity, but poor reliability. Older forms of written assessments are weak in both validity and reliability. Methods for combining marks have often been inadequate.

Interrogating Practice

List all the types of assessment with which you are familiar. For each type consider if it assesses knowing, thinking, technical skills, attitudes and/or behaviour.

Key to the changes introduced has been the 'objectification' of medical assessment (Van der Vleuten, Norman and De Graaff, 1991) and with it, the increase in reliability. Newer assessments claiming increased validity have also been introduced. Another change has been the move away from a 'big bang' graduating examination toward continuous assessment. This has shifted the emphasis of final examinations to 'fitness to practise'. As a result of these changes there are now many, newer types of assessment. The key to good assessment is making it compatible with learning outcomes and realizing that few types of test are perfect; a range is often needed.

Updating clinical assessment: (a) the short case

The typical traditional medical and dental short case involved a candidate seeing four or five patients in front of a pair of examiners and being asked to carry out a clinical examination or provide a diagnosis. The first major change in clinical assessment came with the description of the **objective structured clinical examination (OSCE)** (Harden and Gleeson, 1979). Since the early 1990s the OSCE has become widely used in both undergraduate and postgraduate assessment.

The OSCE consists of a circuit made up of a number of cubicles or stations through which each candidate must pass. At each station the candidate is required to perform a given task. This may be observed and assessed by an examiner, or may require the candidate to answer some questions. Tasks may include communication skills, history taking, informed consent, clinical examination of real and simulated patients, clinical procedures performed on manikins, and data interpretation. Stations may assess various attitudes and behaviours, something the older assessments often failed to address. Each student is assessed on the same task by the same examiner. To further objectivity, the observer is provided with a checklist that has a breakdown of the task into its component items. The observer is requested to mark the candidate on each of these items. More recently, global rating scales have been advocated and employed. Despite fears that their use would be a retrograde step toward the old, subjective marking system, they have been shown to be as reliable as their detailed counterparts (Allen, Heard and Savidge, 1998).

The OSCE remains an assessment in evolution. Debate continues about the maximal duration of the stations, the minimum testing time required for a reliable examination and the number of stations and tasks assessed. In most institutions these details are governed by the practical considerations of the number of students to be examined, the facilities available and, perhaps most importantly, the financial constraints. At present, most UK undergraduate high-stake OSCEs consist of 20 to 30 stations, each of approximately 5–10 minutes in length. It should be stressed that OSCEs of less than two and a half hours become increasingly unreliable and should not be used summatively. However, the 5–10 minute station format limits the type of task assessed and is probably more applicable to the assessment of students in the earlier years, when single tasks need to be assessed in isolation to ensure **competence**. At graduation, and indeed probably earlier in dentistry, one is more interested in a holistic approach and extended or paired stations may be employed to assess a range of skills within a single clinical scenario.

> ## Case Study 2: OSCE station used at the Dental School, Barts and the London, Queen Mary's School of Medicine and Dentistry

This five-minute, final-year, undergraduate station uses freshly mixed alginate (impression material) to simulate soft tissues. The usual surgical instruments are available to carry out the procedure. There are separate sets of examiner and candidate instructions.

Task: You are going to carry out inverse bevel flap periodontal surgery (modified Widman flap) to treat periodontal pocketing at the misial and distal aspects of the lower first molar tooth. Make the incisions you would use on the buccal aspect of the model provided, and elevate the flap appropriately.

The examiner's mark-sheet details 10 aspects the candidate needs to perform correctly. For each aspect a single mark is awarded if it is done as detailed on the mark sheet; no mark is given when it is not done as detailed. The 10 points are:

- selects correct instrument for incision (number 15 scalpel blade);
- uses finger rest on tooth;
- preserves gingival contour/'knife edge' papillae;
- makes inverse bevel incision 1 mm from the gingival margin;
- makes incision at correct angle to the long axis of the tooth;
- extends incision down to the alveolar bone;
- makes appropriate extension of the flap by extending flap to distal of second molar and to first premolar *or* uses appropriate relieving incision(s);
- makes second incision in gingival crevice;
- elevates flap with correct instrument (periosteal elevator);
- uses periosteal elevator correctly (convex curvature pointing medially).

(Dr Elizabeth Davenport)

Case Study 3: An example of a medical OSCE station

This five-minute station would also include a background script for the simulated patient and a separate set of examiner and candidate instructions.

Task: You are a medical student attached to a general medical outpatient clinic. The next patient is a 72-year-old man complaining of palpitations. Please take a history of the presenting complaint and any further relevant history with a view to making a diagnosis.

The examiners' mark-sheet from this OSCE uses a three-point scale of 'good'; 'adequate'; 'not done' and contains items relating to both communicating with the patient (such as introducing oneself and inviting the patient to ask questions) and to asking the correct questions of a patient with these symptoms. The station concludes with the examiner asking the candidate to offer a differential diagnosis. The simulated patient participates in examining the candidate by being asked to respond to two questions on the mark sheet: Did the candidate treat you in a professional manner? Did the candidate allow you to express your concerns?

(Adapted from Feather, Visvanathan and Lumley, 1999)

The main problems with the OSCE format are the financial costs and the manpower required. The administration, logistics and practicalities of running an undergraduate OSCE are comprehensively described in Feather and Kopelman (1997). The experience of the authors is that OSCEs are approximately 30–50 per cent more expensive than traditional examinations. However, this must be set against their reliability, which is far superior to the traditional short case.

Updating clinical assessment: (b) the long case

The traditional long case in medicine and dentistry started with a one-hour unobserved session in which the candidate was required to clerk a patient and formulate a management plan. Examination by a pair of examiners followed. This assessment has probably changed little since the days of Paget in Cambridge in the 1840s. However, it too has recently been subjected to review and more objective formats have been developed; these include the observed long case (Newble, 1991) and the **objective structured long examination record**, the **OSLER** (Gleeson, 1992). These changes have led to candidates seeing similar patients with parts or all of the clerking being observed by the examiners and identical aspects being assessed. Performance is graded against a checklist, similar to that used in an OSCE. Wass and Jolly (2001) argue that the observed long case can produce an equally reliable and valid assessment as the OSCE, while testing a more holistic approach to the patient. The authors maintain that a combination of an extended (45–60 minutes) observed, long case examination should be used in combination with an OSCE in high stakes clinical assessment.

Until recently, medical students and postgraduates clerking patients were observed rarely. Formative and summative use of the updated long case should rectify this and be a useful tool, when applied over several disciplines, in picking up common problems. It has equal potential in dental assessment. Teachers and students alike will have to prepare for this form of assessment.

In the United States, a further development has been the focused patient encounter (FPE) also known in postgraduate education as mini-clinical examination exercise (mini-CEX). This involves the student being asked to focus his or her history and examination to one key point of the clinical problem, eg, dental or chest pain. It may be used formatively and summatively.

Updating clinical assessment: (c) the viva voce

The **viva voce** is often used as a summative assessment tool but is regarded by many as educationally defective and indefensible. It is the least reliable of any form of clinical assessment because it uses only two examiners and its unstructured format can result in a very variable interaction. Its content validity is also questionable and issues of content specificity have major effect on its reliability. Despite its poor reliability, it is still used in assessment within the UK. It is often used in making pass/fail decisions and decisions of 'excellence'. Its defenders quote it being 'like real life' and 'useful in gauging a candidate's all round knowledge', but much of what is gauged about a candidate is actually covered by other, more reliable forms of assessment. In an attempt to bring its supporters and detractors together, it too has been subject to some 'objectification'.

Updating clinical assessment: (d) log books and reflective writing

Log books have long been used to record clinical practice, exposure and events in both undergraduate and postgraduate education. However, in their traditional form, they were often subject to abuse, even in the more supervised dental environment. This abuse was often a result of short cuts, poor objectives and unrealistic targets. In response to this criticism, the use of the log book has changed. Students should now be encouraged to use them to reflect upon clinical events in which they have taken part. Entries in the log book should be monitored and commented upon, so directing the student's learning. Thus, they may be used as a formative assessment tool. (With the introduction of the Calman recommendations, most senior house officers and specialist registrars are required to keep training logs. These are used to ensure all trainees reach nationally agreed standards but are also useful for trainees to reflect upon their areas of strength and those that require improvement.)

Developing written assessment: extended matching questions

Much change to written assessment over the past 30 years has been driven by the use of computer-assisted marking schedules and the need for increased reliability and validity. **Multiple-choice (MCQ)** and short answer questions are common to many disciplines, but **extended matching questions (EMQs)**, have been developed to assess higher levels of cognition, including diagnostic reasoning (Case and Swanson, 1996).

Case Study 4: The EMQ format

Theme: anaemia

Options

A	Acquired non-immune haemolytic anaemia	G	Iron deficiency anaemia
B	Anaemia of chronic disease	H	Leukoerythroblastic anaemia
C	Aplastic anaemia	I	Pernicous anaemia
D	Autoimmune haemolytic anaemia	J	Sickle cell disease
E	Congenital spherocytosis	K	Sideroblastic anaemia
F	Folate deficiency	L	Thalassaemia major

Please select from the list above the most appropriate diagnosis for each of the patients below:

A 55-year-old woman presents with lassitude and tingling in her limbs. On examination she is pale and has a peripheral sensory neuropathy. The serum contains autoantibodies to parietal cells and intrinsic factor.

A 64-year-old man presents with pain in the upper right quadrant of his abdomen. He had an aortic valve replacement 10 years ago. Investigations reveal a normochromic, normocytic anaemia with fragmented red cells and a reticulocyctosis. A direct Coomb's test is negative.

A 44-year-old woman presents with lassitude. Her full blood count reveals a hypochromic, microcytic anaemia. Her serum ferritin is low.

Assessment is one of the fastest-changing areas in medical and dental education and one in which continuing professional development is crucial. Figure 23.2 lists some of the most common types of assessment.

OVERVIEW

Medical and dental teaching and learning has recently undergone 'major surgery' with the aim of 'anastamozing' sound educational theory with traditional teaching and learning methods. New curricula, with student-driven learning, 'objectification' and innovation within assessment, and the changing postgraduate structure have left much for the 'jobbing' clinician to keep up with. The Learning and Teaching Subject Centre has much to offer, as explained in Case Study five.

Written Assessment	Practical Assessment	Others
Free response essays	Objective structured clinical examination (OSCE)	Special projects Video/photographic journalistic, artistic
Structured/short answer questions (SAQ)	Long cases observed OSLER	360-degree appraisal (appraisal is a particular type of assessment with a formative emphasis)
Multiple choice questions (MCQ)	Observation of student – real life	Team/firm assessment – judgements of a trainee made by 1–10 members
Extended matching questions (EMQ)	Moulage –simulated action scenario	Viva voce Structured Unstructured
Log books	Video of 'real life'	Self-assessment/review
PBL case write-up		
Reflective practice diaries		
Portfolios/progress files		
Project reports		

Figure 23.2 Forms of assessment used in medical and dental education in the UK

Case Study 5: Supporting learning and teaching in medicine and dentistry

The Subject Centre for Medicine, Dentistry and Veterinary Medicine (LTSN-01) is one of 24 Subject Centres comprising the Learning and Teaching Support Network (LTSN) established in January 2000.

Based in the Faculty of Medicine at the University of Newcastle-upon-Tyne, with partners in the Faculty of Veterinary Medicine at the University of Edinburgh and the Royal College of Physicians, London, LTSN-01 is funded from the higher education budget and responsible directly to the LTSN Executive and the UK Higher Education Funding Councils.

Our mission is to support all staff involved in learning and teaching medicine, dentistry and veterinary medicine in higher education, including academic staff, senior managers, learning technologists, educational development staff and staff developers. Our office is open Monday–Friday, 9 am – 5 pm, at:

LTSN-01 Catherine Cookson Centre for Medical Education & Health Informatics, University of Newcastle 16/17 Framlington Place, Newcastle upon Tyne NE2 4AB Tel: +44 (0) 191 222 5888 Fax: +44 (0) 191 222 5016 e-mail: enquiries@ltsn-01.ac.uk

We offer a range of services, from access to learning materials (eg, links to image banks, guides to teaching and learning software); and news on curricular review and higher education issues (eg, benchmarking statements); to the 'knowledge base' of good practice; learning resources; frequently asked questions (FAQs); events and funding opportunities. All are available from the Web site (http://www.ltsn-01.ac.uk), where you will also find opportunities to get involved in a number of subject specific and generic educational projects.

Our priorities are:

- To provide easy access to the existing body of knowledge and add value to existing resources through promoting research and development.
- To identify and promote innovation and build capacity in the sector by seeking funds, facilitating new networks and collaboration with established groups and networks.
- To develop and implement a proactive R&D agenda based on priority outcome areas (such as assessment) identified through initial consultation with the constituency.
- To facilitate understanding/implementation of the new quality assurance processes, subject benchmarks, statutory body recommendations, and help the constituency to manage change.

Practical examples of our work include funding mini-projects, answering enquiries about software for specific teaching requirements, facilitating meetings/partnerships for development and research projects in teaching and learning, a regular e-mail newsletter, school visits, brokering access to 'expert consultants', materials, etc, for events and conferences. These are only a few of the ways in which we come into contact with our constituents, and we look forward to more in the future.

(Professor R K Jordan, Director)

Many in the older schools question whether the revolution in medical and dental education is worthwhile. Evidence, although measured on older criteria, suggests that these major changes are not producing a 'better' graduate but are producing a different, perhaps more rounded, individual, but one in whom the public can place confidence.

As professionals, we are coming under increasing public scrutiny and this is never truer than in education. We must apply the same evidence-based approach to our teaching practice as we do to scientific research or clinical practice. Traditional methods do not necessarily need to be thrown away, but can be improved and brought into line with modern educational theory and practice.

REFERENCES

Albanese, M and Mitchell, S (1993) Problem-based learning: a review of literature on its outcomes and implementation issues, *Academic Medicine*, **68** (1), pp 52–81

Allen, R, Heard, J and Savidge, M (1998) Global ratings versus checklist scoring in an OSCE, *Academic Medicine*, **73** (5), pp 597–98

Barrows, H (1993) An overview of the uses of standardized patients for teaching and evaluating clinical skills, *Academic Medicine*, **68**, pp 443–53

Berkson, L (1993) Problem-based learning: have expectations been met? *Academic Medicine*, **68** (10), pp S79–88

Boud, D and Feletti, G (eds) (1996) *The Challenge of Problem-Based Learning*, Kogan Page, London

Bouhuijs, P, Schmidt, H and van Berkel, H (eds) (1987) *Problem-Based Learning as an Educational Strategy*, Network Publications, Maastricht, Netherlands

'Calman Report' (1993) *Hospital Doctors: Training for the future*, Report of Working Group on Specialist Medical Training, Department of Health, London

Case, S and Swanson, D (eds) (1996) *Constructing Written Test Questions for the Basic and Clinical Sciences*, National Board of Medical Examiners, Philadelphia

Crosby, J (2002) Assessment, in *Effective Learning and Teaching in Medical, Dental and Veterinary Education*, eds S Huttly, J Sweet and I Taylor, Kogan Page, London

Davenport, E, Davis, J, Cushing, A and Holsgrove, G (1998) An innovation in the assessment of future dentists, *British Dental Journal*, **184** (4), pp 192–95

Feather, A and Kopelman, P (1997) A practical approach to running an OSCE for medical undergraduates, *Education for Health*, **10**, pp 333–50

Feather A, Visvanathan, R and Lumley, J (1999) *OSCEs for Medical Undergraduates*, Pastest, Cheshire

General Dental Council (GDC) (1997) *The First Five Years*, GDC, London

General Medical Council (GMC) (1993, 2002) *Tomorrow's Doctors*, GMC, London

GMC (1997) *The New Doctor*, GMC, London

GMC (2001) *Draft Recommendation on Undergraduate Medical Education*, GMC, London

Gleeson, F (1992) Defects in postgraduate clinical skills as revealed by the objective structured long examination record (OSLER), *Irish Medical Journal*, **85**, pp 11–14

Harden R, and Gleeson, F A (1979) Assessment of clinical competence using an objective structured clinical examination (OSCE), *Medical Education*, **13**, pp 41–54

Kolb, D A (1984) *Experiential Learning*, Prentice Hall, Englewood Cliffs, New Jersey

Medical Workforce Standing Advisory Committee (1997) *Planning the Medical Workforce*, Medical Workforce Standing Advisory Committee, Third Report, Department of Health

Neufeld, V and Barrows, H (1974) 'The McMaster Philosophy': an approach to medical education, *Journal of Medical Education*, **49**, pp 1040–50

Newble, D (1991) The observed long case in clinical assessment, *Medical Education*, **25** (5), pp 369–73

Norman, G and Schmidt, H (1992) The psychological basis of problem-based learning: a review of the evidence, *Academic Medicine*, **67** (9), pp 557–65

Peyton, J W R (1998) *Teaching and Learning in Medical Practice*, Manticore Europe Limited, Rickmansworth, Herts

Quality Assurance Agency for Higher Education (QAA) (2002) Subject Benchmark Statement for Medicine; QAA, Gloucester

QAA (2002) Subject Benchmark Statement for Dentistry; QAA, Gloucester

Schmidt, H, Dauphinee, W and Patel, V (1987) Comparing the effects of problem-based and conventional curricula in an international sample, *Journal of Medical Education*, **62**, pp 305–15

Smits, P, Verbeek, J and Buisonjé, C (2002) Problem-based learning in continuing medical education: a review of controlled evaluation studies, *British Medical Journal*, **324**, pp 153–56

Stanton, F and Grant, J (1999) Approaches to experiential learning, course delivery and validation in medicine: a background document, *Medical Education*, **33** (4), pp 282–97

Stark, P, Delmotte, A and Howdle, P (1998) Teaching clinical skills using a ward-based teacher, presentation at the ASME Conference, Southampton, September

Suvinen, T, Messer, L and Franco, E (1998) Clinical simulation in teaching pre-clinical dentistry, *European Journal of Dentistry*, **2** (1), pp 25–32

Turner, T, Collinson, S and Fry, H (2001) Doctor in the house: the medical student as academic, attendant and apprentice? *Medical Teacher*, **23** (5), pp 514–16

Van der Vleuten, C, Norman, G and De Graaff, E (1991) Pitfalls in the pursuit of objectivity: issues of reliability, *Medical Education*, **25**, pp 110–18

Vernon, D and Blake, R (1993) Does problem-based learning work? A meta-analysis of evaluative research, *Academic Medicine*, **68** (7), pp 551–63

Wass, V and Jolly, B (2001) Does observation add to the validity of the long case? *Medical Education*, **35** (8), pp 729–34

FURTHER READING

Albanese and Mitchell (1993) See above. The best place to gain an idea of the strengths of PBL and possible variations in its use.

Case and Swanson (1998) See above. For different types of examination questions.

Jolly, B and Grant, J (eds) (1997) *The Good Assessment Guide*, Joint Centre for Medical Education in Medicine, London. Probably the best single source of explanation about suitable types of assessment.

Sweet, J, Huttly, S and Taylor, I (eds) *Effective Learning and Teaching in Medical, Dental and Veterinary Education*, Kogan Page, London. An overview compendium of basic approaches. (In press.)

Jolly, B and Rees, L (eds) (1998) *Medical Education in the Millennium*, Oxford University Press, Oxford. Many useful chapters, especially student learning.

Newble, D and Cannon, R (1994) *A Handbook for Medical Teachers*, Kluwer Publishers, London. A basic 'how to do medical education'; also useful for dentistry.

Peyton, J W R (ed) (1998) See above. Some aspects helpfully described.

Key aspects of teaching and learning in accounting, business and management

Ursula Lucas and Peter Milford

INTRODUCTION

This chapter aims to identify the distinctive features of education in accounting, business and management and the way in which they may impact upon teaching, learning and assessment strategies. Business education forms a significant sector within higher education. In 1999–2000, 157,000 undergraduate students (some 10 per cent of the total) were enrolled on business and management honours degree programmes (including accounting degrees). To this total should be added those students who study business subjects as part of their own specialist degree studies. These students vary widely in their aspirations and modes of study.

Business education embraces a wide variety of disciplines and stakeholders. The diversity of students, disciplines and stakeholders in business education produces tensions that are not easily resolved and creates a complex and challenging environment for lecturers. This chapter explores the implications of this environment for the development of learning, teaching and assessment strategies within business education, primarily at undergraduate level.

DISTINCTIVE ASPECTS OF BUSINESS EDUCATION

The Quality Assurance Agency (QAA) **subject benchmark** statements (QAA, 2000a) identify the purpose of general and business management programmes as:

- The study of organizations, their management and the changing external environment in which they operate.
- Preparation for and development of a career in business and management.
- Enhancement of lifelong learning skills and personal development to contribute to society at large.

The accounting benchmark statements are similar. They do not assume that all accounting students wish to qualify as accountants. Thus an accounting degree programme is seen to provide 'A useful introduction to the worlds of business and finance' (QAA, 2000b).

These objectives may appear straightforward but, in fact, a closer review reveals distinctive features and tensions which should be taken into account when designing teaching, learning and assessment strategies. Perhaps the most notable feature (and tension) of business education lies within the first two objectives. In 1983, Tolley (in a much-quoted statement) reflected: 'It is not clear whether the underlying concern of staff and students in these courses [ie, Business Studies degrees] is a study of business or a study for business' (Tolley, 1983: 5).

It is apparent from the benchmark statements that business education is seen by the QAA to incorporate both of these aspects. A study *for* business recognizes that there is a vocational aspect to education. Students should be adequately prepared for employment in business. A study *about* business recognizes that education can fulfil a wider role, that of allowing students to study the role of business in society, incorporating sociological, legal, economic or ethical aspects. This dichotomy in educational objectives goes back a long way and reflects the contrasting values of a vocational versus a liberal education (for an overview and discussion of contrasting educational perspectives, see Grey and French, 1996).

The business lecturer works within a complex and dynamic environment. Despite the view taken by the benchmark statements, business educators have to acknowledge and respond to competing demands: from government, employers, professional bodies and students. Moreover, the tradition and culture of higher education institutions and the lecturers who work within them also affect the way in which business education is provided. While there are strong influences that support a more vocational approach to business education there are also influences that support a shift towards a more liberal approach. This environment, which is illustrated in Figure 24.1, will be discussed in more detail below.

Lecturers bring with them a particular orientation to the teaching of their subject. The study of business and management does not constitute a single

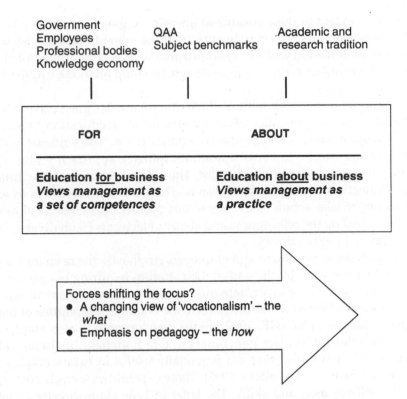

Figure 24.1 The 'for–about spectrum' in business education

discipline. Rather, it comprises some traditional disciplines such as economics, mathematics, law and sociology and newer subjects such as marketing, accounting and strategy which derive their knowledge base from a variety of traditional disciplines. Some lecturers will have come through a traditional higher educational route of doctoral specialism, tending possibly to a view of business education as being *about* business. Whereas other lecturers will have entered higher education after substantial professional and business experience, tending possibly to a view of business education as being *for* business (Macfarlane, 1997). Thus even within one institution there are likely to be differing perspectives about the role of business education.

Students, too, bring with them a particular orientation to learning. There is great diversity within the business student population. In 1999–2000 some 22 per cent of the population was represented by students studying part-time. Many of these combine employment with study. A substantial proportion of business students undertake some form of **placement**. These two categories of students bring a contextual perspective to their studies quite different from those who enter full-time undergraduate education at the age of 18. Students also vary according to the extent of their vocational interest: ranging from those who wish to obtain a broad specialism in management to those who ultimately wish to gain a professional qualification within a specialist area such as accounting. All of these factors have implications for curriculum design, teaching methods, approaches to teaching and assessment.

The institutional framework within which courses are designed can exacerbate the tensions between an education *about*, as opposed to an education *for* business. The use of modular courses is widespread within the UK. The tendency within a modular structure can be towards a multidisciplinary approach within which subjects may become insular and specialist. Thus the student may have difficulty in seeing connections between the subjects. There are various ways in which universities might take action to overcome this problem (discussed below). But they are dependent on the willingness and ability of lecturers (with diverse views) to work in a more integrated way.

Funding agencies, government and employers emphasize the need for business graduates to be *employable* by the end of their studies, requiring business-related knowledge and skills. Employer demands for skills development in business programmes were reflected in submissions to the National Committee of Inquiry into Higher Education (**NCIHE,** 1997). Skills development is also emphasized heavily in the relevant subject benchmarks. 'Graduateness' includes subject knowledge and 'capabilities' that are potentially useful in future employment (Association of Graduate Recruiters, 1995). These capabilities include both attributes, such as self-reliance, and skills. The latter include skills directly related to business and accounting practice, such as business problem-solving and use of financial language, and more generic skills, such as numeracy, communication and team working (see Chapter 9). A review of the educational literature shows a multitude of projects that have enquired into the nature of skills, their transferability and the means of assessing them. Atkins (1999) provides a concise review of these). A key tension arises from the competition for 'space' in the curriculum: will an emphasis on skills development compromise the development of subject knowledge and conceptual understanding? Higher National Diploma programmes in business and accounting traditionally emphasize skills development heavily, with undergraduate degree programmes moving more recently to such approaches.

Interrogating Practice

Consider the balance between the development of subject knowledge and 'skills' development in a business or accounting award that you have knowledge of. Is the balance appropriate? To what extent do the skills developed enhance employability? To what extent do the skills developed support learning and hence the development of subject knowledge and understanding?

The changing nature of knowledge in business is an important influence on business education. Relevant knowledge includes technical expertise (eg, accounting standards, human resource management practices) and critiques of management and accounting practices in their organizational and social context. A growing body of research on the market for ideas in business (eg, Huczynski 1993) reveals the contested nature of knowledge in business and management, the elements of 'fashion' both in management practices and academic approaches and the insatiable thirst of managers for new ideas to help them to deal with a complex and turbulent environment. Business curricula must therefore take account of the diversity and dynamism of subject knowledge; approaches that emphasize technique over context will develop only partial knowledge and understanding. Yet business educators are also under pressure to include 'useful' knowledge within the curriculum.

The trend in recent years has been for there to be a shift in focus towards an education that is *for* business. However, despite the strength of demands from government, employers, professional bodies and students, there are other forces that support a shift in focus towards an education *about* business. The first of these is a changing view of what vocationalism means. The current emphasis on **life-long learning** acknowledges a perception by employers that business graduates require the ability to act autonomously and to think critically. For example, during the 1990s the US-based Accounting Education Change Commission worked to incorporate principles of a liberal education into the accounting undergraduate curriculum for these reasons. This shifting view of vocationalism not only focuses on what is studied but how it is studied. Thus learning and teaching strategies are expected to support the development of independent learners.

A second force that shifts the focus towards an education about business comprises two elements: a more formal approach to programme design and an emphasis on pedagogy. The QAA requires that **programme specifications** are produced for each degree course. Programme designers have to demonstrate how the aims and the learning outcomes of the degree programme are achieved across the spectrum of modules or courses studied. This requires a clear statement of **learning outcomes** for each course and a description of how knowledge and skills are developed and assessed. In particular, the classification of skills includes cognitive skills of 'critical thinking, analysis and synthesis' which include the 'capability to identify assumptions, evaluate statements in terms of evidence ...' (QAA, 2000a: 3) and so on. There is a growing emphasis on pedagogy as evidenced by the creation of the **Institute for Learning and Teaching** (ILT) and the growing expectation that lecturers will have engaged in some form of professional pedagogic development. Consequently there is much more support available than previously for business educators who wish to change the *how* of business education as well as the *what*.

Interrogating Practice

Consider your own institution in the light of the factors discussed above. Where does it lie in terms of an orientation towards an education *about* or *for* business? How does the programme *structure* influence the orientation adopted by the programme? What do *you* think the aims of a business education should be? What orientation do you adopt and why?

A STARTING POINT: LISTENING TO STUDENTS

One of the features of business education noted above is the diversity in the student population. Students bring with them different motivations for, and different orientations to, the study of business. Some wish for an all-round business course, some already have a particular interest in certain subjects such as accounting, marketing or human resource management. Thus a lecturer may find a class is composed of students who are predisposed to view their study in quite distinctive ways. Moreover, while the lecturer may have taken a view about where a course lies on the 'for–about spectrum' but this may differ significantly from the view of some (or all) of the students. Case Study 1 addresses this issue. It looks at how lecturers have ascertained students' perceptions of the development of skills. In this case study the unexpected findings provided lecturers with a challenge.

Case Study 1 : Ascertaining students' perceptions of skills development

Skills development

There has been much discussion about the nature of **key skills** and the ways in which they may be developed within the curriculum. An important decision is whether skills development should be addressed separately within the curriculum or incorporated into modules. However, even if key skills are developed separately, it is important that students recognize when these skills may be relevant within individual modules.

At the University of the West of England, as part of the University's Key Skills and Graduate Capability Project, a working group was established to design a programme specification describing the skills currently developed within the programme. Having done this, students were provided with an opportunity to discuss these skills in some depth. They were asked, 'To what extent has your course helped you in developing these skills?'

The findings of the study were unexpected. Students experienced skill development as a tacit developmental process and, in some cases it was so tacit that students did not perceive it as a process of development at all. For example, having a skill was associated with being the 'kind of person you are'. Either you have a skill or you don't. Or a skill is something that 'you pick up over time', as part of the maturing process – or is developed unconsciously in higher education 'just by being here'. And whether a skill is developed within higher education 'depends on how good you are at doing that anyway'. Students varied enormously in the extent to which they arrived at university with some skills already developed. Finally, students found the language of the skills descriptors rather alien. Consequently one exclamation was, 'Who writes this stuff?' (For further information about this project, see Lucas *et al*, 2001.)

Taking student perceptions into account

How can a lecturer, even in dealing with large groups of students, take account of diverse student perceptions? First, the most positive finding of the study described above was that students found the opportunity to discuss perceptions of immense value. It forced them to reflect and they started to see the course in a new light. 'It wouldn't have occurred to me that I even had those skills ...' was a typical response. Finding that other students saw skills in a different way was, in itself, an eye opener for students. Even in large groups, it is not difficult to give time for students to identify, discuss and compare their perceptions of learning or the subject. Second, the lecturer can then design learning and teaching approaches with a broader awareness of the different ways in which students approach their learning of the subject. Workshop or lecture activities can be used to address perceptions that may adversely affect learning. Third, knowledge learnt from this exercise can be referred to later in the course. Students can then review how their perceptions have (or have not) changed during the course. An interesting account of such an approach is available in Mladenovic (2000). Although it describes an approach taken in an accounting course, it could be adopted within any other subject.

(Dr Ursula Lucas, University of the West of England)

Case Study 2: Developing personal transferable skills for undergraduate students at the University of Bradford Management Centre

While it is important that lecturers listen to students and take account of different student perceptions, it is equally important that students listen to themselves. Students need to develop self-awareness and the ability to reflect on their experience. The approach used to develop skills in the Practice of Management Skills module at the University of Bradford School of Management contrasts the use of stand-alone skills modules with skills integration through other taught modules. The case highlights problems of transferability of skills from one environment to another, due to lack of feedback, insufficient opportunities to demonstrate skills, and 'shallow' learning.

The module was developed in recognition of the fact that students develop skills in a variety of situations, both in the classroom and through other life experiences, such as part-time work. Students are given the opportunity to reflect on the way that they demonstrate and develop transferable skills in any of these situations. The module aims to achieve integration across a broad range of life experiences, thereby enhancing the potential for transferability.

Students need the opportunity to identify areas for improving skills, practising these skills, receiving feedback and reflecting in order to demonstrate learning through changed behaviour (adopting Kolb's Learning Cycle, as seen in Chapter 2).

The taught content of the module covers a broad range of skill areas:

- self-development and planning;
- presentation skills;
- time management;
- interviewing;
- active listening;
- group working;
- stress management;
- leadership;
- CV preparation;
- decision making;
- giving feedback.

Assessment for the module has been devised to increase the opportunities to students to demonstrate and develop their skills in a range of situations:

- Two reflective pieces of work on self-awareness, one identifying weaknesses and plans for turning them into strengths and the other evaluating the success of the plans and proposing areas for future development.
- One reflective assignment on personal experience in a chosen skill area.
- A reflective group presentation to their peers (students have a choice of four option titles, eg, 'What have we learnt regarding interpersonal skills?').

The case demonstrates two key innovations:

1. Opportunities for student ownership and involvement are created through a balance of choice and compulsion. Self-awareness is compulsory, but there is an emphasis on student reflection to identify personal skill areas for further development. Students choose what to be assessed on and are given some choice over assessment timings.

2. Assessment structures are used to encourage transferability of skills. Students are able to apply learning during the module to their personal experiences in other situations as well as reflect upon their experiences from other areas (eg, presentation skills used in assessments in other modules; skills developed in part-time work). The assessment is adaptable to student needs, but the mechanism of planning and the plan content are constant.

Students have capitalized on opportunities for reflection through high commitment and engagement. Student feedback has been positive. Further benefits have been gained through a student focus on the links between self-development and career development. Reported tutor benefits include: relating better to students through knowledge of their needs and issues, making learning more effective, and achieving personal satisfaction in their teaching.

The module has proved to be resource intensive in tutor time, providing in turn a stimulus to developing more effective criteria-driven feedback forms. The module tutors have also been faced with control issues, finding it hard to manage student perceptions. The module was also judged less effective for those who have a theorist or activist **learning style**. These issues have been partly overcome by giving full advice on assessment and criteria, in order to enable all students to select assessment topics that suit their personal needs. For further information about this case, see Morgan (2001a, b).

Issues/questions
To what extent can skills be regarded as 'transferable' between situations and settings?
Should skills be developed through stand-alone modules or integrated throughout all modules?
Does reflection facilitate skills development?

(Dr Peter Morgan, University of Bradford)

DESIGN OF LEARNING, TEACHING AND ASSESSMENT STRATEGIES

This section considers ways in which learning, teaching and assessment strategies can be used to shift the focus along the 'for–about spectrum' at both the level of the programme and the level of the individual module. Any attempt to counter the multidisciplinary tendencies of business education with a holistic approach requires integration strategies at the programme design level. However, individual lecturers can also shift the focus of teaching along the 'for–about spectrum' in a variety of ways. Suggestions as to how the focus might be shifted are outlined in Figure 24.2 and discussed below.

Learning outcomes

The starting point for the design of learning, teaching and assessment strategies is the identification of learning outcomes. Generic educational advice on learning outcomes often refers lecturers to Bloom's taxonomy (see Chapter 3).

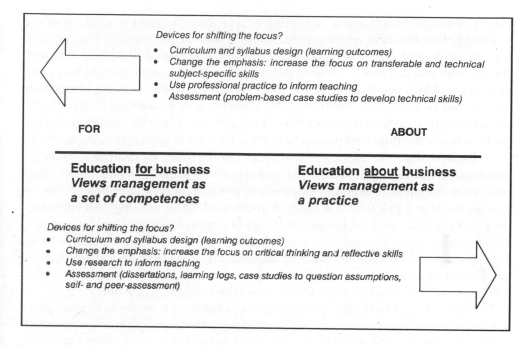

Figure 24.2 Shifting the focus along the 'for–about spectrum'

However, alternative taxonomies may be more relevant to vocational and professional education. For example, Carter's (1985) taxonomy of objectives for professional education and Eraut's (1994) analysis of competences analyse the different types of knowledge and skills that are found within professional practice. In particular, they distinguish, as Bloom does not, between knowing how to do something and being able to do it. Thus **experiential knowledge** (see Chapter 10) is addressed as well as the importance of attitudes and values. Decisions about learning outcomes have to be taken in conjunction with a decision about where the programme might lie on the 'for–about spectrum'. Individual courses may vary in their orientation but there will be an overall approach adopted by the programme specification.

Integration

Regardless of where a programme lies on the 'for–about spectrum', the issue of integration must be addressed. There are several ways in which integration may be achieved. First, cross-curricular themes may be identified: for example, the environment, ethics, globalization, the knowledge economy. These themes can be addressed in all modules, preferably in assessed activity. Second, team teaching might be adopted, such that a marketing or accounting lecturer is involved in the teaching of the business environment. Third, where the programme incorporates a work placement, then the mode of assessment may require the student to link theory with practice and to identify the relevance of various subjects to his or her experience. However, the role of the individual lecturer in achieving integration should not be neglected. Students need constant help in locating where in the broad picture a particular subject 'fits'. Lecturers can assist by identifying other parts of the curriculum that provide a context for what is currently being studied.

Shifts along the 'for–about spectrum' can also be made by changing the skills emphasis of individual modules. A decision must be made as to how far learning outcomes can embrace both development of practical skills and critical review of management as a practice. It is rarely a question of 'all or nothing'. An emphasis on practical skills may be tempered by some element of critical review or vice versa. For example, assessments might be designed which expect students to be able to question the assumptions and theoretical frameworks underlying technical approaches. Or students might be expected to question the means by which 'professional' techniques and practice come to be accepted as the norm.

The placement period can be a valuable opportunity for students to place their academic learning in context and for them to experiment with the development of skills. This chapter will not consider the role of work experience further. However, Foreman and Johnston (1999), in the first edition of this Handbook, discuss the use of university learning in the workplace and it is the subject of their third case study.

Synergy between research, teaching and professional practice

Lecturers can also use their professional or research practice to inform the context within which their students study. The orientation of a lecturer can be an important influence on the student's perception of the subject. Thus a lecturer might design a course that is essentially *about* business, addressing the theoretical frameworks underpinning a subject. However, even in this context, it is possible for a lecturer's professional or business experience to provide practical contexts in which that theoretical knowledge becomes relevant and thus might be effectively challenged. Similarly, a course may be essentially *for* business, and involved with the development of technical skills. However, it is again possible for a lecturer to apply a knowledge of research in the area to question the relevance and efficacy of techniques.

Once learning outcomes have been specified, assessment becomes central to the development of teaching and learning strategies. Not only should it relate directly to the learning outcomes already identified but modes of assessment should be valid, reliable and fair (see Chapter 4). Since assessment is a prime determinant of student motivation, it provides an opportunity for lecturers to channel the energies of students into what are deemed to be appropriate activities.

Assessment strategies

For a good generic introduction to assessment see Chapter 4 and Macfarlane and Ottewill (2001: 53). This section discusses aspects of assessment most pertinent to business education. The tensions created by diversity within business education have already been identified. A key question that might be posed is 'Can assessment assist in resolving some of these tensions?'. There are various ways in which assessment may shift the focus along the 'for–about spectrum'.

Where a course emphasizes an education about business, assessment may focus on problems within a particular context, encouraging students to place knowledge and theories in a practical scenario. Thus case studies and business games are a valuable learning and assessment resource. Similarly, where a course emphasizes an education for business, then assessment may encourage students to place their practical studies in a conceptual framework. Dissertations and theses may provide students with opportunities to identify and critique the theory and knowledge underlying their practical studies.

Assessment may encourage students to make links between subjects studied independently within individual modules. Again case studies are an obvious choice, expecting students to take a more holistic approach to problem-solving. However, a collaboration between modules to develop a joint assessment strategy is another valuable way forward.

Assessment can support the development of employment-related skills such as communication, group work or planning and organization. However, it is critical that marking criteria fully assess the levels of those skills. In some cases, the outcome of that development may not be easily observable. Thus the student may be asked to reflect about the development and exercise of a particular skill, perhaps through the writing of a reflective piece or a learning log. Where there is already an emphasis on employment-related skills, then assessment can shift the focus to critical thinking and reflection. Students who have been assessed on the quality of their technical skills might be required to critically review the relevance or adequacy of those skills in a work context.

Assessment can support the development of students as critically reflective individuals. Feedback on assessments is central to the development of a student understanding of how they have performed. A part of the assessment might involve a reflective student piece of writing on what they have learnt from the assessment (see Case Study 3 below).

An important outcome of business education is often stated to be the development of students who will become autonomous individuals with a capacity to engage in lifelong learning. One might consider the development of an assessment strategy which allows a student to engage more independently within the assessment process throughout the three or four years of the degree course. Students can be involved in the design of assessment exercises and their marking (through self- and peer review) such that it becomes a collaborative exercise.

Case studies are a widely used means of teaching and assessment within business education. However, it should be borne in mind that they can be used in varying ways and may achieve quite different learning and assessment outcomes. For example, a case might be used solely for illustrative purposes, thus giving life to a highly theoretical approach. It might also be used as a problem to be 'solved'. Alternatively, the case can be used to provide a complex context where problems are not 'bounded' and not necessarily 'solvable'. This chapter does not address case studies further; the first edition of this Handbook addressed them in more detail (Foreman and Johnston, 1999). Another helpful overview of the use and relevance of the case method in business education is available in Booth *et al* (2000).

Interrogating Practice

Review a course that you currently teach. To what extent do the written learning outcomes for your course reflect what you are actually trying to achieve? How might you change your assessment strategy in order to change the focus of your course or the motivation of students?

ENCOURAGING REFLECTION AND SELF-AWARENESS IN STUDENTS

An essential goal of education is to encourage reflection and self-awareness in students. This is critically important considering the diversity and tensions inherent within business education. However, students need an opportunity to link not just theory with practice, but to link an *ever-expanding* theory with *their* practice. As discussed above, the business environment has seen a huge expansion in the knowledge base. Moreover, we have become much more aware of the importance of students being able to identify their own personal knowledge and experience bases.

Case Study 3: Developing student understanding of research at Bristol Business School

Both accounting and general business and management undergraduate subject benchmarks require students to develop threshold knowledge and understanding of current research on contemporary issues (QAA, 2000a, b). The latter emphasizes that students should have the ability to conduct research. This requirement is often *traditionally* managed through the medium of the dissertation (see Chapter 8), but this learning approach can make heavy use of academic staff time. Staff resource constraints are making the dissertation less easy to sustain in an academic subject that is required to provide teaching coverage across a broad range of underpinning subject disciplines but which attracts the lowest level of HEFCE funding support. Furthermore, students may be required to conduct primary as well as secondary research, which poses questions of access to research subjects and data. Some institutions encourage or require students to collect primary data during the placement year, but this may not be suitable for all students, and many business and accounting awards do not require a placement period.

Background
Undergraduate BA Business Studies students were required traditionally to take a final year dissertation using primary data gathered during their placement year. A new non-sandwich BA Business Administration was introduced in 1993, students being required to undertake an independent study project using secondary data only. Some students excelled, but many were unable to complete the project without substantial staff support. With increasing student numbers, the project became unsustainable. A new core module, Developing Business Knowledge, was developed in 1998.

Objectives and approaches of module
There is a choice between teaching students how to do research and teaching them how to evaluate it. This module aims to develop students as critical, self-aware, reflexive consumers and readers of published research and attempts to provide students with the tools needed to evaluate research. The module focuses on:

- Interpretation and evaluation of published research.
- Issues of epistemology and methodology rather than method.

- The multi- and interdisciplinary nature of management research.
- Placing management research in its economic, political and social context.
- Current and pervasive issues in research.

The emphasis is on appreciating cross-disciplinary themes and approaches by focusing on business and management research as a whole, thereby helping students to develop an informed understanding of issues underpinning all the management sub-disciplines. The module uses traditional weekly lectures focusing on issues of methodology, epistemology and research context. Workshops provide a focus for students to appreciate and critically evaluate published research cases. Assessment takes place through an end of year examination (40 per cent) and a literature review and reflective learning journal (60 per cent). Students are able to choose a topic for their review from a list of wide-ranging contemporary issues and are provided with individual tutor support to guide their choice, and critical review, of literature. The students attend a lecture series and workshops in which they evaluate published research cases.

Issues and questions
- Do students need to do research in order to learn how to appreciate it?
- Is the dissertation an indispensable component of undergraduate business awards?
- To what extent should business and accounting students be required to develop knowledge and understanding of research methodology in order to become effective consumers of research?

(Charles Booth and Jane Harrington, University of the West of England)

Case Study 4: Linking theory and practice: the leadership model at Bristol Business School

Background
'Leadership' is seen as central to successful business practice and of interest to both academics and managers. The leadership module therefore sits at the boundary between theory and practice. The module is designed to enable students to explore this boundary and develop relevant subject knowledge and skills. The module is a level 3 option offered to general business and accounting students, and has grown in popularity since it

was designed in 1997. The module is both innovative and integrative through its design, delivery and assessment.

Objectives and approaches

The design of the module is informed by Kolb's (1984) experiential Learning Cycle and requires students to reflect and experiment actively. The module contains four integrated types of activity:

- Concrete experience – exposing students to outdoor management and teamworking exercises focusing on leadership issues. Visiting business leaders talk to students about their leadership practice, with students being required to consider how theory informs and explains practice.
- Reflective observation – requiring students to keep learning diaries that reflect on each contact session. Each student performs a leadership skills audit at the end of each exercise, reflecting on his or her beliefs and those of the leader using an action-centred leadership framework.
- Abstract conceptualization – using traditional lectures covering concepts and theories with a textbook and guided reading.
- Active experimentation – through an assessment that requires students to interview a leader and analyse the data using current leadership theory.

Evaluation of the module has demonstrated positive student feedback and evidence of **deep approaches to learning** in a mutually supportive learning environment owned and controlled by the learners. The experiential nature of the module has helped students to develop a strong sense of self-awareness, creativity in learning and their own leadership skills. For further information about this case, see Grisoni and Beeby (2001).

Issues/questions

- How can students be exposed to practice and theory in ways that facilitate development of theoretical knowledge, application of knowledge and self-awareness?
- How central is the notion of 'experimentation' to learning?

(Louise Grisoni and Mick Beeby, University of the West of England)

THE USE OF ICT IN BUSINESS EDUCATION

There is such a wide application of information and communication technologies (ICT) within education that it is easy for the business educator to feel overwhelmed. However, a valuable resource is available in the body of the Business Education Support Team (BEST), the Learning and Teaching Support Network for Business, Management and Accountancy. Its role is to support business educators in all aspects of teaching and learning. However, supporting the use of ICT is one of the most important aspects of its work.

Case Study 5: How BEST can support lecturers

As a focus for its work, BEST carried out an initial fact-finding survey among lecturers. The use of ICT and e-learning were identified as the two most important areas for support, followed closely by assessment. BEST provides a variety of services in all three of these areas.

A wide range of e-learning materials is available to lecturers. So BEST identifies and reviews new computer-based materials which have the potential for enhancing learning and teaching. In addition, examples of good practice in the implementation of ICT have been identified, written up and published as a series of 'stories'. This dissemination to lecturers is important to provide practical examples of what can be done. Lecturers use resources differently, but knowing how other people use materials can spark off innovations appropriate to an individual setting. This is an activity which BEST will maintain, and new examples are continually being sought.

Recent years have seen an explosion of interest in virtual learning environments (**VLEs**) (see Chapter 11). Making effective use of these in teaching and learning requires some new skills on the part of both learner and teacher. In supporting lecturers to think about these skills, BEST runs workshops bringing together those with experience and novices, so that all can learn from each other. The potential that these systems offer for interesting and challenging learning experiences is great, but requires vision and careful planning. These benefits will not be attained simply by putting resource material online. Students need to have a clear idea of what lecturers expect of them and how they are expected to interact with the system. Collaborative work and online discussion between students and between students and lecturer can be beneficial but need skilful handling to be successful.

For business educators the opportunities offered by VLEs and the wider World Wide Web are legion and rest in the hands of the creative teacher. Real company data is available online and can be useful in accounting, finance, marketing and other business options. Many aspects of company Web sites can be compared, online marketing policy, customer focus, etc. Online case studies are available and students have access to teaching material from other sources. In particular BEST can advise on the range of case study and simulation material available.

This wide access is, of course, not without its problems. One of these is plagiarism. However, by ensuring that students understand the need to reference sources and by setting criteria for work that requires a substantial critical input, this problem can be significantly reduced. Teaching students to be critical of the resources found is also essential and is a skill that undergraduates are expected to develop whether they are working online or offline.

(Ailsa Nicholson, BEST, LTSN for Business, Management and Accountancy, University of East Anglia, http://www.business.ltsn.ac.uk)

As discussed earlier, many business students have jobs and therefore have difficulty attending all formal sessions. The use of VLEs or Intranets provides a valuable means of supporting these students, including the many MBA students who may have work commitments that prevent them from getting to scheduled classes.

In the last 10 years there have been major changes in the ICT resources available for higher education. While the formats have changed, the basic principles of implementation remain the same. Pedagogy must take precedence over the technology. Technology simply provides a new set of tools to support learning and teaching. It is important that educators do not lose sight of this.

Interrogating Practice

Access and browse the BEST Web site (http://www.business.ltsn.ac.uk). Explore the links provided on the Resources page. How might BEST's workshops, publications and resources support your own teaching?

For those new to lecturing (but not necessarily new to business, management and accounting) the challenge of teaching is exciting. Yet the complexity of factors to be taken into account when preparing for teaching may be rather daunting. Yet there is no need for any individual lecturer to 'go it alone' when deciding on content and approaches to teaching. For example:

- Draw on the experience of colleagues and ask for advice. It takes some time to build up a personal portfolio of teaching materials and experience. All lecturers have benefited at some time from helpful mentors and most are willing to assist new colleagues. It is important to adopt teaching approaches that are personally meaningful but there is no need to fully 'reinvent the wheel'.
- A significant amount of teaching within business education takes place in teams. Ascertain the various skills and expertise which are available in your particular team and identify just a few aspects of teaching (or of the subject) where you would like to take responsibility for further development.
- The business syllabus is ever-expanding. Do not feel that you have to 'cover' everything (thus taking the responsibility on yourself, rather than giving it to the student). Be realistic when identifying topics for inclusion in the syllabus. More experienced lecturers often find that they reduce the number of topics as time goes on, realizing that subject-specific skills are more important than comprehensive content coverage.
- Bear in mind that you do not have to be the 'expert'. Teaching is often more about facilitation than providing subject expertise. When faced with a diverse student group, draw explicitly on their experiences (and expertise). Let the students tell their own 'stories' or identify their own perspectives. Equally, share your own enthusiasm but also your difficulties with the subject. This sharing can support the mutual identification of areas for further study.

OVERVIEW

Business education is a complex, but potentially very rewarding, area in which to teach. This chapter has identified distinctive aspects of business education which must be taken into account by business educators, both at the level of the programme and at the level of the individual module. The tensions produced by the different demands of students and stakeholders and by the changing nature of the business disciplines are not, in their nature, ever likely to disappear. It is not expected that degree programmes can, or should, be created at identical points along the 'for–about spectrum'. The benchmark statements do not have to be viewed as a form of national curriculum. Indeed, the diversity of students, stakeholders and educators ensures that each institution can make its own unique contribution somewhere along the spectrum. The challenge for business educators lies not in resolving such tensions but in acknowledging their nature in their own particular institutional context and in responding to these tensions creatively as they decide on their own particular approach.

REFERENCES

Atkins, M J (1999) Oven-ready and self-basting: taking stock of employability skills, *Teaching in Higher Education*, **4** (2), pp 267–80

Association of Graduate Recruiters (AGR) (1995) *Skills for Graduates in the 21st Century*, AGR, Cambridge

Booth, C *et al* (2000) The use of the case method in large and diverse undergraduate business programmes: problems and issues, *International Journal of Management Education*, **1** (1), pp 62–75

Carter, C (1985) A taxonomy of objectives for professional education, *Studies in Higher Education*, **10** (2), pp 135–49

Eraut, M (1994) *Developing Professional Knowledge and Competence*, Falmer Press, London

Foreman, J and Johnston, T (1999) Key aspects of teaching and learning in business and management studies, in *A Handbook of Teaching and Learning in Higher Education*, 1st edn, eds H Fry, S Ketteridge and S Marshall, pp 372–90, Kogan Page, London

Grey, C and French, R (1996) Rethinking management education, in *Rethinking Management Education* eds R French and C Grey, pp 1–16, Sage, London

Grisoni, L. and Beeby, M. (2001) Experiential leadership development at undergraduate level, in *Innovations in Teaching Business and Management*, eds C Hockings and I Moore, pp 39–50, SEDA, Birmingham

Huczynski, A A (1993) *Management Gurus*, Routledge, London

Kolb, D A (1984) *Experiential Learning*, Prentice Hall, Englewood Cliffs, New Jersey

Lucas, U (2000) Worlds apart: students' experiences of learning introductory accounting, *Critical Perspectives on Accounting*, **11**, pp 479–504

Lucas, U, *et al* (2001) Implementing a skills framework for learning and teaching: taking account of students' perceptions, in *Improving Student Learning Strategically*, ed C Rust, pp 282–94, Oxford Centre for Staff Development, Oxford

Macfarlane, B (1997). In search of an identity: lecturer perceptions of the business studies first degree, *Journal of Vocational Education and Training*, **49** (1), pp 5–20

Macfarlane, B and Ottewill, R (eds) (2001) *Effective Learning and Teaching in Business and Management*, Kogan Page, London

Mladenovic, R (2000) An investigation into ways of challenging introductory accounting students' negative perceptions of accounting, *Accounting Education*, **9** (2), pp 135–54

Morgan, P G (2001a) The case of the involved students: developing personal transferable skills, in *Innovations in Teaching Business and Management*, eds C Hockings and I Moore, pp 53–60, SEDA, Birmingham

Morgan, P G (2001b) *Implementing Skills Development in Higher Education: Reviewing the territory*, Proceedings of the 2nd Annual Skills Conference, University of Hertfordshire, 11–12 July.

National Committee for Inquiry into Higher Education (NCIHE) (1997) (Dearing Report) *Higher Education in the Learning Society*, NCIHE, HMSO, London (also to be found at: http://www.leeds.ac.uk/educol/ncihe)

Quality Assurance Agency (QAA) (2000a) *Benchmark Statement for General Business and Management,* (Online) http:www.qaa.ac.uk/crntwork/benchmark/business.pdf

QAA (2000b) *Benchmark Statement for Accounting,* (Online) http:www.qaa.ac.uk/crnt-work/benchmark/accounting.pdf

Tolley, G (1983) Foreword, in *The Hidden Curriculum in Business Studies: Proceedings of a conference on values in business education,* ed D Graves, p 5, Higher Education Foundation, Chichester

FURTHER READING

Albrecht, W S and Sack, R J (2000) *Accounting Education: Charting the course through a perilous future*, American Accounting Association, Sarasota, Fla. This booklet addresses the challenges faced by accounting education, particularly the requirement for graduates who possess a broader range of skills than just the technical. While it specifically considers the US context, most of its discussion is pertinent to accounting education internationally.

Grey, C and French, R (1996) See above. This text offers alternative ways of viewing the business and management curricula; in particular, management is viewed as a complex social, political and moral practice rather than simply as a collection of competencies.

Hockings, C and Moore, I (eds) (2001) *Innovations in Teaching Business and Management,* SEDA, Birmingham. An interesting collection of recent innovations in business education, presented in a way that makes them easily accessible. Some of these can be adapted to a lecturer's individual needs quite quickly. Others may need more extensive adaptation, such as a change of course documentation or departmental policy.

Macfarlane, B and Ottewill, R (eds) (2001) See above. This provides an excellent overview of issues affecting teaching in business and management and contains individual chapters on the teaching of particular functional areas.

<table>
<tr><td>25</td></tr>
</table>

25 Key aspects of teaching and learning in mathematics and statistics

Joe Kyle

INTRODUCTION

Recent years have seen a greater focus on learning and teaching in mathematics and its applications in higher education. Old assumptions are being re-examined and there are new political agendas to be addressed. What should the typical undergraduate programme contain and how should it be taught? How best do we serve the needs of those who require mathematics as part of their study of another discipline? There will, no doubt, be many valid answers to these questions and this chapter attempts to cover a good cross-section of the issues involved.

There are in the UK what might be referred to as the 'official' answers embodied in the March 2002 Quality Assurance Agency for Higher Education (QAA) **bench-marking** statement which covers mathematics, statistics and operational research (QAA, 2002). In this a 'modal level' graduate should be able to:

- demonstrate a reasonable understanding of the main body of knowledge for the programme of study;
- demonstrate a good level of skill in calculation and manipulation of the material within this body of knowledge;

- apply a range of concepts and principles in loosely defined contexts, showing effective judgement in the selection and application of tools and techniques;
- develop and evaluate logical arguments;
- demonstrate skill in abstracting the essentials of problems, formulating them mathematically and obtaining solutions by appropriate methods;
- present arguments and conclusions effectively and accurately;
- demonstrate appropriate transferable skills and the ability to work with relatively little guidance or support.

The authors of this statement go to some lengths to qualify and set the context for this list. In particular it is stressed that 'students should meet this standard in an overall sense, not necessarily in respect of each and every of the statements listed'. Clearly there has been no attempt to set a 'national curriculum'; rather we are presented with generic descriptions of the type of skills and qualities we should look to be fostering in our programmes.

Not surprisingly, a number of themes surface again and again in debates about learning and teaching in mathematics and statistics. In workshops and publications in this area, a number of sub-headings arise almost naturally. These are:

- teaching and the support of learning;
- design and planning of learning activities;
- assessment and giving feedback to students;
- effective environments and student learning support systems;
- reflective practice and personal development.

Although in many cases the final point is often implicit and assumed, reflection is increasingly being addressed in its own right (Mason, 2002). However, in this contribution, another approach has been chosen. After a short section setting the scene, one of the major issues facing higher education in the coming years – the transition to university – is looked at. The chapter then moves on to consider pure mathematics, applied mathematics and statistics, the current impact of technology on learning and teaching in the discipline, and finally there is a short section on the relationship with mathematical education. It is acknowledged that there has been a major growth in service teaching for disciplines, but this is not dealt with in what follows.

SETTING THE SCENE

Throughout this chapter, the underlying aim is to concentrate on discipline-specific issues facing those engaged in facilitating learning and teaching in mathematics and statistics at higher education level, drawing upon other contributions that are firmly grounded in the discipline. Consequently, there will be little focus on generic aspects of learning and teaching in higher education, which is covered by Part 1 of this book. Nor is there a catalogue of immediately 'consumable' classroom resources. Up-to-date materials of this nature are available, in abundance, at the Web site of the Learning and Teaching Support Network (LTSN) Mathematics, Statistics and Operational Research Network located at www.mathstore.ac.uk. Instead, this contribution seeks to explain the challenges that are presented by mathematics and statistics education and give examples of good practice from experienced facilitators in the field. Hence, it provides a guide for reflective practice and offers avenues for exploration wherein readers may develop their own pedagogic principles.

Focusing on the nature of mathematics presents a dilemma. In one guise, it is the science of strict logical deduction and reasoning which are very severe taskmasters both for the learner and the teacher. On the other hand the breadth of the applicability of mathematics is immense. Mathematics is fundamental not only to much of science and technology but also to almost all situations that require an analytical model-building approach, whatever the discipline. In recent decades there has been an explosive growth of the use of mathematics in areas outside the traditional base of science, technology and engineering. Even in considering the development of Web-based resources, mathematics, with its specialist symbols and fonts, presents challenges that do not disturb many other disciplines or, it would seem, those developing commercial software (see below).

A further factor is the rather conservative range of approaches for teachers and learners. In the UK at least, 'most teaching comprises formal lectures' and more innovative methods are only used 'occasionally'. Similarly, most assessment strategies rely on formal examinations and, more damagingly, in some cases on too narrow a range of assessment methods, which had led to deficiencies in the measurement of learning (QAA, 2001). There is clearly some value therefore in exploring tried and tested alternatives to the traditional approaches.

There are clear signs that the wider world is becoming aware of the issues, many of them international, that currently surround the discipline. Whether it is as a result of changing policy affecting school mathematics or whether it is the impact of rapidly developing technology, mathematicians face many new challenges in our discipline. Furthermore, the range and diversity of those engaged in learning the subject is considerable and is destined to become wider still in the near future. This will range from foundation level material, preparing students for entry to other numerate disciplines, to advanced level specialist mathematical study at or near the contemporary frontiers of the subject. It is the intention therefore that the tone of this chapter is both contemporary and inclusive.

A major issue for the mathematical community arises in generic discussion of what might be deemed to be good practice in working with students. Put most starkly, young colleagues embarking upon a university career feel that they are obliged to embrace an ideology of learning that is completely foreign to the core values of the discipline. For example, faced with the assertion that *Hamlet* is a lousy play, it may be reasonable and effective to adopt a strategy that respects this as a valid personal view that should be respected and debated alongside other views – all deserving of equal respect. Consider on the other hand, a new lecturer faced with the claim that the recurring decimal 0.99999… is less than 1. One may sympathize with a student who might think this is true and adopt an understanding approach, but no one can, in all honesty, pretend that it has equal validity with the view that 0.99999… is equal to 1.

Of course things need not be as extreme as may be implied here. All of us in the knowledge economy should treat students with sympathy and respect, whatever our subject. But at the same time, those charged with 'training' our new young colleagues must be aware that there is, within mathematics, very restricted room for movement when attempting to allow students 'ownership' of the subject. Perhaps it for reasons such as this that there has been the emergence of an interest in 'discipline-based' staff development, whether this is for new or experienced colleagues (see for example Durkin and Main, 2002).

THE TRANSITION TO HIGHER EDUCATION

The transition from one educational stage to another can often be a fraught and uncertain process. In mathematics there has been a great deal of recent publicity about the issues around the transition to higher education. Notable among these are the report from the London Mathematical Society (1992) and the more recent publication by the Engineering Council (2000). Major factors include changes in school/pre-university curricula, widening access and participation, the wide range of degrees on offer in mathematical subjects, IT in schools, and sociological issues. Problems arising in the transition are mentioned in many Maths, Stats & OR (MSOR) Subject Review reports, and also in some engineering subject review reports. The very recent (February 2002) establishment of the Advisory Committee on Mathematics Education (ACME) and other current government initiatives indicate that there is still work to be done here. Various reports, including those listed above, point to the changes in schools as the source of problems in the transition, and make recommendations as to how things could be put right there. Indeed, in response to wider concerns about literacy and numeracy, recent government initiatives have, perhaps, partially restored some of the skills that providers of numerate degrees need; these might feed into higher education in the next decade (however, as this is being written, there are worrying signs that these changes may end up being the scapegoat for the recent (2001) problems surrounding the introduction of the new system of AS-level examinations in England). But it is doubtful that there will ever be a return to the situation where school qualifications are designed solely as a preparation for higher education.

However, if some of the difficulties in transition lie outside the control of those of in higher education, others can be tackled. These include curriculum design and pastoral support, both of which may need attention if those who choose our courses are to have the best chance of success. We might also usefully consider what our students know about our courses when they choose them, and how they might prepare themselves a little before they come – in attitude as well as in knowledge. For example, Loughborough University sends new engineering students a pre-sessional revision booklet as part of their support for incoming students (Croft, 2001). Since 50 per cent of providers have been criticized for poor progression rates in QAA Subject Reviews and as the government moves to set targets for widening participation *and* retention, there is much scope for other institutions adopting similar methods. A number of the reports and publications listed above offer more detailed suggestions, but common themes which emerge repeatedly include:

- Use of 'pre-sessional' material before arrival.
- Initial assessment (or 'diagnosis') of mathematical skills. This is a key recommendation of the report *Measuring the Mathematics Problem* (Engineering Council, 2000).
- Ongoing attention to the design of early modules.
- Strategic monitoring use of early items of coursework.
- Some overarching form of academic support: a recent report (Lawson, Croft and Halpin, 2001) shows that some 50 per cent of providers surveyed offer some form of 'mathematics support centre'.

Of course, the local circumstance of each institution will influence the nature of initial and continuing support. However, the following have been identified in QAA Subject Review reports (and elsewhere) as effective and worthy of consideration.

Additional modules or courses

Some providers mount specific modules/courses designed to bridge the gap, ranging from single modules focusing on key areas of A-level mathematics to one-year foundation courses designed to bring under-qualified students up to a level where they can commence the first year proper. Specific modules devoted to consolidate and ease the transition to university should be integrated as far as possible with the rest of the programme so that lecturers on parallel modules are not assuming too much of some students. Foundation years should provide a measured treatment of key material; a full A-level course is inappropriate in one year.

There are a number of computer-based learning and assessment packages that can help. (For example *Mathwise*, *Transmath*, and *Mathletics*, are all described on the Maths, Stats & OR Network Web site – www.mathsore.ac.uk.) Again, these are best when integrated fully within the rest of the curriculum, linked strategically with the other forms of teaching and with the profiles and learning styles of the individual students. It is widely accepted that simply referring students with specific weaknesses to 'go and use' a CAL package is rarely effective. On the other hand many middle-ability students may be happy to work through routine material on the computer, thus freeing up teachers to concentrate on the more pressing difficulties.

Streaming

Streaming is another way in which the curriculum can be adapted to the needs of incoming students as a means of easing the transition. 'Fast' and 'slow' streams, practical versus more theoretical streams, etc, are being used by a number of providers who claim that all students benefit (eg, Savage, 2001).

Use of coursework

Regular **formative** (if you can get them to do it!) coursework is often a strong feature of good support provision. Fast turnaround in marking and feedback is seen to be very effective in promoting learning. Subject Reviews often cite tardy return of coursework and unhelpful or non-existent feedback as prime weaknesses in this area. Another regular criticism is the similarity of coursework to examination questions. This and generous weightings for coursework may generate good pass rates, but often simply sweep the problem under the carpet. There is a nice judgement to make: avoid being too 'helpful' for a quick short-term fix, but encourage students to overcome their own weaknesses.

Support centres

Variously called **learning centres**, drop-in clinics, surgeries, etc, they all share the aim of acting as an extra-curricular means of supporting students in an individual and confidential way. Lawson, Croft and Halpin (2001) outline some excellent examples of good practice here, and the concept is commendable and usually a very cost-effective use of resources. One can spread the cost by extending the facility to cover all students requiring mathematical help across the institution. An exciting recent development is the emergence of the UK Mathematics Learning

Support Centre which will, through the agency of the Maths Stats & OR Network, freely make available to all staff and students in higher education a large number of resources via a variety of media.

> ### Interrogating Practice
>
> Reflect on how your department addresses the changing needs of students entering higher education. What do you do to address 'gaps' in knowledge, skills and understanding?
>
> Could you do more? If so, what?

Pastoral support

These mechanisms tend to be generic (see Chapter 12), but are included here as mathematicians have been slow to adopt some of these simple and successful devices. There is a growing trend in the use of second- and third-year students in a mentoring role for new students, supporting, but not replacing, experienced staff. Such student mentors go under a number of names – peer tutors, 'aunties', 'gurus', etc – but the main idea is for them to pass on their experience and help others with their problems. In at least one institution such students receive credit towards their own qualifications in terms of the development of transferable skills that the work evidences. Subject Reviews record that both parties usually benefit – the mentors from the transferable skills they develop, and the mentored from the unstuffy help they receive. It is of course essential that the mentors are trained for their role, and that this provision is monitored carefully. Suggestions are enlarged and expanded upon in Appleby and Cox (2002).

ISSUES PARTICULAR TO PURE MATHEMATICS

What are the special and particular problems that lie in the way of effective teaching and learning in pure mathematics? There are, of course, the issues of transition and mathematical preparedness touched upon above. Lack of technical fluency will be a barrier to further work in pure mathematics. However, there are deeper more fundamental issues concerning reasoning skills and students' attitudes to proof. Certainly, within the context of higher education in the UK, there are a number of signals and signs that can be read. Among these are current issues in mathematical education, reported problems in contemporary literature (a good recent example is Brakes (2001), and – to a lesser extent – the results of the QAA Subject Review reports.

So what can be done? There is little evidence that a dry course in logic and reasoning itself will solve the problem. Some success may be possible if the skills of correctly reading and writing mathematics together with the tools of correct reasoning can be encouraged through the study of an appropriate ancillary vehicle. The first (and some would still claim, the foremost) area was geometry. The standard parade of the standard Euclidean theorems was for many the *raison d'être* of logic and reasoning. However, this type of geometry is essentially absent from the school curriculum, geometry generally is in some state of crisis and there is little to be gained from an attempt to turn the clock back. It is worth noting however that students' misuse of the ⇔ symbol and its relatives were less likely through exposure to the traditional proof in geometry – most commonly lines were linked with 'therefore' or 'because' (with a resulting improvement in the underlying 'grammar' of the proof as well). Mathematicians may not want to bring back classical geometry, but should all regret the near passing of proper use of 'therefore' and 'because' which were the standard features of geometrical proofs.

At one time, introductory mathematical analysis was thought to be the ideal vehicle for exposing students to careful and correct reasoning. Indeed for many the only argument for the inclusion of rigorous analysis early in the curriculum was to provide a good grounding in proper reasoning. Few advance this case now. Indeed some workers in mathematical education have recently cast doubt on the need for proof itself in such introductions to mathematical analysis (see, for example, Tall, 1999). Recently the focus has passed to algebra. Axiomatic group theory (and related algebraic topics) is thought by some to be less technical and more accessible for the modern student. Unfortunately, there is not the same scope for repeated use over large sets of the logical quantifiers ('for all' and 'there exists') and little need for contra-positive arguments. Number theory has also been tried with perhaps more success than some other topics.

However, most success seems to come when the mathematics under discussion is well inside a certain 'comfort zone' so that technical failings in newly presented mathematics do not become an obstacle to engagement with the debate on reasoning and proof.

Interrogating Practice

Reflect on your practice. What do you do to assist students move beyond their 'comfort zone'? What do you do when it becomes apparent that students are floundering with newly presented mathematics? Are there any specific approaches that you feel you would like to improve?

This is the approach, for instance, adopted in Kahn (2001). Examples might include simple problems involving whole numbers (as opposed to formal number theory), quadratic equations and inequalities and trigonometry. (At a simple level we can explore how we record the solutions of a straightforward quadratic equation. We may see the two statements:

'$x = 3$ or $x = 4$ is a root of the equation $x^2 - 7x + 12 = 0$'

'the roots of the equation $x^2 - 7x + 12 = 0$ are $x = 3$ or $x = 4$'

as two correct uses of 'and' and 'or' in describing the same mathematical situation. But do the students see this with us? Is it pedantic to make the difference, or is there a danger of confusing the distinction between 'or' and 'and'? By the time the solution to the inequality

$$(x - 3)(x - 4) > 0$$

is recorded as the intersection of two intervals rather than the union, things have probably gone beyond redemption (see also Brake, 2001).

One possible way forward, which has had some limited success, is to use a workshop-style approach at least to early sessions when exploring these issues. But a real danger for such workshops at the start of university life lies in choosing examples or counter-examples that are too elaborate or precious. Equally it is very easy to puncture student confidence if some early progress is not made. Getting students to debate and justify proofs within a peer group can help here. One way of stimulating this is outlined in the workshop plan given in Kyle and Sangwin (2002).

Students can also be engaged by discussing and interpreting the phraseology of the world of the legal profession. Much legislation, especially in the realm of finance, goes to some length to express simple quantitative situations purely, if not simply, in words. Untangling into symbolic mathematics is a good lesson in structure and connection. Further, one can always stimulate an interesting debate by comparing and contrasting proof in mathematics with proof as it is understood in a court of law.

ISSUES PARTICULAR TO APPLIED MATHEMATICS

The author is a pure mathematician and therefore writes with some trepidation on applied mathematics. This section, therefore, draws heavily on views expressed by others in writing and at conferences, particularly the work of Hibberd (2002). Mathematics graduates, whether they embark upon postgraduate study or enter a career outside academic life, are expected to possess a range of abilities and skills embracing subject-specific mathematical knowledge, the use of mathematical and computational techniques. They are also expected to have acquired other less subject-specific skills such as communication and team-working skills. For most mathematics degree programmes within the UK the acquisition of subject-specific knowledge, essential IT skills, the use of mathematical and statistical software and subject-specific problem-solving skills are well embedded in the curriculum (QAA, 2000). Typically these are delivered through formal lectures supported by a mixture of tutorials, seminars, problem classes and practical workshop sessions. As noted earlier, assessment is often traditional, making much use of examinations. Increasingly it is recognized that these approaches do not provide students with the valuable non-mathematical skills that are much valued by employers. This has prompted a search for some variety of learning and teaching vehicles to help students to develop both subject-specific and transferable skills. This has been achieved with some success over several years at the University of Nottingham in a project upon which Case Study 1 is loosely based.

Case Study 1: Mathematical modelling

A typical goal in implementing a modelling element is to stimulate student motivation in mathematical studies through 'applying mathematics' and to demonstrate the associated problem-solving capabilities. It also offers the chance to provide a synoptic element that brings together mathematical ideas and techniques from differing areas of undergraduate studies that often students meet only within individual modules. This in itself can lead students into a more active approach to learning mathematics and an appreciation and acquisition of associated key skills.

The underlying premise in this type of course can be accommodated through activities loosely grouped as 'Mathematical modelling'. Associated assessments and feedback designed around project-based work, either as more extensive coursework assignments through to substantial reports, can allow students to demonstrate their understanding, problem-solving abilities and enhance both mathematical and key skills. Often quoted attributes gained by graduates are the subject-specific, personal and transferable skills gained through a mathematics-rich degree.

Increasingly, students are selecting their choice of degree to meet the flexible demands of a changing workplace and well-designed MSOR programmes have the potential to develop a profile of the knowledge, skills abilities and personal attributes integrated alongside the more traditional subject-specific education.

A mathematical model is typically defined as a formulation of a real-world problem phrased in mathematical terms. Application is often embedded in a typical mathematics course through providing well-defined mathematical models that can enhance the learning and understanding within individual theory-based modules through adding reality and interest. A common example is in analysing predator–prey scenarios as motivation for studying the complex nonlinear nature of solutions to coupled equations within a course on ordinary-differential equations; this may also extend to obtaining numerical solutions as the basis of course-work assignments. Such a model is useful in demonstrating and investigating the nature of real-world problem by giving quantitative insight, evaluation and predictive capabilities.

Other embedded applications of mathematical modelling, particularly within applied mathematics, are based around the formal development of continuum models such as found for instance in fluid mechanics, electromagnetism, plasma dynamics or relativity. A marked success in MSOR within recent years has been the integration of mathematics into other less traditional discipline areas of application, particularly in research, and this has naturally lead to an integration of such work into the modern mathematics curriculum through the development of mathematics models. Applied mathematics has always been a strong part of engineering and physical sciences but now extends to modelling processes in biology, medicine, economics, financial services and many more.

The difficulties often inherent in practical 'real world' problems requires some pre-selection or guidance on initial problems to enable students to gain a threshold level of expertise. Once some expertise is gained then exposure to a wider range of difficulties provides students with a greater and more realistic challenge. In general, modelling is best viewed as an open-ended, iterative exercise. This can be guided by a framework for developing the skills and expertise required together with the general principle 'solve the simple problems first', which requires some reflection on the student's own mathematical skills and competencies to identify a 'simple problem'.

As with most learning and teaching activities the implementation of modelling can be at a variety of levels and ideally as an integrated activity throughout a degree programme. The learning outcomes that can be associated with an extensive modelling provision include:

- knowledge and understanding;
- analysis;
- problem solving;

- creativity/originality;
- communication and presentation;
- evaluation;
- planning and organization;
- interactive and group skills.

In practice most will only be achieved through a planned programme of activities.

According to Hibberd (2002), mathematical modelling is the process of:

- translating a real-world problem into a mathematically formulated representation;
- solving this mathematical formulation, and then
- interpreting the mathematical solution in a real-world context.

The principal processes are about how to apply mathematics and how to communicate the findings. There are however, many difficulties that can arise.

For those with an interest in exploring the ideas offered in Case Study 1, the article by Hibberd (2002) contains a couple of case studies illustrating the application of these principles.

Interrogating Practice

Reflect on the different teaching and learning approaches used to deliver your modules. Do these address, at various stages, the skills as highlighted above? If not, consider how you might apply the use of modelling to your practice.

ISSUES PARTICULAR TO STATISTICS

This section has benefited greatly from many fruitful meetings and conversations with Professor N Davies, Director of Royal Statistical Society Centre for Statistical Education.

Statistics is much younger than mathematics. Two strands can be identified in tracing its origins. First, discussions about the theory of gambling in the middle of the 17th century led to the first attempts to found a theory of probability. Second, the gradual increase in the collection of what would nowadays be called official statistics throughout the 19th century led to new developments in the display, classification and interpretation of data. Many signal advances in public policy were made through the application of what might now be seen as very elementary techniques of descriptive statistics but which were at the time truly visionary. These included, famously, the identification of a single pump mainly responsible for a cholera outbreak in London, and the work of Florence Nightingale in establishing the antecedents of today's extensive medical statistics.

During 2000, teachers of statistics in UK higher education were asked about their needs to enhance their teaching skills so that, in due course, the learning experience of their students could be enhanced. From the results of this information-gathering exercise, and using evidence from elsewhere, this chapter discusses some ideas of how learning and teaching standards in statistics could be raised. A summary of the feedback from the statistical community was reported in Maths, Stats & OR Newsletter (February 2000) and can be viewed at www.mathstore.ac.uk.

How students learn statistics

Statistics is often regarded as being difficult to understand, especially by non-specialist students of the subject. However, since society is being increasingly exposed to more and more data across a broad range of disciplines, it is vitally important that people involved in those disciplines get at least a basic understanding of what variability means. For many, an appreciation of how that variability within their subject area can be managed is vital for success. Very often there will be just one opportunity to learn statistics, and this is usually at school or higher education level. It is therefore very important for teachers of statistics, whether specialist statisticians or other subject experts who teach it within their own curriculum area, to know how best to approach teaching the subject. Research into the optimal and best-balanced approach to teaching different client groups has not been undertaken, but on a generic level a number of papers have been written. The most influential of these was published around seven years ago. In a wide-ranging paper Garfield (1995) reported results of a scientific study of how some students best learn statistics. Inter alia, she concluded that the following five scenarios needed to be part of the learning environment so that students could get the optimal learning gain for the subject:

- activity and small group work;
- testing and feedback on misconceptions;
- comparing reality with predictions;
- computer simulations;
- software that allows interaction.

When the mathematical foundations of statistics are being studied, it is often necessary to go into the sometimes deep theoretical foundations of the subject. Students who have a strong mathematical background will be able to cope with this. However, many experienced teachers of statistics have come to the conclusion that these five above points work best with a data-driven approach to the subject. Many would claim that this is the only method that is likely to work on a large scale with non-specialist students of the subject. Even so, some scholars advocate that, at the same time as teaching data handling, probability concepts must be taught as well, and as early as possible. See, for example, Lindley (2001), who argues convincingly that even at school level, probability concepts should be taught. Others maintain that probability is such a difficult and sophisticated topic to teach properly that its treatment should be left until students have reached a more mature appreciation of the subject (see, for example, Moore and McCabe, 1998). There appears to be little experimental data to support either claim at present.

Innovative use of real data

As well as a discipline in its own right, statistics is an essential science in many other subjects. Consequently, at some stage data will need to be collected for and on behalf of each of those disciplines. This could comprise primary and/or secondary data. When consulted, the statistics community of teachers in higher education institutions expressed a need for exemplar data-based material for routine use by both themselves and their students. They looked for realistic scenarios, useful to both the teacher for good practice teaching material and students for effective learning material. The Web-based random data selector, described in Davies (2002), provides a useful tool to create just such a rich resource of learning and teaching material. The CensusAtSchool project is delivered from: http://censusatschool.ntu.ac.uk.

A Web facility permits the selection of a random sample of the raw data collected for CensusAtSchool. These data are for use in the classroom or in pupil's projects. Users may choose from four databases consisting of responses from the UK, Queensland, South Africa or a combined database of directly comparable responses. This may be a selection from all data or geographical regions of the chosen country. Selections can be restricted to responses from a particular age or gender. Sample sizes allowed are up to 200 per country and 500 from the combined database. A full range of graphical and spreadsheet accessories may be brought to bear upon the data.

THE ROLE OF TECHNOLOGY

There is an increasing focus on the use of technology in higher education and a lively debate on the effective e-delivery and e-learning. Sadly we have to note that few of the generic developments in this area are well aligned with the needs of learners in mathematics and statistics. To a certain extent these problems also have an impact upon those studying engineering and the sciences. For example, most of the software for computer-based assessment is very restrictive when used in mathematics. Common problems are:

- inefficient or poor display of mathematical expressions;
- restricted choice of question types;
- failure to recognize mathematically equivalent solutions;
- difficulty in allowing students to input complex mathematical responses.

As a result, technological developments in the discipline have tended to follow a distinct but parallel path. The important extra ingredient which enhances the power and ease of access of computer technology usually involves some form of computer algebra system (CAS), by which is meant software systems can perform symbolic as well as numerical manipulations and which includes graphical display capabilities. Examples include **Maple**, Mathematica, **Macsyma**, and **Derive**. Some of these systems are available not only on personal computers but also on hand-held 'super calculators' such as the TI–92 plus and the TI–89.

Much has been spoken and written about the use of a **CAS** in learning and teaching over the last few decades. See, for example, the International Congress for Mathematics Education (ICME) Proceedings since 1984, and journals such as the *International Journal of Computer Algebra in Mathematics Education* (IJCAME)). Yet there still seems to be a range of views about the effectiveness of these systems in the learning and teaching of mathematics. Certainly, the strong emphasis on the use of calculator technology, especially in schools, has been blamed for 'the mathematics problem in society' and this 'bad press' has contributed to the debate that the use of technology such as a CAS may be linked to falling mathematical standards among graduates.

On the other hand, there have been several studies citing students gaining a better conceptual understanding of mathematics with no significant loss in computational skills. For example, Hurley, Koehn and Gantner (1999) cite a National Science Foundation report that states:

> Approximately 50% of the institutions conducting studies on the impact of technology reported increases in conceptual understanding, greater facility with visualization and graphical understanding, and an ability to solve a wider variety of problems, without any loss of computational skills. Another 40% reported that students in classes with technology had done at least as well as those in traditional classes.

Thus matters stood as the 20th century was drawing to a close. However, in 2000 an exciting new development emerged from when Belgian mathematicians found hidden possibilities in the CAS Maple which is explored in Case Study 2.

Case Study 2: AIM

What emerged from Belgium was a great idea with a lousy acronym (for those who must know, AIM stands for Alice Interactive Mathematics in which Alice herself is another acronym for Active Learning in a Computer Environment). In essence it is a package that exploits the full power of computer algebra to allow users an incredible amount of flexibility in authoring tasks for students. At the same time answers may involve arbitrary mathematical expressions couched in Maple syntax. That is to say, AIM goes a long way in overcoming the obstacles listed at the start of this section. Within two years AIM had been adopted in the US, Australia, Canada, Norway, and by at least 10 institutions in the UK. When asked why they had adopted AIM (as opposed to many other very good alternatives) colleagues highlight:

- free availability – AIM is owned and develop by the academic community, there is no AIM licence and the package is freely downloadable;
- ease and flexibility in use – AIM can be easily customized to reflect the particular style or approach of an individual lecturer;
- ease of access for students – AIM is accessible with a standard browser (no extra plug-ins required) over any Internet connection.

More about AIM, including how to download it, may be found at the original Belgian site (http://allserv.rug.ac.be/ nvdbergh/aim/docs/) or at the English site www.mat.bham.ac.uk/aim.

The articles by Strickland (2002), Kyle and Sangwin (2002) and Hermans (2002) elaborate on AIM, describing students' reactions. However, in Sangwin (2002) the power of AIM to help develop higher mathematical skills is outlined. This signals a major new role for technology in learning mathematics. In particular, it is now possible to challenge students to produce 'instances' (as Sangwin calls them) which is a task that has always probed more deeply into students' understanding, but has always been seen to be very demanding on staff (for example, it is very instructive for a student to construct an example of a 4 by 4 singular matrix, with no two entries the same – but who wants to mark 200 when they can all be different and all still correct!).

Other contributions to the role of technology (some with special reference to higher skills) may be found in the 'e-journal' *Computer-Aided Assessment in Mathematics* at:

http://ltsn.mathstore.ac.uk/articles/maths-caa-series/index.htm

RELATIONS WITH MATHEMATICAL EDUCATION

Unfortunately, there is little evidence of a close working relationship between mathematicians and those working in mathematical education. Of course, there are a few notable exceptions, but the generality of the situation has been captured recently by Mogens Niss in his opening address to the Ninth International Congress in Mathematical Education:

> One observation that a mathematics educator can hardly avoid to make is the widening gap between researchers and practitioners in mathematical education. The existence of a gap is neither surprising nor worrying.
>
> The cause for concern lies in the fact that it is widening. For the health and welfare of our field we have to do our utmost to reduce the gap as much as possible. If we are unsuccessful in this, research in mathematical education runs the risk of becoming barren dry swimming, while the practice of teaching runs the risk of becoming more naïve, narrow-minded and inefficient than is necessary or desirable.
>
> (Niss, 2000)

Perhaps if we all do our bit to 'mind the gap', we can improve the lot of those at the heart of our endeavours – our students.

AND NOW...

Read the chapter again! Engage with it and reflect upon it. Consider how you might apply or adapt the ideas proposed to your own practice. There are plenty of other suggestions in the references. Disagree if you wish, but at least engage and know why you teach the way you do. If we have given you something to think about in your own approach, then we will be well on our way to improving the learning experiences of students as they study one of the most inspiring and most challenging subjects in higher education.

REFERENCES

Appleby, J and Cox, W (2002) The transition to higher education, in *Effective Learning and Teaching in Mathematics and its Applications*, eds P Kahn and J Kyle, Kogan Page, London

Brakes, W (2001) Logic, language and life, *Mathematical Gazette*, **85** (503), pp 255–66

Croft, A (2001) *Algebra refresher booklet*, Loughborough University of Technology, Loughborough

Davies, N (2002) Ideas for improving learning and teaching statistics, in *Effective Learning and Teaching in Mathematics and its Applications*, eds P Kahn and J Kyle, Kogan Page, London

Durkin, K and Main, A (2002) Discipline-based skills support for first-year undergraduate students, *Active Learning in Higher Education*, **3** (1), pp 24–39

Engineering Council (2000) *Measuring the Mathematics Problem*, The Engineering Council, London

Garfield, J (1995) How students learn statistics, *International Statistics Review*, **63**, pp 25–34

Haines, C and Dunthorne, S (1996) *Mathematics Learning and assessment: Sharing innovative practice*, Edward Arnold, London

Hermans, D (2002) *Whatsums*, International Symposium on Symbolic and Algebraic Computation (submitted)

Hibberd, S, (2002) Mathematical modelling skills, in *Effective Learning and Teaching in Mathematics and its Applications*, eds P Kahn and J Kyle, Kogan Page, London

Hurley, J F, Koehn, U and Gantner, S L (1999) Effects of calculus reform: local and national, *American Mathematical Monthly*, **106** (9), pp 800–11

Kahn, P E (2001) *Studying mathematics and its applications*, Palgrave, Basingstoke

Kyle, J and Sangwin, C J (2002) AIM – a parable in dissemination, *Proceedings of the Second International Conference on the Teaching of Mathematics*, J Wiley & Sons, Inc, New York

Lindley, D V (2001) Letter to the editor, *Teaching Statistics*, **23** (3)

Lawson, D, Croft, A and Halpin, M (2001) *Good practice in the provision of Mathematics Support Centres*, LTSN Maths Stats and OR Network, Birmingham

London Mathematical Society (1992) *The Future for Honours Degree Courses in Mathematics and Statistics*, The London Mathematical Society, London

Mason, J (2002) Reflections in and on practice, in *Effective Learning and Teaching in Mathematics and its Applications*, eds P Kahn and J Kyle, Kogan Page, London

Moore, D and McCabe, G P (1998) *Introduction to the Practice of Statistics*, W H Freeman, New York

Niss, M (2000) Key issues and trends in research on mathematical education, in *Proceedings of the Ninth International Conference on Mathematics Education, (to appear)*

Quality Assurance Agency for Higher Education (QAA) (2001) *QAA Subject Overview Report for Mathematics, Statistics and Operational Research*, QAA, Bristol, http://www.qaa.ac.uk/revreps/subjrev/All/QO7_2000.pdf

QAA (2002) *Benchmarking Document for Mathematics, Statistics and Operational Research*, QAA, Bristol, http://www.qaa.ac.uk

Sangwin, C J (2002) New opportunities for encouraging higher level mathematical learning by creative use of emerging computer aided assessment, *Journal of Mathematical Education* (submitted)

Savage, M D (2001) Getting to grips with the maths problem, in *A Maths Toolkit for Scientists* (See http://dbweb.liv.ac.uk/ltsnpsc/workshop/reports/mathtoo2.htm)

Strickland, N P (2002) Alice Interactive Mathematics, *MSOR Connections*, **2** (1), pp 27–30

Tall, D O (1999) The cognitive development of proof: is mathematical proof for all or for some?, in *Developments in School Mathematics Education Around the World*, **4**, ed Z Usiskin, pp 117–36, National Council of Teachers of Mathematics, Virginia

FURTHER READING

Baumslag, B (2000) *Fundamentals of Teaching Mathematics at University Level*, Imperial College Press, London. Based primarily on the UK higher education experience.

Kahn, P E and Kyle, J (2002) *Effective Learning and Teaching in Mathematics and its Applications*, Kogan Page, London. Based primarily on the UK higher education experience.

Krantz, S G (1999) *How to Teach Mathematics*, 2nd edn, American Mathematical Society, Providence, Rhode Island. Offers a US perspective and is full of solid, down-to-earth, sensible advice.

Mathematical modelling is well represented in the literature. Three sources of particular note that provide direct advice and gateway information to other articles are:

Townend, M S, *et al* (1995) *Mathematical Modelling Handbook: A tutor guide*, Undergraduate Mathematics Teaching Conference Workshop Series, Sheffield Hallam University Press, Sheffield. A handbook designed to provide initial support and guidance for lecturers new to mathematical modelling. The handbook was developed from three working groups of experienced modellers at an Undergraduate Mathematics Teaching Conference and includes an extensive bibliography of relevant contemporary publications (prior to 1996) which the reader can reference for guidance, advice and examples.

Haines, C and Dunthorne, S (1996) *Mathematics Learning and Assessment: Sharing innovative practices*. Developed under the HEFCE Effective Learning and Assessment Programme this pack of five books and supporting videotape was developed from a consortium of staff from 15 universities. The books contain extensive practical advice and further references to projects, writing reports, oral presentations, working in groups, assessment.

MathSkills, a DfEE (as it then was) funded Discipline Network, is aimed at facilitating the dissemination of information on innovations in teaching and learning with the particular emphasis on the enhancement of transferable skills. (MathSkills may be found at http://www.hull.ac.uk/mathskills/)

Glossary

This glossary provides two types of information. First, it provides the reader with simple explanations and definitions of technical and educational terms used in this book. Second, it provides a dictionary of many commonly used abbreviations and acronyms. The glossary has been carefully assembled by the editors. In the text, the first mention in each chapter of a glossary item appears in **bold**. The entries reflect current usage in higher education in the UK.

Academic practice   A term used to describe the collective responsibilities of academic staff in higher education, namely those: for teaching, learning and communicating the subject, discipline-specific research/scholarship, academic management activities and for some service requirements.

Academic Review   The name for current QAA quality assurance procedure.

Access course   A qualification for non-traditional, usually mature, students, as a route into higher education.

Accreditation   Certified as meeting required standards; eg, an accredited teacher implies the teacher has achieved predetermined and agreed standards or criteria.

Achievement motivation   A desire to succeed at a task; eg, obtaining high grades, even when the task does not inspire interest (*see also* extrinsic motivation, intrinsic motivation).

Achieving approach to learning   *See* strategic approach.

Action learning   An approach to learning involving individuals working on real projects with the support of a group which meets regularly to help members reflect on their experience and to plan next actions.

Active learning   A process of engaging with the learning task at both the cognitive and affective level.

Adult learning theory   A range of theories and constructs claimed to relate specifically to how adults learn. Includes self-directed learning. Much of the work on reflection and experiential learning is also part of this area. Concerns over validity of some of the theories and how far they are applicable to younger learners in higher education.

Affective domain   One of the major areas of learning, the learning of values.

AIM   (Alice Interactive Mathematics)   ALICE stands for Active Learning In a Computer Environment.

Aims (learning aims)   At the top of the hierarchy of description commonly used to define a learning experience. They are intended to provide the student, teacher and other interested parties with an understanding of the most overarching general statements regarding the intended consequences of a learning experience (*see also* objectives, learning outcomes).

Amotivation   Absence of tangible motivation.

Andragogy   The theory of adult learning, associated with the work of Malcolm Knowles.

AP(E)L   Accreditation of prior (experiential) learning. Taking into account previous 'certificated' learning gained either as whole or part of a programme, towards all or part of a new qualification. Also the counting of experience [experiential] towards obtaining a qualification.

API Age Participation Index

Appraisal (as used in higher education) A formal, regular, developmental process in which the one being appraised is encouraged to review and reflect upon performance in the workplace. Usually based on a focused interview between the one being appraised and the appraiser, who may be a peer, head of department or line manager. At the interview, objectives (linked to strategic aims of the department) are set and development needs identified. Performance against these objectives is reviewed at the next appraisal interview.

Approaches to studying inventory A device used to identify student approach to study.

Assessment Measurement of the achievement and progress of the learner.

Audio-visual/audio-lingual methodology Structural methodologies in language teaching developed in the 1950s and 1960s based on drilling, the formation of habit and avoidance of error.

Audit (academic/continuation/institutional) A verification of academic procedures. Institutional audit is conducted by the Quality Assurance Agency on a cyclical basis.

Autonomy (of student/learning) Commonly refers to students taking more responsibility for and control of themselves and their learning, including being less spoon-fed. May also include elements of students taking more responsibility for determining and directing the content of their learning.

Blueprinting (of assessment) Ensures that assessment tasks adequately sample what the student is expected to have learnt.

Bulletin board An electronic version of the notice board. Messages are left and questions asked or answered by contributing to themed or 'threaded' discussions – also called 'asynchronous communication'.

Buzz group A small group activity, typically within a large group, in which students work together on a short problem, task or discussion. So called because of the noise the activity generates.

C&IT Communication and information technologies.

CAL (computer-assisted learning) Use of computers for education and training, sometimes referred to as computer-assisted instruction (CAI) or computer-based learning (CBL). In this context the computer is usually used for a discrete item of teaching.

CALL Computer-assisted language learning.

CAS Computer algebra system.

CILT Centre for Information on Language Teaching and Research.

Code of Practice A 'series of system-wide expectations' for a range of areas, eg assessment, set out by the QAA.

Cognitive domain The major area of learning in most disciplines, to do with knowledge, understanding and thinking.

Common skills *See* Key skills

Communicative approach An approach to the teaching and learning of languages which emphasizes the primacy of meaning and communication needs.

Competence Most contemporary use in education relates to performing a task or series of tasks, with debate over how far such activities also require underpinning knowledge and understanding. (1) May be used generically to mean demonstrated achievement with respect to any clearly defined set of outcomes. (2) Is used to indicate both a high level of achievement and a just acceptable level of activity (*see also* novice, expert). (3) Something which a person in a given occupational area should be able to do.

Computer-based learning *See* CAL.

Constructivist A number of theories attempting to explain how human beings learn. Characterized by the idea of addition to, and amendment of, previous understanding or knowledge. Without such change, learning is not thought to occur. Theories of reflection and experiential learning belong to this school.

Content-based language learning Surrounding and exposing students to examples of language in real situations rather than focusing on the learning of vocabulary and grammar.

Core skills *See* Key skills.

Course This outdated term is used to refer to both smaller module-sized units of study and, confusingly, to larger units encompassing a set of modules that comprise a programme of study, leading to an academic award (*see also* module).

Courseware Software designed to be used in an educational programme. Refers to programmes and data used in CAL, computer-based learning.

Credit accumulation and transfer (CATS) Assigning a numerical value to a portion of learning, often based on a number of notional learning hours earning one credit point. Thus modules can be said to be worth 30 credits and rated at level M (Masters). Used as a currency for purposes of transfer and equivalence, with many different schemes in existence.

Criterion-referenced assessment Judges how well a learner has performed by comparison with predetermined criteria.

Critical incident (analysis) An event which, when reflected on, yields information resulting in learning from experience.

CVCP *See* UUK.

Dearing Report, *see* National Committee of Inquiry into Higher Education.

Deductive teaching/learning Working from general premises; presenting grammar rules in isolation and encouraging learners to generate specific examples based on the rules.

Deep approach to learning Learning which attempts to relate ideas together to understand underpinning theory and concepts, and to make meaning out of material under consideration (*see also* surface approach, strategic approach).

DfES Department for Education and Skills.

Derive A computer algebra system.

Diagnostic test A test used (possibly at the start of an undergraduate module) to identify weaknesses, eg, in grammatical knowledge or numeracy, and used so that these might be addressed in a more focused manner.

Distance learning Learning away from the institution, as exemplified by the Open University. Most often students work with learning resource materials that can be paper-based, on videotape, available on broadcast TV or accessed through the World Wide Web.

Domain A particular area (type) of learning. Much associated with categorizing learning outcomes and the use of hierarchical taxonomies within each domain. Considerable dispute on the number and range of domains and the hierarchies of learning within them. In the original Bloom taxonomy of 1956, the three domains identified were the cognitive, affective and psychomotor.

EMI/Q (extended matching item/question) A written assessment (eg, testing diagnostic investigation and reasoning). Each question has a theme from which lists of possible answers are placed in alphabetical order. The candidate is instructed to choose the best matching answer(s) to each of a series of scenarios, results, etc.

Evaluation Quantitative and qualitative judgement of the curriculum and its delivery, to include teaching.

Exemplification lecture A lecture designed around a series of analytical examples.

Experiential learning Learning from doing. Often represented by the Kolb Learning Cycle.

Expert Can be used with either a general or specific meaning, to indicate complete mastery at level 5 of a five-stage classification of progression. Expert practitioners do not rely on rules and guidelines as they have an intuitive grasp of situations based on deep understanding, and an analytical approach to new situations (*see also* novice, competence).

Explicatory lecture A lecture which seeks to mediate and make more comprehensive a difficult area.

External examiner/examining External examiners are part of universities' self-regulatory procedures and play a key role in maintaining standards between institutions in a particular discipline. Usually distinguished members of the profession who have the respect of colleagues and students alike. For taught courses they typically act for a defined number of years (often three). External examiner reports form the basis of institutional review of courses and programmes for quality assurance purposes. They play a similar role in examination of postgraduate dissertations and theses, leading discussion in viva voce examinations.

Extrinsic motivation   Typifies students who are concerned with the grades they get, external rewards, and whether they will gain approval from others (*see also* achievement motivation, intrinsic motivation).

Facilitator   As opposed to teacher, tutor or mentor, a role to encourage individuals to take responsibility for their own learning, through the facilitation of this process.

Fair (of assessment)   Fair with respect to: 1. Consistency between different markers. 2. Transparency and openness of criteria and procedures. 3. Procedures that do not disadvantage any group of learners in the cohort.

FAQ   Frequently asked question.

Feedback   Oral or written developmental advice on performance so that the recipient has a better understanding of values, standards, criteria, etc. *See also* formative assessment.

Field trip/coursework   Practical or experimental work away from the university designed to develop practical skills, eg, observation of natural environments or surveying, which may be for a single session or coherent period of study lasting several days. Most common in life and environmental sciences, geography, civil engineering, construction.

FL(A)   Foreign language (assistant).

Flexible learning   Often used interchangeably with the term 'open learning', but may be distinguished from it by the inclusion of more traditional modes of delivery (such as the lecture) involving meeting with a tutor. The idea of open access irrespective of prior educational achievement is also often absent.

Focus group   A technique for pooling thoughts, ideas and perceptions to ensure equal participation by all members of a group. Requires a group leader and 8 to 15 participants. Some versions of the method aim to obtain a consensus view, others the weight and thrust of opinion. More accurately called nominal group technique.

Formative assessment   This is assessment that is used to help teachers and learners gauge the strengths and weaknesses of the learners' performance while there is still time to take action for improvement. Typically it is expressed in words rather than marks or grades. Information about learners is used diagnostically (*see* summative assessment).

Framework of Higher Education Qualifications   *See* Level.

Functional notional syllabus/approach   A syllabus designed on the basis of an analysis of language 'meanings', ie, notions (such as time and place) and functions (such as asking, informing, denying).

Graduate demonstrators   A teaching intervention, using graduates to demonstrate the practical skills prior to students application of the new knowledge, skills and understanding.

Grammar-translation   A structural teaching approach whereby a grammatical point is explained and learners are drilled in its use by means of translation of numerous examples into and out of the target language.

HEFCE   Higher Education Funding Council for England.

HEFW   Higher Education Funding Council for Wales.

HESDA   Higher Education Staff Development Agency (formerly UCoSDA).

HESA   Higher Education Statistical Agency.

ILTHE/ILT   Institute for Learning and Teaching in Higher Education. Professional body created in the UK in 1999 as an NCIHE recommendation – originally ILT.

Immersion learning   Student interaction with authentic language through long periods of exposure to the second language.

Independent learning (study) Often used interchangeably with the terms 'open learning', 'self-directed learning' and 'autonomous learning'. Has a flavour of all these. Perhaps most strongly associated with programmes of study created individually for each learner.

Induction Initial period on joining an organization as an employee or as a new student joining a programme of study/research. During induction, basic information is provided through short courses, small group activities or one-to-one meetings. The purpose is to equip staff members or students with background information so that they might become effective in their role or in their study as soon as possible.

Inductive teaching/learning Working from particular cases to general conclusions; learners identify recurrent use and pattern in context and work towards the formulation of rules.

Industrial placements A learning experience offered to students to assist them to gain applied knowledge, understanding and skills through an extended period of time based in industry.

Institutional audit *See* Audit.

Interpersonal domain One of the major areas of learning, the learning of behaviour involved in interacting with others.

Intranet Any network which provides similar services within an organization to those provided on the Internet, but which is not necessarily connected to the Internet. The commonest example is the use by an institution of one of more WWW server on an internal network for distribution.

Intrinsic motivation Typifies students who enjoy a challenge, want to master a subject, are curious and want to learn (*see also* achievement motivation, extrinsic motivation).

IWLP Institution-wide language project.

JISC Joint Information Systems Committee.

Key/core/common/transferable skills Various definitions, eg, communication, numeracy, IT and learning to learn ('we see these as necessary outcomes of all higher education programmes' (NCIHE, 1997). Values and integrity, effective communication, application of numeracy, application of technology, understanding of work and the world, personal and interpersonal skills, problem-solving, positive attitudes to change (Confederation of British Industry).

L1 (of language teaching) Learner's mother tongue.

L2 (of language teaching) A second or foreign language, learnt either in the classroom or naturalistically in the country concerned.

Laboratory/practical class A type of teaching session, usually included in curricula in experimental sciences, biomedical sciences and engineering disciplines, which is broadly intended to offer training in techniques and learning how to carry out experimental investigations.

Learning and Teaching Strategy What an institution wishes to achieve with regard to learning and teaching, how it will achieve it and how it will know when it has succeeded.

Learning Centre A centre to which students may go to gain support for their learning, eg, via computer-aided applications.

Learning contract A contract drawn up between teacher and learner, whereby each agrees to take on certain roles and responsibilities, eg, the learner to hand in work on time and the teacher to return corrected work within a specified period of time. May specifically concern setting out the learning outcomes the learner undertakes to achieve.

Learning cycle Theory describing the stages of learning from concrete experience through reflection and generalization to experiment towards new experience, often attributed to David Kolb.

Learning objectives *See* objectives.

Learning outcomes Specific statements which define the learning students are expected to have acquired on completion of a session, course, programme, module, or unit of study.

Learning style Used to describe how learners differ in their tendencies or preferences to learn. Recognizes learning differences; a mix of personality and cognitive processes which influence approaches to learning.

Level (of award)/level descriptor Used to describe a hierarchy of learning outcomes across all domains, usually L1, 2, 3, M and D. Most commonly follows classification from QAA (Framework of Higher Education Qualifications) or SEEC.

Lifelong learning A concept based on the premise that everyone is involved in learning, from cradle to grave, and that there should be not only opportunities afforded for all to engage in learning activities, irrespective of age, but where appropriate, linkages and progression between certain learning activities should be articulated.

Log book A book in which learners record their reflections on learning activities.

LTSN Learning and Teaching Support Network.

Macsyma A computer algebra system.

Managed learning environment (MLE) An MLE is used to support electronically the learning and learning management processes of an institution. It brings together the VLE and other administrative electronic systems and databases, providing an overarching and integrated learning management system. It is usually delivered via a standard Web browser.

Maple A computer algebra system.

Mathematica A computer algebra system.

MCQ Multiple choice question.

Mentor Most often a colleague who acts as a supporter and adviser to a new member of an institution, eg, by helping him or her adapt to institutional culture, acting as a sounding board for ideas and encouraging reflection on practice.

Mixed skills teaching/testing The integration of the four language skills (listening, speaking, reading and writing) in tasks which replicate real-life language use, eg, relaying written stimuli orally, making a written note of a spoken message.

Module A discrete unit of study, often credit rated and part of a larger award-bearing programme of study. (The term 'course' used to be used with the same sense.)

National Committee of Inquiry into Higher Education (NCIHE) The Dearing Report, set up under Sir Ron (now Lord) Dearing by the Conservative Government in February 1996 to make recommendations for the next 20 years about the purposes, shape, structure, size and funding of higher education. Essentially a product of the deepening crisis in university funding. Reported in July 1997. The extensive report included aspects such as organization of programmes, quality matters, staff development and funding, etc.

Norm-referenced assessment Judges how well the learner has done in comparison with the norm established by their peers.

Novice Can be used with either a general or specific meaning to indicate a beginner. Level 1 of a five-stage classification of progression (*see also* expert, competence).

Objectives Originally developed by educational psychologists and known as behavioural objectives. Definition and use have become less and less precise in recent years. Their meaning has ranged from exact, measurable outcomes of specific learning experiences to more generalized statements of outcomes for courses of study. The term is often used interchangeably (but loosely) with the term 'learning outcomes'.

OMR (optical mark reader) A special scanning device that can read carefully placed pencil marks on specially designed documents. OMR is frequently used to score forms, questionnaires and answer-sheets.

Open learning Learning organized to enable learning at own pace and at time and place of choice. Usually associated with delivery without a tutor being present and may or may not be part of a formal programme of study. Will often allow learning in order of own choice, in a variety of media and may also imply no entry barriers (eg, no prior qualifications).

Oral examination *See* viva voce examination.

OSCE (objective structured clinical examination) Clinical assessment made up of a circuit of short tasks, known as stations.

Several variations on the basic theme. Typically, candidates pass through a station where an examiner grades them according to an itemized checklist or global rating scale.

OSLER (objective structured long examination record) Clinical assessment with some similarity to an OSCE, but involving one or more long case.

Passive learning/approach As opposed to active. Learning or an approach to learning that is superficial and does not involve full engagement with the material.

Peer assessment Assessment by fellow (peer) students, as in peer assessment of team activities.

Peer support A system whereby students support one another in the learning process. Students may be in informal groups (sometimes known as learning groups) or more formal, designated groups (as in SI groups) when the course leader divides the class into groups.

Peer tutor/tutorial Tutorial facilitated by fellow students (peer tutors).

Placement/Placement Learning Placing students outside their home institution for part of their period of study, often work-placement in which the student 'learns on the job'.

Portfolio (teaching portfolio) A personal collection of evidence of an individual's work, eg, to demonstrate achievement and professional development as a university teacher.

Probation The initial phase in employment with a new organization in which a member of staff 'learns the job'. In higher education, this usually involves periods of formal training and development and often the probationer is supported by a mentor. Many institutions set formal requirements that staff are expected to meet for satisfactory completion of probation.

Problem class Typically a session in the teaching of mathematics, engineering and physical science in which students work through problems and derive solutions with the support of a teacher and/or tutor/demonstrator. Not to be confused with PBL sessions.

Problem-based learning (PBL) A pedagogical method introduced in the 1960s, much used in medicine. Curriculum design involves a large amount of small group teaching and claims greater alignment with sound educational principles. Learning and teaching come after learners identify their learning needs from a trigger in the form of a scenario ('the problem').

Programme of study An award-bearing collection of modules or programme of teaching and learning, typically running over a defined period of time (eg, BA, MEng).

Programme specification A succinct way of describing the attributes and outcomes of a named programme of study, written to follow QAA guidelines.

Progress file A term given prominence by the NCIHE. Comprises a transcript, or formal record of academic achievement and a developmental aspect enabling students to monitor, plan and reflect on their personal development.

Psychomotor domain One of the major areas of learning, the learning of certain types of skill.

QAA Quality Assurance Agency for Higher Education.

Quality assurance An ongoing process by which an institution (department, school or faculty) monitors and confirms that the conditions are in place for students to achieve the standards set.

Quality control Refers to the detailed checks on procedures and activities necessary for the attainment of high quality and standards.

Quality enhancement Refers to all the activities and processes adopted to improve and develop the quality of higher education and of practice.

Rationalist The belief that reason is the basis of knowledge.

Reflection Consideration of an experience, or of learning, to enhance understanding or inform action.

Reflective practitioner Someone who is continually involved in the process of reflecting on experience and is capable of reflecting in action, continually learning from experience to the benefit of future actions.

Reliable (of assessment) A test which is consistent and precise in terms of factors, such as marking, quality of test and test items. The assessment process would generate the same result if repeated on another occasion with the same group, or if repeated with another group of similar students.

Role play A planned learning activity where participants take on the role of individuals representing different perspectives (eg, a mock interview) to meet specific learning objectives, such as to promote empathy or to expose participants to a scenario in which they will have to take part in the near future.

SAQ (structured/short answer question) Also known as modified essay questions or short answers. SAQs test knowledge recall in a directed, but non-cueing manner.

SEDA Staff and Educational Development Association.

SEEC Southern England Consortium for Credit Accumulation and Transfer.

Self-directed learning (SDL) The learner has control over educational decisions, including goals, resources, methods and criteria for judging success. Often used just to mean any learning situation in which the learner has some influence on some of these aspects.

Semester A period of study in a modular programme of study, over which a set of modules are taught. Typically the academic year is divided into two semesters of equal length. Of variable length across the sector.

Seminar Used with different meanings according to discipline and type of institution. May be used to describe many forms of small group teaching. Traditionally one or more students present formal academic work (a paper) to peers and a tutor, followed by discussion.

SENDA Special Educational Needs and Disability Act 2002. Spells out requirements for HEIs regarding disability.

SHEFC Scottish Higher Education Funding Council.

SI (supplemental instruction) Imported from the United States. A means of supporting learners through the use of trained SI instructors who are also students. SI instructors take the role of facilitator and operate within a framework determined initially by the course leader. Usually SI instructors are more senior students selected for the role.

Signpost Statements in teaching sessions that help students to see the structure and direction of the teaching, and the links. Typically in a lecture, signposts will be used to give the big picture and then to signal the end of one section, the start of the next and where it is going.

Simulated patient (SP) An actor or other third party who plays the role of the patient in a clinical encounter with dental, medical or similar student.

Simulation Often associated with role play, but increasingly used in the context of ICT, a learning activity that simulates a real-life scenario requiring participants to make choices which demonstrate cause and effect.

Situated cognition/situated learning Relates to the environment and context, eg, in the case of language learning, assistance with vocabulary would be offered in the context of the environment rather than the other way around.

Skills for transferability The ability to transfer applicability of a particular skills from one context to another.

SLA Second language acquisition.

Small group teaching A term used to encompass all the various forms of teaching involving 'small' groups of students, ranging from one-to-one sessions to groups of up to 25 (or even more) students. Includes tutorials, seminars, problem classes.

Standards The term used to refer to levels of student attainment compared to comparators (or criteria).

Strategic approach to learning Typifies students who adapt their learning style to meet the needs of the set task. Intention is external to the real purpose of the task, as it focuses on achieving high marks for their own sake, not because they indicate high levels of learning. Also known as the achieving approach.

Subject benchmarking A collection of discipline-specific statements relating to undergraduate programmes as published by the QAA.

Subject Review The quality assessment process for higher education provision, at subject level, undertaken by the QAA in England and Northern Ireland 1998–02.

Summative assessment The type of assessment that typically comes at the end of a module or section of learning and awards the learner with a final mark or grade for that section. The information about the learner is often used by third parties to inform decisions about the learner's abilities.

Surface approach to learning Learning by students which focuses on the details of the learning experience and which is based on memorizing the details without any attempt to give them meaning beyond the factual level of understanding. *See also* deep approach, strategic approach.

Target language The particular foreign language being taught/learnt.

Team teaching A system whereby learning is designed, delivered and supported by two or more teachers who may share the same session.

Thesis lecture A lecture which builds up a case through argumentation.

Transferable skills *See* Core skills.

Tutorial Used with different meanings according to discipline, type of institution, level, and teaching and learning method. Involves a tutor and one or more students. May focus on academic and/or pastoral matters.

UCoSDA Universities' and Colleges' Staff Development Agency, now HESDA.

UUK Universities UK (formerly CVCP).

Valid (of assessment) Adequacy and appropriateness of the task/test in relation to the outcomes/objectives of the teaching being assessed, ie, it measures what it is supposed to measure.

Video-conference A synchronous discussion between two individuals or groups of people who are in different places but can see and hear each other using electronic communications.

Virtual seminar A seminar which takes place over the Web.

Viva voce examination An oral examination, typically at the end of a programme of study. One part of assessment strategy if used in undergraduate programmes, principal means of assessment of postgraduate degrees. Can be used to test communication, understanding, capacity to think quickly under pressure and knowledge of procedures.

Virtual learning environment (VLE) A VLE is an electronic tool which facilitates online learning and teaching. It provides an environment in which tutors and students can develop learning content and participate in online interactions of various kinds. Typically, a VLE includes a discussion board, chat facilities, a learning tracking mechanism, assessment features, and a tool for tutors to design content without hand-coding html. A VLE is usually delivered via a standard Web browser, and can form an integral component of a larger MLE when integrated with other systems.

Webcast A live or delayed video or audio broadcast delivered throught the Internet.

Website poster board A 'virtual' poster board on which both teachers and learners can offer questions, observations, etc.

Work-based learning A type of curriculum design allowing content and learning to arise from within real working contexts. Students, usually employees, study part-time and use their workplace to generate a project. Unlike PBL, work-based learners are working on real problems in real time.

Index

(Numbers in *italics* refer to figures in the text)

441